Understanding Election Law and Voting Rights

CAROLINA ACADEMIC PRESS

Understanding Series

UNDERSTANDING ADMINISTRATIVE LAW
Seventh Edition
Kristin E. Hickman

UNDERSTANDING ALTERNATIVE DISPUTE RESOLUTION,
Second Edition
Kristen M. Blankley and Maureen A. Weston

UNDERSTANDING ANIMAL LAW
Adam Karp

UNDERSTANDING ANTITRUST AND ITS ECONOMIC IMPLICATIONS
Eighth Edition
Christopher R. Leslie, E. Thomas Sullivan, and Jeffrey L. Harrison

UNDERSTANDING BANKRUPTCY
Fifth Edition
Jeffrey Ferriell and Edward J. Janger

UNDERSTANDING CALIFORNIA COMMUNITY PROPERTY LAW
Second Edition
Jo Carrillo

UNDERSTANDING CAPITAL PUNISHMENT LAW
Fifth Edition
Linda E. Carter, Ellen S. Kreitzberg, Scott W. Howe, and Celestine Richards McConville

UNDERSTANDING CIVIL PROCEDURE
Seventh Edition
Gene R. Shreve, Peter Raven-Hansen, and Charles Gardner Geyh

UNDERSTANDING CIVIL PROCEDURE
The California Edition
Walter W. Heiser, Gene R. Shreve, Peter Raven-Hansen, and Charles Gardner Geyh

UNDERSTANDING CIVIL RIGHTS LITIGATION
Third Edition
Howard M. Wasserman

UNDERSTANDING CONFLICT OF LAWS
Fourth Edition
William M. Richman, William L. Reynolds, and Chris A. Whytock

UNDERSTANDING CONSTITUTIONAL LAW
Sixth Edition
William D. Araiza

UNDERSTANDING CONTRACTS
Fifth Edition
Jeffrey Ferriell

UNDERSTANDING COPYRIGHT LAW
Eighth Edition
Marshall A. Leaffer

UNDERSTANDING CORPORATE LAW
Sixth Edition
Arthur R. Pinto and James A. Fanto

UNDERSTANDING CORPORATE TAXATION
Fifth Edition
Leandra Lederman and Emily Cauble

UNDERSTANDING CRIMINAL LAW
Ninth Edition
Joshua Dressler

UNDERSTANDING CRIMINAL PROCEDURE VOL. 1: INVESTIGATION
Eighth Edition
Joshua Dressler, Alan C. Michaels and Ric Simmons

UNDERSTANDING CRIMINAL PROCEDURE VOL. 2: ADJUDICATION
Fifth Edition
Joshua Dressler, Alan C. Michaels. and Ric Simmons

UNDERSTANDING DISABILITY LAW
Fourth Edition
Mark C. Weber

UNDERSTANDING
ELECTION LAW AND VOTING RIGHTS
Second Edition
Michael R. Dimino, Bradley A. Smith, and Michael E. Solimine

UNDERSTANDING
EMPLOYEE BENEFITS LAW
Second Edition
Kathryn L. Moore

UNDERSTANDING
EMPLOYMENT DISCRIMINATION LAW
Fourth Edition
Thomas R. Haggard and Bruce N. Cameron

UNDERSTANDING
EMPLOYMENT LAW
Fourth Edition
Richard A. Bales, Jeffrey M. Hirsch, and Paul M. Secunda

UNDERSTANDING
ENVIRONMENTAL LAW
Fourth Edition
Kevin A. Reilly and Philip Weinberg

UNDERSTANDING
ESTATE AND GIFT TAXATION
Third Edition
Brant J. Hellwig and Robert T. Danforth

UNDERSTANDING EVIDENCE
Sixth Edition
Paul C. Giannelli and Jules Epstein

UNDERSTANDING FAMILY LAW
Fourth Edition
John Gregory, Peter N. Swisher, and Robin Wilson

UNDERSTANDING
FEDERAL AND CALIFORNIA EVIDENCE
Paul C. Giannelli

UNDERSTANDING
FEDERAL COURTS AND JURISDICTION
Second Edition
Linda Mullenix, Martin H. Redish, and Georgene Vairo

UNDERSTANDING
FEDERAL INCOME TAXATION
Seventh Edition
J. Martin Burke and Michael K. Friel

UNDERSTANDING
THE FIRST AMENDMENT
Ninth Edition
Russell L. Weaver

UNDERSTANDING
IMMIGRATION LAW
Fourth Edition
Kevin R. Johnson, Raquel Aldana, Bill Ong Hing, Leticia M. Saucedo, and Enid Trucios-Haynes

UNDERSTANDING
INSURANCE LAW
Seventh Edition
Robert H. Jerry, II and Douglas R. Richmond

UNDERSTANDING
INTELLECTUAL PROPERTY LAW
Fourth Edition
Tyler T. Ochoa, Shubha Ghosh, and Mary LaFrance

UNDERSTANDING
INTERNATIONAL BUSINESS AND FINANCIAL TRANSACTIONS
Fourth Edition
Jerold A. Friedland

UNDERSTANDING
INTERNATIONAL CRIMINAL LAW
Fourth Edition
Ellen S. Podgor, Roger S. Clark, and Lucian E. Dervan

UNDERSTANDING
INTERNATIONAL LAW
Third Edition
Stephen C. McCaffrey

UNDERSTANDING JEWISH LAW
Second Edition
Steven H. Resnicoff

UNDERSTANDING JUVENILE LAW
Fifth Edition
Martin Gardner

UNDERSTANDING LABOR LAW
Sixth Edition
Douglas E. Ray, Robert N. Strassfeld, and Ariana R. Levinson

UNDERSTANDING
THE LAW OF TERRORISM
Second Edition
Erik Luna and Wayne McCormack

UNDERSTANDING
THE LAW OF ZONING AND
LAND USE CONTROLS
Fourth Edition
Barlow Burke

UNDERSTANDING LAWYERS' ETHICS
Sixth Edition
Monroe H. Freedman and Abbe Smith

UNDERSTANDING
LOCAL GOVERNMENT
Second Edition
Sandra Stevenson

UNDERSTANDING
MODERN REAL ESTATE
TRANSACTIONS
Fourth Edition
Alex M. Johnson, Jr.

UNDERSTANDING
NEGOTIABLE INSTRUMENTS AND
PAYMENT SYSTEMS
Second Edition
William H. Lawrence

UNDERSTANDING
NONPROFIT AND TAX EXEMPT
ORGANIZATIONS
Third Edition
Nicholas P. Cafardi and
Jaclyn Fabean Cherry

UNDERSTANDING
PARTNERSHIP AND LLC TAXATION
Fifth Edition
Jerold A. Friedland

UNDERSTANDING PATENT LAW
Fourth Edition
Amy L. Landers

UNDERSTANDING PRODUCTS
LIABILITY LAW
Second Edition
Bruce L. Ottley, Rogelio A. Lasso,
and Terrence F. Kiely

UNDERSTANDING PROPERTY LAW
Fifth Edition
John G. Sprankling

UNDERSTANDING REMEDIES
Fourth Edition
James M. Fischer

UNDERSTANDING
SALES AND LEASES OF GOODS
Third Edition
William H. Henning, William H. Lawrence,
and Henry Deeb Gabriel

UNDERSTANDING
SECURED TRANSACTIONS
Sixth Edition
William H. Henning, R. Wilson Freyermuth,
and Brook E. Gotberg

UNDERSTANDING SECURITIES LAW
Eighth Edition
Marc I. Steinberg

UNDERSTANDING SPORTS LAW
Timothy Davis and N. Jeremi Duru

UNDERSTANDING
TAXATION OF BUSINESS ENTITIES
Second Edition
Walter D. Schwidetzky and Fred B. Brown

UNDERSTANDING TORTS
Seventh Edition
John L. Diamond, Lawrence C. Levine,
and Anita Bernstein

UNDERSTANDING
TRADE SECRET LAW
John G. Sprankling and
Thomas G. Sprankling

UNDERSTANDING
TRADEMARK LAW
Fourth Edition
Mary LaFrance

UNDERSTANDING
TRUSTS AND ESTATES
Seventh Edition
Roger W. Andersen and Susan N. Gary

UNDERSTANDING
WHITE COLLAR CRIME
Fifth Edition
J. Kelly Strader and Todd Haugh

Understanding Election Law and Voting Rights

SECOND EDITION

Michael R. Dimino
PROFESSOR OF LAW
WIDENER UNIVERSITY COMMONWEALTH LAW SCHOOL

Bradley A. Smith
JOSIAH H. BLACKMORE II/SHIRLEY M. NAULT
PROFESSOR OF LAW, EMERITUS
CAPITAL UNIVERSITY LAW SCHOOL

Michael E. Solimine
DONALD P. KLEKAMP PROFESSOR OF LAW
UNIVERSITY OF CINCINNATI COLLEGE OF LAW

CAROLINA ACADEMIC PRESS
Durham, North Carolina

Library of Congress Cataloging-in-Publication Data

Names: Dimino, Michael author | Smith, Bradley A. author |
Solimine, Michael E., 1956- author
Title: Understanding election law and voting rights / Michael R. Dimino, Sr.,
Bradley A. Smith, Michael E. Solimine.
Description: Second edition. | Durham, North Carolina : Carolina Academic
Press, LLC, 2025. | Series: Understanding series |
Includes bibliographical references and index.
Identifiers: LCCN 2025032360 | ISBN 9781531019082 paperback |
ISBN 9781531019099 ebook
Subjects: LCSH: Election law--United States | Political parties--Law and
legislation--United States | Campaign funds--Law and legislation--
United States | LCGFT: Textbooks
Classification: LCC KF4886 .D565 2025 | DDC 342.73/07--dc23/eng/20250721
LC record available at https://lccn.loc.gov/2025032360

Carolina Academic Press
700 Kent Street
Durham, North Carolina 27701
(919) 489-7486
www.cap-press.com

Printed in the United States of America

To everyone who has taught me to see politics as a cynical game—
and to the politicians who prove the wisdom of those lessons.

—M.R.D.

To my wife and children.

—B.A.S.

To my late father, Eugene Michael Solimine, Esq.,
and to my late professor, James L. Walker.

—M.E.S.

Contents

Preface

The key insight of election law is that laws regulating the political process are not "neutral"; rather, they affect political outcomes in predictable ways and therefore favor predictable interests. Politics is, thus, a "game"—not in the sense that its outcomes are trivial, but in the sense that winners and losers are determined by the strategic decisions and actions that are taken within a context created by a system of rules. Election law is about the creation and implementation of those rules.

This book is written principally as a casebook companion or study aid, although it is also designed to be used as a stand-alone course book or treatise. We anticipate that most users of this book will be law-school or political-science students who are taking a course or seminar on a portion of election law. Nevertheless, some users of this book will be practicing lawyers or others researching the legal regulation of the political process. We have tried to make this book useful and accessible to all who might wish to learn more about the subject.

This text is, therefore, designed with two complementary purposes in mind: First, we desire to provide students with a coherent narrative of the various aspects of election law and to help them synthesize and apply election-law doctrines to typical problems and situations faced by practicing attorneys and policymakers. Second, we wish for this text to serve as a concise treatise on election law for practicing lawyers and for students and scholars in political science and other fields.

Naturally, this book can be used as a companion to our casebook, VOTING RIGHTS AND ELECTION LAW (3d ed. 2021; 4th ed. forthcoming 2026), published by Carolina Academic Press. Students who are using one of the field's other casebooks, or whose classes do not use casebooks, however, should have no problem adapting this book to their own studies. The organization of this book largely follows that of our casebook. Subjects are presented in rough chronological order through the election process, beginning with setting the ground rules for elections, including voting qualifications, districting, and Congress's power to protect voting rights. We then progress to the regulation of campaigns, including political parties' rights, access to the ballot, free speech and the First Amendment rights to participate in campaigns and to run for office, campaign-finance regulation (including a practical guide to the reporting and regulatory obligations concerning different modes of political spending and expression), and disclosure requirements. Our chronology finishes with the election itself and post-election challenges, and we consider issues of ballot-casting and vote-counting, as well as the role of courts in adjudicating disputes about political power and litigation involving election "irregularities."

We have tried to present election-law doctrine with an accompanying discussion of major theoretical principles. Along the way, we note areas where the doctrine is unclear or in tension with other areas. Readers will come away from this text knowing not only the holdings of cases and the meanings of important statutes such as the Voting Rights Act but also understanding the contending views of free speech, equality, judicial authority, and political fairness that are present throughout the field. Our primary goal in presenting the material this way is to prepare students for class (if they are reading this book along with their course material) or for exams (if they are reading this book to aid in reviewing the course). Such a discussion, of course, also might prove useful for litigators who are confronted with questions where the doctrine is unclear.

Election law is largely applied constitutional law (with some statutes, such as the Voting Rights Act and the Help America Vote Act, playing substantial roles as well). Much of election law applies the First and Fourteenth Amendments to the regulation of politics. Basic constitutional doctrine concerning the freedom of speech, equal protection, and fundamental rights, therefore, provides valuable background to the law of elections and voting rights. Although we try to explain basic principles and doctrine of constitutional law when they are relevant, we expect that most people reading this book have had some exposure to them already. Those readers who need more background in constitutional law may consult one of the excellent secondary sources available, including the one in this *Understanding* series: William D. Araiza, Understanding Constitutional Law (6th ed. 2025).

The authors wish to thank the editors and publishing staff for their help. Author Dimino is additionally grateful for the hard work and goodwill of his co-authors, who have been exceptional partners throughout their collaboration, both on the casebook and on this volume.

We welcome comments about how we might improve this book in future editions. Please contact us with suggestions.

MICHAEL R. DIMINO
mrdimino@widener.edu

BRADLEY A. SMITH
bsmith@law.capital.edu

MICHAEL E. SOLIMINE
solimime@ucmail.uc.edu

Understanding Election Law and Voting Rights

Chapter 1

Voting Qualifications

A. Introduction

Much of this book considers the law governing fairly sophisticated ways of affecting the distribution of political power. From regulations of campaign finance to methods of drawing electoral districts, and from the structure of the ballot to the methods of tabulating votes, we will address how choices made by political actors affect the functioning—and the results—of the political process.

We start, however, with an issue that is (at least on the surface) easy to understand. Perhaps the simplest way to limit someone's political power is to exclude him or her from participating in politics. It is for this reason that Chief Justice Warren considered the voting-rights cases of the 1960s to be the most important ones decided during his tenure:[1] If minorities could be guaranteed access to the ballot, it was thought, government officials would have to pay attention to their interests. This attitude was overly optimistic; there are other ways of limiting a disfavored group's political influence, and we will see attempts to use several of them.

Nevertheless, "first-generation" barriers to voting—those involving a hindrance or bar to participating in politics, as opposed to "second-generation" barriers involving diminution of the political *influence* of persons who are permitted nominally to participate—are an undeniably powerful way of limiting a group's political power. In this chapter, we examine the foundational Supreme Court cases establishing the constitutional right to vote as well as cases that have helped to clarify the scope of that right.

B. Constitutional Text and Pre-Civil-Rights-Era Cases

Considering the importance of voting rights to the operation of a democratic republic, it may be surprising that the text of the Constitution does so little to guarantee those rights. Rather, the Constitution largely leaves it to states to set rules governing voter eligibility.

1. Earl Warren, The Memoirs of Earl Warren 306 (1977).

There is no explicit "right to vote" in the Constitution. Rather, the Constitution protects individuals' right to vote by requiring states to adopt a "Republican Form of Government,"[2] implicitly requiring states to hold some elections, and by limiting states' ability to exclude certain categories of persons from the franchise. Further, Article I, § 2, and the Seventeenth Amendment provide that the qualifications for voters in elections for Congress shall be identical to the qualifications of voters in elections for the largest branch of the state legislature. In other words, states are granted considerable latitude in establishing qualifications for voters, but if a person is permitted to vote in state elections, he must also be permitted to vote in congressional elections.

Initially, the Supreme Court confirmed what appeared to be the plain meaning of the text. For example, in *Minor v. Happersett*,[3] a case decided before the adoption of the Nineteenth Amendment, the Court held that states could exclude women from voting and noted that the Constitution "does not confer the right of suffrage upon any one."[4]

Similarly, in the more recent case of *Lassiter v. Northampton County Board of Elections*,[5] the Court upheld North Carolina's English literacy test against constitutional challenge. The Court deferred to the state legislature's judgment as to the value of such a test and noted that "[t]he ability to read and write ... has some relation to standards designed to promote intelligent use of the ballot."[6] Although *Lassiter* has never been overruled, in subsequent decades, the Supreme Court has assumed a more active role in protecting voting rights and has required states to extend the franchise to nearly all persons who want to vote, so long as they satisfy minimal requirements of age, citizenship, and residency. The remainder of this chapter discusses the history and details of this voting-rights expansion.

C. Equal Protection and Due Process

You will recall from the survey course in Constitutional Law that laws challenged under the Fourteenth Amendment will ordinarily be evaluated using "rational basis scrutiny." Under that extremely deferential standard, laws will be held constitutional as long as they are "rationally" (or sometimes "reasonably") related to a "legitimate" government interest. Occasionally, however, a much different standard than rational basis applies. Under "strict scrutiny," laws must be "necessary" (or "narrowly tailored") to achieve a "compelling" government interest.

---

2. U.S. Const. art. IV, § 4.
3. 88 U.S. (21 Wall.) 162 (1875).
4. *Id.* at 178.
5. 360 U.S. 45 (1959).
6. *Id.* at 51.

Strict scrutiny is thus more difficult for the government in two respects: First, the interest the government is trying to achieve—the goal of the law—must be much more important than it needs to be under rational basis scrutiny. Whereas any "legitimate" goal is enough under rational basis scrutiny, strict scrutiny requires that the government have a "compelling"—read, super-important—goal. Second, the connection between the law and that interest must be much closer under strict scrutiny than under rational basis scrutiny. In the parlance of constitutional law, the law must not be overinclusive or underinclusive. That is, the law must not over-regulate or under-regulate, relative to the goal the government is trying to achieve.

For example, imagine a law that imposes voting qualifications in an attempt to restrict the franchise to those people who are mature enough to understand the issues in elections. In order to be narrowly tailored, the law must allow *all* mature people to vote, and it must allow *only* mature people to vote. If the law banned some mature people from voting, the qualifications would be overinclusive because banning those mature people would be overregulation; banning those mature people from voting would not be necessary to achieve the goal of a mature electorate. If the law allowed some immature people to vote, it would be underinclusive because the law would have achieved only part of its goal.

Some laws are both underinclusive and overinclusive. Consider a law establishing a minimum voting age of 18 in an attempt to limit the franchise to people who are mature enough to understand the issues in an election. The law is underinclusive in that it fails to exclude some adults who are immature or incapable of appreciating issues, and it is overinclusive in that it excludes some minors who are unusually mature for their ages.

A minimum voting age of 18 is, however, a *rational* way of achieving the government's legitimate goal of promoting a mature electorate. In general, people mature as they age, and the average 18-year-old is more mature and capable of voting intelligently than the average 17-year-old is.

Thus the constitutionality of a law often depends on the level of scrutiny applied. A minimum voting age is surely a rational way of screening voters for maturity, but it is not a narrowly tailored way of achieving that goal. Therefore, it is constitutional if evaluated under rational basis scrutiny, but it is unconstitutional if strict scrutiny is applied.

The crucial question, then, is when strict scrutiny will apply. The Supreme Court has held that laws will trigger strict scrutiny in two types of cases. First, if a law is challenged as violating the Equal Protection Clause, strict scrutiny will apply if the law discriminates against a "suspect class," with the most important suspect classification being race. Most classifications, however, are not suspect, so laws that discriminate based on age, income, geography, hair color, etc., are evaluated under rational basis scrutiny.

Sometimes it is not clear whether a law discriminates against a suspect class. Suppose, for example, a law imposes a burden on people living in a certain area—an area inhabited overwhelmingly by members of a racial minority. The law's "facial" classification is one of geography, not race. But the law clearly has a disproportionate *impact* on members of the minority race—as do countless other laws. For example, tax laws, labor laws, zoning laws, and laws requiring a certain education for government employment have disproportionate racial impacts because members of different races tend to earn different incomes, hold different types of jobs, live in different areas, and have different levels of education.

When evaluating such "facially race-neutral laws," should we apply strict scrutiny because of the disparate racial impact, or should we apply rational basis because of the law's facially nonracial classification? The Court has held that laws with a facially race-neutral classification trigger rational basis unless the laws both create a racially disparate impact and were enacted or maintained for a racially discriminatory purpose.[7] This test is a difficult one to meet, and accordingly most facially race-neutral laws are evaluated using rational basis scrutiny.

Second, a law will trigger strict scrutiny if it abridges a fundamental liberty protected by the Due Process Clauses. Many fundamental liberties are specifically enumerated in portions of the Bill of Rights that have been incorporated against the states. For example, the freedoms of speech and religious exercise protected by the First Amendment are considered fundamental rights. The government may not abridge them unless the abridgement is a narrowly tailored way of achieving a compelling governmental interest. Other fundamental rights are not explicitly enumerated in the Constitution but are protected anyway. There is nothing in the Constitution explicitly protecting the right to marry, for example, but the Court has held that unless a law passes strict scrutiny, it may not abridge someone's right to marry.[8]

As with strict scrutiny under the Equal Protection Clause, strict scrutiny under the Due Process Clauses is rarely applied. Most rights are not fundamental in the constitutional sense, even if they are extremely important to our lives. The right to welfare benefits or the right to a high-quality public education, for example, might be vitally important to the people who want those benefits, but, because the Constitution does not implicitly or explicitly protect them, they are not fundamental.[9]

The right to vote, the subject of this chapter, is generally considered one of the unenumerated fundamental rights. The Constitution does not explicitly grant a right to vote, but nevertheless the Court has applied strict scrutiny to laws that deprive people of the right. Curiously, however, the Court has *not* applied strict scrutiny to laws that impose age, citizenship, and residency qualifications on voters. Stated differently, the right to vote is fundamental for adult citizens who reside in the jurisdiction holding the election. As we will see below, it is hard to say that such qualifications are narrowly tailored ways of achieving compelling government interests, but nevertheless the Court has indicated that those three types of qualifications are constitutional. The following sections will examine how the Supreme Court arrived at that balance.

---

7. *See, e.g.*, Washington v. Davis, 426 U.S. 229 (1976).

8. *See* Obergefell v. Hodges, 576 U.S. 644, 664–65 (2015); Zablocki v. Redhail, 434 U.S. 374, 383–88 (1978); Loving v. Virginia, 388 U.S. 1, 12 (1967).

9. *See* San Antonio Indep. Sch. Dist. v. Rodriguez, 411 U.S. 1, 33–39 (1973).

D. Excluding Unqualified Voters

Although the Supreme Court has considered the right to vote to be fundamental, everyone agrees that government must be able to draw some lines between those people who are permitted to vote and those who are not. A state need not allow *everyone* to vote; for example, persons who live outside the state, as well as young children and noncitizens, are routinely and uncontroversially excluded from voting. If government were entirely free to make decisions about who could vote, however, there would be very little remaining of the right. Further, by limiting the electorate, government officials would be able to increase the chances of their own reelection and thereby undermine the ability of elections to serve as a check on government.

It is therefore crucial to identify the grounds on which the government may deny someone the ability to register and to vote. The text of the Constitution places a few limits on the ability of states to set voting qualifications. While the constitutional text nowhere says that any particular persons must be permitted to vote, it forbids states from denying the right to vote on account of "race, color, or previous condition of servitude" (Amendment XV);[10] "sex" (Amendment XIX);[11] and "age," for those U.S. citizens who are at least 18 years old (Amendment XXVI).[12] In addition, the Twenty-Fourth Amendment forbids states from denying the right to vote to anyone "by reason of failure to pay any poll tax or other tax," but the Amendment's terms apply only to federal elections.[13] Beyond those limits, the Constitution requires only that every person who is permitted to vote for the most numerous branch of the state legislature be permitted to vote for Congress.[14]

The more controversial grounds for exclusion, which are discussed below, are those not explicitly forbidden by the Constitution. The Court has held that the Fourteenth Amendment's Equal Protection Clause prohibits states from excluding certain categories of people from the franchise where the states' reasons are not closely related to ensuring the proper functioning of democracy.

---

10. U.S. Const. amend. XV, § 1 ("The right of citizens of the United States to vote shall not be denied or abridged by the United States or by any State on account of race, color, or previous condition of servitude.").

11. U.S. Const. amend. XIX, § 1 ("The right of citizens of the United States to vote shall not be denied or abridged by the United States or by any State on account of sex.").

12. U.S. Const. amend. XXVI, § 1 ("The right of citizens of the United States, who are eighteen years of age or older, to vote shall not be denied or abridged by the United States or by any State on account of age.").

13. U.S. Const. amend. XXIV, § 1 ("The right of citizens of the United States to vote in any primary or other election for President or Vice President, for electors for President or Vice President, or for Senator or Representative in Congress, shall not be denied or abridged by the United States or any State by reason of failure to pay any poll tax or other tax.").

14. U.S. Const. art. I, § 2, cl. 1 (providing that voters for the House of Representatives "have the Qualifications requisite for Electors of the most numerous branch of the State Legislature"); *id.* amend. XVII ("The electors [for U.S. Senators] in each State shall have the qualifications requisite for electors of the most numerous branch of the State legislatures."). *See* The Federalist No. 52 (James Madison).

1. The Poor

In *Harper v. Virginia State Board of Elections*,[15] for example, the Court struck down Virginia's requirement that voters in state elections pay a $1.50 poll tax (equivalent to slightly more than $15 today). According to the Court, the poll tax was a kind of wealth discrimination. There were a few problems with this argument. First, the law did not exactly discriminate on the basis of wealth. It required all voters to pay the fee, and of course it is easier for wealthy people to pay a fee than it is for poor people to do so. But the Court held that it was unconstitutional to exclude people from voting based on either "wealth *or* payment of a fee."[16] Thus, the state had to permit a voter to cast his ballot, even if his only reason for not paying the $1.50 tax was that he thought it too much trouble to get change for a $50 bill. The second problem with the Court's methodology was that even if the poll tax were a form of wealth discrimination, wealth is not a suspect class. Accordingly, a law discriminating against the poor would ordinarily be thought to trigger mere rational basis scrutiny.

The Court got around both of these problems by announcing that the poll tax was unconstitutional because it was "capricious or irrelevant." In other words, excluding voters for failing to pay a poll tax was irrational—and therefore unconstitutional—even under the rational-basis test. In reaching that conclusion, the Court had to distinguish *Lassiter v. Northampton County Board of Elections*, in which the Court upheld North Carolina's English-literacy test against a similar equal-protection challenge.[17] The *Harper* Court summarized the crucial difference by stating that "unlike a poll tax, the 'ability to read and write ... has some relation to standards designed to promote intelligent use of the ballot.'"[18]

This explanation, however, was specious, as Justice Harlan pointed out in dissent.[19] A voter's willingness to pay a tax is an indication of how much the voter cares about the election—and, therefore, how much effort the voter is likely to expend educating himself about the issues and candidates. Further, as Justice Harlan noted,

> It is also arguable, indeed it was probably accepted as sound political theory by a large percentage of Americans through most of our history, that people with some property have a deeper stake in community affairs, and are consequently more responsible, more educated, more knowledgeable, more worthy of confidence, than those without means, and that the community and Nation would be better managed if the franchise were restricted to such citizens.[20]

---

15. 383 U.S. 663 (1966).
16. *Id.* at 668 (emphasis added).
17. 360 U.S. 45 (1959).
18. 383 U.S. at 666 (quoting *Lassiter*, 360 U.S. at 51) (ellipsis in *Harper*).
19. *See* 383 U.S. at 684–86 (Harlan, J., dissenting).
20. *Id.* at 685.

To be sure, there is not a perfect correlation between the willingness to pay a poll tax and the "intelligent use of the ballot." Some people who are too poor to pay a poll tax or who simply do not want to spend the money would vote in an "intelligent" manner. And some who are willing to pay a poll tax would not take voting seriously.

But the same could be said of literacy tests, which, to repeat, the Court upheld in *Lassiter*. Surely people who are able to read and write are more likely than illiterates to vote intelligently, but literacy is a very imprecise proxy for intelligent voting. Plenty of people who cannot understand English would be able to get their information in other languages, and plenty of people who cannot read or write any language can get information by radio, television, or word of mouth. And plenty of literate people choose not to invest the effort to vote intelligently. None of that imprecision mattered in *Lassiter*, however. Rather, it was enough that there was "some relation" between English literacy and intelligent voting; in modern terms, literacy tests passed the rational-basis test.

Accordingly, *Harper*'s real significance lies not in its questionable conclusion that poll taxes fail the rational-basis test, but rather in its implicit application of a more demanding test. The Court has never overruled *Lassiter*, although the Voting Rights Act's (VRA) prohibition of literacy tests has made such a ruling unnecessary.[21] Nevertheless, *Lassiter* has been left behind as a relic from the days when laws limiting the franchise to certain preferred classes of voters would be upheld as long as the laws were rational or reasonable. *Harper*, therefore, raises the question of which level of scrutiny should apply to other laws that make it difficult for some elements of the population to vote or otherwise to participate in politics—a topic that will be addressed in the remainder of the chapter.

Additionally, *Harper* raises the question of which laws will be deemed to constitute discrimination against the poor. Many laws impose implicit costs on voters even if the state does not charge a fee directly. Requirements that voters register in advance of an election and that they vote in person at the polling place on election day require voters to pay transportation costs and to take time off of work. Poor persons can be expected to face more difficulty in complying with such requirements than the inconvenience faced by those who have more money. Typically, such requirements are not viewed as discrimination against the poor, and they are not subject to strict scrutiny.

Recently, however, there has been substantial controversy over requiring voters to present identification at the polls. Even where the state provides such identification free of charge, some have argued that the costs associated with obtaining the identification (transportation to the facility plus perhaps a fee for obtaining documents, such as a birth certificate, to prove one's identity) create an effect similar to a poll tax. Identification requirements are discussed in more detail in Chapter 10, § B[1].

21. *See* 52 U.S.C. § 10501(a).

2. The Uneducated, Unintelligent, or Mentally Disabled

Lassiter remains the Court's last word on the constitutionality of tests that screen out voters for their perceived inability to vote intelligently. Thus it is not clear whether additional tests of intelligence or civic knowledge would be constitutional.

Of course, literacy tests and the like have been used to enable discrimination, such as racial discrimination, that is clearly unconstitutional. Tests were often applied unfairly so that racial minorities were given much harder tests than whites were given. Because the plaintiff in *Lassiter* refused to take the test, the Court assumed that the North Carolina test would have been fairly administered and upheld the test only on that assumption.

The Voting Rights Act, however, has forbidden states from using "any test or device" to disqualify voters, whether or not those tests are fairly administered.[22] Specifically, the Act's prohibition includes

> any requirement that a person as a prerequisite for voting or registration for voting
>
> (1) demonstrate the ability to read, write, understand, or interpret any matter,
>
> (2) demonstrate any educational achievement or his knowledge of any particular subject,
>
> (3) possess good moral character, or
>
> (4) prove his qualifications by the voucher of registered voters or members of any other class.[23]

Accordingly, the VRA makes illegal not merely literacy tests but also educational qualifications and other kinds of screening to ensure the "intelligent use of the ballot," whether or not such qualifications are used as a subterfuge for racial discrimination or are otherwise unconstitutional.

The Supreme Court has upheld and applied the VRA's bans on "any test or device" in two cases: *South Carolina v. Katzenbach*[24] and *Katzenbach v. Morgan*.[25] In both cases, the Court held Congress to be acting within its power to enforce the Fourteenth and Fifteenth Amendments,[26] even though the tests did not themselves violate the Constitution. *South Carolina v. Katzenbach* applied a very broad standard that permitted Congress to adopt "any rational means to effectuate the constitutional prohibition of racial discrimination in voting."[27] *Morgan*'s standard was equally broad, if not more

---

22. 52 U.S.C. § 10501(a).
23. 52 U.S.C. § 10501(b).
24. 383 U.S. 301 (1966).
25. 384 U.S. 641 (1966).
26. Both the Fourteenth (in § 5) and Fifteenth Amendments (in § 2) give Congress the power "to enforce the provisions of" the respective Amendments.
27. 383 U.S. at 324.

so. The Court held that it was up to Congress to balance the need to protect voters against the state interests in favor of the tests, concluding that "[i]t is enough that we be able to perceive a basis upon which Congress might resolve the conflict as it did."[28]

Note, however, that the tests reviewed in those two cases were different from the permanent, nationwide test ban that is now in effect.[29] *South Carolina v. Katzenbach* upheld a temporary five-year ban, which applied only to certain states with particularly bad histories of voting discrimination. The ban at issue in *Katzenbach v. Morgan* also had limited application; it involved a provision giving an exemption from English-literacy tests to people educated through the sixth grade in Puerto Rico. Accordingly, it is unclear how much authority the two cases give Congress to override state laws establishing voter qualifications.

Because the standards established in those cases were so broad, Congress could conceivably rely on them to justify nearly any voting law. In recent years, however, the Court has been determined to ensure that Congress's power to enforce the Fourteenth and Fifteenth Amendments not expand into a power to reinterpret the Amendments themselves. In other words, Congress, under the guise of protecting voting rights, remedying voting discrimination, or "enforc[ing]" the Amendments, must not effectively try to amend the Constitution by creating rights that are not already in the Constitution, thereby encroaching on state authority.

To make sure that Congress does not abuse its enforcement powers, the Court has cut back somewhat on the expansive language of *South Carolina v. Katzenbach* and *Katzenbach v. Morgan*. Under the Court's 1997 decision in *City of Boerne v. Flores*, Congress's enforcement power gives it authority to enact laws that are "proportional" and "congruent" responses to violations of the constitutional provision being enforced.[30] Congress can still outlaw actions (such as administering literacy tests) that are not themselves unconstitutional, but Congress's law must be a reasonable response to actions (such as the discriminatory use of literacy tests) that the *Court* recognizes to be constitutional violations.

Even more recently, in *Arizona v. Inter Tribal Council of Arizona, Inc.*,[31] the Court indicated that Congress's power to regulate the times, places, and manner of federal elections extends "to regulat[ing] *how* federal elections are held, but not *who* may vote in them."[32] The Court went on to say that "it would raise serious constitutional doubts if a federal statute precluded a State from obtaining the information necessary to enforce its voter qualifications."[33] Thus, there is renewed interest on the part of the Court in limiting Congress and protecting state authority to regulate the qualifications of voters.

---

28. 384 U.S. at 653.
29. *See* 52 U.S.C. § 10303(e)(2), 89 Stat. 400 (1975).
30. 521 U.S. 507 (1997).
31. 570 U.S. 1 (2013).
32. *Id.* at 16.
33. *Id.* at 17.

In Chapter 3, when we consider preclearance under § 5 of the Voting Rights Act, and in Chapter 4, when we consider the use of race in districting, we will revisit Congress's controversial enforcement power in additional contexts. Jurisdictions that were subject to preclearance had to gain federal approval before changing their voting laws—even if the new laws were perfectly constitutional. And under both § 2 and § 5 of the VRA, states are sometimes required to take account of race to ensure that minorities have adequate political power. Critics have charged that Congress exceeded its power by purporting to "enforce" constitutional rights when it was really changing the meaning of those rights and creating rights that were not actually in the Constitution.

Despite the VRA's ban on tests of knowledge or understanding and the Americans with Disabilities Act's (ADA) prohibition against discrimination on the ground of disability,[34] most states continue to deny the franchise to some people with mental disabilities that may affect their ability to vote intelligently.[35] The Supreme Court has not yet spoken to whether such exclusions violate the Constitution, the VRA, or the ADA.[36]

3. The Disinterested

The 1969 decision in *Kramer v. Union Free School District No. 15* further refined the Court's approach to laws limiting the class of people eligible to vote.[37] *Kramer* involved a challenge to a state law that limited the franchise in school-district elections to people who were either parents of schoolchildren or property owners or lessees in the district. The government's rationale was that people affected by the school board's decisions would be more likely to vote intelligently in school-district elections. In the view of the state, parents had the requisite interest because school policies affected their children, and property owners and lessees paid property taxes that were set by the school boards.

Mr. Kramer, however, fell into neither category. He wished to vote, but he had no children of his own, and he lived with his parents, so he paid no property taxes. Accordingly, he was not permitted to vote. The Supreme Court held the exclusion unconstitutional. In doing so, the Court distinguished "reasonable citizenship, age, and residency requirements" from the additional requirement imposed by the state that voters be interested in the school-district elections' outcomes. The Court accepted the constitutionality of restricting the franchise to U.S. citizens who have attained a certain age and who reside in the jurisdiction, but it held that "if a challenged state statute grants the right to vote to some *bona fide* residents of requisite age and citizenship and denies the franchise to others, the Court must determine whether the

34. *See* 42 U.S.C. § 12132.

35. *See* Bazelon Center for Mental Health Law, *State Laws Affecting the Voting Rights of People with Mental Disabilities*, https://www.bazelon.org/wp-content/uploads/2017/11/2016_State-Laws-Affecting-Voting-Rights-of-PWD.pdf.

36. *See* Doe v. Rowe, 156 F. Supp. 2d 35 (D. Me. 2001).

37. 395 U.S. 621 (1969).

exclusions are necessary to promote a compelling state interest."[38] Thus, instead of asking whether the law was "irrational," was "capricious," or imposed an "irrelevant" requirement, *Kramer* announced that voting exclusions (beyond age, citizenship, and residency requirements) could be sustained only if they passed strict scrutiny. Toward the end of its opinion, the Court made its rejection of the rational-basis standard explicit: "[T]he issue is not whether the legislative judgments [creating voting qualifications] are rational. A more exacting standard obtains. The issue is whether the [qualifications] do in fact sufficiently further a compelling state interest. . . . " Thus, whatever doubt remained after *Harper* seemed to be resolved in *Kramer*: Voting qualifications other than age, citizenship, and residency trigger strict scrutiny.

The Court went on to hold that the law in *Kramer* failed strict scrutiny because it was not narrowly tailored. The government argued that the law served to limit the electorate to those voters "primarily interested in school affairs." The Court held that even if such a purpose were important enough to satisfy strict scrutiny, the law did "not accomplish this purpose with sufficient precision to justify denying [Kramer] the franchise."[39] According to the Court, the law permitted "many persons" to vote "who have, at best, a remote and indirect interest in school affairs and, on the other hand, exclude[d] others who have a distinct and direct interest in the school meeting decisions."[40] In a footnote, the Court further explained that the law was both over- and under-inclusive. While Kramer—who "resides with his parents in the school district, pays state and federal taxes and is interested in and affected by school board decisions"—was excluded from voting, "an uninterested unemployed young man who pays no state or federal taxes, but who rents an apartment in the district" could vote.[41]

The Court was being deceptive in its comparison of Kramer and the hypothetical "uninterested unemployed young man." The justification for the law was that it limited the electorate to only those people "interested" in the outcomes of the elections, *i.e.*, those people who had a stake in the elections, either financially or as parents. The Court nowhere attempted to show that Kramer was interested in the elections in this sense. Instead, the Court said that Kramer was interested in the elections in the subjective sense—he found them interesting. Because the "uninterested unemployed young man" paid rent that would include the cost of district taxes, he *was* interested in the elections in the way in which the government used that term. The Court's use of the term "uninterested" meant only that he subjectively did not care about the elections (so he might have been unlikely to vote anyway). Thus, the Court held that the law did not adequately distinguish between the subjectively "interested" and those who were indifferent to the outcome of the elections. But that was not the law's objective. The law was trying to distinguish between the "interested"—those with a stake in the outcome—and the *dis*interested. It is not surprising that the law did a bad job of achieving an objective different from the one it was trying to accomplish.

---

38. *Id.* at 627.

39. *Id.* at 632.

40. *Id.*

41. *Id.* at 632 n.15.

Nevertheless, the Court's holding that the law violated strict scrutiny is a reminder of how difficult it is for a law to pass that standard. Because the Court believed that the law did not precisely distinguish between those persons who were "primarily interested in school affairs" and those who were not, the law was unconstitutional.

Kramer's rule of strict scrutiny for all voting exclusions (save age, citizenship and residency requirements) has the advantage of clarity and calls into further question the viability of *Lassiter*. Literacy tests bear a rational relationship to intelligent voting, but surely they are not a narrowly tailored way of distinguishing worthy from unworthy voters. Thus, one would think that *Kramer* would portend the constitutional invalidity of literacy tests.

Indeed, *Kramer* would seem to invalidate *every* kind of voting qualification except for age, citizenship, and residency, which the Court expressly exempted from the strict scrutiny the case otherwise required. The Court disclaimed that interpretation, saying that perhaps states could limit the electorate to those "primarily interested" or "primarily affected," so long as the means adopted were narrowly tailored to that end. But it would appear that no means would satisfy such a demanding standard; every possible voter qualification is both over-inclusive and under-inclusive in relation to the goal of producing an ideal electorate.

What is more, age, citizenship, and residency requirements themselves are vulnerable to the same objection; they are all overinclusive and underinclusive relative to that goal. As to age, young people are *generally* less mature than adults, but there are plenty of youths who are mature and knowledgeable about government, and there are plenty of adults who know next to nothing about government and care even less. As to citizenship, it may be that citizens tend to take seriously the responsibility of choosing our leaders and deciding public issues, but certainly many do not. And many noncitizens (for example, permanent-resident aliens) are knowledgeable about public affairs and are quite invested in American society. Similarly, people may tend to be most affected by government policies in the jurisdictions where they live, but often people are affected as much or more by policies in other jurisdictions, such as the ones in which they work.

Nevertheless, *Kramer* exempted age, citizenship, and residency restrictions from the general rule that strict scrutiny applies to laws that bar classes of people from the ballot; therefore, those restrictions are constitutional despite their over- and underinclusivity. The reason for this exemption is unclear. Because Mr. Kramer was an adult, a citizen, and a resident, it was unnecessary for the Court to explain why children, aliens, and nonresidents should be able to be excluded without the government's proving that the exclusions were narrowly tailored to a compelling state interest. Most likely, the Court found those restrictions to be familiar and common, and it may have realized that applying strict scrutiny to those restrictions would require the Court to eliminate even those most commonplace limits on the electorate, leaving elections open to just about anyone who wanted to participate. It surely would have been surprising for the Court to announce a constitutional right for young children and foreign nationals living overseas to vote in American elections. And once one acknowledges that some people should not be able to vote, then the question becomes where to draw the line—and *any* line is going to be over- and underinclusive.

Even after *Kramer*, states can exclude disinterested people from voting in a small category of elections. In elections for so-called "special purpose" districts, the Court has allowed states not only to exclude disinterested voters but also to weigh votes based on the voters' respective interests in the functioning of the district. Special-purpose districts, such as water, sewer, and community development districts, exercise limited authority over a discrete policy area. For example, the water development district at issue in *Salyer Land Co. v. Tulare Lake Basin Water Storage District*[42] exercised certain governmental powers relating to ensuring the availability of water for farming, but "[i]t provide[d] no other general public services such as schools, housing, transportation, utilities,[43] roads, or anything else of the type ordinarily financed by a municipal body."[44] Only landowners were permitted to vote, and instead of each voter casting an equal vote, votes in this special-purpose district were "apportioned according to the assessed valuation of the land."[45]

Because the district exercised such limited authority and its actions disproportionately affected landowners, the Court held that neither *Kramer* nor the Court's one-person, one-vote cases called for the application of strict scrutiny. Rather, once the Court held the district to be a limited, special-purpose district, the only question was "whether '... any state of facts reasonably may be conceived to justify'" the electoral scheme.[46] The Court easily found a rational basis for the law, noting that the benefits and burdens of the district fell not to each resident equally but rather according to the value of the land. Accordingly, the decision to allocate votes on the same basis was "rationally based."[47]

4. Nonresidents

As we saw in *Kramer v. Union Free School District No. 15*, the Court refused to accept New York's attempt to distinguish between voters based on their "interest" in the outcome of an election, as evidenced by whether they owned or leased property in the district and whether they had children in the district.[48] Accordingly, one might think that

42. 410 U.S. 719 (1973).

43. The implication of this statement might have been that governmental bodies that do exercise these powers would be subject to one-person, one-vote. At least as to utilities, however, this has proven incorrect. In *Ball v. James*, 451 U.S. 355 (1981), the Court permitted a deviation from the one-person, one-vote rule in elections for a special-purpose district that stored and delivered water and that also sold electric power. The district thus affected far more people than just landowners and it did provide utility service, but the Court held that the crucial fact was that the district's water was "distributed according to land ownership," so voting power could be distributed on the same basis. *Id.* at 367.

44. 410 U.S. at 728–29.

45. *Id.* at 725.

46. *Id.* at 732 (quoting McGowan v. Maryland, 366 U.S. 420, 426 (1961)).

47. 410 U.S. at 734.

48. 395 U.S. 621 (1969).

the Court would be similarly suspicious of state attempts to distinguish between voters based on their interest in the outcome of an election as evidenced by whether they reside within the limits of the jurisdiction. In fact, however, the Court has been deferential to residency limits that exclude people from voting in neighboring jurisdictions' elections even when those elections have a demonstrable impact on their lives.

In *Holt Civic Club v. City of Tuscaloosa*, the Court considered an Alabama law that permitted cities to exercise some governing authority over a "police jurisdiction" that extended beyond the city limits.[49] The case involved the unincorporated community of Holt, which was located within the police jurisdiction of Tuscaloosa. As the Court explained, residents of Holt were "subject to the criminal jurisdiction of the city's court, and to the city's power to license businesses, trades, and professions."[50] Residents of Holt sued, arguing that it was unconstitutional for them to be governed by the City of Tuscaloosa if they had no ability to vote in city elections. They therefore argued that the Equal Protection Clause demanded that they be given the right to vote, just as if they were residents of the city proper.

The Supreme Court disagreed. The Court concluded that because the Holt residents were not residents of Tuscaloosa, they had no right to vote in Tuscaloosa elections. The Holt residents, drawing on the American revolutionaries' complaints about taxation without representation, had argued that if a jurisdiction was able to exercise power affecting an individual, that individual should have the constitutional right to vote in the jurisdiction's elections. The Court concluded that such an argument "prove[d] too much": "A city's decisions inescapably affect individuals living immediately outside its borders" without extending voting rights beyond the city limits.[51] The Court provided several examples of decisions producing extraterritorial effects, including decisions about zoning, law enforcement, and taxation. Because those effects do not give voting rights to the affected residents of nearby communities, the Court held that Tuscaloosa's exercise of power over its police jurisdiction should likewise not trigger a constitutional right to vote in Tuscaloosa's elections.

Both *Kramer* and *Holt*, then, seem to employ a formalistic methodology in treating residency as a proxy for a voter's interest in an election. Whereas *Kramer* indicated that residents of a particular jurisdiction would conclusively be presumed to be interested in the jurisdiction's elections, *Holt* conversely indicated that *non*residents would be presumed *not* to be interested in the jurisdiction's elections.

Holt was not exclusively formalistic, however. In a footnote, the Court indicated that nonresidents might have a constitutional right to vote in a jurisdiction's elections if the jurisdiction had "annexed outlying territory in all but name, and is exercising precisely the same governmental powers over residents of surrounding unincorporated territory as it does over those residing within its corporate limits."[52] Because

49. 439 U.S. 60 (1978).
50. *Id.* at 61–62.
51. *Id.* at 69.
52. *Id.* at 72 n.8.

Tuscaloosa exercised only a portion of such powers over Holt, however (Tuscaloosa did not exercise "the vital and traditional authorities of cities and towns to levy ad valorem taxes [*i.e.*, taxes, such as those on real property, based on the value of the item taxed], invoke the power of eminent domain, and zone property for various types of uses"[53]), the suggestion did not affect the outcome of the case. It remains to be seen whether the Court will find a jurisdiction that exercises so much extraterritorial power that it must provide nonresidents with voting rights.

Because the Court concluded that Holt residents possessed no fundamental constitutional right to vote in Tuscaloosa elections, the Court applied the rational-basis test to determine whether it was constitutional for Alabama to provide voting rights to Tuscaloosa residents but to deny such rights to residents of the police jurisdiction. The Court upheld Alabama's distinction between city residents and residents of police jurisdictions, noting that people living in police jurisdictions may well prefer to receive basic services, such as police protection, from nearby cities (which have established police departments and can therefore offer such services more economically) without joining those cities for all purposes.[54] *Holt*'s significance in clarifying the constitutional right to vote, however, is not in its application of the rational-basis test; rather, the significant part of *Holt* is its conclusion that, in most instances, the right to vote ends at the jurisdiction's limits and does not extend to nonresidents, even if the jurisdiction's actions tangibly affect them.

5. New Residents

Suppose a state imposes a waiting period on voting.[55] That is, imagine that a state requires a voter not only to be a resident at the time of the election but also to *have been* a resident for some time in advance of the election. Is there any constitutional prohibition on such a durational residency requirement?

Originally, the Court held that states were free to impose such requirements as they saw fit. Because there was (and remains) no right to vote protected by constitutional text, *Pope v. Williams* held that it was up to the states to define the franchise.[56] As the Court said, "[T]he privilege to vote in a state is within the jurisdiction of the state itself,

53. *Id.*

54. *Id.* at 74.

55. This section concerns the constitutional limits on durational residency requirements for *voting*. Even though "laws affecting candidates always have at least some theoretical, correlative effect on voters," *Bullock v. Carter*, 405 U.S. 134, 143 (1972), courts have been much more willing to permit states to impose durational residency requirements on candidates for state (not federal) office. *See, e.g.*, Sununu v. Stark, 420 U.S. 958 (1975) (upholding a seven-year durational residency requirement for the state senate); Chimento v. Stark, 414 U.S. 802 (1973) (upholding a seven-year durational residency requirement for governor). Durational residency requirements for federal candidates are unconstitutional because they would add to the Constitution's exclusive list of qualifications. *See, e.g.*, Schaefer v. Townsend, 215 F.3d 1031 (9th Cir. 2000); *cf.* U.S. Term Limits, Inc. v. Thornton, 514 U.S. 779 (1995) (striking down a state's attempt to term limit candidates for Congress).

56. 193 U.S. 621 (1904).

to be exercised as the state may direct, and upon such terms as to it may seem proper, provided, of course, no discrimination is made [on the ground of race, color, or previous condition of servitude in violation of the Fifteenth Amendment]."[57] Through such reasoning, the *Pope* Court upheld Maryland's one-year durational residency requirement.

In modern times, however, the Court has given more stringent protection to the right to vote and has done more to limit a state's ability to exclude some of its own residents from the franchise. *Carrington v. Rash* began the modern trend.[58] *Carrington* struck down a provision of the Texas Constitution that excluded members of the military from voting. Texas had argued that the provision was necessary to prevent its other citizens from being overwhelmed by the large, concentrated populations at military bases, but the Court was unmoved. The Court stressed that states have the right to insist that voters be *bona fide* residents who intend to live in the state indefinitely—not short-term visitors who would have little interest in the state's long-term future. But the Court held that states could not prevent some of those *bona fide* residents from voting when the basis for such exclusion is a fear of the way they may vote: "'Fencing out' from the franchise a sector of the population because of the way they may vote is constitutionally impermissible."[59]

Carrington might have been grounded on a narrow rationale: The state unconstitutionally discriminated against members of the military. Whereas other would-be voters were permitted to show that they intended to stay in the state indefinitely, only members of the military were categorically and irrebuttably presumed to be temporary visitors.[60] A few years later, however, the Court was presented with another challenge to a durational residency requirement that presented a more direct challenge to the holding of *Pope v. Williams*. *Dunn v. Blumstein* involved a Tennessee law that permitted residents to register to vote only if, by the time of the next election, they would have been residents of the state for one year and residents of the county for three months.[61] The state's objective was to ensure that voters had sufficient time to be acquainted with local issues and politics, and perhaps sufficient time to become acclimated to the local culture and attitudes.

The Court rejected this justification and concluded that, while a brief residency period—perhaps thirty days[62]—might be necessary for the state to compile a list of registered voters in advance of the election, a state could not require a residency period so as to impress the community's philosophies onto new residents. The Court drew on *Carrington*'s concern about "fencing out" people because of their political

57. *Id.* at 632.

58. 380 U.S. 89 (1965).

59. *Id.* at 93–94.

60. *Id.* at 95.

61. 405 U.S. 330 (1972).

62. In *Marston v. Lewis*, 410 U.S. 679 (1973), the Court upheld a fifty-day durational residency and registration requirement for certain elections. The Court held that, under the facts of that case, the state had shown that it would be unable to register voters in time for the election if the registration period were not closed fifty days before the election. *Marston*, therefore, did not accept a fifty-day requirement as a general matter but rather allowed it only in a particular context.

attitudes and concluded that Tennessee's interest in ensuring a "common interest" among its voters was no different.[63]

6. The Lawbreaking

Although *Kramer* stated that strict scrutiny would apply to all restrictions besides age, citizenship, and residency, that statement proved not to be exactly correct. In *Richardson v. Ramirez*,[64] the Court upheld provisions of California law that excluded felons from voting, whether or not they had completed their sentences. There are several reasons that a jurisdiction might want to exclude felons and other convicts from voting, some of them quite controversial. Note that some of the arguments for excluding lawbreakers from voting parallel the reasons (stated and unstated) for excluding the poor.[65]

The first of these reasons draws on the social compact theory of government. Under this theory, individuals form societies to take advantage of the security and other benefits that can be provided by the collective. In exchange, those individuals (constructively) agree to be bound by the rules made by the rest of society. For example, we agree to limit our ability to take other people's property in exchange for society's protection of our property. Law-breakers, however, seek to gain the benefits of the collective without agreeing to be bound by rules that protect the rights of others. They want society to protect their property, but they don't abide by those same rules. States may reason that individuals who are not willing to abide by society's rules should not participate in the process of making rules for others. In response, opponents of felon disenfranchisement may take issue with the assumption that people voluntarily choose to abide by a society's rules, and they may further argue that those rules tend to favor wealthy interests, such that disenfranchisement laws operate to cement those interests' control over government.

Additional reasons center on concerns about the ways that felons may choose to vote. Some people worry that if felons or other criminals were permitted to vote, then politicians would cater to a pro-criminal agenda. Under this rationale, felon disenfranchisement might be a way of lessening the chance of enacting policies that would decriminalize certain conduct, increase trial rights of defendants, improve prison conditions, or the like. Felon disenfranchisement laws thus serve an interest in promoting a particular policy objective (law and order). Judge Friendly of the Second Circuit wrote in support of both these reasons in *Green v. Board of Elections*:

> A man who breaks the laws he has authorized his agent [the legislature] to make for his own governance could fairly have been thought to have abandoned the right to participate in further administering the compact. On a less theoretical plane, it can scarcely be deemed unreasonable for a state to

63. 405 U.S. at 354–56.
64. 418 U.S. 24 (1974).
65. *See* § D[1], *supra*.

> decide that perpetrators of serious crimes shall not take part in electing the legislators who make the laws, the executives who enforce these, the prosecutors who must try them for further violations, or the judges who are to consider their cases. This is especially so when account is taken of the heavy incidence of recidivism and the prevalence of organized crime. A contention that the equal protection clause requires New York to allow convicted mafiosi to vote for district attorneys or judges would not only be without merit but as obviously so as anything can be.[66]

Others argue, however, that felons are merely one kind of interest group among many in society, and there is nothing unusual about interest groups' using the electoral process to advantage their interests. Thus, felons who favor their interests might not be any different from welfare recipients who vote for politicians who promise more benefits for the poor, from millionaires who vote for politicians who promise to lower tax rates, or from outdoors enthusiasts who vote for politicians who promise to improve state parks.

Because law-breakers tend to be disproportionately poor, male, and young, and because they are disproportionately of minority races, some may adopt felon disenfranchisement laws as a way to suppress the voting power of those groups or to lessen the chance that policies favored by those groups would be adopted. Others, however, argue that such use of voting qualifications to affect the results of elections is illegitimate and quite possibly unconstitutional because it might be thought to undermine elections' ability to serve as a check on the government.[67]

Some people argue that felons should be re-enfranchised after finishing their sentences simply because they have "paid their debt to society." Under this theory, the punishment for a crime might include imprisonment, fines, restitution, community service, or whatnot, but once the convict has completed those steps, he should be permitted to rejoin society and should no longer be treated as an outsider—at least as to the convict's ability to exercise fundamental rights, such as the right to vote. (Presumably few people would object to prohibiting ex-cons from holding some government jobs; for example, we would hardly be surprised if the Drug Enforcement Administration rejected job applications from convicted drug kingpins.) In actuality, ex-cons face other disabilities besides disenfranchisement (consider, for example, sex-offender registration laws), but the paid-their-debt-to-society argument has emotive appeal for some people. The theory also has a circularity problem. It depends on one's characterizing imprisonment and fines as part of an offender's "real" punishment, while characterizing disenfranchisement as something imposed in addition to that punishment. Perhaps, however, it is appropriate to see disenfranchisement as part of the punishment, so that the criminal's "debt" is not fully "repaid" upon his release from prison.

---

66. 380 F.2d 445, 451–52 (2d Cir. 1967).

67. *See* Carrington v. Rash, 380 U.S. 89, 94 (1965) ("'Fencing out' from the franchise a sector of the population because of the way they may vote is constitutionally impermissible.").

Lastly, some people may support or oppose felon disenfranchisement because of the effect of such laws on the criminal-justice process. Perhaps (though it seems unlikely), disenfranchisement laws improve criminal law's deterrent effect. If would-be offenders know that their crimes will be punished not only by imprisonment or fines but also by disenfranchisement, then perhaps some will be less likely to commit the crimes. Alternatively, one may believe that re-enfranchising criminals will aid in the rehabilitative process; allowing criminals to rejoin civil society by taking part in government may encourage them to commit themselves to reforming their lives after their punishment has concluded.

Regardless of whether one concludes that felon-disenfranchisement laws represent good policy, *Ramirez* held that such laws are constitutional. On the constitutional question, *Ramirez* explained that the exclusion of felons was implicitly authorized by the Fourteenth Amendment itself. Section 1 of the Amendment requires each state to provide "all persons within its jurisdiction the equal protection of the laws." Section 2, however, provides an implicit limit on states' equal-protection obligations. That section announces that states should be given representation in the House of Representatives based on population, except that a state's representation can be reduced if the state prevents certain of its citizens from voting:

> [W]hen the right to vote at any [federal or state] election . . . is denied to any of the male inhabitants of such State, being twenty-one years of age, and citizens of the United States, or in any way abridged, except for participation in rebellion, *or other crime*, the basis of representation therein shall be reduced in the proportion which the number of such male citizens shall bear to the whole number of male citizens twenty-one years of age in such State.[68]

Thus, a state that excluded certain of its citizens (racial minorities, for example) from voting would have its representation in the House reduced. But even that mild sanction would not apply unless the excluded persons were male citizens over age twenty-one who were excluded for some reason other than their participation in crime. Interestingly, therefore, the Fourteenth Amendment—which contains the Equal Protection Clause—itself contains discrimination against females, noncitizens, and persons younger than twenty-one. The sex and age limitations were abrogated by the Nineteenth and Twenty-Sixth Amendments, respectively, but there has been no constitutional amendment granting voting rights to criminals or noncitizens.

Accordingly, the challengers of felon disenfranchisement in *Ramirez* had to argue that the Equal Protection Clause contained in § 1 of the Fourteenth Amendment prohibited states from barring felons from voting, even though § 2 of the same Amendment provided that the exclusion of criminals would not even trigger a reduction in

---

68. U.S. CONST. amend. XIV, § 2 (emphasis added).

representation.[69] The Court unsurprisingly held that the Equal Protection Clause did not require states to permit felons to vote.[70]

In addition to the text of the Amendment itself, the Court examined the legislative history of the Amendment (finding only "scant" legislative history, all of which supported the view that § 2 "was intended by Congress to mean what it says"),[71] and it relied on historical practice in holding that felon disenfranchisement was consistent with the constitutional requirement of equal protection. The Court noted that at the time the Fourteenth Amendment was adopted, twenty-nine states had felon-disenfranchisement laws.[72] Further, the Court analyzed the enabling acts permitting states to rejoin the Union after the Civil War. Those acts forbade the readmitted states (Arkansas, North Carolina, South Carolina, Louisiana, Georgia, Alabama, Florida, Virginia, Mississippi, and Texas) from depriving their citizens of the right to vote, except as punishment for felonies.[73] The implication, therefore, was that there was nothing objectionable—and certainly nothing unconstitutional—about felon disenfranchisement.

Many commentators have argued for the repeal of felon-disenfranchisement laws, noting that such laws have a disproportionate impact on racial minorities. Just because a law produces a racially disproportionate *effect*, however, is not enough to trigger strict scrutiny of the law on the ground that it is a racial classification. Rather, a law that does not explicitly create different rules for different races will be treated as a racial classification only if it has a discriminatory purpose or intent in addition to a racially disproportionate effect.[74]

The Court's jurisprudence on felon-disenfranchisement laws has followed this settled doctrine. Felon-disenfranchisement laws classify people on the basis of their criminal convictions, not their race. So even if such laws disqualify a disproportionate number of racial minorities, strict scrutiny applies only when the laws were adopted for the *purpose* of disproportionately disqualifying certain races. Proving such a discriminatory purpose is difficult, given that politicians often hide their true motives, but the Court has struck down one ancient Alabama law as motivated by such a purpose. That case, *Hunter v. Underwood*,[75] involved the Alabama Constitution of 1901, which excluded from voting any person convicted of "any crime . . . involving moral turpitude"—a class of offenses believed to be committed disproportionately by blacks.

When considering felon disenfranchisement, it is important to remember that the issue is not as simple as whether or not to disenfranchise felons (and perhaps some misdemeanants as well). States vary considerably in their laws, from Maine and Vermont, which permit felons to vote while in prison, to the twelve states that

69. *See* 418 U.S. at 43.
70. *See id.* at 54, 56.
71. *See id.* at 43.
72. *See id.* at 48.
73. *See id.* at 48–52.
74. *See, e.g.*, Washington v. Davis, 426 U.S. 229 (1976).
75. 471 U.S. 222 (1985).

disenfranchise at least some felons after they have completed their terms of prison, parole, and probation. Between those extremes are states that disenfranchise felons while they are in prison, states that disenfranchise felons while they are in prison or on parole, and states that disenfranchise felons while they are in prison, on parole, or on probation.

Felon disenfranchisement has been an especially active area of law reform over the last generation. In recent years, some states have liberalized their laws and permitted more felons to vote. Others have tightened up their laws, imposing greater restrictions on voting than had been in place beforehand. Overall, there seems to be a slight trend toward permitting more criminals to vote—a trend the Obama administration supported, with former Attorney General Holder urging states to restore the voting rights of anyone who has completed his term of prison, parole, and probation and has paid all his fines.[76]

E. Conclusion

Through the Supreme Court's interpretation of the Equal Protection and Due Process Clauses, the constitutional right to vote has expanded greatly since the mid-twentieth century. But, whereas laws abridging other fundamental rights invariably trigger strict scrutiny, the right to vote is subject to more nuanced treatment.

The modern Court has shown an intolerance for restrictions on voting rights that suppress the political power of disfavored groups or that entrench the position of powerful interests. On the other hand, the Court has not made the right to vote fundamental *per se*. Rather, only certain people—those who are adults, citizens, and residents—possess a fundamental right to vote, such that their exclusion from the franchise triggers strict scrutiny. And even those people may be barred from voting if, for example, they are convicted of a crime or they wish to vote in an election for a special-purpose district but lack the requisite interest in the outcome.

Thus, the right to vote is far more complex than one might have imagined . . . as is the rest of this subject. Welcome to election law.

---

76. *See* Matt Apuzzo, *Holder Urges States to Lift Bans on Felons' Voting*, N.Y. Times, Feb. 12, 2014, at A17.

Chapter 2
Redistricting and One Person, One Vote

A. Introduction

The phrase "one person, one vote" is familiar to most Americans. The right to vote and the right to equal voting power seem so fundamental to democracy and to the constitutional ideal of equality that we may imagine that the one-person, one-vote doctrine is easy, or even obvious. After all, doesn't "equal protection of the laws" require equality? What good is a democracy if the people vote but the government can determine the value of each vote? The doctrine is a great deal more complex than most people realize, however, and it raises questions about the nature of political equality and about judicial competence, to which few people give serious thought.

Until the landmark case of *Baker v. Carr*,[1] the federal courts considered reapportionment claims to be nonjusticiable political questions, *i.e.*, questions properly resolved by the "political" branches of government rather than the judiciary. When a case presents a political question, federal and state courts will refuse to reach the merits of those cases, even if the cases are otherwise properly before them. The political question doctrine has the potential, depending on how broadly and rigorously it is applied, to prevent many election-law disputes from being resolved by the courts. Whether this result is good or bad depends on what one thinks about the appropriateness of courts' deciding election issues.

The political question doctrine in the federal courts has a venerable, if confusing and controversial, history. The doctrine can be traced back to no less than *Marbury v. Madison*, in which Chief Justice John Marshall spoke of certain powers of the President lying in his sole discretion, beyond the control of courts—"[q]uestions, in their nature political" and unfit for judicial resolution.[2] The Supreme Court has since considered whether the political question doctrine applies to issues besides the unique facts presented in *Marbury*. Some of these cases involved various aspects of election

1. 369 U.S. 186 (1962).
2. 5 U.S. (1 Cranch) 137, 170 (1803).

law, and the Court has variously held that they did[3] or did not[4] present nonjusticiable political questions.

The doctrine has generated a large amount of scholarly commentary. Some writers defend the doctrine, arguing that federal judges should be able to exercise prudential judgment to defer reaching the merits of particularly difficult or contentious issues that are better resolved by the other, more democratically accountable, branches of government.[5] In contrast, other writers argue that judges should decide the merits of cases when they have jurisdiction, particularly when constitutional rights are implicated. On this account, the doctrine is unprincipled and based on "political" considerations that judges should not take into account.[6]

In this chapter, we consider the establishment of the one-person, one-vote principle—starting with the Court's determination that reapportionment cases are justiciable—and then examine the one-person, one-vote principle's doctrinal development. We will see that although the Court invokes the ideal of political equality, in practice it is not possible to achieve perfect equality—and the attempt to achieve it would involve the courts in extensive, perhaps never-ending, disputes of the sort that Justice Frankfurter feared when he warned the Court to stay out of the "political thicket."[7] Accordingly, the Court has accepted some deviation from the equality ideal, particularly in districts for choosing state and local representatives.

B. The Political Thicket: The Political Question Doctrine in Redistricting Cases

1. In General

Since the iconic decision of *Marbury v. Madison*,[8] federal courts have held that they cannot resolve "political" questions, but they have not been clear about what satisfies that term. Some cases, like *Marbury*, seem to hold that such questions are those that the Constitution by its terms assigns for resolution to another branch of government.

3. *E.g.*, Vieth v. Jubelirer, 541 U.S. 267 (2004) (challenge to political gerrymandering of congressional districts); Rucho v. Common Cause, 588 U.S. 684 (2019) (same).

4. *E.g.*, Nixon v. Herndon, 273 U.S. 536 (1927) (challenge to racial discrimination in party primary); Baker v. Carr, 369 U.S. 186 (1962) (challenge to malapportioned state legislature).

5. *E.g.*, Alexander Bickel, The Least Dangerous Branch (1962).

6. *E.g.*, Martin H. Redish, *Judicial Review and the Political Question Doctrine*, 79 Nw. U. L. Rev. 1031 (1985). *See generally* Rachel E. Barkow, *More Supreme Than Court? The Fall of the Political Question Doctrine*, 102 Colum. L. Rev. 237 (2002); Jesse Choper, *The Political Question Doctrine: Suggested Criteria*, 54 Duke L.J. 1457 (2005).

7. Colegrove v. Green, 328 U.S. 549, 556 (1946) (plurality opinion).

8. 5 U.S. (1 Cranch) 137 (1803).

Other cases, in contrast, seem to apply the concept in broader terms, and permit courts discretion to decline to rule on a case based on pragmatic and prudential factors. Both approaches are reflected in the modern synthesis announced in *Baker v. Carr*.[9] There, the Court held that application of the political question doctrine contemplates a case-by-case inquiry, and that inquiry turns on no less than six factors: (1) a "textually demonstrable constitutional commitment of the issue to a coordinate political department"; (2) a "lack of judicially discoverable and manageable standards for resolving it"; (3) the "impossibility of deciding without an initial policy determination of a kind clearly for nonjudicial discretion"; (4) the "impossibility of a court's undertaking independent resolution without expressing lack of the respect due coordinate branches of government"; (5) "an unusual need for unquestioning adherence to a political decision already made"; and (6) the "potentiality of embarrassment from multifarious pronouncements by various departments on one question."[10] In *Baker*, the Court held that a challenge in federal court to malapportioned state legislative districts was not a political question, since federal courts would not be questioning decisions of another branch of the federal government, and courts could develop manageable standards under the Equal Protection Clause to resolve such disputes.

The *Baker* criteria continue to be applied in numerous cases, although, as in *Baker* itself, different courts emphasize various elements of the test. Thus, in *Nixon v. United States*,[11] the Court held that an impeached federal judge could not come to court and thereafter challenge the impeachment procedures used in the Senate. Judge Nixon claimed that the Senate's constitutional power to "try" his impeachment meant that he had the right to present evidence to the entire Senate, and, therefore, the Constitution was violated when a committee of the Senate heard evidence and reported that evidence to the rest of the Senate. The Court applied the first two *Baker* factors and noted that a court must "interpret the text" of the Constitution to determine if an issue is committed for resolution to another branch. In the Court's view, the second factor was related to the first because the lack of judicially manageable standards "may strengthen the conclusion that there is a textually demonstrable commitment to a coordinate branch."[12] The Court concluded that Judge Nixon's case presented a political question because the Constitution vested sole discretion in the Senate on how to "try" an impeachment; that the choice between the various meanings of "try" was ultimately a nonjusticiable determination because the term "try" "lacks sufficient precision to afford any judicially manageable standard of review"; and that if an impeached official succeeded in court, it could place courts in the awkward position of ordering the reinstatement of an official whose position had already been filled.

9. 369 U.S. 186 (1962).

10. *Id.* at 217.

11. 506 U.S. 224 (1993).

12. *Id.* at 228–29.

Foreign-affairs issues are often thought to raise political questions.[13] But that is not always the case. Thus, in *Zivotofsky v. Clinton*,[14] the Court considered whether the President could, in the context of issuing passports, refuse to recognize the status of Jerusalem as the capital of Israel, despite a federal statute that called on him to do so. The Court held that the issue was not a nonjusticiable political question. Characterizing the political question doctrine as a "narrow exception" to its presumptive duty to hear cases that satisfied ordinary jurisdictional requirements, the Court focused on the first two *Baker* factors. The Court held that there was not an exclusive commitment to the Executive to resolve the constitutionality of such a statute, and that courts could resolve conflicts between the President and Congress. Also, the resolution of whether the President had the sole authority to recognize foreign governments, as compared to Congress's authority to regulate immigration, involved "familiar principles of constitutional interpretation" that did not leave federal courts lacking in manageable standards.

2. Guarantee Clause Cases

Article IV, § 4, of the U.S. Constitution states that "[t]he United States shall guarantee to every State in this Union a Republican Form of Government." Since *Luther v. Borden*,[15] the Supreme Court has held that federal courts cannot hear legal challenges to state governmental structures or processes on the ground that they violate the Guarantee Clause. *Luther* involved a series of changes to the state constitution of Rhode Island, which resulted in controversy and confusion about the proper governmental authority in that state. The case came before the Court due to a challenge to a search by a sheriff of the Rhode Island government. The challenger argued that the search was unlawful, since it was undertaken on behalf of a government that was not in a republican form. The Court held that the challenge was nonjusticiable, since it was up to Congress to enforce the Guarantee Clause. Among other things, the Court observed that it was unclear how to determine whether or not a state had a republican form of government.

While *Luther* has long stood for its apparent conclusion that Guarantee Clause challenges in federal court are barred by the political question doctrine, that understanding has not prevented litigants, or the Court, from revisiting the issue. For example, in *Pacific States Telephone & Telegraph Co. v. Oregon*,[16] the Court considered a challenge to state initiatives and referenda on the basis that they violated the Guarantee Clause.

---

13. *E.g.*, Goldwater v. Carter, 444 U.S. 996 (1979) (challenge to presidential termination of a treaty held nonjusticiable).

14. 566 U.S. 189 (2012). While the Supreme Court rarely expressly invokes the political question doctrine, a recent study demonstrates that it is more frequently applied in the lower federal courts, especially in cases with foreign-affairs implications. *See* Curtis A. Bradley & Eric A. Posner, *The Real Political Question Doctrine*, 75 Stan. L. Rev. 1031 (2023).

15. 48 U.S. (7 How.) 1 (1849).

16. 223 U.S. 118 (1912).

First enacted in states during the Progressive Era, initiatives and referenda are types of "direct democracy," respectively permitting voters to enact laws by placing them on the ballot or to review laws passed by the state legislature. By taking away power from elected legislatures, the argument ran, these provisions unconstitutionally deviated from a republican form of government by making the government too democratic. The Court dismissed the case without reaching the merits. Citing *Luther*, the Court held that how much popular control of lawmaking was consistent with republican government was a nonjusticiable political question. The attack on the statute passed by direct democracy was of a "political nature" since it concerned the "framework and political character of the government," and the Guarantee Clause reserved those issues to Congress.[17] *Luther* and *Pacific States* have largely prevented Guarantee Clause challenges from proceeding in federal court.[18]

3. Malapportionment and the Equal Protection Clause: Pre-*Baker v. Carr*

Litigants and judges engaged in various efforts—some successful, some not—to circumvent the limits of *Luther* and other Guarantee Clause cases. These efforts often placed more explicit reliance on other constitutional provisions, particularly the Equal Protection Clause of the Fourteenth Amendment. But the jurisprudential shift to the Equal Protection Clause raised complications of its own and did not automatically dispose of concerns raised by the political question doctrine.

The urbanization of many states in the twentieth century caused an increasing disparity between the populations of many urban and rural electoral districts. Many districts for state legislatures and for the U.S. House of Representatives had been drawn early in the century. Districts in rural areas often lost population and those in urban areas gained. But unless the district boundaries were periodically redrawn, legislators in rural areas represented (and could be elected by) far fewer constituents than their counterparts in urban districts. It is not surprising that, in many states, rural legislators resisted efforts to redraw district lines. They were often able to succeed because

---

17. *Id.* at 150.

18. For a rare counterexample, see *Kerr v. Hickenlooper*, 744 F.3d 1156 (10th Cir. 2014) (holding that the *Baker v. Carr* criteria limit categorical exclusion of all Guarantee Clause issues, in a case involving a state taxpayer bill of rights requiring voter approval of all tax increases). The decision was vacated and remanded by the Supreme Court on other grounds, 576 U.S. 1079 (2015), and the Tenth Circuit eventually held that a political subdivision could not sue a state in federal court to enforce the Clause. Kerr v. Polis, 20 F.4th 686 (10th Cir. 2021). For further discussion of the doctrine as it pertains to the Guarantee Clause, see, *e.g.*, Deborah Merritt, *The Guarantee Clause and State Autonomy: Federalism for a Third Century*, 88 COLUM. L. REV. 1 (1988); Robert G. Natelson, *A Republic, Not a Democracy? Initiative, Referendum, and the Constitution's Guarantee Clause*, 80 TEX. L. REV. 807 (2002) (originalist argument that initiative and referendum do not violate the Clause); and Jacob M. Heller, Note, *Death by a Thousand Cuts: The Guarantee Clause Regulation of State Constitutions*, 62 STAN. L. REV. 1711 (2010) (arguing that micromanagement of state budgets by direct democracy can violate the Guarantee Clause).

they retained their disproportionate power in malapportioned legislatures. By the 1960s, virtually all state legislatures were malapportioned to some extent.[19]

Before then, in 1946, a legal challenge reached the Supreme Court in *Colegrove v. Green*.[20] That case involved plaintiff voters from Illinois who sought injunctive relief from the federal courts' requiring the state to redraw malapportioned congressional districts, which the state legislature had not redrawn since 1901. The plaintiffs argued that living in heavily populated districts diluted their vote in violation of Article I and of the Equal Protection Clause of the Fourteenth Amendment. A majority of the Supreme Court held their claim to be nonjusticiable and ordered the case dismissed. A plurality opinion by Justice Frankfurter emphasized that the plaintiffs were asking for federal judges to make essentially political decisions, intruding on the political contests and structure of a state. Congress had ample constitutional authority under Article I, §4, Clause 1,[21] to regulate the drawing of congressional districts, and the plaintiffs' remedy was there. Frankfurter famously concluded that "[c]ourts ought not to enter this political thicket. The remedy for unfairness in districting is to secure State legislatures that will apportion properly, or to invoke the ample powers of Congress." Reapportionment claims were similar, he added, to the Guarantee Clause claims that had already been held to be nonjusticiable.[22]

Justice Black, joined by Justices Douglas and Murphy, dissented. He noted how the differences between the district populations had grown since 1901 to the hundreds of thousands, and how attempts to make the state legislature redraw districts had failed. He concluded that an Equal Protection Clause violation was stated, since different voters, in effect, had differently weighted votes. He contended that calling reapportionment a "political question" was a mere "play on words" because the plaintiffs were simply asking courts to vindicate the "right of a voter to cast an effective ballot."[23]

Despite the loss in *Colegrove*, a legal attack on gerrymandered districts unanimously succeeded in the Court in 1960 in *Gomillion v. Lightfoot*,[24] in an opinion authored by none other than Justice Frankfurter. The case involved the redrawing in 1957 of the boundaries of the City of Tuskegee, Alabama, so as to exclude almost all black voters. The shape of the city had been changed from a square to a 28-sided figure, which had the effect of excluding almost "400 Negro voters while not removing

---

19. Stephen Ansolabehere & James M. Snyder, Jr., The End of Inequality: One Person, One Vote and the Transformation of American Politics 3 (2008).

20. 328 U.S. 549 (1946).

21. U.S. Const. art. I, §4, cl. 1 (giving Congress the authority to "make or alter" rules concerning the "Times, Places and Manner" of congressional elections).

22. 328 U.S. at 556 (plurality opinion). The vote was 4–3, as Justice Jackson did not participate in the case and Chief Justice Stone had passed away earlier in the Term. Justice Rutledge wrote a short concurring opinion.

23. *Id.* at 573 (Black, J., dissenting). The "play on words" language was a quote from *Nixon v. Herndon*, 273 U.S. 536, 540 (1927), which held that a suit against racial discrimination in a Texas Democratic primary was not a nonjusticiable "political" question, despite its connection to politics.

24. 364 U.S. 339 (1960).

a single white voter or resident."[25] The Court held that the suit's allegations, if proven, would constitute racial discrimination in violation of the Fifteenth Amendment's right against racial discrimination in voting. *Colegrove*, the Court held, was distinguishable. That case involved decades of state legislative inaction, while here there was affirmative legislation action, with ample evidence of racial discrimination. "These considerations," the Court observed, "lift this controversy out of the so-called 'political' arena and into the conventional sphere of constitutional litigation."[26]

4. Malapportionment and the Equal Protection Clause: *Baker v. Carr*

While *Gomillion* was being litigated, lower court litigation that would culminate in the Court's historic decision in 1962 in *Baker v. Carr*[27] was already underway.[28] Plaintiffs were Tennessee voters who brought an equal-protection challenge to that state's legislative districts, which had not been redrawn since 1901 and were severely malapportioned by the urbanization of the succeeding decades. The lower court[29] dismissed the case as a nonjusticiable "political question," citing *Colegrove*. The Supreme Court, in a majority opinion authored by Justice Brennan, held that the case was not a political question, properly understood. He articulated the criteria that earlier cases had identified as characteristics of a political question,[30] and he proceeded to explain why the criteria were not satisfied. Political question cases, the Court explained, typically involve a clash between the coordinate branches of the federal government, and that was not involved here. *Colegrove* was distinguished as a Guarantee Clause case, which clause was not implicated in this case. The Court held that "[j]udicial standards under the Equal Protection Clause [in contrast to those under the Guarantee Clause] are well developed and familiar,"[31] and it invoked the recent case of *Gomillion* as an

---

25. *Id.* at 341.

26. *Id.* at 346–47. In a concurring opinion, Justice Whittaker argued that the Fifteenth Amendment was not violated because the plaintiffs still retained their ability to vote, albeit in a redrawn district, but he concluded that the redrawing had been accomplished in a racially discriminatory manner and, therefore, violated the Fourteenth Amendment.

27. 369 U.S. 186 (1962).

28. For overviews of all of the reapportionment cases, including lower-court decisions and the strategies of the litigants, see Ansolabehere & Snyder, *supra* note 19; Richard C. Cortner, The Apportionment Cases (1970); and Robert G. Dixon, Jr., Democratic Representation: Reapportionment in Law and Politics (1968).

29. The lower court was a three-judge district court, with a direct appeal to the Supreme Court. As the statute, 28 U.S.C. § 2284, was then written, such a court was convened to hear most constitutional attacks on statewide statutes or practices. In 1976, the statute was amended to limit the convening of such courts to only reapportionment cases. All of the reapportionment cases discussed in this chapter were initially litigated before a three-judge district court. *See* Michael E. Solimine, *The Three-Judge District Court in Voting Rights Litigation*, 30 U. Mich. J.L. Reform 79 (1996).

30. *See* Chapter 2, § B[1], *supra*.

31. 369 U.S. at 226.

example of a similar constitutional attack on redrawing of electoral boundaries that was not barred as a political question.

The majority opinion purported not to reach the merits,[32] but Justice Clark's concurring opinion did. He argued that the Equal Protection Clause was violated since there was no rational basis for the malapportionment of the state legislative districts. The discrimination among the legislative districts was a "crazy quilt," the result of favoring the *status quo*, not the product of a "rational design."[33] He also emphasized that judicial relief was appropriate since, as he saw it, the people of Tennessee had no other avenue for relief; there was no initiative or referendum in the state, and the makeup of the legislative districts locked in the malapportionment.

Justice Frankfurter, joined by Justice Harlan, wrote a long and impassioned dissent. He argued that the Court was improperly injecting itself into the political processes of the states. *Colegrove*, he argued, was not an aberration and represented settled doctrine. Distinguishing that decision as merely a Guarantee Clause case, as the majority did, was unconvincing. This case, Frankfurter argued, had all the nonjusticiable elements of that case, and was a "Guarantee Clause claim masquerading under a different label."[34] Similarly, cases like *Gomillion* were distinguishable, as they involved discrimination against black voters, which was explicitly forbidden by the Equal Protection Clause and the Fifteenth Amendment. Here, in contrast, no one's right to vote or to have his vote counted was impaired. He argued that, throughout American history, legislative apportionment had been done in a variety of ways, not all on the basis of the sort of population equality demanded by the plaintiffs. The Equal Protection Clause, he argued, provided no clearer guide to the redrawing of districts than the Guarantee Clause did, and he argued that the Court's decision would embroil the federal courts in partisan controversies.

Justice Frankfurter's dissent ostensibly did not reach the merits of the equal-protection challenge, but Justice Harlan's dissent (which Justice Frankfurter joined), in effect, did. He argued that the case was based on a "difference of opinion as to the function of representative government" and that the drawing of legislative districts was a "classic legislative judgment" to which courts should defer. In his view, there were rational reasons for the state's apportionment, in that the legislature might have wanted to take into account rural, agricultural interests when drawing (or refusing to redraw) districts.[35]

32. Justice Stewart wrote a brief concurring opinion noting that the majority did not reach the merits, and, although the other separate opinions did discuss the merits, in his view it was not necessary to do so.

33. 369 U.S. at 257–58 (Clark, J., concurring).

34. *Id.* at 297 (Frankfurter, J., dissenting).

35. *Id.* at 333, 336 (Harlan, J., dissenting).

5. The Political Question Doctrine and Political Gerrymandering, Post-*Baker v. Carr*

The holding in *Baker v. Carr* unleashed the reapportionment revolution in federal courts. In the wake of *Baker*, litigants filed numerous cases challenging the drawing of congressional and state legislative districts on what came to be "one-person, one-vote" grounds. Freed of the restraints of the political question doctrine, the Supreme Court and lower courts ordered that legislative districts in many states be redrawn.[36] While initially controversial, at least in Congress and in state legislatures, *Baker* and its progeny came to be accepted and rather easily implemented.[37]

More controversial was continued political gerrymandering by state legislatures. Gerrymandering is the practice of dividing electoral districts, often into highly irregular shapes, to give one party an advantage over the other by packing supporters into the district and excluding supporters of the other party. The Supreme Court's consideration of the political question doctrine as applied to partisan gerrymandering is discussed in § E, *infra*.

Although the political question doctrine is occasionally raised in election-law contexts other than gerrymandering, it is rarely successful.[38]

6. The Political Question Doctrine in State Courts

The political question doctrine has sometimes been applied in state courts, when those courts consider legal challenges to the actions of other branches of the state government. To the extent they apply the doctrine, some state courts borrow from the criteria developed in federal courts. But, on the whole, the doctrine has been applied less robustly by many state courts, in part because state constitutions are typically much longer and more detailed than the U.S. Constitution and seem to call for more judicial interpretation of those provisions.[39] Moreover, in the redistricting context,

---

36. For an overview of those cases, see §§ C and D, *infra*.

37. Barry Friedman, The Will of the People 268–70 (2009); Michael E. Solimine, *Congress, the Solicitor General, and the Path of Reapportionment Litigation*, 62 Case W. Res. L. Rev. 1109 (2012).

38. *See, e.g.*, Jacobson v. Secretary of State, 974 F.3d 1236 (11th Cir. 2020) (challenge to order of names on ballot deemed nonjusticiable); Kim v. Hanlon, 99 F.4th 140 (3d Cir. 2024) (challenge to order and grouping of names on ballot justiciable, and noting different result in *Jacobson*); Castro v. Scanlan, 86 F.4th 947 (1st Cir. 2023) (affirming, on lack-of-standing grounds, a district court decision holding that a challenge to Donald Trump's eligibility as an alleged insurrectionist under § 3 of the Fourteenth Amendment to run for President failed for plaintiff's lack of standing and because it was a nonjusticiable political question).

39. *E.g.*, Robert F. Williams & Lawrence Friedman, The Law of American State Constitutions 336 (2d ed. 2023); Helen Hershkoff, *State Courts and the "Passive Virtues": Rethinking the Judicial Function*, 114 Harv. L. Rev. 1833 (2001); Nat Stern, *Don't Answer That: Revisiting the Political Question Doctrine in State Courts*, 21 U. Pa. J. Const. L. 153 (2018).

some state provisions explicitly call for state courts (often, the state supreme court) to review the work of the state body or committee that engages in the redistricting.[40]

C. The Constitutional Basis for One Person, One Vote

Until the 1960s, the Supreme Court did not interpret the Constitution to contain any requirement that electoral districts be equally populated. In fact, as discussed in § B[3], *supra*, the Court considered apportionment controversies to be nonjusticiable. In 1962, however, the Court decided *Baker v. Carr*,[41] which held that courts could hear equal-protection challenges to the apportionment of districts. That case did not, however, establish what limitations, if any, the Equal Protection Clause (or any other provision of the Constitution) placed on electoral districting. The Court left the formulation of those substantive standards to later cases.

Almost immediately after *Baker v. Carr* opened the door, cases came to the Court challenging electoral systems that seemed to give more political power to some voters than to others. The very next year after *Baker*, the Court decided *Gray v. Sanders*.[42] That case considered Georgia's "county unit" system for statewide elections. The county unit system was similar to the Federal Electoral College, which is used for selecting the President. Under the county unit system, the victorious candidate was the one who received the most unit votes—not the greatest number of total individual votes cast. Each county was allotted a certain number of unit votes, which roughly—but only roughly—corresponded to the counties' populations. In other words, the winner was the candidate who won in enough counties to give him a majority of the total number of unit votes. Thus, candidates effectively competed in simultaneous county-wide elections, even though they were running for statewide office.

In an opinion by Justice Douglas, the Court held that this system violated the Equal Protection Clause. Stressing that the county-unit system weighted certain (rural) areas of the state more heavily than others, the Court compared that weighting to undoubtedly unconstitutional systems that gave more voting power to males or whites than to females or blacks.[43] The Court concluded, without much analysis and without specifying a standard of review, that the unit system was similarly unconstitutional because

---

40. James A. Gardner, *A Post-*Vieth *Strategy for Litigating Partisan Gerrymandering Claims*, 3 Election L.J. 643 (2004); David Schultz, *Redistricting and the New Judicial Federalism: Reapportionment Litigation Under State Constitutions*, 37 Rutgers L.J. 1087 (2006).

41. 369 U.S. 186 (1962).

42. 372 U.S. 368 (1963).

43. *See id.* at 379 (noting that the county-unit system in Georgia "in end result, weights the rural vote more heavily than the urban vote, and weights some small rural counties heavier than other larger rural counties").

it violated the principle of "one person, one vote."[44] *Gray* was thus the first Supreme Court case to use the iconic phrase.

As to the constitutional basis for the one-person, one-vote principle, the Court was vague. The Court invoked a "conception of political equality" which it found reflected in texts "from the Declaration of Independence, to Lincoln's Gettysburg Address, to the Fifteenth, Seventeenth, and Nineteenth Amendments," but it did not explain how any of those sources rendered the county-unit system unconstitutional.[45]

The Court rejected Georgia's argument that the county-unit system should be upheld because of its similarity to the Electoral College, which, of course, is delineated in the Constitution itself.[46] According to the Court, the Electoral College reflected a "conception of political equality [that] belongs to a bygone day, and should not be considered in determining what the Equal Protection Clause of the Fourteenth Amendment requires in statewide elections."[47] The Court treated the Electoral College as an exception to the general rule requiring equality of voting strength. In the Court's view, the compromise resulting in the Electoral College "validated the collegiate principle despite its inherent numerical inequality, but implied nothing about the use of an analogous system by a State in a statewide election."[48]

Although *Gray* was less than clear in its reasoning, it was quite clear about its conclusion that it was unconstitutional to give certain votes within a given constituency more weight than others; the Court read the Equal Protection Clause to require states to adhere to "one person, one vote."[49] Importantly, however, the Court did not hold that populations had to be equal *across* districts. Rather, the Court held that the population within each electoral area must be given equal voting power: "Once the geographical unit for which a representative is to be chosen is designated, all who participate in the election are to have an equal vote."[50] It was left to later cases to apply the one-person, one-vote rule where there was a disparity of voting power between voters in different districts.

Wesberry v. Sanders was the first such case.[51] It applied *Gray*'s one-person, one-vote rule to congressional districts. Rather than rest its holding on the Equal Protection Clause, however, *Wesberry* relied on article I, § 2, of the Constitution. That section provides that the members of the House of Representatives shall be chosen "by the People of the several States." According to the Court, that section requires congressional

---

44. *Id.* at 381.

45. *See id.* at 381. Compare the Court's opinion two years later, also written by Justice Douglas, in *Griswold v. Connecticut*, 381 U.S. 479, 484 (1965) (finding constitutional rights in "penumbras, formed by emanations from" the specific guarantees of the Bill of Rights); *id.* at 485 (holding that there is a "zone of privacy created by several fundamental constitutional guarantees").

46. *See* U.S. Const. art. II, § 1, cls. 1–4 & amend. XII.

47. *Gray*, 372 U.S. at 376 n.8.

48. *Id.* at 378.

49. *Id.* at 381. *See also id.* at 382 (Stewart, J., concurring) ("Within a given constituency, there can be room for but a single constitutional rule—one voter, one vote.").

50. *Id.* at 379.

51. 376 U.S. 1 (1964).

districts to be apportioned so that "as nearly as practicable one man's vote in a congressional election is to be worth as much as another's."[52]

Wesberry's analysis was largely historical and rested primarily on the Framers' decision to base representation in the House on population, rather than giving each of the states equal representation in the entire Congress, as the small states had favored. Although most of the history cited by the Court related to the allocation of representatives *between* the states based on the states' populations rather than the allocation of representatives *within* the states, the Court took the point one step further than the Framers had. According to the Court, "It would defeat the principle solemnly embodied in the Great Compromise—equal representation in the House for equal numbers of people—for us to hold that, within the States, legislatures may draw the lines of congressional districts in such a way as to give some voters a greater voice in choosing a Congressman than others."[53] In the view of the Court, the point of allocating seats in the House of Representatives by population was to make the representatives responsible "to the people as individuals."[54] If states were able to draw districts on a basis other than population, they could undermine this objective.

As formulated in *Wesberry*, the right to equipopulous districts was vague. It wasn't quite "one person, one vote"; rather, the right was watered down so as to require equality only "as nearly as is practicable."[55] The Court accepted the possibility that it might "not be possible to draw congressional districts with mathematical precision."[56] Nevertheless, the Court held that equality was "the fundamental goal for the House of Representatives," requiring states to adhere to equality unless "[im]practicable" or "[im]possible."[57] Later cases would further refine the standard, moving it closer to a guarantee of precise mathematical equality.

Reynolds v. Sims,[58] which was decided four months after *Wesberry*, is the most important case of the "reapportionment revolution." It instantly placed courts at the center of never-ending controversies about the distribution of political power—a position courts have held for the last sixty years.

Unlike *Gray* and *Wesberry*, which involved statewide elections and congressional districts, respectively, *Sims* involved an equal protection challenge to state legislative districts. *Sims* could not, therefore, rest on article I, § 2, which deals only with elections for the federal House of Representatives. Neither could *Sims* rely on *Gray*'s rationale, which required equal voting power only among voters participating in the same election. Finding existing precedent insufficient to attack malapportionment in state legislative districts, *Sims* expanded the precedent by holding that "the Equal

52. *Id.* at 7–8.
53. *Id.* at 14.
54. *Id.*
55. *Id.* at 7–8.
56. *Id.* at 18.
57. *Id.*
58. 377 U.S. 533 (1964).

Protection Clause requires that the seats in both houses of a bicameral state legislature must be apportioned on a population basis."[59]

The districts for Alabama's House of Representatives and Senate had not been reapportioned since 1900, and population shifts had been so dramatic that by the time of *Sims*, the districts' populations varied as much as 41-to-1 in the Senate and 16-to-1 in the House. Voters in one of the more populated districts challenged the apportionment, and during the course of the litigation, the Alabama legislature passed a proposed constitutional amendment patterned on the "Great Compromise" reflected in the composition of the two houses of the U.S. Congress. Under the proposed amendment, each of the state's 67 counties would receive one senator and at least one seat in the 106-member House of Representatives, with the remaining 39 seats allocated by population.

The Court struck down Alabama's existing districting plan and further announced that the proposed amendment would not meet constitutional standards either. Both plans, the Court argued, contravened the democratic principle of majority rule by allowing a minority of voters—those living in under-populated districts—to control a majority of legislative seats. Alabama had argued that such under-population was a rational way of protecting the rights of rural residents, but the Court instead characterized it as discrimination against urban voters. And discrimination against voters based on their place of residence, the Court held, was no more constitutional than discrimination on the basis of "race or economic status."[60]

One might have thought that the Warren Court, which did so much to protect the rights of minorities such as blacks, the poor, and criminal defendants, would be receptive to a representational structure designed to protect the interests of a minority. The Court, however, told states that it was unconstitutional to manipulate groups' political influence to protect minorities' rights. Rather, the Court said, "[o]ur constitutional system amply provides for the protection of minorities by means other than giving them majority control of state legislatures."[61]

The Court's holding was based on the idea that voters in an over-populated district have had the value of their votes "debased" or "diluted" by the presence of the additional voters. But, as Justice Harlan argued in dissent, the Court's analysis was conclusory: One cannot tell whether the value of a vote has been "debased" or "diluted," or even whether a district is "over-populated," without first deciding how many voters should be in the district.[62] The majority did not, and could not, dispute the point; rather, it appeared to treat the issue as self-evident. In the majority's view, equal protection demanded that states accord voters equal influence, therefore guaranteeing that districts contain (at least "substantially") equal population.[63] Justice

59. *Id.* at 568.

60. *Id.* at 566 (citations omitted). *See also id.* at 576.

61. *Id.* at 566. It is worth noting that the "minorities" protected by the malapportioned districts—white rural voters—were hardly the minorities whose rights the Warren Court was interested in protecting.

62. *See id.* at 590 (Harlan, J., dissenting).

63. *Id.* at 565–66 (opinion of the Court).

Harlan further protested that population deviations had existed during the entire history of the United States and convincingly demonstrated that the Equal Protection Clause had not been understood to call those deviations into question, but the majority ignored the historical argument and forced states to redraw their district lines to equalize population.

As in *Gray v. Sanders*, where the Court rejected the argument that the state's electoral system was constitutional because it was modeled on the electoral college, *Reynolds v. Sims* rejected the argument that Alabama's proposed amendment was constitutional because it was based on the Great Compromise. Under the proposed amendment, Alabama's House of Representatives would have been apportioned loosely based on population but with each county guaranteed at least one representative. Alabama's Senate would have contained one senator from each of the state's counties. Such a plan appeared to mirror the apportionment of Congress, as article I, § 2, clause 3 of the Constitution bases apportionment of the House on population but provides that "each State shall have at Least one Representative"; and article I, § 3, clause 1 provides for an equal number of senators from each state. Nevertheless, the distribution of congressional seats did not control this case, the Court held, because while the Great Compromise was necessary to the foundation of the nation (small states would have refused to ratify the Constitution if representation were based strictly on population), states had no comparable reason to subordinate population equality.[64]

Further, because *Sims* conceived of the right to an undiluted vote as "personal in nature," that is, possessed by each voter individually, the Court was unwilling to tolerate such discrimination even if the voters in a state approved a districting plan that contained some population deviations.[65] Accordingly, even if the proposed constitutional amendment in *Sims* had passed and been ratified by voters, it would still have been unconstitutional. The Court made that conclusion clear in *Lucas v. Forty-Fourth General Assembly of Colorado*,[66] which was decided on the same day as *Sims*. *Lucas* involved a Colorado plan that was passed by a referendum and modeled on the

64. *See Sims*, 377 U.S. at 572–75. The *Federalist* championed the benefits of dividing the legislature "into different branches; and to render them by different modes of election, and different principles of action, as little connected with each other, as the nature of their common functions, and their common dependence on the society, will admit." The Federalist No. 51 at 350 (Jacob E. Cooke ed. 1961) (James Madison). Those benefits would apply equally to state legislatures and to Congress. Nevertheless, in a later paper, Publius provided some support for the *Sims* Court's conclusion that the mixed representation of the Great Compromise was appropriate for the national government because of the unique demands of federalism. *See id.* No. 62 at 416 ("If indeed it be right that among a people thoroughly incorporated into one nation, every district ought to have a *proportional* share in the government; and that among independent and sovereign states bound together by a simple league, the parties however unequal in size, ought to have an *equal* share in the common councils, it does not appear to be without some reason, that in a compound republic partaking both of the national and federal character, the government ought to be founded on a mixture of the principles of proportional and equal representation."). Because Alabama's people were "thoroughly incorporated into one" state, rather than being a "simple league" of independent counties, the Court (and perhaps the *Federalist* too) concluded that "every district ought to have a *proportional* [*i.e.*, population-based] share in the government."

65. 377 U.S. at 561.

66. 377 U.S. 713 (1964).

congressional apportionment system. Not only did the plan get the approval of two-thirds of the state's voters, but it also received majorities in every county. Nevertheless, the Court struck down the plan, holding that individual voters' right to an undiluted vote could not be denied simply because most of the state approved of a plan with unequally populated districts.[67]

Sims and *Lucas* notwithstanding, the concept that there is an *individual* right to an undiluted vote is an odd one, as individual voters do not elect candidates. Therefore, the right not to have one's vote diluted seems to be geared toward protection of the interests of voters collectively, rather than individually.[68]

Reynolds v. Sims left the details of its holding vague, just as *Wesberry v. Sanders* had done. *Sims* demanded that districts be "substantially equal" in population but did not clarify the degree of inequality that would be constitutionally tolerable.[69] Further, although the Court said that some variation in districts' populations would be permissible, the Court did not explain which reasons would justify a deviation. In fact, the Court appeared to reject nearly every potential reason for deviating from one person, one vote. As Justice Harlan noted disapprovingly in dissent, the Court held that it was unconstitutional to vary the population of districts so as

> to give effective consideration to any of the following . . . : (1) history; (2) "economic or other sorts of group interests"; (3) area; (4) geographical considerations; (5) a desire "to insure effective representation for sparsely settled areas"; (6) "availability of access of citizens to their representatives"; (7) theories of bicameralism (except those approved by the Court); (8) occupation; (9) "an attempt to balance urban and rural power" [and] (10) the preference of a majority of voters in the state.[70]

The only exception—the only reason that the Court appeared to accept as justifying a slight deviation from equal population—was the desire to have district lines track the lines of political subdivisions. And even that interest would not be sufficient, the Court indicated, to justify more than an incidental population deviation.[71]

---

67. Similarly, the *Sims* Court was unimpressed with the argument that differences in districts' populations should be held constitutional because Congress accepted states into the union when those states' districts had population deviations. The Court held that congressional approval could not insulate states' districts from judicial review. *See Sims*, 377 U.S. at 582.

68. For an expanded treatment of this issue, see Heather K. Gerken, *Understanding the Right to an Undiluted Vote*, 114 Harv. L. Rev. 1663, 1681–89 (2001), and Samuel Issacharoff, *Groups and the Right to Vote*, 44 Emory L.J. 869 (1995).

69. *See* 377 U.S. at 568; *see also id.* ("[A]n individual's right to vote for state legislators is unconstitutionally impaired when its weight is *in a substantial fashion* diluted when compared with votes of citizens living in other parts of the State.") (emphasis added).

70. *Id.* at 622–23 (Harlan, J., dissenting) (footnotes omitted and paragraphing altered).

71. *See id.* at 580–81 (opinion of the Court) ("[A] State can rationally consider according political subdivisions some independent representation in at least one body of the state legislature, as long as the basic standard of equality of population among districts is maintained."). As noted in the next section of this chapter, the Court later held that small or moderate deviations in the populations of state

One issue left unresolved by *Sims* was *which populations* must be equalized across state legislative districts. The phrase "one person, one vote" implies that it is voting strength that must be equalized, which would mean that the number of *voters* should be the same in each district.[72] Because it is impossible to tell how many people will cast ballots in any election until election day itself, however, states cannot equalize districts' voters if districts are drawn in advance of the election. States could approximate that result, however, by equalizing the number of *registered voters* in each district. Alternatively, states could equalize the number of persons *eligible* to vote in each district, a category that would include all residents that have reached voting age but exclude ineligible felons and noncitizens. Another option is to equalize the entire *voting-age* population or the *citizen voting-age population* (CVAP) of each district.

Finally, states could draw state legislative districts so as to equalize *total* population, which is the basis of allocating congressional seats among the states.[73] State legislative districts are usually drawn on the basis of total population, as reflected in the census, but doing so is not an attempt to make "one man's *vote* . . . worth as much as another's."[74] Rather than equalizing voting strength, a focus on total population equalizes representation—the constituent's access to his representative and the per capita distribution of government benefits that the constituents may expect from their representatives.[75]

Until 2016, the Supreme Court's only word on the issue was the *sui generis* case of *Burns v. Richardson*.[76] *Burns* involved a challenge to legislative districts in Hawaii, which had a substantial military and tourist population that skewed some of its census numbers. The Court held that the state could base its plan on the number of registered voters, rather than total population. *Burns*, however, did not hold that states *must* equalize the number of registered voters. In fact, the Court appeared to permit Hawaii to use registered voters instead of total population or citizen population only because the plan used by Hawaii "produced a distribution of legislators not substantially different from that which would have resulted from the use of a permissible population basis."[77]

---

legislative districts could be justified by this desire to give representation to political subdivisions *qua* political subdivisions. *See* Mahan v. Howell, 410 U.S. 315 (1973), discussed in § D[2], *infra*.

72. Other ways of phrasing the right also imply equality of voting strength. *See, e.g.*, Reynolds v. Sims, 377 U.S. at 565 ("equally effective voice in the election of members of [the] state legislature").

73. *See* U.S. Const. amend. XIV, § 2 ("Representatives shall be apportioned among the several States according to their respective numbers, counting the whole number of persons in each State, excluding Indians not taxed.").

74. Wesberry v. Sanders, 376 U.S. 1, 7–8 (1964) (emphasis added).

75. *See* Evenwel v. Abbott, 578 U.S. 54, 74 (2016) ("[R]epresentatives serve all residents, not just those eligible or registered to vote. . . . By ensuring that each representative is subject to requests and suggestions from the same number of constituents, total-population apportionment promotes equitable and effective representation."); *see also* Garza v. County of Los Angeles, 918 F.2d 763, 781–82 (9th Cir. 1990) (Kozinski, J., concurring and dissenting in part).

76. 384 U.S. 73 (1966).

77. *Id.* at 93.

For fifty years the Supreme Court said nothing more about whether states could (or must) equalize total population, registered voters, CVAP, or something else. Finally, in *Evenwel v. Abbott*, the Court held that the Constitution permits a state to draw districts that equalize total population, even where such districts contain deviations in voting-age population.[78] The Court explained that while "constituents have no constitutional right to equal access to their elected representatives," "a State certainly has an interest in taking reasonable, nondiscriminatory steps to facilitate access for all its residents."[79]

Evenwel does not hold that states *must* equalize total population; rather, it merely *allows* states to use total population. It remains unclear whether (absent an unusual situation, as in *Burns*) states may use another population basis, such as registered voters or CVAP.[80]

D. How Equal Must Districts' Populations Be? (Or, One-Person, One-Vote . . . More or Less)

As noted in the previous section, the Supreme Court's initial one-person, one-vote cases were vague concerning exactly how "equal" the districts' populations had to be. *Wesberry v. Sanders* said that the populations had to be "as nearly [equal] as is practicable,"[81] and *Reynolds v. Sims* said that districts' populations had to be "substantially equal."[82] It was not long before the Court had to define the right with more specificity.

1. Variations in Congressional Districts

Five years after *Sims*, the Court decided *Kirkpatrick v. Preisler*[83] and *Wells v. Rockefeller*,[84] which involved population deviations between congressional districts in Missouri and New York that were much smaller than the population deviations between the districts that the Court invalidated in *Wesberry v. Sanders*. The largest district in *Kirkpatrick* had a population of approximately 3% over the "ideal" district, and the smallest had a population of approximately 3% below the "ideal," creating a total deviation of 6%. In *Wells*, the total deviation was 13%. Although the deviations

78. 578 U.S. 54 (2016).
79. *Id.* at 74 n.14.
80. *Id.* at 75.
81. 376 U.S. 1, 7–8 (1964).
82. 377 U.S. 533, 568 (1964).
83. 394 U.S. 526 (1969).
84. 394 U.S. 542 (1969).

in *Kirkpatrick* and *Wells* were too small to yield a noticeable difference in voting strength between voters in different districts (it would have amounted to the difference between being one of 400,000 constituents and being one of 425,000), the Court nonetheless invalidated them.

Rather than treating the 6% deviation as *de minimis*, the Court required the states to justify *any* deviation from precise equality, interpreting *Wesberry*'s "as nearly as practicable" standard to "require[] that the State make a good-faith effort to achieve precise mathematical equality."[85] After all, the Court noted, "as nearly as practicable" is inconsistent with the establishment of any safe harbor that insulates population deviations from challenge. Further, the Court cited two practical problems with establishing a safe harbor for population deviations. First, the extent of such a safe harbor—the population variation that would be permitted—would necessarily be arbitrary. If a 6% variation were *de minimis*, why not 10%? Why not 15% or 25%? Second, the Court predicted that if states were able to take advantage of a safe harbor, legislators would strive for the safe harbor rather than for precise equality.[86]

The Court's refusal to treat a 6% deviation—or any other deviation—as *de minimis* did *not* mean that all population deviations in congressional districts were necessarily unconstitutional. It meant instead that states were required to *justify* all such deviations. Accordingly, the remainder of the Court's opinion in *Kirkpatrick v. Preisler* considered (and ultimately rejected) the state's proffered justifications for its 6% deviation. Missouri first contended that its districts were designed to provide representation for "areas with distinct economic and social interests."[87] But the Court rejected that justification, noting that *Sims* held that individuals—not group "interests"—had to be the basis of representation.

Missouri also argued that its plan was based not merely on where populations lived at the time the districts were drawn but also on predictions about where populations would be living during the ten-year period when the districting plan would be in effect. The Court acknowledged that states could constitutionally base districting decisions on "systematic" attempts to take account of population trends, but it held that such an attempt could not be *ad hoc* or applied to only part of the state.[88]

The Court also rejected the arguments that the variations were necessary to keep political subdivisions intact and to keep districts compact. The Court found the interest in compact districts to be minimal, given "'modern developments and improvements in transportation and communications,'" which permitted constituents and representatives to have sufficient access to each other even across districts covering

85. Kirkpatrick v. Preisler, 394 U.S. at 530–31.

86. *See id.* at 531.

87. *Id.* at 533. Note that this interest is subtly different from one that the Court earlier rejected in *Wesberry* and *Sims*—under-populating certain districts in order to give increased representation to the people in those districts. Missouri's argument in *Preisler* was that areas with those "distinct" interests should be kept in the same district (irrespective of the districts' populations) so that the representatives elected from those areas would pay attention to the distinct interests.

88. *Id.* at 535.

vast territory.[89] The Court also rejected the interest in not splitting political subdivisions across congressional districts, even though *Reynolds v. Sims* had noted that such an interest might justify some population deviations across state legislative districts. Missouri argued that keeping political subdivisions intact would reduce the risk of gerrymandering, but the Court pointed out that "opportunities for gerrymandering are greatest when there is freedom to construct unequally populated districts."[90]

The Court extended *Kirkpatrick v. Preisler* to its logical conclusion in *Karcher v. Daggett*,[91] which upheld a challenge to a congressional districting scheme with an average population deviation of 726 people (0.1384% of the average district) and whose most-populous district had 3,674 more people (0.6984%) than the least-populous district. The Court reiterated that states were required to justify *all* population deviations no matter how small, even though nobody would seriously contend that a voter's right to an equally weighted vote was meaningfully abridged by a districting plan with such a minuscule population deviation.

The Court further explained the burden shifting that occurs when a one-person, one-vote violation is alleged: First, the challengers of a districting law must show that the legislature could have adopted an apportionment scheme with a smaller population variance between districts. Challengers therefore routinely come to court with alternate plans containing smaller population variations than the one actually adopted. Often those challengers have already submitted similar alternative plans to the legislature, only to see the legislature adopt a different plan with more variation. In the modern era of computer-aided districting, it is virtually always possible for a challenger to develop a plan with zero population deviation, so this burden is often an easy one to meet.

Assuming that the challengers are able to suggest an alternative plan with less population variation than the plan adopted by the state, the burden shifts to the government. At that point, "the State must bear the burden of proving that each significant variance between districts was necessary to achieve some legitimate goal."[92] Such a

---

89. *Id.* at 535–36 (quoting Reynolds v. Sims, 377 U.S. 533, 580 (1964)).

90. 394 U.S. at 354 n.4. The Court was surely correct that gerrymandering would be easier logistically if the districts did not need to have equal populations. Missouri's point (and Justice Harlan's point in dissent, *see* Wells v. Rockefeller, 394 U.S. 542, 551 (1969) (Harlan, J., dissenting)) was more practical. *See also* Reynolds v. Sims, 377 U.S. 533, 622 (1964) (Harlan, J., dissenting) ("Recognizing that 'indiscriminate districting' is an invitation to 'partisan gerrymandering,' [*Sims*, 377 U.S. at] 578–579, the Court nevertheless excludes virtually every basis for the formation of electoral districts other than 'indiscriminate districting.'"). Missouri's point was that if the Court interpreted the Constitution to require mathematical equality, it would force states to split political subdivisions across districts. They would do so, and they would do so in such a way as to achieve a partisan advantage. If, however, it were constitutional for states to draw districts that conformed to political subdivisions despite small population deviations, then map-makers would feel pressure to follow the lines of political subdivisions and thereby avoid the charge of gerrymandering. In such a situation, there would be a norm against gerrymandering, even if there would be no legal prohibition on it. A demand for mathematical equality, however, would undermine such a norm.

91. 462 U.S. 725 (1983).

92. *Id.* at 731.

phrasing (particularly the reference to a "legitimate" state goal) might lead one to believe that states could satisfy their burden fairly easily, but in fact, the task of justifying population deviations is quite difficult. In the context of congressional redistricting, the Court has been willing to accept very few justifications for population deviations, holding that population equality must trump states' desires to protect the political influence of any group of its citizens.

2. Variations in State Legislative Districts

In the context of state legislative districting, however, the Court has been more willing to allow states to draw districts that track the lines of political subdivisions, even if doing so requires some departure from the ideal population distribution. The Court announced the new standard in *Mahan v. Howell*, using language that it quoted from *Reynolds v. Sims*: "'[S]o long as the divergences from a strict population standard are based on legitimate considerations incident to the effectuation of a rational state policy, some deviations from the equal-population principle are constitutionally permissible. . . . '"[93] Recall that although *Sims* rejected nearly all potential justifications for varying from the equal-population ideal, it did suggest that it might be permissible to allow districts to track the lines of political subdivisions—so long as population was not "submerged as the controlling consideration."[94]

The Court found three reasons for applying this more lenient standard: First, states have more state legislative districts than congressional districts. Because of their size, most congressional districts have to cross political subdivision lines; very few political subdivisions have enough people to fill a congressional district. Therefore, congressmen necessarily have their loyalties divided across different political subdivisions. State legislatures, on the other hand, have enough members that districts can be small enough so that a representative's district can be confined to a single city, town, or county.

Second, state legislatures, unlike the U.S. Congress, pass much "local legislation"—laws that are "directed only to the concerns of particular political subdivisions."[95] It makes sense, then, that districts would be drawn so as to encourage representatives to be loyal to a single political subdivision.

Third, the Court suggested that allowing states to track the lines of political subdivisions might "deter the possibilities of gerrymandering."[96] As noted above, the Court rejected the same argument in the context of congressional districting.[97]

In *Mahan v. Howell* itself, the districts for the Virginia House of Burgesses varied in population by as much as 16.4%. That variance was necessary, however, if Virginia

93. 410 U.S. 315, 325 (1973) (quoting Reynolds v. Sims, 377 U.S. 533, 579 (1964)).

94. 377 U.S. at 581.

95. *Id.*

96. *Id.*

97. *See supra* note 90 and accompanying text.

was to keep its political boundaries intact. The Court applied its new standard to the Virginia districting scheme and upheld it. The Court held that the plan did "advance the rational state policy of respecting the boundaries of political subdivisions."[98] Even so, the Court offered that a larger population variance would be unconstitutional: "While [the 16.4% maximum deviation] may well approach tolerable limits, we do not believe it exceeds them."[99] Thus, under *Mahan*, state legislative districts can have moderate population variances if they rationally advance a legitimate state policy, such as the policy of keeping political subdivisions intact.

Mahan v. Howell established a more lenient standard for assessing the justifications for differences in the populations of state legislative districts than the Court had earlier established for congressional districts. Sometimes, however, states do not even need to offer *any* justification for population variations in state legislative districts. Since *Gaffney v. Cummings* was decided in 1973,[100] the Court has allowed states to have small (10%) population deviations in the apportionment of their legislatures' districts without even having to justify those deviations.[101] This rule stands in stark contrast to the one applied to congressional districts in *Kirkpatrick v. Preisler* and *Karcher v. Daggett*, which requires states to justify any difference in population, no matter how small.

In *Gaffney*, the Court considered a Connecticut reapportionment that had a maximum population deviation of 2% in the state senate and 8% in the state house of representatives. In an opinion by Justice White, the Court scoffed at such minor deviations, concluding that there was no need to invoke judicial supervision of the districting process to "eliminat[e] the insignificant population variations involved in this case."[102] Indeed, because the census is a snapshot of a population that is constantly changing (and an imprecise snapshot at that), the Court believed that "it ma[de] little sense"[103] to hold "that any person's vote is being substantially diluted" because of a slight difference in the census figures.[104] Note, however, that in considering congressional redistricting, *Kirkpatrick* rejected the identical argument, made by Justice White in dissent and by Justice Fortas in his concurrence in the judgment, about the fallibility of the census.[105]

98. Mahan v. Howell, 410 U.S. 315, 328 (1973).

99. *Id.* at 329.

100. 412 U.S. 735 (1973).

101. *See* Brown v. Thompson, 462 U.S. 835, 842 (1983) (acknowledging the 10% threshold for "minor deviations"). *Compare* White v. Regester, 412 U.S. 755 (1973) (holding that a 9.9% deviation did not need to be justified), *with* Abate v. Mundt, 403 U.S. 182 (1971) (holding that an 11.9% violation did require a justification).

102. 412 U.S. at 748.

103. *Id.* at 745.

104. *Id.* at 746.

105. Kirkpatrick v. Preisler, 394 U.S. 526, 538–40 (1969) (Fortas, J., concurring in the judgment); Wells v. Rockefeller, 394 U.S. 542, 554 (1969) (White, J., dissenting) ("As Mr. Justice Fortas demonstrates, the 1960 census figures were far from accurate when they were compiled by professional enumerators, and statisticians bent on precision, in 1960. Massive growth and shifts in population since 1960 made the 1960 figures even more inaccurate by 1967. That is why a new census is taken

Rather than apply a standard of precise mathematical equality that would subject nearly all reapportionments to judicial oversight, the *Gaffney* Court argued that redistricting typically should be left to legislatures, and that routine judicial involvement in redistricting would bog the courts "down in a vast, intractable apportionment slough."[106] The Court was especially wary of having the judiciary draw district lines when the population deviations in legislatively drawn plans were minor, and therefore "there [was] little, if anything, to be accomplished by" involving the courts.[107]

The plaintiffs claimed that the districting plan was an unconstitutional political gerrymander, even leaving aside the population differences between districts. The Court was unmoved, however, and was more sympathetic to the state's characterization of its motives as seeking "political fairness." By "political fairness," the state meant "that the composition of both Houses would reflect 'as closely as possible . . . the actual [statewide] plurality of vote on the House or Senate lines in a given election.'"[108] The Court found no constitutional impediment to considering political factors in districting, particularly "when a State purports fairly to allocate political power to the parties in accordance with their voting strength."[109]

Gaffney's holding that small population variations do not make out a *prima facie* violation of the one-person, one-vote requirement is incompatible with *Kirkpatrick v. Preisler* and *Karcher v. Daggett*. Unlike *Mahan*, which offered some plausible reasons for evaluating congressional districts differently from state legislative ones, *Gaffney* made no such effort. Rather, each of the arguments that *Gaffney* made was equally applicable in the congressional context but did not carry the day. *Gaffney*'s outcome is less the result of any distinction between the cases than the result of new appointments to the Court. Between 1969, when *Kirkpatrick* was decided, and 1973, when *Gaffney* was decided, four new Justices had been appointed. Three members of *Kirkpatrick*'s five-Justice majority had left the Court, replaced by Justices who all joined the *Gaffney* majority. Justices Stewart and White went from the *Kirkpatrick* dissent to the *Gaffney* majority, with Justice White authoring the opinion of the Court.

In 2004, the Court revisited the *Gaffney* standard in *Cox v. Larios*, a cryptic summary affirmance.[110] In that case, Georgia redrew its state legislative districts with a maximum population disparity of 9.8%—seemingly within the 10% safe harbor established by earlier cases. The state's apparent reason for the population disparity was strictly partisan; it wanted to promote the election of Democrats and the reelection of Democratic incumbents. The Supreme Court affirmed the lower court's invalidation of the plan, but without writing a majority opinion. The Court's failure

every 10 years. When the Court finds a 3% variation from substantially inexact figures constitutionally impermissible it is losing perspective and sticking at a trifle.").

106. 412 U.S. at 750.

107. *Id.*

108. 412 U.S. at 738 (quoting the testimony of one of the officials who constructed the districts) (alteration and ellipsis in *Gaffney*).

109. *Id.* at 754.

110. 542 U.S. 947 (2004), *aff'g* 300 F. Supp. 2d 1320 (N.D. Ga.) (three-judge court).

to explain its reasoning leaves one to speculate on the case's meaning and significance. Because the case is binding precedent, however, it is important to analyze its potential implications.

Justice Stevens wrote a concurring opinion in *Cox* that was joined by Justice Breyer, and Justice Scalia wrote a dissent. Justice Stevens's opinion attacked partisan gerrymandering and decried the Court's opinion in *Vieth v. Jubelirer*,[111] which held that partisan-gerrymandering claims were nonjusticiable.[112] Justice Stevens argued that one-person, one-vote claims had to be strictly enforced when there was a partisan motivation for varying districts' populations, especially because *Vieth* held that courts would not police partisan districting if districts' populations were equal.[113] Justice Scalia, the author of the plurality opinion in *Vieth*, treated partisan gerrymandering as a normal, traditional part of politics. He argued that allowing political-gerrymandering claims to masquerade as one-person, one-vote claims involving "minute population deviations" would do more "to encourage politically motivated litigation than to vindicate personal rights."[114]

Cox v. Larios appears to have undermined the safe harbor established by *Gaffney*. The point of *Gaffney*'s holding was that states need not offer any explanation for population deviations under 10% in state legislative districts, yet *Cox* seemed to hold (albeit without a majority opinion) that if the state is motivated by partisanship, then even a deviation of less than 10% is unconstitutional.

Perhaps the Court sees this peculiar context as the one way in which a political-gerrymandering case can be justiciable.[115] Courts may not have judicially manageable standards for determining the percentage of legislative seats one party should receive, but it is certainly possible for the judiciary to apply manageable standards to ensure equality of populations across districts.

The Supreme Court brought some clarity to this issue in 2016 when it decided *Harris v. Arizona Independent Redistricting Commission*.[116] In *Harris*, the districting commission slightly overpopulated Republican-leaning districts and underpopulated Democratic-leaning ones. Republicans complained that the districts violated the one-person, one-vote principle for partisan reasons and argued that the Court should hold the districting unconstitutional, just as it had done in *Cox*. Arizona, however, argued that the population variations were not created to protect Democrats for partisan reasons but rather because the state wanted to comply with § 5 of the Voting Rights Act,

---

111. 541 U.S. 267 (2004).

112. In *Vieth*, four Justices would have held that partisan-gerrymandering claims were inherently nonjusticiable. Justice Kennedy concurred in the judgment but suggested that perhaps a judicially manageable standard could be developed in the future. In *Rucho v. Common Cause*, 588 U.S. 684 (2019), the Court eliminated the ambiguity that remained after *Vieth* by holding squarely that partisan-gerrymandering claims are political questions and therefore nonjusticiable in federal court. *See* § E, *infra*.

113. 542 U.S. at 949–50 (Stevens, J., concurring).

114. *Id.* at 952 (Scalia, J., dissenting).

115. *See generally* § E, *infra* (discussing the justiciability of political-gerrymandering claims).

116. 578 U.S. 253 (2016).

which protects against laws that reduce the percentage of districts in which minorities have the ability to elect their candidates of choice. (Although *Shelby County v. Holder* held in 2013 that Arizona did not need to comply with § 5,[117] the districting decisions involved in *Harris* had already been made.)

The Supreme Court upheld the districting, explaining that "those attacking a state-approved plan must show that it is more probable than not that a deviation of less than 10% reflects the predominance of illegitimate reapportionment factors."[118] The Court left open the question whether partisanship was one of those "illegitimate reapportionment factors," but it is hard to explain *Cox* any other way.

In *Harris*, although "partisanship played some role" in the districting decisions,[119] the Court held that "the deviations predominantly reflected Commission efforts to achieve compliance with the federal Voting Rights Act, not to secure political advantage for one party."[120] Thus, even though the Democratic districts were under-populated and Republican districts were overpopulated, the Court concluded that Democrats were the incidental beneficiaries of a plan to benefit minorities. Because minorities preferred Democrats, a plan designed to protect minority voting strength would tend to help Democrats, but that political impact was not enough to prove that the districting plan was implemented for "illegitimate" reasons. Finally, note that the Court upheld the districting without concluding that the deviations were *necessary* to comply with the Voting Rights Act; rather, the Court held that it was sufficient that the districting decisions were thought likely to ease the preclearance process.[121]

Harris illustrates the interplay between race, districting, partisanship, and political ideology—a topic that we address more thoroughly in Chapters 4 and 5.

E. The Political Question Doctrine and Political Gerrymandering, Post-*Baker v. Carr*

After *Baker v. Carr*, judicial review of one-person, one-vote claims became almost routine. Few people doubted that there was a judicially manageable standard for adjudicating such claims—after all, it was seemingly just a matter of comparing the numbers of people in different districts. Although, as we have already seen, one-person, one-vote cases are a bit more complicated than that, analysis of those claims had a mathematical quality to them, making the population-equality rule administrable.

---

117. 570 U.S. 529 (2013), discussed in Chapter 3, § D[2], *infra*.

118. 578 U.S. at 259.

119. *Id.* at 263 (quoting the opinion below, 993 F. Supp. 2d 1042, 1046 (D. Ariz. 2014) (three-judge court)).

120. 578 U.S. at 259.

121. *See id.* at 262–63.

By contrast, claims about gerrymandering have never been that simple. A gerrymandering claim is based on the idea that district maps are drawn in such a way as to advantage one group of people (such as a party in a partisan-gerrymandering case) and to disadvantage another, even though every district has the same number of people. For example, suppose that a city is to be divided into five city-council districts, and 60% of the city's population favors Party A, while 40% favors Party B. If each party were represented proportionately, Party A would win three seats on the city council and Party B would win two. But if Party A were in control of the districting, it would try to draw districts so that Party A had its 60/40 majority in each of the districts. That is to say, the mapmakers would try to spread out the Party B supporters across all of the districts so that they would not be able to win a single seat on the council.

Partisan gerrymandering not only can lead to electoral results that are disproportionate but can permit those people who hold political power to use the districting process to keep themselves in power. As a result, many citizens find political gerrymandering at best distasteful, and some have argued that it is unconstitutional—either because gerrymanders violate the Equal Protection Clause by purposefully reducing the political power of the minority party or because they violate the First Amendment by discriminating against people who have political views contrary to the group in power.

But whereas one-person, one-vote claims could use population figures as a benchmark against which to measure the constitutional requirement of equality, that benchmark is unavailable in partisan-gerrymandering claims because the number of voters in each district is equal. Further, whereas *Sims* interpreted the Equal Protection Clause to require population equality across districts, it is hard to find in the Constitution a demand that a minority party receive a number of legislative seats proportionate to the number of votes it receives in the jurisdiction as a whole. Critics of partisan gerrymandering, then, have been forced to argue that, although the Constitution permits some amount of partisan gerrymandering, excessive gerrymandering is unconstitutional. It is difficult to establish a judicially manageable standard for determining how much gerrymandering is "too much," however, and it is perhaps impossible to explain how any potential threshold could be divined from the Constitution.

The constitutionality of political gerrymanders first reached the Supreme Court in the 1986 case of *Davis v. Bandemer*.[122] That case involved the drawing of districts for the state legislature in Indiana. All the districts complied with the equal-population mandate, but the Democratic plaintiffs alleged that the Republican majority in the legislature deliberately drew district lines to disadvantage Democrats. After examining evidence of the passage of the plan, the lower court held for the plaintiffs and found a violation of the Equal Protection Clause.

The Supreme Court reversed on appeal. Justice White's opinion (which spoke for a majority on this point) first concluded that the case did not present a nonjusticiable

122. 478 U.S. 109 (1986).

political question (an issue not explicitly addressed by the lower court). He first observed that the Court had decided racial-gerrymandering cases, and affirmed lower-court decisions involving racial-gerrymandering, without the barrier of the political question doctrine.[123] If the Court could hear cases where states were alleged to have violated the Constitution because they placed too much emphasis on race when they drew districts, it was not clear why the Court could not hear cases challenging an undue consideration of politics.

The plurality nonetheless reversed on the merits, finding that plaintiffs in this context needed to show "intentional discrimination against an identifiable political group and an actual discriminatory effect on that group."[124] On the latter point, plaintiffs were required to demonstrate that the gerrymandering will "consistently degrade a voter's or a group of voters' influence on the political process as a whole."[125] Evidence of mere disproportionate representation was not enough, and the higher threshold of proof was not present in the case. Thus, the opinion explained that partisan-gerrymandering claims were justiciable, but plaintiffs could not succeed in such a claim merely by pointing to one party's lack of success in an election or two; the disadvantaged group would have to suffer a lack of influence on the entire political process. Practically speaking, it was very difficult for either party to meet that standard, and, in fact, in the years since *Bandemer*, the Supreme Court never found the standard to have been met.

Justice O'Connor, joined by Chief Justice Burger and then-Justice Rehnquist, concurred in the result, on the basis that the case presented a political question. Unlike the plurality, she concluded that the racial-gerrymandering cases were distinguishable, given the purpose of the Equal Protection Clause to combat racial discrimination. In contrast, she concluded that the Clause did not present an easily applicable baseline against which to measure claims of disproportionate political influence or over which time period to make such measurements. Any such inquiry would inevitably evolve into a requirement of rough proportional representation, a result which, she said, would improperly involve federal courts in political and policy choices that were best left to state authorities.[126]

The Court revisited the issue in *Vieth v. Jubelirer* but was again unable to reach a definitive resolution.[127] The facts in *Vieth* were very similar to those in *Bandemer*,

---

123. Both the plurality opinion and the concurring opinion by Justice O'Connor noted that the Court had been inconsistent and unclear, in earlier opinions and in summary affirmances of three-judge district court decisions, regarding whether cases of political gerrymandering were political questions. *Bandemer* was the first time the Court gave the issue extended consideration.

124. 478 U.S. at 127.

125. *Id.* at 132.

126. Justice Powell, joined by Justice Stevens, concurred in part and dissented in part. He agreed with the plurality that there was no political question, but on the merits he argued that a broader set of factors should be considered by a court, including the process and results of the alleged gerrymander. After applying that broader set of factors in the context of *Bandemer* itself, he concluded that the plaintiff should have prevailed.

127. 541 U.S. 267 (2004).

the exception being that the *Vieth* plaintiffs challenged a political gerrymander of Pennsylvania congressional districts, rather than state legislative districts. The lower court dismissed the suit on the basis that it was a political question, and the Supreme Court affirmed. As in *Bandemer*, there was no majority opinion. The lengthy plurality opinion by Justice Scalia began by noting the long history of such gerrymanders in American politics and finding it "significant" that Congress possessed constitutional authority under Article I, § 4, to "make or alter" congressional districts drawn by states. Congress has periodically exercised that authority, including by such means as the current requirement that each district elect only one member of Congress.[128] Congress has not acted, however, to limit partisan gerrymandering.

The plurality opinion then revisited *Bandemer*. It began by observing that there was no majority opinion in the case, which caused lower courts to struggle with determining which standard to apply. Those courts had typically applied the standard of the plurality opinion in *Bandemer* and rarely found for plaintiffs, usually because the effects prong of the *Bandemer* plurality was so difficult to satisfy. Lower courts applying *Bandemer* had been unable to generate judicially discernible and manageable standards to adjudicate challenges to political gerrymanders, the plurality concluded, so such claims should be held nonjusticiable, and *Bandemer* should be overruled.

Even though lower courts had not developed judicially manageable standards under *Bandemer*, the plurality and the rest of the Court addressed whether such standards might be developed in *Vieth* itself. The plaintiffs in *Vieth* proposed their own test, similar to that of the *Bandemer* plurality but requiring that the intent to achieve partisan advantage "predominate" and using a multi-factor inquiry to ascertain whether districts were systematically drawn to pack or crack[129] voters of the rival party as well as whether the map thwarted the plaintiffs' ability to translate a majority of votes into a majority of seats. The plurality was not impressed by this refined test, which it believed was too vague, whether the test was used to evaluate the constitutionality of a specific district or a statewide plan. Further, the plurality doubted whether partisan factors could be distinguished from others, such as contiguity, compactness, or preservation of neighborhoods, each of which might produce the same effect. The proposed effects test was hampered by the possibility of changing political affiliations of voters and by its resemblance to proportional representation. *How much* proportionality the plaintiffs' test would require (that is, how closely the number of legislative seats would have to reflect voters' partisan preferences), the plurality concluded, was impossible for courts to say.

The *Vieth* plurality also rejected each of the tests proposed by the other Justices.[130] Justice Stevens concurred in the result on the basis that the plaintiffs lacked standing,

---

128. 2 U.S.C. § 2c.

129. "Packing" refers to filing a district with a supermajority of the opposition party, while "cracking" refers to splitting a group's voters among several districts to deny them a majority in any district. 541 U.S. at 286 n.7.

130. The *Vieth* plurality also concluded that Justice Powell's proposed totality-of-the-circumstances test in *Bandemer* suffered from indeterminacy.

but he argued that "severe political gerrymanders" were inconsistent with democratic principles (a conclusion that the plurality agreed with in the abstract) and that the racial-gerrymandering cases were precedent for judicial intervention. The plurality responded that discrimination on the basis of race receives strict scrutiny, while discrimination on the basis of politics does not.

In dissent, Justice Souter (joined by Justice Ginsburg) proposed a multipart test, requiring, among other things, that plaintiffs first show that they were part of a cohesive political group and that traditional districting principles had not been followed. If that showing were made, the burden would shift to defendants to justify the districting "by reference to objectives other than naked partisan advantage."[131] The plurality found a lack of objective, measurable criteria in each step of this test and concluded that its ultimate goal of preventing "at least the worst cases of gerrymandering" was judicially unmanageable.

In his dissent, Justice Breyer focused on the "unjustified use of political factors to entrench a majority in power." Not surprisingly, the plurality responded that this test was full of subjective inquiries, adding that Justice Breyer "gives no instance (and we know none) of permanent frustration of majority will."[132]

Finally, in an opinion concurring in the judgment, Justice Kennedy agreed that in this case the litigants presented no manageable standards to govern political gerrymanders, but (unlike the plurality) he refused to rule out the possibility of such standards emerging in future litigation. While the Equal Protection Clause may not be a useful source of possible standards, Justice Kennedy suggested that the First Amendment might be. Such an inquiry might examine "whether the legislation burdens the representational rights of the complaining party's voters for reasons of ideology, beliefs, or political association. The analysis allows a pragmatic or functional assessment that accords some latitude to the States."[133]

The Supreme Court finally brought an end to this confusion and uncertainty in 2019 with its decision in *Rucho v. Common Cause*.[134] A five-Justice majority held that there are no judicially manageable standards discoverable in the Constitution for resolving partisan-gerrymandering claims. Accordingly, the Court held, such claims present political questions that may not be decided by the federal courts. The Court's major point was not that it was impossible to create a standard that could be managed by courts; rather, the Court held that any test of partisan gerrymandering would

---

131. 541 U.S. at 351 (Souter, J., dissenting).

132. 541 U.S. at 300 (plurality opinion).

133. *Id.* at 315 (Kennedy, J., concurring). The Court briefly revisited the political question doctrine in *LULAC v. Perry*, 548 U.S. 399 (2006). Plaintiffs there challenged an unusual mid-decade redistricting in Texas of the boundaries for congressional seats, both on constitutional grounds and under the Voting Rights Act. On the former point, a plurality opinion by Justice Kennedy concluded that a challenge to mid-decade redistricting as such was a political question, though apparently leaving open the possibility that, at some point in the future, such a claim would not be a political question.

134. 588 U.S. 684 (2019).

ultimately depend on a normative assessment of political fairness—an assessment that federal courts were ill-equipped to make.[135]

Although the Court characterized its holding as jurisdictional,[136] there is reason to think that the basis of the Court's holding was actually a judgment on the merits that the Constitution contained no right against partisan gerrymandering.[137] The Court's determination that there was a lack of judicially *discoverable* and manageable standards was based on the belief that there was no such standard in the Constitution, not that it was impossible to create a manageable standard. More directly, the Court acknowledged that federal courts had jurisdiction to adjudicate *racial*-gerrymandering cases, where the key question is whether race was the "predominant factor" in districting. The *Rucho* Court held that it could not simply adopt a predominant-factor test for partisan gerrymandering because partisanship, unlike race, was a "permissible" basis on which to draw district lines.[138] Thus, the Court appeared to decide that "securing partisan advantage" was substantively permissible (not just insusceptible of a judicially manageable standard), even "when that permissible intent predominates."[139]

Despite the fact that partisan-gerrymandering claims may not be adjudicated by the courts (at least the federal courts[140]), the other branches of government, both federal and state, have tools to combat gerrymandering. These include Congress itself directing the drawing of districts for the U.S. House of Representatives, or bipartisan or nonpartisan redistricting commissions in individual states.[141] Some states also have constitutional or statutory provisions limiting partisan gerrymandering, and those provisions are enforced in state courts.[142]

---

135. *See id.* at 705 ("[P]laintiffs inevitably ask the courts to make their own political judgment about how much representation particular political parties *deserve*—based on the votes of their supporters—and to rearrange the challenged districts to achieve that end. But federal courts are not equipped to apportion political power as a matter of fairness, nor is there any basis for concluding that they were authorized to do so.").

136. *See id.* at 718 ("We conclude that partisan gerrymandering claims present political questions beyond the reach of the federal courts."); *see also id.* at 719 ("Our conclusion does not condone excessive partisan gerrymandering.").

137. *See* Michael R. Dimino, *You've Got (Political) Questions? We've Got No Answers*, 71 Mercer L. Rev. 719 (2020).

138. 588 U.S. at 711.

139. *Id.*

140. *See* Michael Solimine, *State Courts as Forums for Partisan Gerrymandering Claims After* Common Cause v. Rucho (Rucho *Symposium*), Election Law Blog (June 30, 2019), https://electionlawblog.org/?p=105902.

141. For overviews, see Bruce E. Cain, *Redistricting Commissions: A Better Political Buffer?*, 121 Yale L.J. 1808 (2012), and David Schultz, *Regulating the Political Thicket: Congress, the Courts, and State Reapportionment Commissions*, 3 Charleston L. Rev. 107 (2008). *See also* Ariz. St. Legis. v. Ariz. Indep. Redistricting Comm'n, 576 U.S. 787 (2015) (holding that an independent commission, created by popular initiative and bypassing state legislature, could redraw congressional districts).

142. *See Rucho*, 588 U.S. at 720 (citing provisions in the laws of Florida, Missouri, Iowa, and Delaware).

Some of those attempts to limit state legislatures' partisan gerrymandering have raised federal constitutional questions. In particular, because the Constitution's Elections Clause gives state legislatures—and not any other aspect of state government—the power to determine the "Times, Places and Manner" of congressional elections (subject to Congress's power to "make or alter such Regulations"),[143] state-law restrictions on the discretion of state legislatures to draw district lines might be thought to be unconstitutional.

The Supreme Court has largely, but not completely, rejected such arguments. In *Arizona State Legislature v. Arizona Independent Redistricting Commission*, the Court held that it was constitutional for Arizona voters, by initiative, to take the power to draw congressional districts away from the state legislature and give it to a commission.[144] And in *Moore v. Harper*, the Court similarly held that the North Carolina Constitution could forbid the state legislature from engaging in partisan gerrymandering when drawing congressional districts.[145] The provision of the state constitution was enforced by the state courts, but the U.S. Supreme Court held that such enforcement would not violate the U.S. Constitution as long as the state courts merely exercised "ordinary judicial review."[146]

It is not clear what kind of action by state courts would violate that proviso, but there seem to be two possibilities. First, state courts would not be exercising "ordinary" judicial review if their interpretation of state law were so outlandish that it would amount to lawmaking.[147] Second, state courts' actions that are not judicial review at all would obviously not be "ordinary judicial review." For example, a constitutional question would appear to arise if (as is the case in some states) state courts were given administrative powers or legislative powers over redistricting, rather than simply the power to hear lawsuits in a traditional form. If it is unconstitutional for a state to give its courts administrative or legislative power in districting, however, that rule would conflict with *Arizona State Legislature*.[148] That is, if the Elections Clause really requires that state *legislatures* have the power to determine the manner of congressional elections (as *Moore v. Harper* appeared to say), it does not make sense for independent commissions (but not state courts) to be able to usurp that authority. Yet *Arizona State Legislature* upheld districting by commissions.

Not surprisingly, efforts to depoliticize the drawing of legislative districts have not drawn universal support. The reaction of the parties in states has often ranged from lukewarm at best to outright opposition at worst, depending on how favorable the

143. U.S. Const. art. I, § 4, cl. 1.

144. 576 U.S. 787 (2015).

145. 600 U.S. 1 (2023).

146. *Id.* at 36.

147. *See* Chapter 10, § C[7], *infra*.

148. The apparent conflict may not be surprising given that *Moore* was authored by Chief Justice Roberts, who dissented in *Arizona State Legislature*. It is surprising, however, that six Justices (Roberts, Sotomayor, Kagan, Kavanaugh, Barrett, and Jackson) formed the *Moore* majority, and none distanced himself from the "ordinary judicial review" passage, even though it was concededly unnecessary to the Court's resolution of the case. *See* 600 U.S. at 36–37.

status quo is to their interests. It appears that voters sometimes act in a similar fashion when asked to approve the creation of redistricting commissions by initiative or referenda.[149] Nonetheless, given the widespread perception that gerrymandered districts have led to protection for incumbents and been an important cause of a heightened partisanship in American politics,[150] it is likely that there will be continued efforts, at least at the state level, to enact nonjudicial limits on such gerrymandering.

---

149. *See* Caroline J. Tolbert *et al.*, *Strategic Voting and Legislative Redistricting Reform*, 62 Pol. Res. Q. 92 (2009).

150. For a skeptical evaluation of this theory, see Richard H. Pildes, *Why the Center Does Not Hold: The Causes of Hyperpolarized Democracy in America*, 99 Calif. L. Rev. 273 (2011).

Chapter 3

Preclearance Under § 5 of the Voting Rights Act

A. Introduction

Until 1964, Southern state officials bent on denying blacks political power could exact enormous costs on opposition forces simply by requiring plaintiffs to litigate. A plaintiff wishing to put a stop to unconstitutionally discriminatory limits on the right to vote, for example, would have to spend resources pursuing a court case. Even if the plaintiff were successful in court, the state could simply replace the challenged law with another discriminatory one, and by staying one step ahead of plaintiffs, the state could significantly delay compliance.

In what was likely the most innovative aspect of the Voting Rights Act of 1965 (VRA), Congress sought to correct this situation by "shift[ing] the advantage of time and inertia from the perpetrators of the evil to its victims."[1] While § 2 of the VRA (discussed in depth in Chapter 4) continued to place the burden on plaintiffs to demonstrate the illegality of election laws, § 5 imposed upon certain governments the obligation to prove the laws' legality *before* those laws could go into effect.[2] Under the preclearance provision, a state or political subdivision wishing to change its election laws had to submit its proposed change to the Attorney General of the United States or obtain a declaratory judgment from a three-judge district court convened in the U.S. District Court for the District of Columbia. Under either route, preclearance would be granted, and the proposed change would be permitted to take effect, only if the change had neither the purpose nor the effect of "denying or abridging the right to vote on account of race or color."[3] (The Act was amended in 1975 to cover laws denying or abridging language minorities' right to vote as well.[4])

---

1. South Carolina v. Katzenbach, 383 U.S. 301, 328 (1966).

2. For discussions of the similarities and differences between § 2 and § 5, see Michael J. Pitts, *Section 5 of the Voting Rights Act: A Once and Future Remedy?*, 81 Denv. U. L. Rev. 225, 230–36 (2003), and Nicholas O. Stephanopolous, *The South After Shelby County*, 2013 Sup. Ct. Rev. 55, 62–66.

3. 52 U.S.C. § 10304.

4. *See* Pub. L. 94-73 § 203 (1975), codified at 52 U.S.C. § 10303(f)(2).

The preclearance provision did not apply to every proposed law that might conceivably affect voting power. Rather, the preclearance obligation extended only to "voting qualification[s] or prerequisite[s] to voting, or standard[s], practice[s], or procedure[s] with respect to voting."[5] Although the Supreme Court recognized that this phrase implied that some category of laws need not be precleared, the Court gave it a broad interpretation, extending its coverage to such matters as the hours and locations of polling places, the drawing of district lines, whether certain government offices should be elective, and limitations on candidates' ballot access.[6]

The preclearance provision was limited also in that it did not apply to the entire country. Its scope was restricted to "covered jurisdictions" identified in § 4(b) of the VRA[7] as those states or political subdivisions that used "tests or devices" in determining voter eligibility and in which fewer than 50% of the voting-age residents were registered or voted in certain presidential elections (originally only the 1964 election, but expanded in 1970 and 1975 to include the 1968 and 1972 elections as well). The Act further defined a "test or device" as "any requirement that a person as a prerequisite for voting or registration for voting (1) demonstrate the ability to read, write, understand, or interpret any matter, (2) demonstrate any educational achievement or his knowledge of any particular subject, (3) possess good moral character, or (4) prove his qualifications by the voucher of registered voters or members of any other class."[8]

Originally, the covered jurisdictions included six entire states (Alabama, Georgia, Louisiana, Mississippi, South Carolina, and Virginia), as well as large portions of North Carolina. By 2013, coverage was extended to include the states of Alaska, Arizona, and Texas, as well as portions of California, Florida, Michigan, New York, and South Dakota.

As the Supreme Court interpreted § 5, preclearance guarded against "retrogressive" changes—laws that reduced the political power of minority groups as compared to the power they held before the proposed change.[9] Preclearance did not demand that states improve the lot of minorities, or even that minorities be given the power to which they were entitled by § 2 of the VRA; it simply required that the proposed change not make the situation worse. If, however, the *purpose* of a proposed change (as distinguished from its effect) was to give minorities less political power than that to which they are entitled, preclearance was denied.[10]

In the previous paragraphs, and the ones that follow, we speak primarily in the past tense because in 2013, in *Shelby County, Alabama v. Holder*, the Supreme Court struck down the coverage formula as unconstitutional.[11] This holding left the preclearance process itself dormant. The majority of the Court reasoned that the coverage formula,

---

5. 52 U.S.C. § 10304.
6. *See* Allen v. State Bd. of Elections, 393 U.S. 544 (1969); § B, *infra*.
7. *See* 52 U.S.C. § 10303(b).
8. 52 U.S.C. § 10303(c).
9. *See* Beer v. United States, 425 U.S. 130 (1976); § C, *infra*.
10. *See* 52 U.S.C. § 10304(c).
11. *See* Shelby County v. Holder, 570 U.S. 529 (2013); § D[2], *infra*.

which was included in Congress's 2006 reauthorization of the VRA in a form unchanged since 1975, was based on old and outdated assumptions and data, and, thus, it violated the equal sovereignty of the states without sufficient reason.

But, for several reasons, the preclearance provision is not simply of historical interest. In the wake of the Supreme Court decision, there were several bills introduced in Congress to modify the coverage formula, in an attempt to satisfy the majority's constitutional concerns. Also, some jurisdictions, even after 2013, defended their redistricting practices against challenges to their legality in part by arguing that they were necessary to comply with the now-unenforced preclearance provisions of the VRA.[12] For these reasons, the preclearance provision had an active and controversial life before 2013, and may yet have an active one in the future.

B. Voting Standards, Practices, and Procedures

The preclearance procedure applied to only a subset of laws passed or administered by covered jurisdictions. Specifically, preclearance was required whenever a covered jurisdiction "enact[ed] or s[ought] to administer any voting qualification or prerequisite to voting, or standard, practice, or procedure with respect to voting."[13] There was little controversy as to the meaning of "voting qualification or prerequisite to voting," but the remaining statutory language was the subject of important litigation.

Disputes concerning the meaning of "standard, practice, or procedure with respect to voting" confronted two competing concerns. On the one hand, all manner of state and local laws can diminish the significance of the right to vote without directly stopping any person from casting a ballot. The purposes of the Voting Rights Act would be undermined by an interpretation that permitted states to avoid its strictures through clever devices that formally did not involve voting. On the other hand, however, Congress did not intend to require *every* state and local law to be precleared. Requiring changes "with respect to voting," in other words, implied a desire to exempt some category of changes in laws not respecting voting. Exactly which laws comprised that category was a matter of considerable dispute.

1. *Allen v. State Board of Elections* and Its Impact

The Supreme Court first confronted the scope of the preclearance provision in the leading case of *Allen v. State Board of Elections*.[14] That case involved changes to election laws in Mississippi and Virginia, all of which concerned various issues

12. *See* § D[3], *infra*.
13. 52 U.S.C. § 10304.
14. 393 U.S. 544 (1969).

regarding the administration of elections, but not the right to vote as such. Plaintiffs brought declaratory-judgment actions in federal court, arguing that preclearance was required. Three-judge district courts that were convened in those states dismissed the cases on the basis that the changes were not "with respect to voting" and thus did not require preclearance. Decisions of such courts can be, and these ones were, directly appealed to the Supreme Court.

The Court first held that private plaintiffs could bring such actions, even though the VRA does not explicitly grant individuals a right of action to bring such suits.[15] The goals of the VRA, the Court held, would be "severely hampered" if citizens were required to rely on the Attorney General to bring suit.[16] Although the Act authorized the Attorney General to bring suits, that office has limited resources and cannot investigate all of the potential changes covered by preclearance, and the Court's holding on this point was supported by an *amicus curiae* brief filed by the Solicitor General.

On the merits, the Court adopted a broad reading of the statutory language governing the coverage of § 5—"any voting qualification or prerequisite to voting, or standard, practice or procedure with respect to voting." This language, the Court concluded, applied to "the subtle, as well as the obvious, state regulations which have the effect of denying citizens their right to vote because of their race."[17] This reading was supported by the "mass of legislative history" as well as the "basic purposes" of the VRA. Thus, the election law changes at issue were required to be precleared, since the "right to vote can be affected by a dilution of voting power as well as by an absolute prohibition on casting a ballot."[18]

The holding in *Allen* led jurisdictions to seek preclearance of many more changes related to election laws. A covered jurisdiction could seek preclearance by choosing one of two routes: administratively, by obtaining the permission of the Department of Justice; or judicially, by obtaining a declaratory judgment in a three-judge court convened in the District Court for the District of Columbia. The former was almost always sought, since it was usually speedier and cheaper for the jurisdiction.[19] Almost

---

15. On the propriety of inferring a private right of action from a statute that is silent concerning the availability of such a suit, see Chapter 11, § D[1], *infra*. *See also* Alexander v. Sandoval, 532 U.S. 275 (2001); Cort v. Ash, 422 U.S. 66 (1975); William Baude et al., Hart and Wechsler's The Federal Courts and the Federal System 881–907 (8th ed. 2025).

16. 393 U.S. at 556.

17. *Id.* at 565.

18. Justice Harlan concurred regarding the availability of a private right of action but dissented on the merits, on the basis that the Court read the § 5 language too broadly. In Justice Harlan's view, § 5 should have been held to cover only "those state laws that change either voter qualifications or the manner in which elections are conducted." *Id.* at 591 (Harlan, J., concurring in part and dissenting in part). Justice Black dissented on the basis of his *South Carolina v. Katzenbach* dissent, that Congress could not require states to ask permission of federal officials to change their laws.

19. If the Attorney General were to deny administrative preclearance, the jurisdiction could in effect appeal that decision by seeking judicial preclearance. On the other hand, if administrative preclearance were granted, then it would be subject to judicial review by any affected party. Morris v. Gressett, 432 U.S. 491 (1977). Finally, in judicial preclearance, the decision of a three-judge district court could be directly appealed to the Supreme Court.

forty years after passage of the preclearance provision, several thousand administrative requests were being received by the DOJ each year, and the vast majority were approved. In contrast, only about two judicial requests were received each year.[20]

Another effect of *Allen* was the use of what came to be called "Section 5 enforcement actions." If a jurisdiction refused to seek any type of preclearance for a change to election laws, then the statute permitted the DOJ to file suit in a local three-judge district court to obtain an order that the jurisdiction must seek preclearance. *Allen* held that private parties could bring suit under an implied right of action to obtain the same relief. In such actions, the only issue was whether a new law should be submitted for preclearance; the merits—whether preclearance should be granted—would be determined by the normal administrative or judicial process.[21]

Preclearance litigation in different courts and at different times led to complications for the jurisdictions involved. For example, states must redraw legislative districts at least every ten years to account for population shifts reported in the census. *Allen*, however, held that changes to voting procedures—including redrawn districts—could not go into effect until they obtained preclearance. As a result, covered jurisdictions found themselves constitutionally compelled to redraw districts but unable to make such changes effective until the preclearance process was complete.

Perry v. Perez[22] presented such a dilemma. As a result of the 2010 census, Texas received four additional congressional districts and was required to draw new district lines before the 2012 elections. The state passed a plan and submitted it to the D.C. District Court for preclearance, but there the process stalled. Not only was no timely decision on preclearance forthcoming, but the plan was challenged in a separate suit in federal court in Texas as violating the Constitution and § 2 of the Voting Rights Act for allegedly diluting the strength of minorities' votes. That suit likewise would not be resolved in time to make whatever adjustments would be required before the 2012 elections. As a result of this simultaneous litigation before different three-judge district courts in the District of Columbia and in Texas, the litigation occurred in a somewhat awkward and confusing posture.

In reviewing the Texas case, the Supreme Court reaffirmed that where a state's existing districts have been rendered unconstitutional by a subsequent census, a federal district court must itself draw interim districts if the political process is unable to yield new districts on its own.[23] But what standards should the district court use in crafting an interim plan? In particular, what consideration should be given to the plan that has been passed but is awaiting preclearance?

---

20. Michael E. Solimine, *Rethinking District of Columbia Venue in Voting Rights Preclearance Actions*, 103 Geo. L.J. Online 29 (2014); Daniel P. Tokaji, *If It's Broke, Fix It: Improving Voting Rights Act Preclearance*, 49 How. L.J. 785 (2006).

21. *See* Perry v. Perez, 565 U.S. 388, 394–95 (2012) (*per curiam*); Lopez v. Monterey Cnty., 519 U.S. 9, 23 (1996).

22. 565 U.S. 388 (2012) (*per curiam*).

23. *See id.* at 392 (quoting Connor v. Finch, 431 U.S. 407, 415 (1977)).

If the district court simply adopted the state's plan, it could be giving effect to an illegal or unconstitutional plan. If, on the other hand, the district court shied away from the state's plan, it would be preventing a state's policies from having effect simply because of an *allegation* of illegality—an action that would have federalism costs and would encourage the filing of meritless allegations in the future. Further, if the district court itself were to decide whether the state's plan should be precleared, it would be usurping the role assigned by the VRA to the D.C. District Court and the Attorney General.

The Supreme Court's answer was that even though such a plan may not have legal effect itself, it is a "starting point" for the district court to use in devising an interim plan. "It provides important guidance that helps ensure that the district court appropriately confines itself to drawing interim maps that comply with the Constitution and the Voting Rights Act, without displacing legitimate state policy judgments with the court's own preferences."[24]

Before deferring to the state's plan, the district court should peek at the merits of the preclearance issue and any other challenges to the new districts but back away from actually deciding their legality. In the Court's words, "Where a State's plan faces challenges under the Constitution or § 2 of the Voting Rights Act, a district court should still be guided by that plan, except to the extent those legal challenges are shown to have a likelihood of success on the merits."[25] Similarly, with regard to the preclearance issue, the district court should be guided by the state's plan, except to the extent it contains elements "that stand a reasonable probability of failing to gain § 5 preclearance. And by 'reasonable probability' this Court means in this context that the § 5 challenge is not insubstantial."[26]

2. Preclearance Coverage After *Allen*

After *Allen*, the Court struggled with applying the "standard, practice, or procedure with respect to voting" language of the VRA. For example, in *Dougherty County Board of Education v. White*,[27] the Court considered whether a board of education in a covered state must seek preclearance of a rule requiring its employees to take unpaid leaves of absence while campaigning for elective office. A majority of the Court concluded that preclearance was required because the change was "not a neutral personnel practice governing all forms of absenteeism" but rather one that "specifically addresses the electoral process."[28] It was akin to other matters subject to preclearance, such as changes to the location of polling places or the procedures for casting write-in

24. *Id.* at 394.
25. *Id.*
26. *Id.* at 395.
27. 439 U.S. 32 (1978).
28. *Id.* at 40.

votes. A dissent argued that the change was not connected to "elections as such," since no one was being denied the right to vote.[29]

A different and narrower view of the VRA language was suggested by the subsequent decision in *Presley v. Etowah County Commission.*[30] There the Court considered changes to the powers of the elected members of certain county commissions in a covered jurisdiction. The changes diminished the authority of individual commissioners and enhanced the power of the commissioners to act collectively. The Court concluded that the changes were not subject to preclearance. In reaching that conclusion, the Court analyzed its prior cases and categorized the types of changes pertaining to "election law" that those cases had held were subject to preclearance. These included changes involving the manner of voting, candidacy requirements and qualifications, the composition of an electorate that may vote for a given office, or the creation or abolition of an elective office. All of these changes, the Court asserted, had "a direct relation to voting and the election process." In contrast, the changes at issue in *Presley* concerned the "internal operations of an elected body," with "no connection to voting procedures."[31] Requiring preclearance of all changes that would affect the power of elected officials would potentially implicate a vast number of governmental decisions far afield from the purpose of the preclearance provisions. A dissent argued that the changes at issue could have the purpose or effect of diminishing the power of representatives of certain political communities and, hence, should be subject to preclearance.[32]

C. Retrogression

Once it was determined that a particular proposed change was "with respect to voting" and therefore required preclearance, it became necessary to examine the standards by which the Attorney General or the D.C. District Court would decide to grant or to deny preclearance. The VRA provides that preclearance should be granted only if the proposed change "does not have the purpose and will not have the effect of denying or abridging the right to vote on account of race or color."[33] This language raised a number of difficult questions. For example, what does it mean to "deny[]" or "abridg[e]" the right to vote? Specifically, what is the baseline against which to compare the proposed change? Should preclearance be denied only if the change makes the existing situation worse, *i.e.*, if it abridges voting power relative to the *status quo*? Or should preclearance be denied to any plan that fails to give racial groups the voting power to which they are entitled, even if the proposed change modestly improves the existing situation?

29. *Id.* at 51 (Powell, J., dissenting).
30. 502 U.S. 491 (1992).
31. *Id.* at 503.
32. *Id.* at 525 (Stevens, J., dissenting).
33. 52 U.S.C. § 10304.

In *Beer v. United States*,[34] the Court interpreted "abridg[e]" to mean a reduction in voting power as compared to the *status quo*. Thus, a proposed change that had the effect of improving the political power of a racial group could not be said to have abridged it, even if neither the proposed plan nor the existing one gave the group the representation to which it was entitled. In *Reno v. Bossier Parish School Board*,[35] the Court applied *Beer* to hold that the "purpose" to discriminate proscribed by § 5 was a retrogressive purpose. Thus, after *Bossier Parish*, preclearance was to be denied only if a proposed change actually reduced a racial minority's voting power relative to the *status quo* or if it was intended to do so.

As we will see in § C[2], *infra*, in 2006, Congress amended the VRA to overrule the Court's holding in *Bossier Parish*, but Congress left *Beer* intact.[36] Thus, the amended statute provides that preclearance should be denied if a proposed change actually reduces a minority group's voting power relative to the *status quo* or if it is intended to discriminate against a minority group by giving it less voting power than it should have received.

1. Effect and Purpose

In *Beer v. United States*, *supra*, the Court considered a reapportionment of the districts for the seven members of the New Orleans city council. The city sought judicial preclearance, but the three-judge district court denied the request on the ground that the change would have the effect of abridging the right to vote on the basis of race. The court found that since elections had been characterized by bloc voting along racial lines, the change would mean that blacks would probably be able to elect only one member of the council, as opposed to the two or three that they might have been able to elect based on their proportion of the electorate. On appeal, the Supreme Court held that preclearance should have been granted. The purpose of § 5, the Court held, "has always been to insure that no voting-procedure changes would be made that would lead to a retrogression in the position of racial minorities with respect to their effective exercise of the electoral franchise."[37] Thus, a change that "enhances the position of racial minorities" cannot be said to have the effect of diluting or abridging the right to vote. The Court noted that, prior to the change, blacks were not a majority in any of the districts. After the change, even assuming bloc racial voting, blacks would likely elect one or perhaps two members. Hence, there was no retrogression.[38]

---

34. 425 U.S. 130 (1976).
35. 528 U.S. 320 (2000).
36. *See* 52 U.S.C. § 10304(c).
37. 425 U.S. at 141.
38. Justices Brennan, Marshall, and White dissented. They argued that the VRA language was meant to track the requirements of the Fifteenth Amendment (except for the shift of the burden of proof from the challenger to the covered jurisdiction) and that the Amendment did not require a retrogressive or ameliorative inquiry. Instead, the inquiry should have been whether there was a discriminatory effect or purpose.

The Court in *Beer* held that because the districting plan was not retrogressive, it did not have the "effect of denying or abridging the right to vote." But a non-retrogressive effect is not enough to satisfy § 5. The statute also demands that the change not have the "purpose . . . of denying or abridging the right to vote on account of race or color."[39] Should this "purpose" requirement be interpreted to require a retrogressive purpose? The Court confronted that question in *Reno v. Bossier Parish School Board*.[40] The case concerned a redistricting plan enacted with a discriminatory but non-retrogressive purpose. Prior to the redistricting, none of the school board's electoral districts were majority-minority, and governmental authorities declined a request to redraw districts so as to add at least one such district. The challengers to the redistricting conceded that there was no retrogression, as the new plan did not worsen the position of minority voters. But they argued that demonstrating retrogression was unnecessary if discriminatory purpose was shown.

The Court disagreed, holding that "the language of § 5 leads to the conclusion that the 'purpose' prong of § 5 covers only retrogressive dilution." The Court reached this conclusion by reasoning that *Beer* should be read as requiring retrogression for both "purpose" and "effect" inquiries, which are drawn from the same sentence in the VRA. This did not make the purpose and effect prongs redundant, the Court explained, because the challenger to the covered jurisdiction could prevail by showing either discriminatory purpose *or* effect. The Court concluded that an inquiry into whether changes to the *status quo* abridged the right to vote necessitated some baseline of comparison, and that baseline was the existing practice.[41]

Whether there was retrogression under § 5 was sometimes itself a complex inquiry, more than simply, say, comparing the numbers of majority-minority districts in a challenged plan and the benchmark plan. One prominent example was the Supreme Court's decision in *Georgia v. Ashcroft*.[42] The case concerned redistricting for the state senate in Georgia. The prior plan had ten or eleven majority-minority districts. In the redistricting that followed the 2000 census, the Democratic majority in the legislature (which had the support of a substantial majority of black voters) sought to maintain the existing number of majority-minority districts but also to increase the number of "influence" districts, where minority voters could exert a significant influence on election outcomes. The new plan decreased the number of majority-minority districts with a black voting-age population of greater than 60% but increased the number of black influence districts.

In *Beer*, the Court held that retrogression consisted of a reduction of racial minorities' "effective exercise of the electoral franchise,"[43] but the Court had not made clear

---

39. 52 U.S.C. § 10304.

40. 528 U.S. 320 (2000).

41. Justices Souter, Stevens, Ginsburg, and Breyer dissented, primarily on the basis that *Beer* was wrongly decided and that the purpose prong should be read concurrently with the Fifteenth Amendment.

42. 539 U.S. 461 (2003).

43. 425 U.S. at 141.

how to assess a group's "effective exercise of the electoral franchise." The Court in *Georgia v. Ashcroft* held that such an inquiry depended "on an examination of all of the relevant circumstances, such as the ability of minority voters to elect their candidate of choice, the extent of the minority group's opportunity to participate in the political process, and the feasibility of creating a nonretrogressive plan."[44] The "comparative ability of a minority group to elect a candidate of its choice" was an "important" but not "dispositive or exclusive" factor in determining retrogression.[45] A court should also consider the minority group's overall participation in the political process, such as in legislative leadership, and in the number of influence districts.[46] Based on these criteria, the Court concluded that Georgia "likely met its burden of showing nonretrogression," meaning that it was probably entitled to preclearance, but the Court remanded for further proceedings.[47]

2. Congressional Reaction

In its reauthorization of the preclearance provisions in 2006, Congress amended § 5 to overturn the *Bossier Parish* holding. Since the amendment, 52 U.S.C. § 10304(c) has provided that "purpose" in the preclearance provisions "shall include any discriminatory purpose." Thus, preclearance should be denied when a covered jurisdiction acts with a "discriminatory," albeit non-retrogressive, purpose, or with a retrogressive effect.

The 2006 amendments to the VRA also added a new provision, codified at 52 U.S.C. § 10304(b), which provides, "Any voting qualification or prerequisite to voting, or standard, practice, or procedure with respect to voting that has the purpose of or will have the effect of diminishing the ability of any citizens of the United States on account of race or color, or [status as a language minority], to elect their preferred candidates of choice denies or abridges the right to vote within the meaning of" the statute, and should therefore result in a denial of preclearance. This language has the effect of overruling, or at least limiting, the holding in *Georgia v. Ashcroft* because it prevents or limits covered jurisdictions from substituting influence or coalition districts for minority-majority districts.[48]

---

44. 539 U.S. at 479.

45. *Id.* at 480.

46. *See id.*

47. *Id.* at 487. Justice Kennedy concurred, but he observed that "race was a predominant factor in drawing the lines" of the new plan and argued that Georgia's new plan showed the tension between § 5 and cases holding that race cannot be a predominant factor in redistricting. *Id.* at 491 (Kennedy, J., concurring). Justice Souter, joined by three other Justices, agreed that increasing the number of coalition or influence districts can be non-retrogressive but dissented on the basis that the majority was "redefin[ing] effective voter power in § 5 analysis without the anchoring reference to electing a candidate of choice." *Id.* at 493 (Souter, J., dissenting).

48. For further discussion of these 2006 amendments, see Abigail Thernstrom, Voting Rights—and Wrongs: The Elusive Quest for Racially Fair Elections 178–82 (2009), and Nathaniel Persily, *The Promise and Pitfalls of the New Voting Rights Act*, 117 Yale L.J. 174, 216–51 (2007).

The language in the 2006 amendment modifying *Georgia v. Ashcroft* was considered by the Supreme Court in 2015 in *Alabama Legislative Black Caucus v. Alabama*,[49] which involved a redistricting plan put in place by the Alabama legislature. In an attempt to gain preclearance, the state tried to ensure that the new plan not only preserved the number of majority-minority districts but also minorities' voting strength within each majority-minority district. For example, if a district under the previous plan was 70% minority, the line-drawers attempted to ensure that the district would continue to be 70% minority; otherwise, Alabama feared, the new plan would diminish minorities' voting strength. Because not all eligible voters turn out, and because of crossover votes, a slim population majority in a district hardly ensures that a group will be able to elect its candidates of choice. Thus, a reduction of minority population from 70% to, say, 55% in a district could diminish the minority's ability to elect its candidates of choice, even as the number of majority-minority districts was maintained. Although the Supreme Court declared the coverage formula unconstitutional two years earlier, thus rendering preclearance unenforceable, the state continued to argue that its plan was justified, in part due to its purpose to comply with the requirements of § 5, as the state understood it.

The Supreme Court held that § 5 of the VRA was not so constraining. In the Court's view, the question of the diminishment of minority voting strength required a more "complex" analysis than simply a comparison of the percentage of minorities in a district before and after the district lines have been redrawn. Rather, it required courts to "take account of all significant circumstances" bearing on minorities' voting power. While reducing the percentage of minorities in a district *might* decrease that group's ability to elect its preferred candidates, it might not. The Court thus made clear that, in adopting the 2006 amendment, Congress "rejected" the holding in *Georgia v. Ashcroft* and adopted the views of the dissent in that case.[50]

---

49. 575 U.S. 254 (2015).

50. Even so, the Court added that the revised language in the 2006 amendment "may raise some interpretive questions," such as "its application to coalition, crossover, and influence districts," that the Court found unnecessary to resolve. Justice Thomas in dissent criticized what he considered the Court's vague standard as "requir[ing] States to analyze race even *more* exhaustively, not less, by accounting for black voter registration and turnout statistics." He added that "States covered by § 5 have been whipsawed, first required to create 'safe' majority-black districts, then told not to 'diminis[h]' the ability to elect, and now told that they have been too rigid in preventing any 'diminishing' of the ability to elect." *Id.* at 305 (Thomas, J., dissenting).

D. The Constitutionality of § 5

1. Introduction

Shortly after the adoption of the Voting Rights Act, the Supreme Court, in *South Carolina v. Katzenbach*, upheld § 5 against a constitutional challenge.[51] Although § 5 unquestionably represented "an uncommon exercise of congressional power" and a federal incursion into an area that had previously been regulated by the state, the Court held that § 5 was within Congress's power.[52] The Fourteenth and Fifteenth Amendments, which respectively guarantee equal protection and forbid racial discrimination in voting, grant Congress the "power to enforce, by appropriate legislation, the provisions of" each Amendment. In *South Carolina v. Katzenbach*, the Court interpreted Congress's enforcement power very broadly, holding that, "[a]s against the reserved powers of the States, Congress may use any rational means to effectuate the constitutional prohibition of racial discrimination in voting."[53] In light of the South's long history of racial discrimination, particularly with regard to voting rights, and in light of the difficulty of remedying that discrimination through case-by-case litigation, the Court held that it was rational to require states with a discriminatory past to preclear changes to their election laws.[54]

The question of § 5's constitutionality would return to the Court more than forty years later, after Congress in 2006 reauthorized the VRA for another twenty-five years but continued to use the same "coverage formula" that had been in place since 1975 for determining which states would be required to preclear their election laws. Under that formula, a jurisdiction would be subject to preclearance if it had used voting tests and it had less than 50% voter registration or turnout in 1964, 1968, or 1972.

A renewed constitutional challenge to § 5, specifically to the 2006 congressional reauthorization of the VRA, reached the Court in 2009, with *Northwest Austin Municipal Utility District Number One v. Holder*.[55] There, a utility district in Texas complained that Congress could not constitutionally require preclearance on the basis of an outdated coverage formula that rendered the state a covered jurisdiction. The Court dodged the constitutional issue, instead holding that the district was eligible to bail out of § 5's preclearance obligations if it could show that it met the requirements of 52 U.S.C. § 10303(a)(1): that within the preceding ten years it had not used a voting test, had not been denied preclearance, and had not been found guilty of other voting-rights violations.

---

51. South Carolina v. Katzenbach, 383 U.S. 301 (1966).

52. *Id.* at 334.

53. *Id.* at 324.

54. *See id.* at 335 (noting that preclearance was an attempt to prevent states from continuing to employ "the extraordinary stratagem of contriving new rules of various kinds for the sole purpose of perpetuating voting discrimination in the face of adverse federal court decrees").

55. 557 U.S. 193 (2009).

Even though the case thus turned on the statutory bailout question, the Court warned that Congress might have exceeded its constitutional power in passing the 2006 reauthorization. The lead opinion by Chief Justice Roberts stated that "[t]hings have changed in the South. Voter turnout and registration rates [of different races] now approach parity. Blatantly discriminatory evasions of federal decrees are rare. And minority candidates hold office at unprecedented levels."[56] He acknowledged that the "improvements are no doubt due in significant part to the Voting Rights Act itself," but warned that "[p]ast success . . . is not adequate justification to retain the preclearance requirements. . . . [T]he Act imposes current burdens and must be justified by current needs."[57] He added that given the "equal sovereignty" of the states, the disparate treatment of the jurisdictions covered by § 5 must be justified by a "showing . . . sufficiently related to the problem it targets."[58]

2. *Shelby County, Alabama v. Holder*

In 2013, the Court faced another constitutional challenge to preclearance, this time by an Alabama county that was ineligible for bailout because it had been denied preclearance within the prior ten years. The Court in *Shelby County, Alabama v. Holder*[59] was thus presented with the constitutional question that it had avoided in *Northwest Austin*.

The majority opinion in *Shelby County* was again authored by Chief Justice Roberts. As in *Northwest Austin*, he emphasized that since the passage of the original VRA, there had been significant gains in black voting and electoral power, undermining the claim that preclearance remained necessary and would continue to remain necessary through the duration of the 2006 reauthorization, which would last until 2031. "At the same time," he acknowledged, "voting discrimination still exists; no one doubts that. The question is whether the Act's extraordinary measures, including its disparate treatment of the States, continue to satisfy constitutional requirements."[60]

The Court held that the constitutional requirements were not satisfied. The opinion by the Chief Justice focused on the coverage formula in § 4, which, in the 2006 reauthorization, focused "on decades-old data relevant to decades-old problems, rather than current data reflecting current needs."[61] The government attempted to argue that even if blacks' access to the ballot was no longer obstructed, preclearance was still necessary to combat "second-generation barriers," that is, "electoral arrangements that affect the weight of minority votes." The Court rejected that argument.

---

56. *Id.* at 202.

57. *Id.* at 202–03.

58. *Id.* at 203. Justice Thomas dissented, arguing that, as a matter of statutory construction, the utility district was not entitled to a bailout and that § 5 was unconstitutional as an unjustified intrusion on the powers of states.

59. 570 U.S. 529 (2013).

60. *Id.* at 536.

61. *Id.* at 553.

The coverage formula, it found, was "based on voting tests and access to the ballot, not vote dilution." The large record of second-generation barriers before Congress in 2006 "played no role in shaping the statutory formula" of § 4. The Court concluded that if "Congress had started from scratch in 2006, it plainly could not have enacted the present coverage formula." The Court's holding left intact the nationwide regulation of § 2 and concerned only the coverage formula, not § 5 itself, so the Court acknowledged that "Congress may draft another formula based on current conditions."[62]

Four dissenters, in an opinion by Justice Ginsburg, saw things quite differently. She emphasized what she called the "voluminous record" of voting discrimination in the affected states that was before Congress in 2006. She concluded that "current needs" did indeed exist to justify maintaining the coverage formula, and she chastised the Court for misapplying an "equal sovereignty" principle in a way that prevented Congress from requiring preclearance for some states but not others based on different states' vastly different histories of racial discrimination in voting. The Court believed, however, that if Congress were to violate the states' presumptively equal sovereignty, it would have to do so based on *currently* unequal conditions across the states.

The Court's decision in *Shelby County* was extremely controversial and resulted in an unusually large outpouring of academic commentary.[63] A matter of particular dispute was the Court's application of the equal sovereignty principle.[64]

3. Impact of and Responses to *Shelby County*

Shortly after *Shelby County* held the coverage formula unconstitutional, pending preclearance litigation was dismissed, and some of the theretofore covered jurisdictions enacted voting regulations (such as voter-ID laws) that likely would have required preclearance before 2013.[65]

With the demise of the coverage formula in § 4 of the VRA, the "bail-in" or "pocket trigger" provisions of § 3 have assumed greater prominence. According to § 3, "[i]f in any proceeding instituted by the Attorney General or an aggrieved person under any statute to enforce the voting guarantees of the fourteenth or fifteenth amendment in any State or political subdivision the court finds that violations of the fourteenth or fifteenth amendment justifying equitable relief have occurred within the territory of

---

62. Justice Thomas concurred, following the reasoning of his *Northwest Austin* dissent, and argued that § 5 itself was unconstitutional, regardless of the coverage formula.

63. For a sampling of the large academic literature, see *Forum: Responses to* Shelby County, 12 ELECTION L.J. 317–45 (2013); William S. Consovoy & Thomas R. McCarthy, Shelby County v. Holder: *The Restoration of Constitutional Order*, 2012–2013 CATO SUP. CT. REV. 31; and Samuel Issacharoff, *Beyond the Discrimination Model on Voting*, 127 HARV. L. REV. 95 (2013).

64. For differing views of the principle, see Thomas B. Colby, *In Defense of the Equal Sovereignty Principle*, 65 DUKE L.J. 1087 (2016), and Leah M. Litman, *Inventing Equal Sovereignty*, 114 MICH. L. REV. 1207 (2016).

65. Richard L. Hasen, *Race or Party? How Courts Should Think About Republican Efforts to Make It Harder to Vote in North Carolina and Elsewhere*, 127 HARV. L. REV. F. 58 (2014).

such State or political subdivision, the court, in addition to such relief as it may grant, shall retain jurisdiction for such period as it may deem appropriate and during such period" preclearance shall be required.[66]

Thus, § 3 permits a jurisdiction-by-jurisdiction identification of the places where preclearance is required, rather than the wholesale approach of § 4's coverage formula, which was struck down in *Shelby County*.[67] Further, the decision whether to require preclearance under § 3 belongs with the courts. Most jurisdictions to have been bailed-in have accepted that status through a consent decree. Prior to *Shelby County*, only one jurisdiction had been bailed-in without such an agreement.[68] After *Shelby County*, more jurisdictions have been bailed-in,[69] some without the jurisdictions' consent.[70]

The bail-in procedure requires a finding of a constitutional violation on the basis of intentional discrimination—not simply a violation of the prophylactic guarantees of § 2, which protect minorities from laws that *result* in an abridgement of their ability to elect their candidates of choice. This requirement of a constitutional violation will make it difficult for "aggrieved person[s]" to win a bail-in suit, but while it may be difficult to force a state or political subdivision to be bailed-in, it is not impossible.

In response to *Shelby County*, bills were introduced in Congress, with bipartisan support, to amend the VRA's coverage formula and to effect other changes, in an effort to revive preclearance and comply with the demands of the majority opinion.[71] Some of these proposals defined away the selective coverage issue by requiring at least some form of preclearance for *all* jurisdictions in the United States. Other proposals less ambitiously redefined and updated the coverage formula or expanded § 3(c)'s bail-in procedure.[72] For example, some created a new coverage formula based on a rolling fifteen-year calendar; states would be covered if they committed five federal voting-rights violations within the preceding fifteen years. Such a provision would cover

66. 52 U.S.C. § 10302(c). On § 3 bailouts, see Travis Crum, Note, *The Voting Rights Act's Secret Weapon: Pocket Trigger Litigation and Dynamic Preclearance*, 119 Yale L.J. 1992 (2010).

67. *See* Michael Ellement, *Preclearance Without Statutory Change: Bail-In Suits Post-*Shelby County, 32 Yale L. & Pol'y Rev. Inter Alia 1 (2013).

68. Jeffers v. Clinton, 740 F. Supp. 585 (E.D. Ark. 1990).

69. *See* Jones v. Jefferson Cnty. Bd. of Educ., 2019 WL 7500528 (N.D. Ala. 2019) (consent decree). *See also* NAACP Legal Defense Fund, *A Primer on Sections 2 & 3(c) of the Voting Rights Act* (Jan. 5, 2021), https://www.naacpldf.org/wp-content/uploads/LDF-Sections-2-and-3c-VRA-primer-1.5.21.pdf.

70. *See* Allen v. City of Evergreen, Ala., 2014 WL 12607819 (S.D. Ala. 2014).

71. *See, e.g.*, S. 1945, 113th Cong. (2014); H.R. 885, 114th Cong. (2015).

72. On the wisdom and constitutionality of expanding § 3(c), compare Richard H. Pildes, *One Easy, but Powerful, Way to Amend the VRA*, Election Law Blog (June 28, 2013), http://electionlawblog.org/?p=52349, and Travis Crum, *The Voting Rights Advancement Act of 2019*, Take Care (Mar. 1, 2019), https://takecareblog.com/blog/the-voting-rights-advancement-act-of-2019, with Hans von Spakovsky, *Destroying Election Integrity: The Unnecessary and Unconstitutional John R. Lewis Voting Rights Advancement Act (S.4/H.R.4)*, Heritage Found. (Oct. 29, 2021), https://www.heritage.org/election-integrity/report/destroying-election-integrity-the-unnecessary-and-unconstitutional-john-r.

only four states: Georgia, Louisiana, Mississippi, and Texas. (Political subdivisions would be covered if they committed three federal statutory violations in the same fifteen-year period.) This rolling fifteen-year calendar was designed to address the *Shelby County* Court's insistence that Congress must be able to point to current evidence—and not just voting data from the 1964, 1968, and 1972 elections—to justify overriding the equal sovereignty of states.

Such updated coverage formulas present their own potential constitutional problems. For example, if preclearance would be triggered by violations of federal statutory law, such as § 2 of the VRA, states might be bailed-in and forced to preclear future election laws on the basis of statutory violations without having committed constitutional violations. Because Congress passed the VRA pursuant to its power to "enforce" the Fifteenth Amendment (and *South Carolina v. Katzenbach* upheld it on the same basis), an amended VRA might be unconstitutional if it imposed preclearance without any showing that rights protected by the Fifteenth Amendment were threatened. The lack of clarity regarding the requirements of *Shelby County*, as well as partisan opposition in Congress, cast uncertainty on early legislative efforts to revive the preclearance process.

Chapter 4
Race-Conscious Districting Under the Constitution and the Voting Rights Act

A. Introduction

Our examination of voting rights began with the constitutional right of people to participate in elections by registering and voting. Our treatment of the subject progressed to consider the constitutional requirement that districts be equally populated. In establishing the one-person, one-vote doctrine, the Court recognized that the right to cast a vote and to have that vote fairly counted was not enough to guarantee that a person or group would have effective political power.

In the last chapter, we began to learn that the one-person, one-vote doctrine was also not sufficient to ensure the equality of voting power.[1] It was for that reason that the Voting Rights Act (especially as interpreted in *Allen v. State Board of Elections*[2]) required covered jurisdictions to preclear all changes to their election laws, as each of those changes might have been a device to minimize the political influence of disfavored groups.

This chapter continues to address the effects that election laws can have on groups' political power, focusing particularly on districting. The term "vote dilution" is often used to express the idea of using districting to reduce voters' political influence. Voters are permitted to vote, but those votes have less value than they would if the districts were organized differently. As we will see, however, the term "vote dilution" is a loaded one because it presupposes that we can determine the proper value of a vote—the amount the vote would be worth if it were "undiluted." But assessing the value of an undiluted vote has been notoriously difficult.

---

1. *See generally, e.g.*, Grant M. Hayden, *The False Promise of One Person, One Vote*, 102 Mich. L. Rev. 213 (2003).
2. 393 U.S. 544 (1969).

There are two principal methods of minimizing a group's political influence through districting: packing and cracking. Packing takes as many of the disfavored voters as possible and places them in as few districts as possible. Under such a scheme, the group may have a controlling influence in a few districts but very limited influence outside of those districts. The group may therefore elect some candidates, but the rest of the representatives might safely ignore their concerns.

Cracking takes the opposite approach. Under this method of diluting a group's political influence, the group is split across several districts so that it possesses very little influence in any of them. Under this kind of scheme, the group may have minimal influence on a large number of representatives, but each of those representatives might be able to ignore their concerns if the remainder of the electorate is sufficient to vote them into office.

So far, we have spoken of effects of districting on the voting power of groups. Groups, however, do not cast votes as such. More importantly, the Constitution does not appear to confer rights on groups; rather, it says that rights of due process and equal protection apply to "person[s]"[3] and the right to be free from racial discrimination extends to "citizens."[4] Individuals, who unquestionably have constitutional rights, have minimal political power by themselves, and so it makes little sense to talk about the diluted value of a single vote. The Court's struggle with balancing the individual nature of voting rights with the political power of groups of voters is a major theme of this chapter.

B. Constitutional Constraints on Minority Vote Dilution

In *Gomillion v. Lightfoot*,[5] which we encountered in Chapter 2, the Supreme Court held that Alabama violated the Fifteenth Amendment when it re-drew the boundaries of the City of Tuskegee from a square to an "uncouth twenty-eight-sided figure"[6] so as to exclude virtually every black person from the city (and thus exclude them from being able to vote in city elections). The case therefore established that people's voting rights could be abridged by laws that drew districts in such a way as to exclude them from the electorate. That is, even though there is no constitutional right to have cities drawn in any particular shape, there is a constitutional right not to have city boundaries drawn so as to deprive racial minorities of voting rights.

Modern cases, of course, present allegations of much subtler discrimination, and those cases have forced courts and Congress to be much more sophisticated in their responses. Congress's chief effort to combat vote dilution is § 2 of the Voting Rights

---

3. U.S. Const. amend. XIV, § 1.
4. U.S. Const. amend. XV, § 1.
5. 364 U.S. 339 (1960).
6. *Id.* at 340.

Act, which will be considered later in this chapter. This section addresses the protection against vote dilution contained in the Fourteenth and Fifteenth Amendments.

1. Multimember Districts and Vote Dilution

The most obvious way to reduce a group's voting power is to make it more difficult for members of that group to register and to vote. In Chapter 1, we considered the constitutionality of several limitations on the right to vote, and we will return to that theme in future chapters. Chapter 5, for example, considers rules that limit people's ability to participate in political parties, and Chapters 10 and 11 respectively address burdens on casting ballots and on having one's vote counted. But even if one is permitted to vote and to have his vote counted, the power of that vote may be affected by laws that govern how society translates votes into political results.

This section considers one such category of laws: multimember districts, *i.e.*, those in which the same voters elect multiple candidates for the same legislative body. Suppose, for example, that a state has one million residents and a legislature of one hundred representatives. If the entire state were divided into single-member districts, each district would include about ten thousand people. If the state had a city with thirty thousand people, then the state could carve that city into three districts, with each district electing one representative. Alternatively, the state could allocate three representatives to that city, and make the entire city a single multimember district, so that every voter in the city would be able to vote for three representatives, and each city resident would be represented by three legislators.

While this triple representation sounds like a benefit for city residents, recall that there are three times as many people in the city than in the average single-member district. So while each resident has a claim on the attention of three different representatives, he must compete with three times as many other residents for the attention of any one of those three representatives. Multimember districts thus introduce a fundamental trade-off that will be a major consideration throughout this chapter: Is it better to have more influence over a small number of representatives or less influence over a greater number of representatives?

Multimember districts present an opportunity to dilute the strength of minority groups within the districts. Using the example discussed above, suppose that a given minority group (whether defined by race, party affiliation, or any other characteristic) has 12,000 members in a city that has a population of 30,000. If the city were carved into three districts of 10,000 persons, and if most members of the minority group were placed in one of those districts, the minority group would be able to control the election of the candidate from that district. By creating a 30,000-person multimember district, however, the city could subsume the minority group within a larger number of people, enabling it to be outvoted. Thus, although that minority group might represent more than one-third of the city population, it might expect to receive far less than one-third of the representatives elected from a district that elects all three representatives at large.

Whitcomb v. Chavis[7] was the first modern case to consider the dilutive effects of multimember districts, and it identified the principal difficulty surrounding vote-dilution issues: how to distinguish mere lack of political success from unconstitutional discrimination. The case involved two very different challenges to the multimember districts that Indiana used to elect members of the state legislature from Marion County. The first challenge was that voters in Marion County were too powerful compared to voters in single-member districts. The second challenge was that the multimember district diluted the votes of racial minorities in Marion County by subsuming them in a larger, majority-white district. The Court rejected both constitutional challenges.

In *Whitcomb*, Indiana had figured that its one-person, one-vote obligation was satisfied so long as a district electing X representatives had X times the number of residents that single-member districts had. The first group of challengers had alleged, however, that, even accounting for the population difference, a voter in a multimember district was more powerful than a voter in a single-member district, because a voter in a multimember district would have a much greater opportunity to cast the critical vote that would determine which representatives would win election. The Court dismissed the challengers' argument as "theoretical,"[8] and held that the challengers had not "sufficiently demonstrated" "[t]he real-life impact of multi-member districts on individual voting power."[9]

The Court also brushed off the challengers' additional argument that multimember districts had an unconstitutional advantage over other districts because voters in such districts would be represented by a greater number of representatives in the legislature and those representatives would tend to vote in a bloc, effectively giving those districts extra power in the legislative body. The Court again relied on the argument that multimember districts' extra power "remains to be demonstrated in practice,"[10] and it also pointed out that bloc voting happens in legislatures all the time, regardless of the type of districts used in selecting representatives.

The Court also rejected the second challenge, which argued that minority votes within Marion County were being unconstitutionally diluted. The challengers noted that a disproportionately low number of legislators came from the area of the county known as "the ghetto," which was populated mostly by poor blacks. The Court was unimpressed. The Court first noted that this was not a case of purposeful discrimination, nor was this a case where minorities encountered "first-generation" problems in gaining access to the ballot. In language that Congress later adopted in amending the Voting Rights Act, the Court held that a minority group's disproportionately low electoral success could not "satisfactorily prove invidious discrimination absent evidence and findings that ghetto residents had less opportunity than did other Marion County residents to participate in the political process and to elect legislators of their choice."[11]

---

7. 403 U.S. 124 (1971).
8. *Id.* at 145.
9. *Id.* at 146.
10. *Id.* at 147.
11. *Id.* at 149.

The Court did not explicitly provide a definition of what it meant "to participate in the political process and to elect legislators of their choice," but it did provide examples of the kinds of opportunities that were available to members of the minority group that challenged the Indiana districts. They could register and vote, join and participate in political parties, and run for election. They failed to receive a proportional share of representatives only because they supported the party that lost most of the elections. Thus, although the challengers complained about vote dilution, the Court concluded that "this seems a mere euphemism for political defeat at the polls."[12]

The potentially far-reaching consequences of the challengers' argument seemed to worry the Court. If Indiana's multimember districts were unconstitutional because they failed to give the ghetto proportional representation, would other groups besides racial minorities be able to invalidate multimember districts whenever they received less representation than they would receive in a system of single-member districts? Such a rule would render virtually all multimember districts unconstitutional, as their very purpose is to select representatives who are acceptable to the entire community rather than those candidates preferred by only a portion of it. The Court was unwilling to mandate such a result, especially considering that multimember districts had been the rule, rather than the exception, at the Framing, and they remained popular since that time.

In dissent, Justice Douglas, joined by Justices Brennan and Marshall, saw no such slippery slope toward recognition of a right of proportional representation for all kinds of minority groups. He pointed out that the Fifteenth Amendment specifically prohibits *racial* discrimination in voting (although the Fourteenth Amendment's Equal Protection Clause is not so limited), and so he argued that there should be no need to worry about other interest groups' claims of a constitutional right against vote dilution. Justice Douglas suggested that there should be a constitutional violation whenever a racial group's "identity is purposely washed out of the system"—an odd basis on which to decide the case, as the majority reached its decision in part because there had not even been any allegation of purposeful discrimination.

Two years later, vote dilution was back before the Court, but this time the Court's holding was quite different. The second case, *White v. Regester*,[13] came from Dallas and Bexar Counties in Texas. Again, the allegation was that although members of minority communities in those counties were permitted to vote, the Texas election laws unconstitutionally reduced the power of those votes. This time, however, the Supreme Court held in favor of the plaintiffs and affirmed the district court's order requiring single-member districts. While acknowledging that, under *Whitcomb*, multimember districts were not *per se* unconstitutional, the Court held that, in this case, the plaintiffs had shown that "the political processes leading to nomination and election were not equally open to participation by" minorities, who "had less opportunity

12. *Id.* at 153.
13. 412 U.S. 755 (1973).

than did other residents in the district to participate in the political process and to elect legislators of their choice."[14]

While the Court's conclusion was clear, its reasoning was not. The Court cited several ways in which the political process in those Texas counties was not equally open to minorities, but the Court did not explain why those reasons amounted to a constitutional violation. The essential difficulty is this: If any Texas law interfered with minorities' voting rights in a way that was itself unconstitutional, then that law could be struck down without the need for any further vote-dilution analysis. If, on the other hand, Texas's "discriminatory" laws, customs, practices, and social conditions did *not* themselves violate the Constitution, then it is hard to understand how they could combine to create a constitutional violation by harming minority voters' political power. In fact, the Court would later confirm that a discriminatory effect alone is not enough to violate the Fourteenth Amendment's Equal Protection Clause or the Fifteenth Amendment; a facially neutral law ordinarily does not violate the Constitution unless it produces a disparate effect *and* is motivated by a discriminatory purpose.[15]

The Court first cited Texas's discriminatory history as one factor limiting the ability of minorities to access the political process. As shown in Chapter 5, Texas's use of the "white primary" prevented blacks from participating in primary elections, even after they were formally granted the ability to vote in the general election. By 1973, however, that discrimination had been eliminated, and it was clear that, by the time of *Regester*, there was no *de jure* impediment to blacks' registering and voting.

The Court then noted that Texas's election laws increased the tendency of multimember districts to shut out minorities and to overrepresent majorities. Specifically, candidates needed to obtain a majority (not just a plurality) of votes to be nominated, and Texas's "place" rule required candidates to run against each other for particular places on the ticket. That is, if the multimember district elected three representatives, there would be head-to-head races for Representative 1, Representative 2, and Representative 3, rather than a single race with the three offices being awarded to the top three vote-recipients. Additionally, there was no requirement that those offices go to people living in different parts of the district, so it was possible to choose all of the district's representatives from outside the area where minorities lived.[16] Again, the Court did not attempt to claim that any of these laws were themselves unconstitutional, but, together with the multimember districts, they made it more difficult for the minority community to exercise political influence.

The Court then turned to the conditions in the two counties. In Dallas County, the district court found that the Dallas Committee for Responsible Government (DCRG), a white-dominated, anti-black organization, was "in effective control of Democratic Party candidate slating." The DCRG did not appeal to black voters, and in fact it

14. *Id.* at 766 (citing Whitcomb v. Chavis, 403 U.S. 124, 149–50 (1971)).

15. *See* City of Mobile v. Bolden, 446 U.S. 55 (1980).

16. *Regester*, 412 U.S. at 766 & n.10.

made racial appeals to encourage white opposition to candidates favored by the black community. The effect was that only two blacks had been elected to the Texas House of Representatives from Dallas County since Reconstruction. Neither the influence of the DCRG nor the resulting minimal success of black candidates was a constitutional violation; indeed, the DCRG (like all political associations) had a constitutional right to engage in political speech, however discriminatory. The district court held that these factors nevertheless combined with the multimember districts to result in blacks' exclusion from the political process in violation of the Constitution, and the Supreme Court affirmed that conclusion.[17]

The district court's conclusion with respect to Bexar (pronounced "Bare") County was similar. That court found that the minority community of Mexican Americans suffered from discrimination throughout disparate areas of life, including "education, employment, economics, health, politics, and others." The Supreme Court also cited Mexican Americans' "cultural and language barrier" that inhibited their participation in the community. With regard to politics in particular, the Court noted that Texas's voter-registration requirements were (in the opinion of the district court) "the most restrictive . . . in the nation," although the Supreme Court did not imply that the registration requirements themselves were unconstitutional. Similarly to the way that the combination of factors in Dallas County led to disproportionately low representation of blacks in the state legislature, the combination of factors in Bexar County led to disproportionately low representation of Mexican Americans. Lastly, the district court concluded "that the Bexar County legislative delegation in the House was insufficiently responsive to Mexican-American interests."[18]

Once again, the cited factors were not themselves constitutional violations. Some discrimination by the government, of course, is unconstitutional, but private discrimination cannot be. The "cultural and language barrier," however regrettable, was also not unconstitutional. While registration requirements could be unconstitutionally burdensome, the Court made no effort to show that Texas's were in fact unconstitutional. And obviously no person and no group has a constitutional right to a legislative delegation that is "sufficiently responsive."

When combined with the use of multimember districts, however, these "cultural and economic realities" produced an unconstitutional suppression of minority voting power, in the view of the district court. Accordingly, the district court ordered the multimember districts replaced with single-member ones, and the Supreme Court affirmed.[19] The Supreme Court argued that deference to the district court was particularly appropriate in determining whether the minority group was unable to exercise equal political power because the decision involved "a blend of history and an intensely local appraisal of the design and impact of the . . . multimember district in light of past and present reality, political and otherwise."[20]

---

17. *Id.* at 766–67.
18. *Id.* at 768–69.
19. *Id.* at 769.
20. *Id.* at 769–70.

This "intensely local" focus on history as well as other details about political, economic, and cultural conditions resulted in a rule that was flexible enough to allow district judges to reach results tailored to the needs and "realit[ies]" of each case.[21] By the same token, it raised the possibility of inconsistent judgments. *Whitcomb* and *Regester*, for example, reached different results, but were the facts of the cases meaningfully different? In both cases, the jurisdictions used multimember districts that led to disproportionately low representation of poor minority communities. In neither case was there any unconstitutional infringement with minorities' ability to register and vote. And in neither case was the multimember districting scheme adopted for a discriminatory purpose. It seems as though the only significant difference between *Whitcomb* and *Regester* was Texas's history of discrimination and Indiana's lack of such a history. Although history undoubtedly produces long-lasting effects, one may question whether a state should be prohibited from using multimember districts because of discrimination that is no longer occurring.

Because of its focus on the specific facts of discrimination in Texas—especially in two Texas counties—and because of the Supreme Court's deference to the conclusions of the district court, *Regester* might appear to have little significance outside the case itself. On the contrary, *Regester* has proven to be of immense significance. As we will see in § C, *infra*, *Regester*'s case-by-case application of its test—whether the political process is equally open to minorities so that they have an equal opportunity

---

21. The most significant lower-court case to expound on *Regester*'s analysis of the factors that could lead to a finding of unconstitutional discrimination was *Zimmer v. McKeithen*, 485 F.2d 1297 (5th Cir. 1973) (*en banc*):

> The Supreme Court has identified a panoply of factors, any number of which may contribute to the existence of dilution. Clearly, it is not enough to prove a mere disparity between the number of minority residents and the number of minority representatives. Where it is apparent that a minority is afforded the opportunity to participate in the slating of candidates to represent its area, that the representatives slated and elected provide representation responsive to minority's needs, and that the use of a multimember districting scheme is rooted in a strong state policy divorced from the maintenance of racial discrimination, Whitcomb v. Chavis would require a holding of no dilution. *Whitcomb* would not be controlling, however, where the state policy favoring multimember or at-large districting schemes is rooted in racial discrimination. Conversely, where a minority can demonstrate a lack of access to the process of slating candidates, the unresponsiveness of legislators to their particularized interests, a tenuous state policy underlying the preference for multimember or at-large districting, or that the existence of past discrimination in general precludes the effective participation in the election system, a strong case is made. Such proof is enhanced by a showing of the existence of large districts, majority vote requirements, antisingle shot voting provisions and the lack of provision for at-large candidates running from particular geographical subdistricts. The fact of dilution is established upon proof of the existence of an aggregate of these factors. The Supreme Court's recent pronouncement in White v. Regester demonstrates, however, that all these factors need not be proved in order to obtain relief.

Id. at 1305 (footnotes and citations omitted). These "*Zimmer* factors" were relied on by Congress in amending § 2 of the VRA in 1982. They were cited in the Senate Report on the VRA amendment, S. Rep. No. 97-417, at 28–29 (1982), and so are also known as the "Senate factors."

to "participate in the political process and to elect legislators of their choice"—has been incorporated into the Voting Rights Act.

Ironically, however, *Regester*'s case-by-case analysis of local conditions and history has been overshadowed in the area where it developed: litigation directly under the Constitution. *City of Mobile v. Bolden*, decided in 1980, purported not to overrule *Regester*, but the plurality opinion by Justice Stewart applied a much simpler rule than *Regester* did and reached a result arguably inconsistent with *Regester*. As we discuss in § C, Congress viewed *Bolden* as an improvident overruling of *Regester*, and Congress amended the Voting Rights Act in an attempt to re-impose *Regester*'s multi-factor test.

City of Mobile v. Bolden,[22] like *Whitcomb* and *Regester*, involved a challenge to a multimember district. The district was the entire city, which elected its three city commissioners at large. Each of the three commissioners ran for a specific post (*i.e.*, the successful candidates were not simply the three highest vote-getters among all the candidates), and a majority vote was necessary for a commissioner to be elected. The result, as in the earlier cases, was that the minority community in Mobile could be outvoted for each spot on the commission. The at-large system thus had a dilutive effect on the power of the minority group's votes compared to the group's share of the population.

The plaintiffs argued that the multimember district violated § 2 of the Voting Rights Act as well as the Fourteenth and Fifteenth Amendments. Despite the dilutive effect of the multimember districting scheme, the Court rejected all of the plaintiffs' claims.

The Court first concluded that § 2 of the VRA protected only those rights that were already protected by the Fifteenth Amendment. At the time *Bolden* was decided, VRA § 2 prohibited only state laws that "den[ied] or abridge[d] the right of any citizen of the United States to vote on account of race or color."[23] The Fifteenth Amendment similarly provided that the right to vote "shall not be denied or abridged by the United States or by any State on account of race, color, or previous condition of servitude."[24] The Court held that this language was equivalent: "[T]he language of § 2 no more than elaborates upon that of the Fifteenth Amendment, and the sparse legislative history of § 2 makes clear that it was intended to have an effect no different from that of the Fifteenth Amendment itself."[25]

Accordingly, the Court turned to the question whether the multimember district violated the Constitution. As to the Fifteenth Amendment, the Court rejected the plaintiffs' arguments easily, noting that minorities could "register and vote without hindrance" and, therefore, "their freedom to vote has not been denied or abridged by anyone."[26]

---

22. 446 U.S. 55 (1980).
23. 79 Stat. 437, 42 U.S.C. § 1973 (1965), now codified at 52 U.S.C. § 10301.
24. U.S. Const. amend. XV, § 1.
25. 446 U.S. at 60–61 (footnote omitted).
26. *Id.* at 65.

Concerning the Fourteenth Amendment, the Court conceded that a dilutive electoral system could violate the Equal Protection Clause, but the Court concluded that no districting scheme could violate the Constitution without *purposeful* discrimination.[27] That conclusion is consistent with standard equal-protection doctrine, which holds that facially discriminatory laws trigger strict scrutiny regardless of purpose, but facially race-neutral laws (such as districting laws) trigger strict scrutiny only if they both produce a racially disparate impact and were adopted or maintained for a racially discriminatory purpose.[28]

The requirement of a discriminatory purpose, however, was arguably inconsistent with *Regester*, which held that a multimember district violated the Fifteenth Amendment even though the Court did not explicitly discuss discriminatory purpose. *Bolden* attempted to reconcile the cases by equating the discriminatory *history* and other barriers to minorities' political participation discussed in *Regester* with a finding of discriminatory purpose.

Nevertheless, in explaining why discriminatory purpose had not been proven in *Bolden* itself, the Court provided reasons that seemingly could have applied in *Regester* as well. The Court said that "gauzy sociological considerations" such as "historical and social factors"—even those that might demonstrate a group's lack of political influence—"have no constitutional basis."[29] It was precisely those kinds of factors, however, that the Court relied on in *Regester* to conclude that the multimember district in that case was unconstitutional. In fact, Justice White, the author of the Court's opinion in *Regester*, dissented in *Bolden* because he believed that the totality of those facts demonstrated a discriminatory purpose.

What seemed most important to the *Bolden* plurality was reaffirming *Whitcomb*'s holding that multimember districts are not *per se* unconstitutional, and clarifying that minority groups do not have a constitutional right to legislative representation in proportion to their populations. The *Bolden* plurality was worried that allowing minority groups to claim a constitutional violation whenever an electoral structure "diluted" their voting strength by giving them disproportionately low representation would in practice become a right to proportional representation.[30]

Justice Marshall's dissent would have gone far toward recognizing such a right. He argued that multimember districts should be held unconstitutional whenever they result in a discriminatory impact[31]—a standard that would have struck down virtually all multimember districts.

It seemed, then, that *Bolden* was a retreat from the expansive right recognized in *Regester*. While *Regester* was vague about the need for plaintiffs to show discriminatory

---

27. *See id.* at 66 ("[O]nly if there is purposeful discrimination can there be a violation of the Equal Protection Clause of the Fourteenth Amendment.").

28. *See* Washington v. Davis, 426 U.S. 229 (1976).

29. *Bolden*, 446 U.S. at 75 n.22.

30. *Id.* at 78 n.26.

31. *Id.* at 104 (Marshall, J., dissenting).

intent, *Bolden* was clear that such a showing was indeed necessary.[32] Further, *Bolden* clarified that discriminatory intent could not be inferred merely from historical factors; some more direct showing of discriminatory purpose was necessary. That requirement made it significantly more difficult for plaintiffs to prove unconstitutional discrimination in the use of multimember districts.

2. Gerrymandering and Vote Dilution Under the Constitution

The use of multimember districts is but one way that the voting power of minority groups can be diluted. Single-member districts can achieve the same dilutive effect if the district lines are drawn in such a way as to minimize minorities' influence. For example, minority communities could be carved up so that small numbers of minority voters are distributed among greater numbers of white voters. Alternatively, minorities could be packed into a small number of districts so as to minimize the minority voters' influence in other districts.

Whichever means are employed to dilute the power of minorities' votes, however, the key issue is the same: Unless minority groups have a right to proportional representation—a right the Court has rejected over and over—how is one to determine whether a minority group's voting power has been diluted? That is, if the Constitution gives groups a right not to have their voting strength diluted, it is necessary to determine how much *undiluted* voting strength the group should have.

At the same time that vote-dilution litigation has struggled with protecting minorities' voting power, other litigants have challenged gerrymandering as unconstitutionally *privileging* the voting power of racial minorities, in violation of *whites'* equal-protection rights.

The Supreme Court first encountered all of these constitutional complexities of gerrymandering in *United Jewish Organizations, Inc. v. Carey* (*UJO*).[33] The issues raised in *UJO*, therefore, reappear in many different kinds of cases involving race and districting.

UJO stemmed from New York's state-legislative redistricting following the 1970 census. Because parts of New York City were subject to preclearance under § 5 of the Voting Rights Act,[34] the state submitted its proposed districting plan to the Attorney General. The Attorney General rejected the proposal because, in his view, it did not adequately protect the voting strength of blacks and Puerto Ricans who were living in parts of Brooklyn. In order to meet the Attorney General's requirement that majority-minority districts contain at least 65% minorities, the state re-drew the districts. A

32. Discriminatory intent could, however, be satisfied by a showing that a discriminatory law was *maintained*, even if not originally enacted, for a discriminatory purpose. *See* Rogers v. Lodge, 458 U.S. 613, 622, 626 (1982).

33. 430 U.S. 144 (1977).

34. *See generally* Chapter 3, *supra*.

community of Hasidic Jews had been in a single district under the proposed plan, but the new plan split that community across two districts so as to increase the districts' percentages of blacks and Puerto Ricans. The Hasidim sued, complaining that their voting power had been reduced solely because of their race.

UJO raised several constitutional arguments, but the Supreme Court rejected them all. The lead opinion was written by Justice White, but although Justice Stevens joined the entire opinion and Justices Brennan, Blackmun, and Rehnquist joined portions of the opinion, the only portion to obtain five votes was the statement of facts. Accordingly, although the opinion raised several important issues, it definitively resolved few of them. It was unsurprising, then, that the issues continued to return to the Court in subsequent decades, as we shall see in the remainder of this chapter.

UJO first argued that the use of race in districting should be prohibited, at least where it was not used to remedy past instances of unconstitutional discrimination. Even if race could be used in drawing districts, UJO next argued, states could not constitutionally use a 65%-minority quota. Justice White's plurality opinion, joined in relevant part by Justices Brennan, Blackmun, and Stevens, relied on past cases to reject this argument. Justice White reasoned that because past cases had validated the Voting Rights Act's guarantee against state laws producing a "retrogression" in minority voting strength, it was permissible for a state to consider race and to "use[] specific numerical quotas in establishing a certain number of black majority districts."[35]

Even though UJO was unsuccessful in arguing for those broad prohibitions on the use of race, it continued to maintain that the use of race in its case was unconstitutional. There, too, however, it was unsuccessful. Justice White's plurality opinion offered two reasons, one of which was joined by Justices Brennan, Blackmun, and Stevens, and the second of which was joined by Justices Rehnquist and Stevens. The plurality's first reason was that the Attorney General's desire for a 65% nonwhite majority was a permissible way of ensuring that minorities' voting strength would not be reduced below the pre-1970 level in violation of VRA § 5. In the plurality's view, New York should not have been held to have acted unconstitutionally when it was merely attempting to comply with the Attorney General's interpretation of the Voting Rights Act.

The plurality's second argument was that New York's use of race was simply not unconstitutional, independent of the effect of the VRA. The plurality's argument on this point crucially treated the Hasidim not as their own race, but as a subgroup of whites. Because the plurality believed that New York's revised districting plan did not discriminate against whites, the plurality concluded that the legislators' conscious use of race was not unconstitutional.

The plurality offered two arguments in support of its conclusion that the districting plan did not unconstitutionally discriminate against whites. First, the plan imposed

35. 430 U.S. at 162 (plurality opinion).

"no racial slur or stigma."[36] Second, members of "the white population" were not excluded from participation in politics, nor was the value of their votes diluted "in the county or in the State as a whole."[37]

The second argument deserves considerable attention. Note that the plurality treated voters as belonging to racial groups, and asked whether the districting plan diluted the political power of the entire race. It therefore treated the right to an undiluted vote as being held by the racial group as a whole, rather than treating the right as being held by voters individually.[38] The consequence of that conception of the right was that discrimination against one group of whites would be upheld as long as it was balanced by preferential treatment of a different group of whites: "[A]s long as whites in Kings County, as a group, were provided with fair representation, we cannot conclude that there was cognizable discrimination against whites or an abridgement of their right to vote on the grounds of race."[39] And, in fact, whites constituted a majority in 70% of the county's districts, even though they represented only 65% of the county's population.

The plurality expanded on this group-based conception of the right to an undiluted vote, invoking what has become known as "virtual representation": "[T]he white voter who as a result of the [revised districting] plan is in a district more likely to return a nonwhite representative will be represented, to the extent that voting continues to follow racial lines, by legislators elected from majority white districts."[40]

The plurality also adverted to another argument that would reappear decades later, when the Court considered the constitutionality of race-conscious districting under *Shaw v. Reno*[41] and its progeny.[42] The *UJO* plurality noted that it does not violate the Constitution for voters to refuse to support candidates of other races, and, if voters favor candidates of their own race, the race comprising a majority of voters will tend to have an electoral advantage. While that result may be regrettable, states are under no constitutional obligation to structure their electoral systems to minimize the effects of voters' discrimination. Nevertheless, the plurality contended, it is *permissible* for states to use their election laws "to achieve a fair allocation of political power between white and nonwhite voters."[43] Thus, the plurality did not believe that race-conscious districting was either *per se* constitutional or *per se* unconstitutional. Rather, the constitutionality of the use of race in districting would depend on the state's purpose. If the state "invidiously minimized" the power of a racial group,[44] the state law would

36. *Id.* at 165.

37. *Id.* at 165, 166.

38. *See generally* Heather K. Gerken, *Understanding the Right to an Undiluted Vote*, 114 Harv. L. Rev. 1663 (2001).

39. 430 U.S. at 166 (plurality opinion).

40. *Id.* at 166 n.24.

41. 509 U.S. 630 (1993).

42. *See* § D, *infra*.

43. 430 U.S. at 167 (plurality opinion).

44. *Id.* (quoting Gaffney v. Cummings, 412 U.S. 735, 754 (1973)).

be unconstitutional; but if the state used race to achieve "a fair allocation of political power," then the action could be upheld.

Is there a limit on states' ability to use race consciously as a way of achieving "fair" political results? The *UJO* plurality hinted that there might be. The plurality offered that it would be constitutional for a state purposely to draw majority-minority districts *if* the state were to "employ[] sound districting principles such as compactness and population equality."[45] Population equality, of course, had been required since *Reynolds v. Sims*,[46] but the plurality did not elaborate on why compactness would be a requirement. Certainly there is no independent constitutional requirement of compact districts. Perhaps non-compact majority-minority districts might betray a "slur or stigma" against whites, but the plurality left the matter for the future, and we will see that the Court returned to the issue in *Shaw*.

UJO was the first case in which the Court dealt with a constitutional challenge to a race-conscious districting scheme that had been imposed to *aid* minorities' voting power, and it came before the Court addressed educational affirmative action (or "reverse discrimination") in *Regents of the University of California v. Bakke*.[47] Justice Brennan's partial concurrence in *UJO* raised several issues relevant to affirmative action more generally. Of particular note, Justice Brennan warned that "benign" discrimination may produce negative consequences for the group that is ostensibly helped, either because the benignity was a sham for invidious discrimination or because the assistance itself might imply the inferiority of the assisted group. Further, "the most 'discrete and insular' of whites often will be called upon to bear the immediate, direct costs of benign discrimination."[48] However, Justice Brennan noted that UJO did "not press any legal claim to a group voice as Hasidim"[49]—in other words, they raised their claim as whites, not as Hasidim—and Justice Brennan thought that the procedures of the Voting Rights Act were sufficient to guard against the possibility that race-conscious districting would lead to invidious discrimination in disguise.

Justice Stewart, joined by Justice Powell, concurred in the judgment. He argued that for the districting plan to be unconstitutional, it would have to be the result of *purposeful* discrimination against whites. Because the revised districting plan was adopted to obtain preclearance from the Attorney General, and not to discriminate, he voted to uphold the plan.[50]

Only Chief Justice Burger dissented, arguing that the deliberate use of racial quotas in districting was unconstitutional. In his view, the use of race to achieve a "predetermined racial result"[51] was unconstitutional, whether the purpose was to advantage

45. *Id.* at 168.
46. 377 U.S. 533 (1964); *see* Chapter 2, *supra*.
47. 438 U.S. 265 (1978).
48. *UJO*, 430 U.S. at 174 (Brennan, J., concurring in part).
49. *Id.* at 178.
50. *Id.* at 180 (Stewart, J., concurring in the judgment).
51. *Id.* at 181 (Burger, C.J., dissenting).

minorities, as in *UJO*, or to harm them, as in *Gomillion v. Lightfoot*.[52] Either way, he feared, the effect of race-conscious districting would be to promote racial isolation, both geographically and ideologically, as such districting "suggests to the voter that only a candidate of the same race, religion, or ethnic origin can properly represent that voter's interests, and that such candidate can be elected only from a district with a sufficient minority concentration."[53] Chief Justice Burger's warning about the divisive effects of race-conscious districting went unheeded in *UJO*, but it had a much more receptive audience in *Shaw*, which we will discuss in § D.

C. The 1982 Amendments to § 2 of the Voting Rights Act

As discussed above in § B[1], the plurality opinion in *City of Mobile v. Bolden* reached two important conclusions. First, as a matter of statutory interpretation, the plurality held that § 2 of the Voting Rights Act prohibited only the kind of discrimination in voting that the Fifteenth Amendment already prohibited. Second, as a matter of constitutional interpretation, the plurality held that the Fourteenth and Fifteenth Amendments prohibited facially race-neutral election laws only if they both produced a racially disparate effect and were motivated by a racially discriminatory purpose.

In 1982, Congress reacted to the Court's decision in *City of Mobile v. Bolden* by amending § 2 of the Voting Rights Act. The amendment was designed to overrule *Bolden*'s holding that § 2 was coextensive with the Fifteenth Amendment and to adopt *White v. Regester*'s multi-factor approach as the test for assessing violations of § 2.

Before the 1982 amendments, VRA § 2 was not divided into subsections. The amendments expanded on it and created an entirely new § 2(b). The changes are shown below, with additions in *italics* and deletions in ~~strikethrough~~:

(a) No voting qualification or prerequisite to voting, or standard, practice, or procedure shall be imposed or applied by any State or political subdivision *in a manner which results in a denial or abridgement of* ~~to deny or abridge~~ the right of any citizen of the United States to vote on account of race or color, or in contravention of the guarantees set forth in section 4(f)(2) [protecting language minorities], *as provided in subsection (b).*

(b) A violation of subsection (a) is established if, based on the totality of the circumstances, it is shown that the political processes leading to nomination or election in the State or political subdivision are not equally open to participation by members of a class of citizens protected by subsection (a) in that

52. 364 U.S. 339 (1960) (holding unconstitutional the redrawing of city boundaries so as to exclude almost the entire black population of the city).

53. 430 U.S. at 186 (Burger, C.J., dissenting).

> *its members have less opportunity than other members of the electorate to participate in the political process and to elect representatives of their choice. The extent to which members of a protected class have been elected to office in the State or political subdivision is one circumstance which may be considered:* Provided, *That nothing in this section establishes a right to have members of a protected class elected in numbers equal to their proportion in the population.*[54]

Subsection (b) provides for the application of a totality-of-the-circumstances test but does not provide much information as to the kinds of circumstances to be considered. The Senate committee report, however, listed several "typical factors," including a history of discrimination, either as to voting or otherwise; the extent of racial polarization in voting; the use of electoral structures that tend to lessen minorities' chances of electoral success, such as unusually large districts, majority-vote requirements, and anti-single-shot rules; racial appeals in campaigns; a small number of successful minority candidates; and a lack of responsiveness among elected officials to the concerns of minorities.[55]

By prohibiting not only those laws enacted with a discriminatory purpose but also those that merely "result[] in" a denial or abridgement of the right to vote, Congress meant to make it easier for plaintiffs to prevail in vote-dilution cases than under the constitutional standard articulated by the plurality in *Bolden*. By expanding on the constitutional protection, however, Congress created another constitutional issue—one that the Supreme Court has not yet resolved. As we discussed in Chapter 1, Congress has the power to "enforce, by appropriate legislation, the provisions of" the Fourteenth and Fifteenth Amendments.[56] But does this power to "enforce" the Amendments give Congress the power to *expand* on the Amendments' protections? The answer is yes, but with limits.

Unfortunately, the Supreme Court has been inconsistent in delineating those limits. In *South Carolina v. Katzenbach*, the Court articulated a very liberal standard, permitting Congress to exercise its enforcement power by enacting any law rationally related to the purposes of the Amendments.[57] *City of Boerne v. Flores* tightened up that standard by requiring Congress's laws to be "congruent" with and "proportional" to the constitutional provision being enforced.[58] Because there is considerable flexibility even in the "congruence and proportionality" standard, however, no one is certain whether the revised § 2 is closely enough related to the coverage of the Fourteenth and Fifteenth Amendments to be constitutional.[59] In 2013, the Court held

---

54. Pub. L. No. 97-205, § 3, 96 Stat. 134, codified at 52 U.S.C. § 10301.

55. *See* Thornburg v. Gingles, 478 U.S. 30, 36–37 (1986) (quoting S. Rep. No. 97-417, at 28–29 (1982)).

56. *See* Chapter 1, § D[2], *supra*.

57. South Carolina v. Katzenbach, 383 U.S. 301, 324 (1966); *see also* Katzenbach v. Morgan, 384 U.S. 641, 653 (1966).

58. City of Boerne v. Flores, 521 U.S. 507, 519–20 (1997).

59. *See generally* Pamela S. Karlan, *Two Section Twos and Two Section Fives: Voting Rights and Remedies After* Flores, 39 Wm. & Mary L. Rev. 725 (1998).

in *Shelby County, Alabama v. Holder*[60] that the coverage formula in § 4 of the VRA exceeded Congress's enforcement power, but the Court has never directly addressed the constitutionality of § 2.

The Court has, however, interpreted the statutory language of the amended § 2, and the most important case in that regard is *Thornburg v. Gingles*.[61] *Gingles* established that success on a § 2 claim would require plaintiffs to prove the existence of three "preconditions" showing that the challenged law had the effect of denying or abridging the right to vote on account of race. Although *Gingles* involved a challenge to a multimember district, the preconditions apply to challenges to any kind of state law, such as particular single-member-districting plans, alleged to abridge the right to vote on account of race.[62]

Each of the preconditions is designed to assess when the challenged "electoral law, practice, or structure interacts with social and historical conditions to cause an inequity in the opportunities enjoyed by black and white voters to elect their preferred representatives."[63] However, because the nature of democracy is that groups with greater numbers are likely to exert greater influence, and because the Court has repeatedly reaffirmed that there is no right to proportional representation, it is not enough simply to point to an inequity in electoral opportunities. Rather, the law accepts some inequality as the inevitable—or at least tolerable—result of groups' differing numerical strength, while it treats other inequalities as excessive or unjustified. The preconditions are an attempt to separate permissible from impermissible inequalities.

The first precondition requires the minority group to be "sufficiently large and geographically compact to constitute a majority in a single-member district."[64] (If the challengers are objecting to the way that single-member districts are drawn, the minority group must be sufficiently large and geographically compact to constitute a majority in a differently drawn—but reasonably compact—district.) The idea behind this requirement is that § 2(b) protects the right of members of the minority group "to participate in the political process and to elect representatives of their choice." If the minority group is so small that it could not constitute a majority in a single-member district,[65] then it would not be able to elect representatives of its choice regardless of the electoral structure.[66] And if its members were so spread out that they could

60. 570 U.S. 529 (2013).

61. 478 U.S. 30 (1986).

62. *See* Johnson v. De Grandy, 512 U.S. 997 (1994); Voinovich v. Quilter, 507 U.S. 146, 153–54 (1993); Growe v. Emison, 507 U.S. 25, 37–42 (1993).

63. *Gingles*, 478 U.S. at 47.

64. *Id.* at 50.

65. *See id.* at 50 n.17 ("The single-member district is generally the appropriate standard against which to measure minority group potential to elect because it is the smallest political unit from which representatives are elected. Thus, if the minority group [cannot constitute a majority in a single-member district], these minority voters cannot maintain that they would have been able to elect representatives of their choice in the absence of the multimember electoral structure.").

66. The Court put aside the question whether a small minority group might be able to challenge laws that limit its ability to influence elections, even if the group were not large enough to control the elections' outcomes. *See id.* at 46 n.12. Ultimately, the Court held that such a claim was not cognizable

not form a majority in a non-gerrymandered district, then they also cannot blame the existing districting plan for their inability to elect their preferred candidates. In either event, then, the challenged law would not be the cause of the group's lack of electoral success.

Although it might make intuitive sense that minority groups need majority-minority districts in order to elect representatives of their choice,[67] that conclusion can be questioned in several different ways. Cumulative voting—allowing voters to allocate multiple votes to individual candidates where multiple offices are being filled—would allow a dispersed minority to elect its chosen candidate, and, accordingly, perhaps the "geographically compact" requirement should be thought unnecessary.[68] Additionally, having a majority of eligible voters in a district is neither necessary nor sufficient to ensure the election of a group's chosen candidate, even in a single-member district. A group with a thin majority may not have a majority of voters in any particular election, and some "crossover" voters within the group may prefer the candidate favored by whites. Conversely, a group whose members do not constitute a majority may nevertheless find that enough whites favor their candidate to result in that candidate's election.

Making the issue more complicated, it may in fact harm the minority's interest to have a large majority in a district. If minorities could achieve electoral success with, for example, 40% of a district's population, then additional numbers of minorities in that district might be considered "wasted." Groups antagonistic to the interests of minorities might, therefore, try to place as many minorities into districts as possible so as to lessen the influence of minorities in surrounding districts. But if minorities were spread too thinly—if too few minorities were placed in individual districts—then they would not have sufficient votes in those districts to exercise meaningful power.[69]

---

under § 2 of the VRA, and it reaffirmed that challengers must establish that their minority group would be sufficiently large and geographically compact to constitute a *majority* in a single-member district. *See* Bartlett v. Strickland, 556 U.S. 1 (2009).

67. Majority-minority districts are those districts in which a majority of residents (or, perhaps, voters or voting-eligible citizens) are members of a minority group. *See Strickland*, 556 U.S. 1 (2009) (voting-age population); League of United Latin Am. Citizens v. Perry, 548 U.S. 399, 429 (2006) ("[T]he parties agree that the relevant numbers must include citizenship. This approach fits the language of [VRA] § 2 because only eligible voters affect a group's opportunity to elect candidates."); Reyes v. City of Farmers Branch, Tex., 586 F.3d 1019, 1023–25 (5th Cir. 2009) (citizen voting-age population). Typically those residents must be members of the same minority group, although the Court has sometimes, as in *UJO*, grouped together different ethnic groups that are believed to have common interests.

68. In fact, cumulative voting has been ordered to remedy violations of § 2 of the VRA. *See* United States v. Village of Port Chester, 704 F. Supp. 2d 411 (S.D.N.Y. 2010). More often, however, cumulative voting has been rejected as a remedy for VRA § 2 violations. *See* Cousin v. Sundquist, 145 F.3d 818, 826 (6th Cir. 1998); Cane v. Worcester County, Md., 35 F.3d 921, 929 (4th Cir. 1994); Nipper v. Smith, 39 F.3d 1494 (11th Cir. 1994). *See generally* Erica L. Mirehouse, *Majority-Minority Voting Rights: Is Cumulative Voting a Valid Remedy for Violations of the Voting Rights Act or an Impermissible Tactic to Advance Racial Politics?*, 14 The Scholar: St. Mary's Rev. L & Soc. J. 521, 535-42 (2011).

69. As early as 1969, Justice Harlan raised this concern about the difficulty of assessing a group's political influence by looking to the way in which its population was spread across districts. *See* Allen v. State Bd. of Elections, 393 U.S. 544, 586 (1969) ("[I]t is not clear to me how a court would go

Gingles's second and third preconditions for a successful §2 suit are together referred to as "racially polarized voting." The second precondition requires the minority group to be "politically cohesive," that is, to have "distinctive . . . interests."[70] The third requires the majority to "vote[] sufficiently as a bloc to enable it . . . usually to defeat the minority's preferred candidate."[71] The rationale for these two preconditions, like the rationale for the first, rests on the minority group's ability to elect its preferred candidates. In the absence of the second precondition—if the minority group were not politically cohesive—it would not have distinct interests that would be threatened by electoral failure. In essence, it would become impossible to determine when there has been electoral failure because the minority group itself would be so divided.

The absence of the third precondition also leads to the conclusion that the electoral structure is not inhibiting the minority group's electoral success, but for a very different reason. If the majority shows so much support for the minority group's interests that the minority group's preferred candidates regularly win, then the minority group can hardly be said to have its ability to elect abridged.

The Court was divided concerning the showing necessary to demonstrate racially polarized voting. Writing only for a plurality on this point, Justice Brennan concluded that racially polarized voting simply meant a difference in voting patterns *correlating* with voters' races, regardless of the cause for that difference. Thus, for Justice Brennan, it made no difference whether black and white voters preferred different candidates because each group would support only candidates of their own race, or whether they preferred different candidates because blacks tended to support candidates of one party and whites tended to support candidates of a different party, regardless of the races of the candidates. The important consideration for Justice Brennan was not *why* voters of different races had different preferences but simply *whether* they did.

Justice Brennan had several arguments for focusing on the existence of a difference in voters' preferences, rather than on the reasons for any such difference. One argument was textual: VRA §2 bans election laws that result in a reduced opportunity for minorities to participate in the political process and to elect candidates of their choice, without any discussion of the reasons why minorities might have chosen those candidates. It does not provide that minorities' electoral opportunities should depend either on the reasons they have for supporting their preferred candidate or on whites' reasons for preferring different candidates.[72]

Another one of Justice Brennan's arguments was more practical (and, indeed, somewhat contrary to the text of §2, which prohibits denials or abridgments of the right

about deciding whether an at-large system is to be preferred over a district system. Under one system, Negroes have some influence in the election of all officers; under the other, minority groups have more influence in the selection of fewer officers. If courts cannot intelligently compare such alternatives, it should not be readily inferred that Congress [in the Voting Rights Act] has required them to undertake the task.").

70. *Gingles*, 478 U.S. at 51.

71. *Id.*

72. *See id.* at 63 (plurality opinion).

to vote only "on account of race or color"[73]): Many characteristics, such as "income level, employment status, amount of education, housing and other living conditions, religion, language, and so forth" are correlated with race.[74] "Where such characteristics are shared, race or ethnic group not only denotes color or place of origin, it also functions as a shorthand notation for common social and economic characteristics."[75] In other words, when VRA § 2 prohibited laws that produced discrimination on the ground of "race or color," it did not mean to permit discrimination on the grounds of other characteristics that are shared by members of a particular race. On the contrary, according to this argument, Congress meant to prohibit those forms of discrimination as well. Further, according to Justice Brennan, sometimes those other socioeconomic characteristics are not just correlated with race, but caused by race: "The opportunity to achieve high employment status and income, for example, is often influenced by the presence or absence of racial or ethnic discrimination."[76]

Consider an example: Imagine that a given districting scheme advantages Republicans over Democrats. In the community under consideration, white voters tend to prefer Republicans and black voters tend to prefer Democrats. Black voters, then, claim that the districting scheme violates § 2 by hampering their ability to elect their favored candidates. The state claims, however, that the law does not interfere with their ability to elect candidates *because of* either the race of the voters or the race of the candidates; rather, the law affects electoral outcomes on the basis of party affiliation and other characteristics that also correlate with party affiliation, such as income level. The state claims, therefore, that black voters are not being harmed because they are black but rather because they are Democratic supporters with low incomes. Justice Brennan would treat this argument as irrelevant. For Justice Brennan, the only thing that matters is that voters of different races prefer different candidates, and therefore Justice Brennan would find racially polarized voting in this instance.

After setting forth the preconditions, the Court turned back to the facts of the *Gingles* case itself. The Court concluded that § 2's totality-of-the-circumstances test could not be met merely by pointing to a small number of elections in which minorities' preferred candidates were defeated, and a state could not rebut a claim of a § 2 violation by pointing to a small number of elections in which minorities' preferred candidates were victorious. Rather, the key question was whether the laws of an area, combined with social and historical factors, led to a consistent diminution in the value of minorities' votes. Applying that standard, the Court held that most of the challenged districts in *Gingles* did dilute the value of minorities' votes in violation of § 2, but in one

---

73. The plurality relied on a footnote in the legislative history to conclude that "'that Congress has used the words 'on account of race or color' in the Act to mean 'with respect to' race or color, and not to connote any required purpose of racial discrimination." 478 U.S. at 71 n.34 (quoting S. Rep. at 27–28 n.109).

74. *Id.* at 64.

75. *Id.*

76. *Id.*

district (District 23), minorities had consistent success and therefore it appeared that, in that district, minorities had the ability to elect candidates of their choice.

Justice Brennan's discussion of racially polarized voting did not command a majority. Justice White and Justice O'Connor, the latter joined by Chief Justice Burger and Justices Powell and Rehnquist, wrote separately to express different views. For them, it was important to distinguish between discrimination on the basis of race, which was prohibited, and "interest-group politics," from which no group, including minorities, should be exempt.[77] Justice White focused on the race of the candidates, believing that there would not be the prohibited discrimination "on account of race" if minority candidates were elected, even if those candidates were not the preferred candidates of minority voters.

For Justice O'Connor, both Justice White and Justice Brennan focused on too narrow a question. Showing a view of the law which was to achieve majority support in *Johnson v. De Grandy* eight years later, Justice O'Connor argued in *Gingles* that election results were only a part of the proper analysis under § 2. She saw the 1982 amendments to § 2 as reinstituting *Regester*'s totality-of-the-circumstances test for determining whether there was not just an impairment of a minority group's ability to elect its favored candidates but also whether members of that group had an equal opportunity to participate in the political process—a much broader question than simply whether elections produced disproportionate outcomes. She criticized Justice Brennan's opinion for appearing to "create[] what amounts to a right to *usual, roughly* proportional representation on the part of sizeable, compact, cohesive minority groups."[78] In her view, such a right to roughly proportional representation was inconsistent with both the Court's repeated statements that there is no constitutional right to proportional representation and § 2's proviso that the VRA does not create "a right to have members of a protected class elected in numbers equal to their proportion in the population."[79]

Rather, for Justice O'Connor, the key was whether a minority group was forced to endure a sustained reduction in political strength. And in answering that question, Justice O'Connor would have treated as relevant far more considerations than simply the three preconditions. Specifically, she agreed with Justice White that the race of the candidates could be relevant, and she argued that the reasons for racially polarized voting could be relevant too: "Evidence that a candidate preferred by the minority group in a particular election was rejected by white voters for reasons other than those which made that candidate the preferred choice of the minority group would seem clearly relevant in answering the question whether bloc voting by white voters will consistently defeat minority candidates. Such evidence would suggest that another candidate, equally preferred by the minority group, might be able to attract greater white support in future elections."[80]

---

77. *Id.* at 83 (White, J., concurring in part).
78. *Id.* at 91 (O'Connor, J., concurring in the judgment).
79. 52 U.S.C. § 10301(b).
80. *Gingles*, 478 U.S. at 100 (O'Connor, J., concurring in the judgment).

When the Court reconsidered vote dilution and VRA § 2 in *Johnson v. De Grandy*,[81] the Justices clarified that the *Gingles* preconditions were "generally necessary to prove a § 2 claim," but they were not sufficient.[82] Under *De Grandy*, even if plaintiffs showed that they were sufficiently numerous and compact to constitute a majority in a single-member district, and even if they further showed that there was racially polarized voting, they still needed to satisfy the statutory totality-of-the-circumstances test before they would be held to have been deprived of their equal "opportunity . . . to participate in the political process and to elect representatives of their choice."[83] *De Grandy* thus validated the interpretation of § 2 that Justice O'Connor had advanced in her separate opinion in *Gingles*: Section 2 plaintiffs must ultimately demonstrate not just that an alternative plan could give them more political influence but also that the existing plan deprives them of the equal opportunity to participate in politics that was guaranteed by *Regester*.[84]

In *De Grandy*, minority voters showed that districts could have been drawn that would have given them more influence than they had under the challenged plan. They also showed that there was racially polarized voting, so all three *Gingles* preconditions were satisfied. The existing plan, however, gave the minority voters control over a number of districts proportional to their percentage of the population. The Court held that proportionality in this case fatally undercut the plaintiffs' claim of a § 2 violation, although the Court refused to read § 2 as establishing an absolute requirement that plaintiffs demonstrate a lack of proportionality in every case.

The *De Grandy* Court conceived of proportionality not as an independent requirement but as part of the totality of the circumstances that a court was bound to consider under subsection (b) of § 2. "[E]qual political opportunity," rather than proportional representation itself, was the ultimate goal of the statute.[85] And although the proviso in § 2(b) seemed explicitly to disclaim a right to proportional representation, the Court drew a distinction between "proportionality"—the relationship between "the number of majority-minority voting districts [and] minority members' share of the relevant population"—and the proportional-representation proviso, which "speaks to the success of minority candidates, as distinct from the political or electoral power of minority voters."[86] Proportionality was thus a tool, though not a determinative one in itself, for assessing vote dilution under § 2.

---

81. 512 U.S. 997 (1994).

82. *Id.* at 1011.

83. 52 U.S.C. § 10301(b).

84. Thus the *De Grandy* Court had no trouble unanimously rejecting the plaintiffs' argument that § 2 entitled them to the maximum number of majority-minority districts that could be created through application of the *Gingles* preconditions, even when that number would provide greater-than-proportional representation. As the Court stated, "[o]ne may suspect vote dilution from political famine, but one is not entitled to suspect (much less infer) dilution from mere failure to guarantee a political feast." 512 U.S. at 1017.

85. *Id.* at 1014.

86. *Id.* at 1014 n.11. As Justice Thomas has pointed out, however, unless the proviso reaches proportional voting power, rather than just the proportional election of candidates, it makes little practical sense. "Only one system would [guarantee the election of a proportionate number of minority

The Court again considered the meaning of "equal political opportunity" in *Brnovich v. Democratic National Committee.*[87] The case concerned two Arizona voting regulations, one applicable to in-person voting on election day and one applicable to mail-in voting. Voters could choose either method of voting, in addition to early in-person voting.

The in-person-voting regulation required voters who chose to vote in person on election day to vote in their respective precincts. Voters whose names did not appear on the precinct's voter rolls would be directed to the correct precinct, but voters could cast a provisional ballot if they believed their names belonged on the precinct's register. Voters who cast provisional ballots in their precincts would have their ballots counted, but voters who cast a provisional ballot in the wrong precinct would not have their ballots counted.

The mail-in voting regulation was a prohibition on "ballot harvesting"—the collection of ballots by supporters of a party or a candidate. Arizona law permitted only three categories of persons to handle anyone else's ballot: a member of the voter's family or household, the voter's caretaker, or a postal worker. Ballot harvesting presents an opportunity for fraud (if, for example, the harvester not only delivers but also completes the ballot) and for intimidation or undue influence. But it also provides an opportunity to get out the vote by permitting campaign workers to go door to door and collect ballots from people who might not have gone to the effort themselves to deliver their ballots on time.

Because the Democratic Party thought that members of minority groups likely to vote Democratic were disproportionately harmed by the regulations, the party brought a § 2 claim. Emphasizing how easy it was to cast a valid ballot in Arizona, the Supreme Court, by a 6–3 vote, rejected the claim. The Court focused on § 2's requirement that voting be "equally open" to members of all races, such that members of all races have an equal "opportunity" to vote. The Court argued that a state might provide all of its citizens with an equal opportunity to vote, even if some races took advantage of that opportunity in greater numbers than did others. Accordingly, the Court concluded, it was improper to base a § 2 violation on the simple fact that a given election law might result in the invalidation of a greater proportion of votes from one racial group than from another.

Rather, the Court identified five nonexclusive factors that, it argued, would help a court determine whether, under the totality of the circumstances, a state's political processes were truly equally open to members of all races: (1) "the size of the burden imposed by a challenged voting rule"; (2) "the degree to which a voting rule departs from what was standard practice when § 2 was amended in 1982"; (3) "[t]he size of any

---

candidates]: a system based on a racial register in which a quota of seats are set aside for members of a minority group. I think it would be preposterous to suggest that the disclaimer in § 2(b) was intended solely to prohibit the use of such a system. Such a device has never, to my knowledge, been proposed in any voting rights case." Holder v. Hall, 512 U.S. 874, 928 n.26 (1994) (Thomas, J., concurring in the judgment).

87. 594 U.S. 647 (2021).

disparities in a rule's impact on members of different racial or ethnic groups"; (4) "the opportunities provided by a State's entire system of voting"; and (5) "the strength of the state interests served by a challenged voting rule."[88] In the Court's view, a state law with a marginally greater impact on one race than another would still give all races an equal opportunity to vote if the burden on voting was small and consistent with the usual burdens on voting in 1982 (the Court thought it unlikely that Congress meant to outlaw election procedures that were common at the time that § 2 was amended), and if the law was justified by a strong state interest, such as the prevention of voting fraud.

In the Court's view, both Arizona voting regulations were consistent with § 2. Although they might have had a greater impact on minorities than on whites (largely because of frequent changes in polling locations in areas with large black populations and because of poor mail service in Native American areas), "Arizona law generally makes it very easy to vote."[89] Further, the burdens of going to the correct polling place on election day, or depositing a mail-in ballot in a mailbox during the four weeks before election day, or voting in person during that same four-week period, were "unremarkable," "modest," and no more onerous than the typical requirement in 1982 that voters appear in person at a polling place on election day.[90] Lastly, those regulations were supported by state interests in preventing fraud, distributing voters among different polling locations, and ensuring that voters cast votes in local races for which they were eligible.

For the dissent, much of the majority's analysis missed the point. The Voting Rights Act meant to ensure that voters of different races had an *equal* opportunity to vote, so even a minimal burden would violate § 2 if that minimal burden were felt unequally by different races.[91] Whereas the majority argued that its multi-factor analysis was necessary to apply the statute's totality-of-the-circumstances standard, the dissent argued that the standard "requires courts to explore how ordinary-seeming laws can interact with local conditions—economic, social, historical—to produce race-based voting inequalities" like those seen under the challenged laws.[92]

Thus, for all its focus on statutory language, the Court's opinion did not provide a strong explanation for why Arizona's voting processes were *equally* open to voters of all races. On the other hand, the dissent was subject to the more practical critique that *all* laws produce a disparate effect on different races, and, therefore, interpreting § 2 to call into question all laws that produce a disparate effect would be to give § 2 a much broader scope than Congress likely expected in 1982—and could paralyze modern election administration.

---

88. *Id.* at 669–72.

89. *Id.* at 654.

90. *Id.* at 678, 679.

91. *See id.* at 704 (Kagan, J., dissenting) ("[E]qual 'opportunity' is absent when a law or practice makes it harder for members of one racial group, than for others, to cast ballots.").

92. *Id.* at 711 (Kagan, J., dissenting).

D. Constitutional Constraints on Majority-Minority Districting

1. The *Shaw* Cause of Action

We have already seen that racial gerrymandering can operate to harm minorities, either by packing minority voters into as few districts as possible or by dispersing minorities into several districts so as to minimize their influence in all of the districts where they are present. Sometimes, as in *Gomillion v. Lightfoot*[93] and *White v. Regester*,[94] drawing boundaries to minimize the political influence of minorities violates the Constitution.[95] Other times, districting that harms minorities' voting power can violate § 2 of the Voting Rights Act.[96]

Ironically, the nation's problems with race-conscious districting that minimizes minorities' political influence have led to more race-conscious districting—this time for the purpose of protecting minorities' political influence. VRA §§ 2 and 5 have required jurisdictions to pay attention to race when drawing district lines, so as to ensure that minorities have the equal access to the political process guaranteed by § 2 and to ensure that their influence is not subject to the retrogression forbidden by § 5.

This race-consciousness, however, can create another constitutional problem. When does the conscious use of race to protect minorities' political power (for example, through the intentional creation of majority-minority districts) violate the constitutional rights of whites or other residents of the gerrymandered jurisdiction?

As with affirmative action in the educational and employment contexts, race-conscious electoral districting uses race to remedy some past act of discrimination or to achieve other benefits (such as a system of fair representation that encourages legislators to take minorities' concerns into account). And as with affirmative action, there is widespread agreement on the long-term desirability of race-neutral decisionmaking but great disagreement about whether it is necessary or beneficial to consider race in the short term.

There are, however, significant differences between majority-minority districting and affirmative action. One such difference is that it is hard to imagine truly race-blind districting unless it is done completely by computer. The politically involved people who draw districts certainly know the racial characteristics of their states and localities; even if they do not emphasize racial considerations, they are certainly aware of them.

---

93. 364 U.S. 339 (1960).

94. 412 U.S. 755 (1973).

95. As discussed in § B[1], *supra*, racial gerrymandering must produce a racially disparate effect and be the result of a racially discriminatory purpose for the Constitution to be violated. *See* City of Mobile v. Bolden, 446 U.S. 55 (1980) (plurality opinion).

96. *See* § C, *supra*.

Another difference is that districting involves—indeed, it is supposed to involve—the grouping of voters with commonalities of interests and backgrounds. We draw districts so that representatives can advocate for the interests that are particularly important to the people in those districts, and so we consciously group people into districts on the basis of perceived commonalities of interest, *e.g.*, farmers, blue-collar workers, young professionals, or suburban families. Indeed, geographical districts themselves are proxies for commonalities of interest because people who live in certain areas tend to have similarities in the way they look at the world and the issues they consider important.

So while in the affirmative-action context it is possible (though, to be sure, the subject of intense argument) to say that decisions about employment and college admission should be based on "race-neutral" criteria, that argument makes less sense in districting, where we are necessarily grouping people based on perceived interests. People who would limit majority-minority districting, therefore, must explain how race is different from these other characteristics—why it is acceptable to use income and employment as a reason to group people into districts, but it is unacceptable to use race for the same purpose.

Yet another difference involves the nature of the injury caused to whites by race-conscious majority-minority districting. When a white person is denied a preference for a job or admission to college, he has suffered an injury that is easy to understand. Even if he might not have gotten the job or been admitted to the college, he was denied an equal opportunity to compete. Majority-minority districting produces no such individual injury, and for that reason many have argued that the courts should not intervene to stop or limit such uses of race in districting. There is, of course, no right to win an election, or to be in a district with like-minded voters. So the fact that whites may be placed in a district designed to allow minorities the ability to elect their preferred candidate cannot itself constitute an injury. Furthermore, as a formal matter, the whites in a majority-minority district have not had their voting power reduced at all. They are still permitted to register and vote. Their preferred candidate may lose, but their situation is no different from that of voters who are stuck in a district populated mostly by members of a different political party or by voters who have an ideology different from their own.

Whites probably have the same constitutional protection against vote dilution that minorities have under *Gomillion v. Lightfoot*, *City of Mobile v. Bolden*, and *White v. Regester*. That is, whites are probably guaranteed the right not to have their political power intentionally diminished because of their race, as well as the right not to be harmed by laws that deny them an equal opportunity to access the political process and to elect representatives of their choice. The Supreme Court has never evaluated such a claim, however, because it would be the rare case where whites could justifiably claim to be the victims of intentional discrimination or to have been shut out of the political process.

Instead, the Court has called into question some racial gerrymanders by creating an entirely new cause of action, independent of vote dilution. The seminal case in this line is *Shaw v. Reno*,[97] which involved a challenge to districts that North Carolina drew after the 1990 census.[98] To address Justice Department objections and to achieve preclearance under § 5 of the Voting Rights Act, North Carolina drew two majority-black congressional districts. Both districts were strangely shaped, and the obvious (and uncontested) purpose of drawing the districts in that way was to place sufficient numbers of blacks in the districts so that black voters would be able to control the elections in those districts. In the state as a whole, however, whites controlled slightly more districts (83%) than their share of the population (76%).

The Supreme Court, by a 5–4 vote, held that even without any vote dilution, a districting plan violates equal protection if it "is so extremely irregular on its face that it rationally can be viewed only as an effort to segregate the races for purposes of voting, without regard for traditional districting principles and without sufficiently compelling justification."[99] "Segregat[ion]" was something of a misnomer, as Justice White pointed out in dissent, because the majority-minority districts themselves contained quite a mix of races.[100] Nevertheless, the Court believed that bizarrely shaped majority-minority districts sent an unconstitutional message to voters and to representatives precisely because of their shapes: "[W]e believe that reapportionment is one area in which appearances do matter. A reapportionment plan that includes in one district individuals who belong to the same race, but who are otherwise widely separated by geographical and political boundaries, and who may have little in common with one another but the color of their skin, bears an uncomfortable resemblance to political apartheid. It reinforces the perception that members of the same racial group—regardless of their age, education, economic status, or the community in which they live—think alike, share the same political interests, and will prefer the same candidates at the polls."[101] Further, the Court thought that "[w]hen a district obviously is created solely to effectuate the perceived common interests of one racial group, elected officials are more likely to believe that their primary obligation is to represent only the members of that group, rather than their constituency as a whole. This is altogether antithetical to our system of representative democracy."[102]

Shaw's focus on the districts' bizarre shapes leads to an important area of debate surrounding the racial-gerrymandering cause of action: Why should it matter what the districts look like? If it is unconstitutional for states to use race in drawing districts, what difference does it make if the state's geography and residency patterns allow majority-minority districts to be drawn in neat rectangles? The Court's answer is in its focus on the message sent by districts. Bizarrely shaped districts result in what has been

---

97. 509 U.S. 630 (1993).

98. For background on the *Shaw* line of cases, see generally Tinsley E. Yarbrough, Race And Redistricting: The *Shaw-Cromartie* Cases (2002), and Melissa L. Saunders, *A Cautionary Tale:* Hunt v. Cromartie *and the Next Generation of* Shaw *Litigation*, 1 Election L.J. 173 (2002).

99. *Shaw*, 509 U.S. at 642.

100. *See id.* at 672 n.7 (White, J., dissenting).

101. *Id.* at 647 (opinion of the Court).

102. *Id.* at 648.

termed an "expressive harm"—a message sent by the state that race is an important determinant of political attitudes and should be an important consideration of representatives.[103] The Court seemed to be saying that districts that adhere more closely to "traditional districting principles such as compactness, contiguity, and respect for political subdivisions" do not send the same kind of race-above-all message.[104]

It was this focus on appearances that the Court used to distinguish *United Jewish Organizations v. Carey*, which had upheld race-conscious majority-minority districting against a claim that it unconstitutionally diluted the political power of a group of white Hasidic Jews.[105] In that case, *Shaw* noted, the state was able to create majority-minority districts while still adhering to traditional districting principles—a fact that was noted by three of the Justices forming the majority in *UJO*.[106] In *Shaw*, by contrast, the state created the majority-minority districts by disregarding those traditional districting principles.[107] Still, one may question whether that fact should make a difference. Surely few voters know the shapes of their districts, and fewer perceive the state as sending a message by drawing the districts that way. Further, the notion of an expressive harm may be too ephemeral to fit with the Court's usual requirement that there be a "concrete and particularized" injury for one to be able to obtain a judicial remedy.[108]

Although the Court acknowledged that districts are regularly gerrymandered for all kinds of purposes, it held that racial gerrymanders—at least obvious ones—were different. In the Court's view, the country's history of racial discrimination and the special constitutional attention to race meant that states faced a greater constitutional burden when attempting to justify the use of race in districting. The Court thought that the message sent by racial gerrymandering—that race could determine political attitudes and was an appropriate way to group voters, irrespective of differences in geography, class, education level, and other characteristics—was particularly offensive. As the Court said, racial gerrymandering "reinforces the perception that members of the same racial group—regardless of their age, education, economic status, or the community in which they live—think alike, share the same political interests, and will prefer the same candidates at the polls."[109]

---

103. Richard H. Pildes & Richard G. Niemi, *Expressive Harms, "Bizarre Districts," and Voting Rights: Evaluating Election-District Appearances After* Shaw v. Reno, 92 Mich. L. Rev. 483 (1993).

104. *Shaw*, 509 U.S. at 648.

105. 430 U.S. 144 (1977).

106. *See Shaw*, 509 U.S. at 651–52 (quoting *UJO*, 430 U.S. at 168 (opinion of White, J.)).

107. *See* 509 U.S. at 652 ("*UJO*'s framework simply does not apply where, as here, a reapportionment plan is alleged to be so irrational on its face that it immediately offends principles of racial equality.").

108. *See, e.g.*, TransUnion, LLC v. Ramirez, 594 U.S. 413 (2021); Spokeo, Inc. v. Robins, 578 U.S. 330 (2016); Lujan v. Defenders of Wildlife, 504 U.S. 555, 560 (1992). The Court subsequently held that only residents of the gerrymandered district have standing to sue on a *Shaw* claim, even though arguably the entire state has suffered the expressive harm that *Shaw* identified. *See* United States v. Hays, 515 U.S. 737, 744–46 (1995); *see also* Sinkfield v. Kelley, 531 U.S. 28 (2000).

109. *Shaw*, 509 U.S. at 647.

The correlation between race and political attitudes may be offensive to some, but it is surely a fact of political life, as even the Court recognized later.[110] Considering the last several presidential elections, for example, the difference in preferences between white and black voters is striking. In 2024, blacks voted for Kamala Harris 86% to 13%, while whites favored Donald Trump by a margin of 57% to 42%. In 2020, the numbers were almost identical, with 87% of black voters supporting Joe Biden and 12% supporting Donald Trump, while white voters favored Trump 58% to 41%. As stark as those differences are, the data from earlier elections show an even greater divide. In 2016, black voters supported Hillary Clinton 89% to 8%, and white voters supported Trump 57% to 37%. In 2012, 93% of black voters voted for Barack Obama and 6% voted for Mitt Romney, while 39% of white voters voted for Obama and 59% for Romney. In 2008, 95% of blacks voted for Obama and 4% voted for John McCain, while among whites, 43% voted for Obama and 55% voted for McCain. In 2004, 88% of blacks voted for John Kerry and 11% voted for George W. Bush, while 41% of whites voted for Kerry and 58% voted for Bush. And in 2000, 90% of blacks voted for Al Gore and 9% voted for Bush, while 42% of whites voted for Gore and 55% for Bush.[111]

There is also a correlation between race and party identification, although black voters' support for Democrats is not as overwhelming as it was before the early 2020s. As of 2023, 66% of blacks identified as Democrats or leaned Democratic, with only 19% identifying as Republicans or leaning Republican. Among whites, Republicans had the edge, 54% to 38%.[112]

Race, of course, is not the only demographic characteristic showing a correlation with political preferences. But race is a much better predictor of votes in presidential elections than is age, education level, or income. One might question the Court's conclusion that there is a constitutional bar on the consideration of race in districting when race does seem to matter empirically.[113] It seems especially anomalous to condemn states for considering race when the Voting Rights Act itself appears to assume

110. *See* Easley v. Cromartie, 532 U.S. 234, 244–45 (2001) (permitting a state to treat black Democrats as more reliable Democratic voters than white Democrats, and for that reason treating a state's decision to group blacks together as a political, rather than a racial, gerrymander); *see also* Hunt v. Cromartie, 526 U.S. 541, 552 (1999) (noting that there may be "a high correlation between race and party preference").

111. The statistics in this paragraph are taken from the Roper Center for Public Opinion Research at Cornell University. They are available online at https://ropercenter.cornell.edu/how-groups-voted-2012, with the final digits of the web address corresponding to the year of the presidential election.

112. *See* Jeffrey M. Jones & Lydia Saad, *Democrats Lose Ground with Black and Hispanic Adults*, Gallup (Feb. 7, 2024), https://news.gallup.com/poll/609776/democrats-lose-ground-black-hispanic-adults.aspx. *See also* Pew Research Center, *Partisanship by Race, Ethnicity and Education* (Apr. 9, 2024), https://www.pewresearch.org/politics/2024/04/09/partisanship-by-race-ethnicity-and-education/.

113. Justice Ginsburg, for one, made this argument. *See* Miller v. Johnson, 515 U.S. 900, 947 (1995) (Ginsburg, J., dissenting) ("[E]thnicity itself can tie people together, as volumes of social science literature have documented—even people with divergent economic interests. For this reason, ethnicity is a significant force in political life. . . . The creation of ethnic districts reflecting felt identity is not ordinarily viewed as offensive or demeaning to those included in the delineation."); *see also id.* at 949 (citing the "political reality" of ethnically defined groups).

that racial groups *do* have identifiable interests. Recall from the discussion of *Gingles* that claims under VRA § 2 require plaintiffs to demonstrate racially polarized voting. If different racial groups did not "share the same political interests" and "prefer the same candidates at the polls," there could be no successful § 2 claims.

Despite its apparent condemnation of racial gerrymandering, the Court did not call into question all uses of race in districting. First, the Court did not hold that all racial gerrymanders—or even all obvious racial gerrymanders—were unconstitutional. Rather, it held that they triggered strict scrutiny, which means that they could be constitutional if they were narrowly tailored ways of achieving a compelling state interest. Second, the Court suggested that compliance with the Voting Rights Act might provide such a compelling interest. But, even so, a state may not justify its race-conscious districting simply by citing its obligations under the VRA. Rather, the state must have a reasonable basis for believing that it was under a statutory obligation to use race as it did.

Shaw raises controversial issues that touch on fundamental conflicts in the law of elections. It shows society's skepticism over governmental uses of race and the distribution of political power among racial groups, even as it balances the need for government intervention to protect the rights of racial minorities. It also raises deep concerns about the capacity of courts to police vaguely defined rights where there is no clearly identifiable harmed party. Finally, it raises important questions about the nature of democratic representation and about the ability of voters to be represented by people of different races and different ideologies or backgrounds.[114] These questions have persisted as the Court has decided more cases in the *Shaw* line—almost all by a 5–4 margin.

The first such case was *Miller v. Johnson*,[115] decided two years after *Shaw*. In facts reminiscent of both *Shaw* and *UJO*, *Miller* involved a back-and-forth interaction between the state and the Department of Justice concerning the state's application for preclearance. The Justice Department required Georgia to re-draw its districts to create three majority-minority districts, which Georgia did by drawing a district that connected black communities that were "260 miles apart in distance and worlds apart in culture."[116]

Miller struck down Georgia's racial gerrymander and, in the process, significantly revised *Shaw* by holding that a district's irregular shape was not itself an element of the constitutional cause of action. Rather, a district's bizarre shape was "persuasive

---

114. The concept referred to here is known as "descriptive representation." A person is descriptively represented in the legislature to the extent that the representative resembles the constituent in terms of race, background, occupation, wealth, or myriad other characteristics. Thus, a minority group is descriptively represented if the group has a representative who is a member of the same minority group, regardless of whether that representative is the choice of the minority voters. Conversely, minority voters who elect a non-minority representative would lack descriptive representation, even as their preferred representative is in the legislature.

115. 515 U.S. 900 (1995).

116. *Id.* at 908.

circumstantial *evidence*" of a constitutional violation. The violation itself (or, to be precise, the condition triggering strict scrutiny) consisted of the use of race as the "dominant and controlling rationale in drawing . . . district lines."[117] Thus, the key was not the shape of the district *per se* but whether the state placed too much emphasis on race when drawing districts.

The Court explained its meaning by describing the burden that plaintiffs in *Shaw* cases would have to meet: "The plaintiff's burden is to show, either through circumstantial evidence of a district's shape and demographics or more direct evidence going to legislative purpose, that race was the predominant factor motivating the legislature's decision to place a significant number of voters within or without a particular district. To make this showing, a plaintiff must prove that the legislature subordinated traditional race-neutral districting principles, including but not limited to compactness, contiguity, and respect for political subdivisions or communities defined by actual shared interests, to racial considerations."[118] This "predominant factor" test, where considerations of race "subordinate[] traditional race-neutral districting principles," has become the key phrase to emerge from *Miller*.[119]

Recall that *Shaw* had distinguished *United Jewish Organizations* by saying that the state in *UJO* adhered to traditional districting principles, whereas the state in *Shaw* drew districts that disregarded them. According to *Shaw*'s interpretation of *UJO*, a state could use race in drawing districts, but only if it did so without sacrificing considerations of compactness, contiguity, and political-subdivision boundaries. *Miller*'s retreat from *Shaw*'s apparent focus on the shape of districts required *Miller* to reevaluate *UJO* and to distinguish it on a different basis. In both *Miller* and *UJO*, the states intentionally created a certain number of majority-minority districts but did so without abandoning traditional districting principles. *UJO* would therefore have appeared to be a controlling precedent, and Justice Ginsburg's dissent argued that it was.[120] *Miller* distinguished *UJO*, however, not by relying on the districts' shapes, as *Shaw* had done, but by claiming that *UJO* was a vote-dilution case—not one raising the "analytically distinct" constitutional claim that *Shaw* recognized.[121] In any event, *Miller* announced, "[t]o the extent that any of the opinions in that 'highly fractured decision' can be interpreted as suggesting that a State's assignment of voters on the basis of race would be subject to anything but our strictest scrutiny, those views ought not be deemed controlling."[122]

---

117. *Id.* at 913 (emphasis added).

118. *Id.* at 916.

119. The Court later clarified that, for a *Shaw* claim to succeed, race must be the predominant factor "in determining *which* persons were placed *in appropriately apportioned districts*," so that a state could not defend against a *Shaw* claim merely by demonstrating that its predominant consideration in drawing district lines was to comply with its one-person, one-vote obligation. Alabama Legislative Black Caucus v. Alabama, 575 U.S. 254, 273 (2015).

120. *Miller*, 515 U.S. at 948 n.11 (Ginsburg, J., dissenting).

121. Shaw v. Reno, 509 U.S. 630, 652 (1993).

122. 515 U.S. at 915 (quoting *Shaw*, 509 U.S. at 652).

As *Shaw* had done, *Miller* accepted that states could make *some* use of race in drawing district lines without triggering strict scrutiny. As long as race was merely *a* factor, and not the *predominant* factor, strict scrutiny would not apply.[123] Although that conclusion was (and remains) controversial, and although there is language in *Miller* that might appear to condemn any use of race in districting, the Court has never required strict scrutiny to be applied unless race was the predominant factor.

Unfortunately, it can be difficult to assess whether race predominates in any particular redistricting. For example, one might think that race must logically predominate whenever a state intentionally creates a majority-minority district. Such a conclusion would mean that states could intentionally create majority-minority districts only when necessary to accomplish a compelling interest (such as compliance with the Voting Rights Act). Perhaps surprisingly, however, the Court has indicated that race does not necessarily predominate in the intentional creation of majority-minority districts.[124]

Subsequent cases have applied *Miller's* predominant-factor test, with arguably inconsistent results. In 1996, the year after *Miller*, the Court decided two *Shaw* cases: *Bush v. Vera*[125] and *Shaw v. Hunt* (*Shaw II*).[126] Both cases involved the question of how to determine when a racial purpose predominates over a political one—a question that is especially difficult because of the correlation between race and political ideology. The Court was clear that the state's mere awareness of the racial characteristics of its districts did not necessarily mean that the state had improperly based its districting decisions on race. As the *Vera* plurality noted, "If district lines merely correlate with race because they are drawn on the basis of political affiliation, which correlates with

---

123. Note that, in this respect, *Miller* departs from the standard applicable to other kinds of race-conscious legislation. When dealing with subjects other than districting, strict scrutiny applies when race is "a motivating factor," even if other, race-neutral, factors predominate. *See* Village of Arlington Heights v. Metro. Housing Dev. Corp., 429 U.S. 252, 266 (1977).

124. In *Bethune-Hill v. Virginia State Board of Elections*, 580 U.S. 178 (2017), the Court remanded to allow the lower court to determine if race had predominated in the intentional creation of a majority-minority district. If race *necessarily* predominated, there would be no need for a remand.

More recently, and more definitively, in *Allen v. Milligan*, 599 U.S. 1, 31–33 (2023), the Court held that race did not predominate in the intentional creation of a majority-minority district because "several other factors . . . such as compactness, contiguity, and population equality" were considered with "equal weighting" to the consideration given to race. *Id.* at 31. As Justices Thomas and Alito pointed out in dissent, however, the case appeared to be one of "textbook racial predominance," *id.* at 63 (Thomas, J., dissenting), in that other considerations were secondary to the one that could not be compromised—the creation of a district that would be controlled by the minority group so as to satisfy VRA § 2. *See id.* at 101–02 (Alito, J., dissenting).

Prior to *Bethune-Hill*, individual Justices had announced disparate opinions on the question. *See* Bush v. Vera, 517 U.S. 952, 958 (1996) (plurality opinion of O'Connor, J., joined by Rehnquist, C.J., and Kennedy, J.) ("Strict scrutiny does not apply . . . to all cases of intentional creation of majority-minority districts."); League of United Latin Am. Citizens v. Perry, 548 U.S. 399, 517 (2006) (Scalia, J., joined by Roberts, C.J., and Thomas and Alito, JJ., concurring in the judgment in part and dissenting in part) ("In my view, . . . when a legislature intentionally creates a majority-minority district, race is necessarily its predominant motivation and strict scrutiny is therefore triggered.").

125. 517 U.S. 952 (1996).

126. 517 U.S. 899 (1996).

race, there is no racial classification to justify. . . . "[127] On the other hand, "to the extent that race is used as a proxy for political characteristics, a racial stereotype requiring strict scrutiny is in operation."[128]

Thus the key difference appeared to be between political classifications that merely correlated with racial differences (which would be evaluated under rational-basis scrutiny) and racial classifications (which would be evaluated under strict scrutiny even if they were used for political purposes). The *Vera* plurality seemed to be most critical of the use of race as a "proxy" or a "stereotype"—the assumption that people of a certain race had certain political views. Both *Vera* and *Shaw II* concluded that the state in each case had indeed given predominant consideration to race.

The difficult task of distinguishing between racial gerrymanders and political gerrymanders was back before the Court three years later in *Hunt v. Cromartie*.[129] Again, the Court held that a state can constitutionally draw politically gerrymandered lines that correlate with racial divisions, even when the state is aware of the racial characteristics of the areas being divided into districts. Thus, where a plaintiff alleges a racial gerrymander and the state defends by claiming that it engaged in mere political gerrymandering, summary judgment is inappropriate. Rather, a trial is necessary to determine whether race or politics was the predominant factor.

Note that the trial on racial predominance is necessary because of the Court's use of the *Miller v. Johnson* predominant-factor test rather than the *Shaw* test, under which the shape of the district was given controlling consideration. If the district's shape were all that were needed to determine whether there was a racial gerrymander, such a determination could be made on summary judgment. Because assessing the weight of various districting considerations is a fact-based inquiry, the predominant-factor test requires a trial and makes the resolution of racial-gerrymandering claims less predictable.

The saga was not yet finished. North Carolina's redistricting in response to the 1990 census and the majority-minority district it had created were already the subject of three Supreme Court cases: *Shaw I*, *Shaw II*, and *Hunt v. Cromartie*. (*Miller* arose from Georgia, and *Vera* came from Texas.) The same North Carolina district would return to the Supreme Court yet again in *Easley v. Cromartie*[130]—eleven years after the census that had instigated the eventful redistricting. This time, however, the Supreme Court held in favor of the state, again by a vote of 5–4.

In *Easley*, the district court had held as a matter of fact that race predominated in the latest round of North Carolina's districting. The state had contended that it was motivated by politics, not race, but the district court pointed out that the majority-minority district included areas with high concentrations of blacks when it could have created a more compact district instead by including areas with an even higher

127. *Vera*, 517 U.S. at 968 (plurality opinion).
128. *Id.*
129. 526 U.S. 541 (1999).
130. 532 U.S. 234 (2001).

concentration of Democrats. Had the state really been trying to draw a heavily Democratic district, rather than one primarily focused on race, it had an available option that adhered more closely to the "traditional districting principle" of compactness.

The Supreme Court found this factual finding "clearly erroneous," however, and reversed. In the Court's view, the state could consider the fact that blacks were particularly loyal Democrats—that is, they were less likely than white Democrats to cross over and vote for Republican candidates.[131] The state may, then, have used race, but in order to create an effective political—not racial—gerrymander. Justice Thomas, in dissent, protested that by allowing the state to use race as a proxy for Democratic Party loyalty, the majority had used the very kind of "stereotype" that the *Shaw* cases had condemned.[132]

2. The Conflict Between *Shaw* and the Voting Rights Act

The combination of *Shaw* and §§ 2 and 5 of the Voting Rights Act places states in a difficult position. On the one hand, the VRA requires states to consider race in drawing district lines. Prior to *Shelby County v. Holder*, covered jurisdictions were not able to enforce changes to their election laws if those changes produced a retrogression in the position of minorities, and every state is subject to a § 2 suit if it draws lines that dilute the votes of minorities. States, therefore, must analyze the racial impact of any proposed election laws, and, sometimes, states must consciously create majority-minority districts to comply with the VRA. On the other hand, if considerations of race predominate in redistricting, courts will apply strict scrutiny and may very well find a constitutional violation under *Shaw*.

If either § 2 or § 5 of the VRA were interpreted to require states to consider race excessively, in violation of *Shaw*, that part of the VRA would raise substantial constitutional questions. Justice Kennedy discussed that concern in arguing for a restrained interpretation of VRA §§ 2 and 5. Most notably, in *Johnson v. De Grandy*, Justice Kennedy was troubled by the possibility that "States might consider it lawful and proper to act with the explicit goal of creating a proportional number of majority-minority districts in an effort to avoid § 2 litigation" or to gain preclearance.[133] He, therefore, concurred with the decision of the Court to reject the plaintiffs' § 2 claim in that case on statutory grounds while specifically reserving the "constitutional implications" of an interpretation of the VRA in which groups would have a right to something approaching proportional representation.[134]

---

131. *See id.* at 244–45.

132. *See id.* at 266–67 (Thomas, J., dissenting).

133. Johnson v. De Grandy, 512 U.S. 997, 1029 (1994) (Kennedy, J., concurring in part and concurring in the judgment).

134. *See id.* at 1028–29.

The Supreme Court was presented with the tension between *Shaw* and the VRA when it decided *League of United Latin American Citizens (LULAC) v. Perry* in 2006, although ultimately the Court was able to avoid the constitutional question.[135] Plaintiffs in that complex case challenged Texas's redistricting, which protected a Republican incumbent congressman by taking Latino voters from his district and creating a different, non-compact Latino district in a different area of the state. The Court held, over the dissent of Chief Justice Roberts, that Texas violated § 2 by diluting the votes of Latinos in the original district, even though the newly created district gave Latinos in the region and the state overall a roughly proportionate share of congressional districts. The Court held that the new district could not compensate for the loss of the old one because the only districts that mattered under § 2, as interpreted in *Gingles*, were compact ones. Thus, Latinos were deprived of a compact majority-minority district, and providing an additional non-compact district did not make the loss of the original district any less of a violation.[136]

The Chief Justice derided the Court's decision as disregarding what, in his view, should have been the most important factor in assessing the totality of the circumstances under § 2—proportionality—in favor of a concern about compactness that did not affect the overall distribution of political power between racial groups. He thought it improper for the Court to "str[i]ke down a State's redistricting plan under § 2, on the ground that the plan achieves the maximum number of possible majority-minority districts, but loses on style points, in that the minority voters in one of those districts are not as 'compact' as the minority voters would be in another district were the lines drawn differently."[137]

The Court further concluded that the totality of the circumstances showed that Latinos were being deprived of an equal opportunity to participate in politics and to elect their candidates of choice because the redistricting occurred just as Latinos were amassing sufficient political power in the original district to oust the incumbent congressman. Incumbency protection, in this instance, was not a traditional redistricting criterion but rather a "troubling blend of politics and race" that was made "to benefit the officeholder, not the voters."[138]

The Court's conclusion that the reduction of Latino voting strength in the original district was illegal made it unnecessary to address the constitutionality of the district that Texas had created to compensate for the loss of the original Latino district. If, however, the Court had held that the loss of the initial Latino district could be balanced by the intentional creation of a Latino district elsewhere, then that new district would itself be vulnerable under *Shaw* because of the state's consideration of race in intentionally creating the new Latino district. Thus, a measure taken to comply with the VRA (the creation of the second Latino district) would raise a constitutional

---

135. 548 U.S. 399 (2006).

136. *See id.* at 430–31.

137. *Id.* at 494 (Roberts, C.J., concurring in part, concurring in the judgment in part, and dissenting in part).

138. *Id.* at 442, 441 (opinion of the Court).

question, although the state could have avoided both issues by not dismantling the first Latino district.

That very issue has returned to the Supreme Court in *Louisiana v. Callais*, which is pending before the Supreme Court as of this writing. After the 2020 census, Louisiana adopted a districting plan that made one of the state's six congressional districts majority-minority. Challengers sued and obtained a preliminary injunction after a district court determined that a second majority-minority district was likely required by VRA § 2. The state redrew the districts and created a second majority-minority district by grouping together black voters across virtually the entire width of the state. A different set of challengers brought suit raising a racial-gerrymandering claim. *Callais* thus presents the Court with the conflict between the VRA (as interpreted in *Gingles*) and the Fourteenth Amendment (as interpreted in *Shaw*) that has troubled this area of the law for thirty years.

The closest the Supreme Court came to addressing the collision course of § 2's race-consciousness and *Shaw*'s right against racial gerrymandering was in 2023, when it decided *Allen v. Milligan*.[139] The case involved Alabama's congressional redistricting following the 2020 census, according to which Alabama was allotted seven seats in the House of Representatives. A three-judge district court held that VRA § 2 required Alabama to draw the congressional districts so that blacks (who comprised two-sevenths of the state's population) could control two of the districts.

Alabama argued that the only way that a second majority-minority district could be drawn was to prioritize race, meaning that the only way to comply with § 2 of the Voting Rights Act was to violate the Fourteenth Amendment. Alabama therefore asked the Court to reinterpret the VRA and revise *Gingles* to hold that a state could comply with § 2 by drawing districts in a race-neutral process. The Court rejected that interpretation and adhered to *Gingles*, which read § 2 to require race-conscious districting.[140]

Alabama responded that if § 2 forced states to draw districts in a race-conscious way, and to adopt districts that would not have been created in a race-neutral process, then § 2 effectively created a right to proportional representation, contrary to the proviso in VRA § 2(b). The Court rejected this argument, finding that "the *Gingles* framework itself imposes meaningful constraints on proportionality."[141] Those constraints were the "traditional redistricting criteria"—most importantly compactness. Because the first *Gingles* precondition weeds out § 2 claims that are brought by groups that are not large or compact enough to constitute a majority in a single-member district, only compact racial minority groups can press a § 2 claim. The Court's implication, however, was that there was indeed a right to roughly proportional representation of racial minority groups—the § 2(b) proviso notwithstanding—if rough proportionality could be achieved with compact districts that adhered (closely enough) to other traditional redistricting criteria.

---

139. 599 U.S. 1 (2023).
140. *Id.* at 23–26.
141. *Id.* at 26.

It is obviously problematic for the Court to interpret § 2 as requiring the kind of race-conscious districting that *Shaw* and its progeny prohibit. Accordingly, it might appear that *Milligan* portends a return to *Shaw*'s concern with districts' shapes and away from *Miller v. Johnson*'s concern with the subjective intentions of the officials drawing district lines. That is, if *Milligan* interpreted § 2 to require, insofar as possible, the race-conscious creation of a proportionate number of compact majority-minority districts, it effectively means that a racial-gerrymandering claim can succeed only if a state creates *non-compact* majority-minority districts or districts that disregard other traditional redistricting criteria—in other words, districts so oddly shaped that they cannot "be understood as anything other than an effort to separate voters into different districts on the basis of race."[142] It is too early to determine if *Milligan* will have that effect, but the Court is not ready to discard the predominant-factor test. The year after *Milligan*, the Court applied the predominant-factor test in *Alexander v. South Carolina State Conference of the NAACP* to hold that politics, not race, was the predominate motive among those who redrew South Carolina's congressional districts.[143]

After *Milligan*, states do not appear to have much flexibility in districting. If, as suggested above, § 2 requires rough proportionality when that can be achieved with (somewhat) compact districts, then states *must* employ race-conscious means to produce the proportionate number of majority-minority districts. But a state cannot play it safe, ignore compactness, and gerrymander districts to ensure a proportional number of majority-minority districts because doing so would open the state to a suit under *Shaw*.

In thinking about the interplay of the Voting Rights Act and *Shaw*, keep in mind that racial predominance is not itself unconstitutional; rather, a finding of racial predominance requires the state to satisfy strict scrutiny in justifying its use of race. The Court has never definitively resolved whether compliance with the Voting Rights Act is a compelling interest that would justify states in using race to an extent that would otherwise violate *Shaw*. The Court has, however, been willing to assume that compliance with VRA § 5 is a compelling interest. Even the Court's conservatives indicated a willingness to go along with that conclusion,[144] but that is far from allowing states a free hand. First, the Court has already held that a state may not justify its use of race by pointing to § 5 unless it has a "strong basis in evidence" for believing that its use of race was required by § 5.[145] On the other hand, the strong-basis-in-evidence standard

142. *Shaw*, 509 U.S. at 649.

143. 602 U.S. 1, 9–10, 19–24 (2024) (referring to partisanship as the legislature's "aim" and "driving force," and referring to "the possibility that politics drove the districting process").

144. *See LULAC*, 548 U.S. at 518 (Scalia, J., joined in relevant part by Roberts, C.J., and Thomas and Alito, JJ., concurring in the judgment in part and dissenting in part) ("I would hold that compliance with § 5 of the Voting Rights Act can be [a compelling state] interest.").

145. Bethune-Hill v. Virginia State Bd. of Elections, 580 U.S. 178, 193–94 (2017) (quoting Alabama Legis. Black Caucus v. Alabama, 575 U.S. 254, 278 (2015)).

does not require the state to show that its consideration of race was *actually* required by the Voting Rights Act—only that there was good reason for so believing.[146]

Second, even if compliance with § 5 were to constitute a compelling interest, it is by no means clear that compliance with § 2 would also be compelling. Section 2 reaches more broadly than § 5—both in that it applies nationwide and in that it outlaws vote dilution that is not itself unconstitutional. Specifically, *Gingles* and *Milligan* appear to read § 2 to create a right to rough proportionality in districting, so long as that proportionality can be achieved with fidelity to traditional districting principles. Such a right is a far cry from the right against purposeful discrimination that, per *City of Mobile v. Bolden*, the Fifteenth Amendment itself guarantees. Accordingly, there is a substantial argument that, if *Gingles* and *Milligan* are correct, § 2 is not "appropriate legislation" to enforce the Fifteenth Amendment because § 2 is not "congruent" with and "proportional" to the constitutional rights that are ostensibly being enforced.

Although the Court has upheld the constitutionality of § 5, it had never squarely addressed the constitutionality of § 2 in its post-1982 amended form until *Allen v. Milligan*.[147] In *Milligan*, the Court tersely invoked a pre-1982 precedent, *City of Rome v. United States*,[148] in concluding that Congress had the power to enact § 2.[149] *City of Rome* had applied the deferential rational-basis test of *South Carolina v. Katzenbach* in permitting Congress to enact any rational means of achieving the goals of the Civil War Amendments. It did not anticipate the more-restrictive congruence-and-proportionality test of *City of Boerne v. Flores*, and *Milligan* did not discuss the conflict between the two standards.

Although five Justices in *Milligan* upheld the constitutionality of § 2, one of the five, Justice Kavanaugh, specifically noted in a concurrence that the strongest argument against § 2's constitutionality was not argued in the case. That argument (which Justice Kavanaugh labeled the "temporal" argument) was that although § 2 was within Congress's power initially, Congress could not obligate states to conduct "race-based redistricting . . . indefinitely into the future."[150] Justice Kavanaugh suggested that he would be willing to consider that argument if it were presented in a future case.

If both §§ 2 and 5 are constitutional, they present a potential conflict with the prohibition on racial gerrymandering established by the *Shaw* line of cases. The Court could avoid a square conflict between those two doctrines by reconsidering *Gingles* and interpreting the VRA in line with *White v. Regester*'s focus on access to the political process rather than proportionality. ALternatively, the Court could hold that strict scrutiny applies to racial gerrymandering but states have a compelling interest in avoiding violations of both § 2 and § 5, as those sections are currently interpreted. Although it is thus possible to reconcile *Shaw* and the VRA, those doctrines place

146. *See id.*

147. 599 U.S. 1 (2023).

148. 446 U.S. 156 (1980).

149. 599 U.S. at 41–42.

150. *Id.* at 45 (Kavanaugh, J., concurring in part).

states in a difficult position, as the VRA requires some consideration of race—even to the point of intentionally creating majority-minority districts. But if race becomes the predominant factor, then the districting will be struck down under *Shaw* and *Miller* unless the state satisfies strict scrutiny by demonstrating at least a substantial basis in evidence for believing that its consideration of race was required by the VRA.

E. Conclusion

This chapter has addressed constitutional and statutory limits on states' ability to consider race in the districting process. After reading it, you should be in a better position to discuss the difficulties that abound in trying to balance the protection of minorities' political power with concerns about the excessive use of race in governmental decision-making. The demands of the Constitution and the Voting Rights Act also require a difficult balance between federal power and states' freedom to structure their own electoral systems. Whether one agrees with Chief Justice Roberts that "[i]t is a sordid business, this divvying us up by race,"[151] surely race-based districting is a complicated business, one that forces us to consider racial justice, federalism, and the very purposes of representation.

151. League of United Latin Am. Citizens v. Perry, 548 U.S. 399, at 511 (2006) (Roberts, C.J., concurring in part, concurring in the judgment in part, and dissenting in part).

Chapter 5
Political Parties

A. Introduction

The Constitution does not explicitly address the place of political parties in the American political system. The Framers were particularly conscious of the dangers of "faction," and parties were considered by many to be examples of the kinds of factions that would coopt the machinery of government and use it to undermine "the rights of other citizens, or . . . the permanent and aggregate interests of the community."[1] On the other hand, the First Amendment protects the right of the people "to assemble" (a right that has been extended to cover the right to "associate" as well),[2] and parties are the result of politically minded individuals' decisions to assemble and to associate with each other "for the common advancement of political beliefs and ideas."[3] It is therefore no surprise that the Supreme Court has held that the First Amendment protects "[t]he right to associate with the political party of one's choice."[4]

A group's membership affects its message. Therefore, if a group has a right to control and express its distinctive message, it must also have the ability to decide *who* will be permitted to participate in developing and expressing that message. For that reason, the Supreme Court has held that the right to associate presupposes not only a freedom to join with others in a common endeavor, but also a "freedom not to associate"—in other words, to decide that the association will be limited to certain people and to exclude outsiders.[5]

But parties are not exactly like other expressive associations. Unlike other private associations, parties carry out essential government functions. They play the principal role in winnowing potential candidates to the few that appear on the general-election ballot. If political parties did not exist, the government would have to come up with

---

1. The Federalist No. 10, at 57 (James Madison) (Jacob E. Cooke ed., 1961). *See generally, e.g.*, Richard Hofstadter, The Idea of a Party System: The Rise of Legitimate Opposition in the United States, 1780–1840 (1969).
2. *See* NAACP v. Alabama, 357 U.S. 449, 460 (1958).
3. Kusper v. Pontikes, 414 U.S. 51, 56 (1973).
4. *Id.* at 57.
5. Roberts v. United States Jaycees, 468 U.S. 609, 623 (1984).

some way itself to disqualify some candidates, lest the general election be unmanageable. Further, parties are subject to considerable state regulation, and, in practice, many of the same people who are influential in parties are influential in government. Thus, there is considerable overlap between the parties and the government. For these reasons, the Supreme Court has held that parties, as state actors, must comply with the Constitution's ban on racial discrimination in voting.

There is an inherent conflict between a legal rule that forbids the government from interfering with a party's membership decisions (because those decisions are protected by the First Amendment) and another rule that forces it to accept racial minorities whom it does not like (because racial discrimination in voting is forbidden by the Fifteenth Amendment). The conflict stems from parties' ambiguous status as both private organizations and cogs in the state's election machinery.

B. State Action

1. In General

With the exception of the Thirteenth Amendment's prohibition on slavery,[6] the Constitution regulates the conduct of government—not private parties. Specifically, the Fourteenth Amendment provides that "[n]o state shall" deprive anyone of due process or equal protection,[7] and the Fifteenth Amendment says that neither "the United States [n]or . . . any State" shall deny or abridge the right to vote on account of race.[8] Accordingly, whether the Constitution is violated or not depends not only on what action is committed but also on who is committing the action. If the conduct is performed by the government, then the Constitution may be violated; if by a private party, then it cannot be.

Because of this "state action" requirement, it is necessary to classify certain persons and groups as either government actors or private parties. That determination is easy when a prosecutor seeks to enforce a statute or when a government agency is taking action against a regulated party. Unfortunately, the choice is not always clear. Sometimes an action ostensibly taken by a private party is enabled or influenced by the government, and the courts have had great difficulty in sorting out the kinds of governmental involvement that are sufficient to satisfy the requirement of state

6. *See* The Civil Rights Cases, 109 U.S. 3, 20 (1883) ("[T]he [Thirteenth A]mendment is not a mere prohibition of State laws establishing or upholding slavery, but an absolute declaration that slavery or involuntary servitude shall not exist in any part of the United States.").

7. U.S. Const. amend. XIV, § 1 ("No state shall make or enforce any law which shall abridge the privileges or immunities of citizens of the United States; nor shall any State deprive any person of life, liberty, or property, without due process of law; nor deny to any person within its jurisdiction the equal protection of the laws.").

8. U.S. Const. amend. XV, § 1 ("The right of citizens of the United States to vote shall not be denied or abridged by the United States or by any State on account of race, color, or previous condition of servitude.").

action. Because political parties have characteristics of both private organizations and government entities, the state-action doctrine has been particularly difficult to apply when parties' behavior forms the basis of a constitutional claim.

2. The *White Primary Cases*

In the beginning of the twentieth century, the Supreme Court heard a series of cases involving the application of the state-action doctrine to political parties. Collectively, these cases are referred to as the *White Primary Cases* because they centered around attempts by branches of the Democratic Party to reserve their primary elections for white voters. Eventually, the Supreme Court held that the party was indeed a state actor—at least when it set qualifications for voting in primary elections—but the Court's reasoning continues to lead to confusion about the place of parties in the constitutional structure.

a. Nixon v. Herndon

The first of the *White Primary Cases* was *Nixon v. Herndon*.[9] In that case, the Supreme Court struck down a Texas law providing that "in no event shall a negro be eligible to participate in a Democratic party primary election held in the State of Texas." Even though the law regulated the conduct of a party, rather than controlling access to a function or activity of the state itself, the exclusion was mandated by the state law. Accordingly, the Court held the law unconstitutional, opining that it was "hard to imagine a more direct and obvious infringement of the Fourteenth" Amendment.[10]

b. Nixon v. Condon

Despite having its exclusionary statute struck down in *Nixon v. Herndon*, Texas was still unwilling to permit blacks to participate in the Democratic primary. In an attempt to maintain its exclusionary policy, the state passed a new law that gave power to each party's executive committee "to prescribe the qualifications of its own members and ... [to] determine who shall be qualified to vote or otherwise participate in such political party." Texas knew full well that the executive committee of the state Democratic Party would vote to exclude blacks, as indeed it did.

L.A. Nixon, the black man who had successfully challenged the earlier Texas statute in *Nixon v. Herndon*, returned to the Supreme Court to challenge the new law. In a 5–4 decision, the Supreme Court in *Nixon v. Condon* agreed with Nixon that the law was unconstitutional.[11] The Court ducked the question of whether parties were state actors, and instead held that the requisite state action was present because the

---

9. 273 U.S. 536 (1927).
10. *Id.* at 541.
11. 286 U.S. 73 (1932).

executive committee was acting under authority granted to it by the state law.[12] In other words, even though the state law did not mandate the exclusion of blacks, it enabled the executive committee to exclude blacks—a power that otherwise would have rested with the party convention. Thus, the Court held the Texas statute unconstitutional. But the case expressly left unresolved the question whether an exclusion imposed by the party convention would contain sufficient state action to implicate the constitutional protection against racial discrimination.[13]

c. *Grovey v. Townsend*

That question arrived three years later, in *Grovey v. Townsend.*[14] *Nixon v. Condon* was decided on May 2, 1932. A mere three weeks later, on May 24, 1932, the Texas Democratic Party convention adopted a resolution restricting party membership and voting rights to whites. The Court unanimously upheld the exclusion, noting that, under state law, political parties were "voluntary associations for political action, and . . . not the creatures of the state."[15] As such, the party convention had the right to determine its rules for membership without interference from the state—a right that was itself inconsistent with status as a state actor. The Supreme Court acknowledged that both parties and party primaries were extensively regulated by the state, but the Court pointed out that the parties and their candidates paid for and implemented the primaries.[16] All in all, the Court concluded that the party was not a state actor.

d. *Smith v. Allwright*

Grovey's holding did not last long. Cracks began to appear as early as 1941, when the Court decided *United States v. Classic.*[17] In that case, the defendants, who had engaged in election fraud in a primary election for Congress, were accused of violating federal statutes that made it a crime to deprive someone of rights protected by the Constitution. Even though the primary election selected only the party's nominee, the Court held that such fraud did in fact deprive the voters of a constitutionally protected right, *viz.*, the right to select representatives to Congress.[18] The Court treated the primary election as simply the first stage in a two-stage election process, and it held that fraud in either the primary or general election deprived the voters of a constitutionally protected right.[19] The result is hard to square with *Grovey*. If, as *Grovey* held, parties are private associations and they have the ability to set membership qualifications and exclude outsiders from their deliberations, then people have no constitutional

12. *See id.* at 84.
13. *See id.* at 84–85.
14. 295 U.S. 45 (1935).
15. *Id.* at 52.
16. *See id.* at 49–50.
17. 313 U.S. 299 (1941).
18. *See id.* at 316.
19. *See id.* at 316–17.

right to participate in primaries (as distinct from general elections). *Classic* did not address this tension at all, and did not even cite *Grovey*. It was clear, however, that the question of political parties' constitutional status would return to the Court yet again.

And it did, in very short order. Only three years after *Classic*, in *Smith v. Allwright*, the Court reconsidered and overruled *Grovey*.[20] The Court that decided *Allwright*, however, was very different from the one that decided *Grovey* nine years earlier. Seven of the nine Justices in *Allwright* had been appointed by President Franklin Roosevelt since *Grovey* had been decided, and the new appointees jettisoned *Grovey* by an 8–1 vote, leaving only Justice Owen Roberts (the author of *Grovey*) in dissent.

Writing for the Court in *Allwright*, Justice Reed relied on *Classic* to explain that the primary and general elections are parts of one system for selecting public officials. Thus, a party's exclusion of blacks was not "a mere refusal by a party of party membership";[21] rather, it was equivalent to denying blacks the opportunity to participate in part of the electoral process—a process set up by the state. Because the state chose to give the parties their role in narrowing the electorate's choice of candidates, the Court concluded "that state delegation to a party of the power to fix the qualifications of primary elections is delegation of a state function that may make the party's action the action of the state."[22]

In addition to this focus on the party's performance of "a state function," *Allwright* noted the extensive state regulation to which parties were subject. The Court explained that not only did the state "direct[] the selection of all party officers" by statute, but the state also extensively regulated the primaries themselves and provided that the names of the parties' nominees shall appear on the general-election ballot.[23] The Court concluded that the state could not delegate the function of choosing candidates to a party and tell the party how to choose those candidates, and then claim that the party's action was solely that of a private association.[24] As the Court summarized its holding,

> [i]f the state requires a certain electoral procedure, prescribes a general election ballot made up of party nominees so chosen and limits the choice of the electorate in general elections for state offices, practically speaking, to those

---

20. Smith v. Allwright, 321 U.S. 649 (1944).

21. *Id.* at 660–61.

22. *Id.* at 660.

23. *Id.* at 662–64. The Court's analysis assumed that it was constitutional for the state to impose such regulations on parties—a question raised, but not fully settled, by the cases discussed in § C, *infra*.

24. *See Allwright*, 321 U.S. at 663 ("[Texas's] statutory system for the selection of party nominees for inclusion on the general election ballot makes the party which is required to follow these legislative directions an agency of the state in so far as it determines the participants in a primary election. The party takes its character as a state agency from the duties imposed upon it by state statutes; the duties do not become matters of private law because they are performed by a political party."). Although it makes some sense that a state-regulated entity would not be fully "private," the Court's analysis "raises the troubling inference that an organization's First Amendment right to autonomy against government control can be limited or eliminated by an exertion of government control." Michael R. Dimino, Sr., *It's My Party and I'll Do What I Want To: Political Parties, Unconstitutional Conditions, and the Freedom of Association*, 12 First Amend. L. Rev. 65, 84 (2013).

> whose names appear on such a ballot, it endorses, adopts and enforces the discrimination against Negroes, practiced by a party entrusted by Texas law with the determination of the qualifications of participants in the primary. This is state action within the meaning of the Fifteenth Amendment.[25]

Allwright did not hold that every action by a party would qualify as state action. In fact, *Allwright* said that party membership "may be ... no concern of a state. But where, as here, that privilege is also the essential qualification for voting in a primary to select nominees for a general election, the state makes the action of the party the action of the state."[26]

Smith v. Allwright held that the Democratic Party itself could not reserve its primaries for whites without violating the Constitution. Other associations besides parties are influential in politics, however. Must those associations, too, comply with the Constitution's anti-discrimination requirements? The Court would provide a partial, but badly fractured, answer to that question in *Terry v. Adams*,[27] the last of the *White Primary Cases*.

e. *Terry v. Adams*

Unlike the rest of the *White Primary Cases*, *Terry v. Adams* did not involve an exclusion from the Democratic Party. Rather, it involved a nominally separate, all-white organization in Fort Bend County, Texas, known as the Jaybird Democratic Association, or Jaybird Party. The Jaybirds held a primary election before the Democratic primary. The Jaybirds' pre-primary was not paid for or regulated by either the state or the Democratic Party. Nevertheless, the winner of the Jaybird primary almost always entered and won the Democratic primary and, because the Democratic Party was dominant in Texas at the time, won the general election as well.

This three-stage election process permitted blacks' votes to be marginalized, just as they were marginalized during their exclusion from the Democratic primary before *Smith v. Allwright*. In the earlier system, blacks were excluded from the Democratic primary, and their votes in the general election were useless because white voters would unify behind the Democratic Party's nominee. Under the Jaybird system, whites chose the Jaybird nominee in an all-white primary and then would unify behind that Jaybird nominee in the Democratic primary, thereby ensuring that blacks' votes in the Democratic primary would be impotent.

The Court held that blacks' exclusion from the Jaybird primary violated the Fifteenth Amendment, and so it held that the Jaybird Party qualified as a state actor. Although eight of the nine Justices agreed on the result, there was no opinion of the Court. Justice Black's lead opinion, which was joined by Justices Douglas and Burton, appeared to announce a purely effects-based test: whether the conduct "produces the

---

25. 321 U.S. at 664.
26. *Id.* at 664–65.
27. 345 U.S. 461 (1953).

equivalent" of the racially discriminatory elections that would be unconstitutional if engaged in by the government directly.[28] Because of the dominance of the Jaybirds within the Democratic Party, and because of the dominance of the Democratic Party in the state as a whole, "[t]he Democratic primary and the general election have become no more than the perfunctory ratifiers of the choice that that has already been made in Jaybird elections from which Negroes have been excluded."[29] All together, Justice Black's opinion concluded that the effect of the three-stage election process was "to do precisely that which the Fifteenth Amendment forbids—strip Negroes of every vestige of influence in selecting" the county's elected officials.[30]

Justice Clark's concurring opinion employed similar reasoning. That opinion, which Chief Justice Vinson, Justice Reed, and Justice Jackson joined, stressed that the Jaybird Association "operate[d] as part and parcel of the Democratic Party"[31] and "as an auxiliary of the local Democratic Party organization."[32] Justice Clark pointed out, as Justice Black had done in the principal opinion, that the effect of the Jaybirds' pre-primary was to exclude blacks from the only election that mattered: "To be sure, the Democratic primary and the general election are nominally open to the colored elector. But his must be an empty vote cast after the real decisions are made."[33]

Justice Frankfurter also concurred. He argued that state action was present because the same elites that controlled the county government and the county Democratic Party "participat[ed] by voting in the Jaybird primary"[34] and thereby contributed to "a wholly successful effort to withdraw significance from the State-prescribed primary."[35]

Justice Minton argued in dissent that the Jaybirds were an interest group like dozens of others that were attempting to influence politics. Justice Minton conceded that the Jaybirds were particularly powerful, but in that respect Justice Minton argued that the Jaybirds' influence was little different "from the situation in many parts of the 'Bible Belt' where a church stamp of approval or that of the Anti-Saloon League must be put on any candidate who does not want to lose the election."[36] In brief, Justice Minton questioned whether the action of a private group should become state action just because it is successful.[37]

More than seventy years later, Justice Minton's question continues to puzzle us. What exactly made the Jaybirds different from any other interest group, and might a private group's activities be considered state action if the group is particularly influential? If a religious organization or a union or an advocacy group is so powerful that

28. *Id.* at 469.
29. *Id.*
30. *Id.* at 470.
31. *Id.* at 482 (Clark, J., concurring).
32. *Id.* at 483.
33. *Id.* at 484.
34. *Id.* at 473 (opinion of Frankfurter, J.).
35. *Id.* at 474.
36. *Id.* at 494.
37. *Id.* at 493.

its preferred candidates usually win the general election, would its endorsements be state action?

There is some language in the various *Terry* opinions that might suggest that whenever the state "permits . . . a duplication of its election processes," there is state action.[38] The better reading, however, is probably much more limited and tied to the extraordinary facts of the case. *Terry v. Adams* came after decades of Southern opposition to blacks' political power. The Court—in the year before it decided *Brown v. Board of Education*[39]—may well have grown impatient with efforts to subordinate blacks. *Terry* may therefore be a stretch by a Court that wanted to end Jim Crow.

Further, the Jaybirds were influential in Fort Bend County only because the Democratic Party was dominant in the South. If another party were competitive in general elections, then that party could have capitalized on the Democrats' willingness to write off blacks. In a jurisdiction where there are two viable parties, if one party allows its nomination process to be controlled by a faction, the other party will be more likely to win. Whereas in *Terry*, the Jaybird primary was the only election that mattered, in a competitive political environment the general election is more than a mere formality. *Terry* may, therefore, have limited precedential force for organizations that endorse candidates but do not hold state-run primary elections.

3. Modern Cases

The Supreme Court has said relatively little about parties and the state-action doctrine since the *White Primary Cases*. The issue resurfaced, however, in 1996, when the Court decided *Morse v. Republican Party of Virginia*.[40] That case involved a fee imposed by the party on voters who wanted to take part in the party's convention for selecting its nominee for the U.S. Senate. The question before the Supreme Court was whether the party's imposition of the fee was subject to preclearance under § 5 of the Voting Rights Act. As discussed in Chapter 3, that section of the VRA required certain covered jurisdictions to submit proposed changes of their election laws to the Attorney General or the U.S. District Court for the District of Columbia. Those changes could not go into effect until either the Attorney General or the court granted preclearance.

The preclearance requirement applied only to "State[s] or political subdivision[s]," however. The question in *Morse* was, thus, whether, within the meaning of the VRA, the Republican Party qualified as the Commonwealth of Virginia or one of its political subdivisions. In answering that question, several Justices addressed the meaning and significance of the *White Primary Cases*. Unfortunately, the Court was badly fractured in *Morse*. So, while the case raises interesting questions about the application of the

---

38. *Id.* at 469 (opinion of Black, J.).
39. 347 U.S. 483 (1954).
40. 517 U.S. 186 (1996).

state-action doctrine in the modern context and the doctrine's applicability to conventions (rather than primaries), the case does little to answer them.

Justice Stevens, in an opinion joined by Justice Ginsburg, equated the VRA's "State or political subdivision" language with the Constitution's state-action requirement. That is, for Justices Stevens and Ginsburg, a "State or political subdivision" included any person or group that would qualify as a state actor under the Fifteenth Amendment.[41] Justice Stevens analogized the Republican convention to the Jaybird primary in *Terry*, suggesting even that the Republican convention presented an easier case for state action because the Jaybird primary "did not involve the State's electoral apparatus in even the slightest way—neither to supply election officials, nor ballots, nor polling places."[42] Finally, Justice Stevens explicitly rejected the idea that the *White Primary Cases* should be limited to situations of one-party dominance. In his view, "[t]he operative test . . . is whether a political party exercises power over the electoral process. . . . That situation may arise in two-party States just as in one-party States."[43]

The other Justices' interpretations of Congress's power and the VRA were less expansive. Justice Breyer, writing also for Justices O'Connor and Souter, cautioned that parties might have a First Amendment right to be free from state interference in conducting their conventions, but he held the VRA applicable in *Morse* because the Republican convention "resembles a primary about as closely as one could imagine," in that it was open to anyone willing to declare loyalty to the party and pay the fee.[44]

Justices Kennedy and Thomas wrote dissenting opinions. In Justice Kennedy's dissent, he argued that the Republican Party was not a "State or political subdivision" within the meaning of the VRA. He did not address whether the party could be considered a state actor under the Constitution.[45]

Justice Thomas wrote a separate dissent, which was joined by Chief Justice Rehnquist and Justice Scalia, in which he argued that the party was not a state actor. Countering Justice Stevens's contention that *Terry v. Adams* controlled the case, Justice Thomas responded that in that case "the Jaybird primary was the *de facto* general election."[46] Because the Republican Party did not dominate Virginia politics like the Democratic Party dominated Texas at the time of the *White Primary Cases*, Justice Thomas did not view those cases as controlling.[47]

The Court was presented with a similar issue in 1972 in *O'Brien v. Brown*, but it did not reach the merits of the case.[48] *O'Brien* involved a controversy over California's delegates to the Democratic National Convention. California had chosen its delegates based on a winner-take-all system, but because the national party's

---

41. *Id.* at 217 (opinion of Stevens, J.).
42. *Id.* at 215. *See also id.* at 216 n.28.
43. *Id.* at 218.
44. *Id.* at 238 (Breyer, J., concurring in the judgment).
45. *See id.* at 250 (Kennedy, J., dissenting).
46. *Id.* at 269 (Thomas, J., dissenting).
47. *See id.* at 269–70.
48. 409 U.S. 1 (1972).

credentials committee objected to that system, it refused to seat the delegates. The delegates challenged the committee's decision. The Court refused to intervene, saying that the limited time before the start of the convention did not allow it to give adequate consideration to the issues involved. The Court did state, however, that interference with the party committee's decision would raise "highly important questions" about the party's "vital rights of association" and "whether the action of the Credentials Committee is state action." Overall, the Court expressed "grave doubts" that the Constitution would give courts the authority to interfere with the party's ability to decide on the qualifications of delegates.[49]

As noted at the outset of this chapter, there is a connection between an association's ability to control its membership decisions and its ability to control its message. A party that is forced to open its primary to unwelcome voters will find that the candidates chosen and the views of the party will change due to the influence of the new voters. Most of the state-action cases deal with exclusionary policies motivated by racial prejudice, but, in principle, the state-action issue is identical regardless of the reason for the party's behavior.

Suppose, for example, that the reason for the exclusion is ideological. In *Republican Party of Texas v. Dietz*, a group of Republicans favoring gay rights sought to lease a booth at the party convention and to take out an advertisement in the convention program.[50] The party refused to permit either action because of a disagreement with the group's position. If the party were a state actor, such viewpoint-based suppression of speech would be clearly unconstitutional. Yet a major reason people join political parties in the first place is to advance their shared ideological agendas. If the party were unable to make such ideologically based judgments about the values it wished to promote, its identity could very well be undermined. Such situations thus starkly illustrate the conflict between voters' rights to participate in parties' decisions and the parties' ability to control their own messages.

In *Dietz*, the Texas Supreme Court held that the party's exclusion of the gay-rights group from the convention was an "internal party affair[]," and so it did not constitute state action. If the gay-rights group were excluded from an "external" affair such as the Republican primary, however, the issues would seem to be very much the same. In both cases, the group's participation in the party would affect the party's message, and, in both cases, the group would be trying to influence the party's attitude and behavior regarding gay rights. It is not clear that the U.S. Supreme Court would accept *Dietz*'s distinction between internal party affairs and actions that are external (whatever that might mean), but perhaps Justice Breyer's opinion in *Morse* can be interpreted as moving in that direction. Justice Breyer thought that the Virginia Republican convention was sufficiently like a primary to fall within the reasoning of the *White Primary Cases*. Perhaps the exclusion of a group or an individual from a convention for ideological reasons would be sufficiently different from a primary that the party's action would be constitutionally protected.

---

49. *Id.* at 3, 4–5.

50. 940 S.W.2d 86 (Tex. 1997).

C. Political Parties' Associational Rights

1. The Right to Associate . . . and Not to Associate

The First Amendment protects the people's ability not only to speak individually but also to "assemble" and to make use of the power that comes from speaking in groups. Political parties—associations of people who wish to influence government through their collective action—are prime examples of expressive associations, whose advocacy is constitutionally protected.[51] Unsurprisingly, then, the First Amendment protects a party's ability to articulate a message, to endorse candidates, and to advocate for its political ideals.[52] Further, the right includes not only the ability to band together for the purpose of expressing a message but also the right *not* to associate with those who might undermine, change, or dilute the message.

The Court has also recognized that threats to a group's ability to advocate for a message come not only from direct restraints on the group's expression but also from interferences with the group's internal organization and deliberations. Without the ability to discuss and develop a message, the right to express a message is meaningless. Thus, in *Eu v. San Francisco County Democratic Central Committee*, the Court not only struck down limits on the ability of party governing boards to endorse candidates but also struck down laws governing parties' internal structures. The challenged laws contained rules about the selection of members of parties' governing committees, required committee chairs to rotate between northern and southern California, and imposed other limits. The Court held that such limits interfered with parties' freedom of association because they "prevent[ed] the political parties from governing themselves with the structure they think best." Because the laws burdened the right of association, they could be sustained only if they satisfied strict scrutiny. The Court could find no compelling interest served by the laws, however, because they did nothing to ensure either "the integrity of the electoral process" or "the civil rights of party adherents."[53] Rather, the state appeared to be "substitut[ing] its judgment for that of the party as to the desirability of a particular internal party structure"—but such a purpose was itself an impermissible interference with parties' autonomy.[54]

---

51. *See, e.g.*, Kusper v. Pontikes, 414 U.S. 51, 56–57 (1973). Parties are by no means, however, the only kind of expressive association that has the First Amendment right to create and distribute a message free of government interference—including the interference that occurs when the government forces a group to associate with unwelcome outsiders. *See* Boy Scouts of Am. v. Dale, 530 U.S. 640 (2000) (holding that the Boy Scouts had a First Amendment right not to associate with a gay scout leader, who, in the view of the Boy Scouts, would have undermined the lesson of morality it wanted to inculcate).

52. *See, e.g.*, Eu v. San Francisco Cnty. Democratic Cent. Comm., 489 U.S. 214 (1989).

53. *Id.* at 231–32.

54. *Id.* at 232.

State rules affecting parties' ability to organize themselves and to choose their leaders present a rather obvious conflict with party members' First Amendment rights. Laws governing party primaries affect the process of choosing parties' standard-bearers—the persons who will most visibly articulate the parties' messages and who will have a powerful influence in crafting those messages. As a result, laws regulating primaries, including laws specifying who shall be permitted to vote in primaries, also implicate party members' right of association.

What about the choice to select leaders via primary elections in the first place? Does a party have a First Amendment right to decide to select its nominees by conventions, caucuses, primaries, or whatever other method it selects? Apparently not. The Court has stated, but never explained, that it was "too plain for argument" that states could require parties to choose their nominees by either primaries or conventions.[55] The Court has never explicitly questioned this conclusion, but it is worth noting that in 1974, when the Court made that statement, parties' right to the freedom of association was hardly recognized at all. After fifty years' development of First Amendment doctrine, states' ability to demand that parties use primaries or conventions is anything but "too plain for argument."

For the time being, however, parties can be made to use primaries. But the Court has interpreted the First Amendment to grant parties significant (though not total) autonomy in the rules governing who shall be permitted to vote in those primaries. In a long line of cases beginning with *Democratic Party of the United States v. Wisconsin ex rel. La Follette*,[56] the Court has recognized that participation in primaries affects party members' rights not to associate with others and to be free from state interference in the selection of their leaders.

Those rights, however, are in great tension with the *White Primary Cases*, discussed above in § B[2]. After all, *Smith v. Allwright* and *Terry v. Adams* do not simply *permit* states to force parties to open their primaries to voters whom the party would rather exclude but rather *require* states to restrict the parties' freedom in that way. The *White Primary Cases* involved race-based exclusions, of course, but it is not evident why that fact should matter. The Court held that parties were state actors when they excluded blacks from voting in primaries because of race; presumably parties are equally "the state" when they exclude someone because of ideology, party membership, or any other reason. And while ideologically based exclusions by state actors do not violate the Fifteenth Amendment, as race-based exclusions do, they might well violate the First Amendment. Quite obviously, a state could not exclude someone from voting on the ground that he is a Libertarian or an anti-war activist; if parties are really "the state," as *Smith v. Allwright* seems to say, they might not be able to exclude someone on those grounds either. Such a result, however, would undermine the very reason for the existence of parties and would, thus, seem to be as clear a violation of the freedom of association as could be imagined. Parties exist to promote an ideology; to maintain

55. Am. Party of Texas v. White, 415 U.S. 767, 781 (1974).
56. 450 U.S. 107 (1981).

that ideological identity, they need to be able to ensure that their leaders are not chosen by voters who have differing viewpoints.

As we have seen, current doctrine is unstable and full of inconsistencies. The Court has said that, as to race-based exclusions from primaries, the party is the state, and, therefore, its discrimination is unconstitutional; as to ideological exclusions, the party has some (but not complete) autonomy to set its own rules; and as to the ability to choose to use primaries or conventions, the party must follow the choice made by the state. The remainder of this section describes the progression of doctrine concerning party members' rights to associate with comrades and not to associate with opponents.

The materials in this section are presented mostly in chronological order, so you should pay attention to the precise issues presented in each of the cases. Some of the cases, for example, involve claims that the party has been forced to associate with outsiders; other cases involve a claim that the party has been prevented from associating with certain individuals. Take note of the Justices' respective views of those different issues and think about how the issues should fit together.

2. When the Party Wants a Closed Primary but the State Wants an Open Primary: *Democratic Party of the United States v. Wisconsin ex rel. La Follette*

Seven years after the Court announced that it was "too plain for argument" that states could require parties to use primaries, the Court held that Wisconsin could not require the Democratic Party to accept delegates to its 1980 national convention who were pledged to vote for the winner of that state's *open* primary. The case involved a conflict between the party's rules, which limited participation in the delegate-selection process to members of the party, and state law, which permitted members of other parties and independents to vote in the primaries. The delegates themselves (the party members who attended the national convention) were chosen at caucuses held after the primaries, but Wisconsin law required the delegates to vote at the convention in accordance with the results of the primary. So the delegates might share the views of the committed Democrats who selected them, but if the primary voters (including Democrats, Republicans, members of third parties, and independents) preferred a more moderate presidential nominee, then the state law required the delegates to vote for the moderate candidate.[57]

---

57. The Party's rule was adopted upon the recommendation of its McGovern-Fraser Commission, formed after the 1968 Democratic National Convention. The Commission complained that the participation of non-Democrats in delegate selection diluted the voice of members of the Party by moderating the Party's nominees and positions. Both Senator George McGovern and Representative Donald Fraser, who chaired the Commission, were quite liberal—which was to be expected because

The Court held that in a conflict between the party's rules and the state law, the party's rules trumped. The Court began by noting that the freedom not to associate with outsiders was essential, lest forced association "seriously distort [parties'] collective decisions."[58]

The Court disclaimed any intent to declare open primaries unconstitutional. In fact, the Court offered that states "may well" have a compelling interest in encouraging voter participation that is served by open primaries.[59] This case was different, the Court asserted, because it presented the question "whether, once Wisconsin has opened its Democratic Presidential preference primary to voters who do not publicly declare their party affiliation, it may then bind the National Party to honor the binding primary results. . . . "[60]

Despite the Court's cautionary language, however, its reasoning appeared to call into question any law that forced party members to choose nominees through a process that involved unwanted outsiders. That reasoning was strongly libertarian, stressing that it was for the party—not the state—to decide whether to choose its nominees through a process that included outsiders: "A political party's choice among the various ways of determining the makeup of a State's delegation to the party's national convention is protected by the Constitution."[61]

Justice Powell's dissent challenged the notion that major parties had associational rights that were undermined by open-primary laws. In his view, major parties were "relatively nonideological,"[62] and, therefore, they had little to lose from the participation of independents.[63] Rather, Justice Powell suggested that parties could even benefit from such laws, by "enlarg[ing] the support for a party at the general election."[64] The majority responded that it was for the party to determine whether the advantages of involving outsiders exceeded the disadvantages; even if the party's choice were believed to be "unwise or irrational," the choice would still be for the party to make.[65]

---

the Commission's members were chosen by the chairman of the Democratic National Committee. Not coincidentally, the rules championed by the Commission favored ideologically extreme candidates, and McGovern himself won the Democratic nomination in 1972, the first year under the new rules. Ideologically extreme candidates are at a disadvantage in the general election, however, as McGovern and the Democrats found out when they were trounced by Richard Nixon.

58. 450 U.S. at 122. *See also id.* ("[T]he freedom to associate for the 'common advancement of political beliefs' necessarily presupposes the freedom to identify the people who constitute the association, and to limit the association to those people only.") (quoting *Kusper v. Pontikes*, 414 U.S. 51, 56 (1973)).

59. 450 U.S. at 121.

60. *Id.* at 120.

61. *Id.* at 124.

62. *Id.* at 134 n.9 (Powell, J., dissenting).

63. *See id.* at 132.

64. *Id.* at 133.

65. *Id.* at 124 (opinion of the Court).

3. When the Party Wants a Semi-Closed Primary but the State Wants a Closed Primary: *Tashjian v. Republican Party of Connecticut*

In *Tashjian v. Republican Party of Connecticut*, the Supreme Court invalidated a Connecticut law that forced parties to use closed primaries. In the process, it expanded parties' First Amendment right to autonomy in their decisionmaking processes and in fashioning their constitutionally protected expression.[66] Thus, between *Democratic Party* and *Tashjian*, the Court held both that parties had a right to limit primaries to party members despite a state law inviting nonmembers to participate and that parties had a right to invite independents to participate in their primaries despite a state law limiting participation to only party members.

As with *Democratic Party*, *Tashjian* relied on party members' First Amendment right to promote "common political goals" through their association with like-minded comrades.[67] Connecticut's closed-primary law interfered with this right, the Court said, because it "limit[ed] the Party's associational opportunities at the crucial juncture at which the appeal to common principles may be translated into concerted action, and hence to political power in the community."[68]

In dissent, Justice Scalia protested that the case did not involve the ability of party members to associate with each other; rather, the party wanted to invite nonmembers to participate in the party's primaries without having them become members of the party. Accordingly, he questioned whether such a fleeting association between the party and the nonmember primary voter was protected by the First Amendment.[69] The Court countered that party membership is "merely one element in the continuum of participation in Party affairs, and need not be in any sense the most important."[70] As the Court suggested, a person may associate with a party, even without becoming a member of the party, by speaking in support of its candidates, contributing money, attending meetings, displaying signs, or by voting.[71]

The state defended its law by arguing that closed primaries were better for the party because it prevented the party from being influenced by outsiders, but the Court ruled that it was not the state's business to "protect[] the integrity of the Party against the Party itself."[72] In other words, it should be the choice of *the party*, not of the state, whether to prefer the ideological purity of closed primaries or the general-election

---

66. 479 U.S. 208 (1986).
67. *Id.* at 215.
68. *Id.* at 216.
69. *Id.* at 235 (Scalia, J., dissenting).
70. *Id.* at 215 (opinion of the Court).
71. *Id.*
72. *Id.* at 224.

advantage that might result from the participation of nonmembers in the party's primaries.

Connecticut also alleged that closed primaries helped to keep the costs of primaries down and limited voter confusion by ensuring that party nominees agreed with the party's ideology, but the Court was unmoved. While the Court acknowledged that both of those interests were legitimate, the Court held that neither was a sufficient reason to limit parties' First Amendment rights. As to costs, the Court held that states did not have to fund primaries at all, but it could not fund primaries that interfered with the party's freedom of association. As to voter confusion, the Court was content to rely on voters' ability to inform themselves about candidates through means other than party labels.[73]

4. When the Party Wants a Closed Primary but the State Wants a Blanket Primary: *California Democratic Party v. Jones*

Justice Scalia dissented in *Tashjian*, but he wrote the opinion of the Court in *California Democratic Party v. Jones*, the next important case concerning parties' associational rights.[74] *California Democratic* held unconstitutional the state's blanket primary because it, like the Wisconsin law in *Democratic Party v. La Follette*, forced the party to accept the participation of outsiders in the selection of its leaders.

A blanket primary resembles an open primary in that members of one party may vote in the primary election of a different party. The difference is this: Voters in an open primary receive a ballot allowing them to vote in a single party's primary for all offices. In a blanket primary, voters receive a ballot that permits them to vote in one party's primary for one office and a different party's primary for a different office.

California Democratic followed *Democratic Party v. La Follette* and *Tashjian* in holding that "a corollary of the right to associate is the right not to associate."[75] And *California Democratic* continued to follow those earlier cases in stressing the particular importance of protecting the "right not to associate" when parties choose their nominees and select the positions they will take on policy issues.[76]

California Democratic explained, in more detail than did any earlier case, the potential danger to parties' identities posed by laws that force parties to involve outsiders in choosing their nominees. As the Court noted, the California law was a conscious attempt to nominate more moderate candidates than the ones who would be favored by party members, who are typically more ideologically extreme than the electorate as a whole. (Note that this rationale is the mirror image of the one favored by the

73. *See id.* at 219–20.

74. 530 U.S. 567 (2000).

75. *Id.* at 574.

76. *See id.* at 575–76.

McGovern-Fraser Commission and adopted by the national Democratic Party, leading to *Democratic Party v. La Follette*.) Thus, the blanket primary would force parties to nominate candidates other than the ones that members of the party would choose. Such a manipulation of the nomination process "has the likely outcome—indeed, in this case the *intended* outcome—of changing the parties' message. We can think of no heavier burden on a political party's associational freedom."[77]

Such burdens must satisfy strict scrutiny to be constitutional, and the Court found each of the state's justifications wanting. The Court placed the state's arguments in two categories. In the first, the state tried to argue that it had compelling interests in producing moderate candidates and giving unaffiliated voters the ability to influence primary elections. The Court rejected these interests out of hand, as they were just different ways of saying that the state wanted to interfere with the parties' messages. The interests in the second category were more generally phrased (they consisted of "promoting fairness, affording voters greater choice, increasing voter participation, and protecting privacy"), but they, too, were largely just alternate ways of claiming an interest in producing more moderate nominees (who, presumably, would provide more choice and, thus, more fairness for unaffiliated voters).[78]

Even if the state had a compelling interest in supporting an electoral system that favored moderate candidates, the Court stressed that there was a more narrowly tailored way of achieving that benefit: a nonpartisan blanket primary. Such a "primary" is really the first stage in a run-off election. Like a traditional primary election, a nonpartisan blanket primary winnows the field of candidates to a small number (generally two). Unlike a traditional party primary, however, a nonpartisan blanket "primary" does not designate those two remaining candidates as the nominees of parties. That is, they compete in the (run-off) general election not as party nominees but as the candidates who received the most votes in the preliminary election. Such a system, the Court explained, "has all the characteristics of the partisan blanket primary, save the constitutionally crucial one: Primary voters are not choosing a party's nominee [and are thus not] severely burdening a political party's First Amendment right of association."[79]

Justice Stevens dissented. He argued that parties' right not to associate should not overcome individuals' ability to vote for the candidates of their choice. He pointed out that the *White Primary Cases* held that the Democratic Party had to permit blacks to vote in their primaries—therefore, blacks' right to vote superseded whatever right the party had to exclude unwanted voters.[80] Aside from the effect of the *White Primary Cases*, Justice Stevens appeared to object to the very existence of what he referred to as "[t]he so-called 'right not to associate'"[81]—at least as applied to elections. In his

---

77. *Id.* at 581–82.

78. *See id.* at 582–85.

79. *Id.* at 585–86.

80. The Court responded that the *White Primary Cases* "simply prevent exclusion that violates some independent constitutional proscription"—a holding that the majority thought irrelevant when the basis for exclusion was not race but party membership. *Id.* at 573 n.5.

81. *Id.* at 595 (Stevens, J., dissenting).

view, the Constitution should not have been interpreted to interpose any bar to states' laws that "broaden voter access to state-run, state-financed elections" and "expand the ability of individuals to participate in the democratic process."[82]

One crucial unresolved question after *California Democratic* is the status of open primaries. As noted, the Court held that parties' right not to associate was unconstitutionally abridged by the blanket primary because the involvement of nonparty members would threaten to change the parties' messages or the individuals who would be leading those parties and championing their messages. Open primaries present the same potential, and so they may also be unconstitutional. *California Democratic* did not, however, drop that other shoe. Instead, it dropped a footnote in which it put the constitutionality of open primaries to the side. In the footnote, the Court suggested that perhaps open primaries could be constitutional despite the reasoning in the rest of the opinion. Its suggestion was based on the fact that voters in open primaries are "limited to voting for candidates of [one] party."[83] Perhaps, the Court mused, limiting one's choices to a single party might "'fairly . . . be described as an act of affiliation with the'" party, whereas a blanket primary does not involve even that level of commitment.[84] The remainder of *California Democratic*, however, focused on the *party's* right *not* to associate, suggesting that even if an open-primary voter did seek to "affiliat[e]" with the party, such an affiliation could be unconstitutional if the party did not want to associate with the voter. In any event, the Court concluded, "[t]his case does not require us to determine the constitutionality of open primaries."[85]

5. When the Party Wants an Open Primary but the State Wants a Semi-Closed Primary: *Clingman v. Beaver*

In a surprising decision issued only five years after *California Democratic*, the Court in *Clingman v. Beaver*[86] appeared to backtrack from its strong protection of parties' associational freedom—particularly from *Tashjian*'s recognition of parties' right to associate with nonmembers. *Tashjian* held that a party had a right to invite independents to participate in its primaries. The Oklahoma law challenged in *Beaver* permitted parties to invite independents to vote in their primaries but forbade them

---

82. *Id.* at 595–96.

83. *Id.* at 577 (opinion of the Court).

84. *Id.* at 577 n.8 (quoting *Democratic Party of the United States v. Wisconsin ex rel. La Follette*, 450 U.S. 107, 130 n.2 (Powell, J., dissenting)).

85. 530 U.S. at 577 n.8. *Democratic Party v. La Follette* involved the constitutionality of open primaries, but as discussed in § C[2], *supra*, the Court's conclusion appeared limited to the constitutionality of a law that imposed a requirement on national delegates to vote in a certain way, *i.e.*, in accordance with the results of the state's open primary. As the Court explained in *California Democratic*, *Democratic Party*'s reason for holding that such a rule violated the party's associational rights suggested that the primary itself was unconstitutional. *See California Democratic*, 530 U.S. at 576 & n.7.

86. 544 U.S. 581 (2005).

from inviting members of other parties. That is to say, Oklahoma law provided for semi-closed primaries, but the party wished to run an open primary. *Beaver* upheld the Oklahoma law, holding that it imposed only a minor burden on parties' association—a burden that was justified by the state interests offered to justify it.[87]

Citing the *dissent* in *Tashjian*, the *Beaver* Court minimized both the parties' interest in associating with members of other parties and the voters' interest in associating with parties other than the ones of which they were members. Note, however, that *Tashjian* held that parties had a constitutionally protected interest in associating with people who were unwilling to join and that voters had a constitutionally protected interest in associating with parties that they were unwilling to join. In *Tashjian*'s words, "The Party's attempt to broaden the base of public participation in and support for its activities is conduct undeniably central to the exercise of the right of association."[88] In the *Beaver* Court's view, however, "a voter who is unwilling to disaffiliate from another party to vote in [a party's] primary forms little 'association' with the [party]—nor the [party] with him."[89]

Although *Beaver* seemed to disapprove of *Tashjian*'s analysis (perhaps unsurprising, since by the time of *Beaver*, none of the members of the *Tashjian* majority remained on the Court), *Beaver* distinguished that case and did not overrule it. *Beaver* noted that while the Connecticut law in *Tashjian* required voters wishing to vote in a party's primary to join the party, Oklahoma's law required only that the voters register as independents.

Calling the associational burden on the party "minimal[]," *Beaver* refused to apply strict scrutiny to the Oklahoma law and upheld it by citing some of the same interests that *Tashjian* found inadequate. The first such interest was in protecting the identity of parties and in ensuring that voters were not misled by having parties nominate candidates who were not representative of the party's prevailing ideology. This interest was the same one that *Tashjian* derided as "protect[ing] the integrity of the Party against the Party itself."[90] The second interest accepted by the Court as justifying Oklahoma's semi-closed primary was aiding parties in communicating with supporters by ensuring that voters' party affiliations reflected their political preferences. The third interest—again, one considered and rejected in *Tashjian*—was in preventing party raiding, *i.e.*, voting in a different party's primary so as to cause the party to select a nominee who would be easy to defeat in the general election.

Justice Stevens dissented in an opinion that was joined in full by Justice Ginsburg and joined in part by Justice Souter. The dissent argued that the Court's opinion was inconsistent with *Tashjian*, and it also argued that the Court gave insufficient protection to the right to vote—a contention that Justice Stevens had earlier made

---

87. *Id.* at 587.

88. Tashjian v. Republican Party of Conn., 479 U.S. 208, 214 (1986).

89. 544 U.S. at 589 (citing *Tashjian*, 479 U.S. at 235 (Scalia, J., dissenting)). *See also* 544 U.S. at 592 ("[R]equiring voters to register with a party prior to participating in the party's primary [which is what the unconstitutional law in *Tashjian* required] minimally burdens voters' associational rights.").

90. 479 U.S. at 224.

unsuccessfully in *California Democratic*. In Justice Stevens's view, the state had no significant interest in preventing willing voters from associating with willing parties, and so the parties' interests and the voters' interests should have prevailed.

Justice O'Connor wrote a concurrence that was joined by Justice Breyer. Despite her conclusion that the Oklahoma law was justified by the state's regulatory interests, she contended that voters had a constitutionally protected interest in maintaining associations with multiple parties, just as parties had an associational interest in inviting nonmembers to participate in party functions, including primaries. That said, Justice O'Connor conceded that such multiple associations could be limited by, for example, laws forbidding individuals from joining multiple parties or forbidding voters from voting in multiple primaries. Thus, even for Justice O'Connor, individuals' associations with parties could be limited in ways that would presumably be unconstitutional if applied to interest groups or, indeed, any organizations other than parties. That result is curious, given the preferred position that political speech and association are supposed to receive under the First Amendment.

To summarize, after *Clingman v. Beaver*, parties have the right to invite independents to participate in their primaries, even if state law prescribes closed primaries. However, parties have no right to invite members of other parties to vote in primaries. It is likely that, for most of the Court, this doctrinal fine line is more the result of the Justices' skepticism of the associational right established in *Tashjian* rather than any belief that there is a meaningful distinction between the associational rights implicated by closed and semi-closed primaries.

The Court's next entry into the area of parties' associational rights came when Washington State accepted the Court's invitation in *California Democratic* and adopted a version of the nonpartisan blanket primary described in that case.

6. When Candidates Want to Identify with Parties but the Parties Don't Want to Identify with the Candidates

California Democratic suggested that, by adopting a nonpartisan blanket primary, states could avoid interfering with parties' associational rights and still allow voters to participate in primaries regardless of party affiliation. Washington attempted to take advantage of that option, but its "top-two" primary contained a complication that brought the law to the Supreme Court. The ballots in the nonpartisan blanket primary contemplated in *California Democratic* would have had no mention of parties. The two candidates with the most votes would advance to the general election, but not as nominees of parties.

Washington's top-two primary, in which all voters could participate, likewise served a winnowing function by paring the general-election ballot to the top two candidates in the primary, regardless of party. However, Washington permitted each of the candidates in the primary to indicate a "party preference." The primary system was challenged as violating *California Democratic* because voters might equate a candidate's "party preference" with the party's endorsement. Thus, even though the top-two primary did not formally choose the parties' nominees, voters might believe that it did. Such a misperception would create a constitutional problem because, by advertising candidates' party preferences, the state's ballot would be forcing the parties to associate with the candidates. After all, although the candidates could use the ballot to express their party preferences, the parties could not use the ballot either to explain that they did *not* support the candidates or to indicate the candidates they *did* support.

The Supreme Court, in *Washington State Grange v. Washington State Republican Party*, rejected a facial challenge to the top-two primary.[91] The Court found the allegations about voter confusion to be "sheer speculation" because the challenge had been brought before it was clear whether the state would adequately explain that party preferences were not the same as party endorsements.[92] After the Supreme Court rejected the facial challenge and Washington implemented the top-two primary, the primary was back in court, this time the subject of an as-applied challenge. The Ninth Circuit rejected that challenge, too, and the Supreme Court denied *certiorari*.[93] The court of appeals held that confusion was not sufficiently likely to render the law unconstitutional, given that the ballot stated that the candidate "Prefers XYZ Party" and explained that a "candidate's preference does not imply that the candidate is nominated or endorsed by the party, or that the party approves of or associates with that candidate."

7. Summary

The disagreements between the Justices about the scope of parties' associational rights reflect differences in philosophy about the place of parties in the First Amendment and in our democratic structure.[94] Some Justices see parties as gatekeepers, institutions through which individuals must act in order to exercise political influence. Seeing parties in this way leads those Justices, as in *Smith v. Allwright* and *Terry v. Adams* (the last two *White Primary Cases*), to elevate voters' interests in accessing the political process above parties' interest in maintaining a uniform identity. Other Justices take a more libertarian approach to parties' associational rights. Those Justices are more likely to analogize parties to voluntary clubs, with the effect that they elevate party autonomy over the desires of nonmembers to influence those parties, their messages, or their candidates. Although cases such as *Tashjian* and *California Democratic* make some noises in that direction, they have not fully applied such a philosophy, and other cases, such as *Clingman v. Beaver*, make clear that states can

91. 552 U.S. 442 (2008).

92. *Id.* at 454.

93. Washington State Republican Party v. Washington State Grange, 676 F.3d 784 (9th Cir.), *cert. denied*, 568 U.S. 814 (2012).

94. *See* Nathaniel Persily & Bruce E. Cain, *The Legal Status of Political Parties: A Reassessment of Competing Paradigms*, 100 Colum. L. Rev. 775, 782–85 (2000).

restrict parties' associational liberty in ways that would probably be unconstitutional if applied to other organizations. Most notably, the Court has not retreated from its view that states can require parties to nominate their candidates in primaries. Thus, the Court's holdings cannot be placed within any single philosophy.

It is also worth asking whether the advantages that the state provides to parties should have any effect on the constitutionality of state laws regulating them. For example, states are under no obligation to guarantee parties' nominees a spot on the general-election ballot. And states are similarly under no obligation to pay for parties' primary elections, if that is how the parties select their nominees. If states do give parties those advantages, could the states then demand that parties give up some of their associational rights in exchange?[95] The cases are equivocal. On the one hand, if, as the *White Primary Cases* seem to hold, states give parties such advantages as to bring party primaries within the state-action doctrine, then one would think that the state should be able to override parties' exclusionary membership rules. And indeed that is what those cases hold by requiring parties to accept primary voters regardless of race. On the other hand, *California Democratic* held that a state could not require parties to open their primaries to nonmembers, even though the primaries were (as Justice Stevens noted) "state-run, state-financed elections" and the winners would receive automatic ballot access.[96]

Thus, we are left with the same ambivalence about parties with which we began our analysis. While parties are unquestionably entitled to some First Amendment protection, they also play an important role—one often dictated by law—in the political process. And as much as we deride partisanship and factionalism, it is undeniable that parties play a crucial role in organizing voters and other political actors. As a result, parties' associational rights have effects on the greater political system—effects that make it important to protect the ideological discussion and conflict resolution that parties facilitate but that also make it important to ensure that they do not shut off others' access to politics. The next chapter, which addresses laws governing third parties and independents, continues this theme.

---

95. *See* Dimino, *It's My Party and I'll Do What I Want To*, *supra* note 24.

96. California Democratic Party v. Jones, 530 U.S. 567, 595 (2000) (Stevens, J., dissenting).

Chapter 6
Ballot Access and Term Limits

A. Introduction

Prior to the late nineteenth century, government did not print ballots. Rather, voters might declare their preference orally, by dropping markers of some type in a box, or, most commonly, by writing the name of their preferred candidates on a piece of paper and depositing it in the ballot box. To facilitate voting by their adherents, and to avoid spelling or other errors that might nullify votes, parties soon began to distribute ballots with the names of their candidates already listed and marked, which a voter could simply drop in the box. (Eventually these ballots came to be printed on colored paper, which had the added advantage—to the parties, anyway—of allowing party whips to see how a person was voting by noting the color of the paper placed in the box). These ballots were called "tickets," a term which survives today and is used when people speak of voting for the Democratic or Republican ticket.

The "Australian ballot"—the government-printed ballot we know today, first adopted in Tasmania around 1856—was implemented statewide by Massachusetts in 1888 and then quickly adopted across the United States. It was believed that a pre-printed ballot listing all qualified candidates would reduce bribery and coercion (party whips could no longer verify a person's vote by the color of the ticket placed in the box) and allow candidates to compete on more even terms, since candidates would no longer need large sums of money simply to print tickets to distribute to voters in order to have a realistic chance to win. The ballot generally achieved the first goal but not the second, as candidates without major-party support still found themselves at a substantial disadvantage in campaigning, and the inexorable fear of "wasting" one's vote still pushed voters toward one of the two major-party candidates.

But if the Australian ballot was successful in combating fraud and intimidation, it created new legal dilemmas. Most notably, which candidates would appear on the ballot? In order to print accurate ballots, states had to develop criteria and deadlines by which candidates would file for or request a place on the ballot; and if the ballot became too cluttered with gadflies and hopeless candidates, it could create both the physical problem of including all candidates on one ballot and the practical confusion of actually making it harder for voters to weed through candidates and cast the vote they wished to make. Typically, these problems were resolved by requiring a candidate to pay a "filing fee" or gather a number of signatures supporting his candidacy, or both.

While it was originally thought that the Australian ballot would equalize campaigns by reducing the importance of spending money to print tickets or to inform voters of one's candidacy, a candidate denied a space on the ballot would typically be worse off competitively than he would be under the old system with no government-printed ballots at all. Legislative bodies—dominated by the major parties—quickly realized that they could reduce electoral competition from new or third parties and independent candidates by setting high thresholds merely to appear on the ballot. And the dilemma affected voters as well as candidates. If a candidate's name did not appear on the ballot, the voter would have to write it in, which was often difficult—and in some cases, impossible—on the machines developed to count the new standardized ballots.[1]

Today, most states guarantee a place on the ballot for the Republican and Democratic parties, typically by automatically placing on the ballot any party whose top candidate in a recent election (typically the candidate for President or Governor) received a percentage of the vote that Republicans and Democrats were likely to have met but other parties were not—typically something over 5%, and, in some cases, as much as 25 or 30%.

This chapter explores limitations on a state's ability to restrict a candidate or party's access to the ballot. Additionally, it covers efforts by states to place requirements on candidates for federal office beyond those specified in the Constitution—the most notable and common of which, by far, is through limiting terms of office.

B. Third Parties, Independent Candidates, and Ballot Access

Almost all laws governing elections in the United States are made by politicians who belong to one of the two major parties. And those laws, of course, have a powerful effect on election results. From laws defining who has the right to vote, to laws drawing district lines, to laws regulating campaign finance, politicians can use their lawmaking power to advance their (and their parties') prospects in future elections. Likewise, laws governing party structure and, especially, laws specifying which candidates shall be listed on general-election ballots have a large effect on the success and even viability of parties, as well as on the fortunes of independent candidates. Politicians belonging to the major parties, therefore, may construct rules that favor a two-party duopoly by making it difficult for minor parties and independents to challenge the dominance of the Democrats and the Republicans. This capacity for political

1. The history of the adoption of the Australian ballot and early ballot-access laws is summarized in Bradley A. Smith, *Judicial Protection of Ballot Access Rights*, 28 HARV. J. ON LEGIS. 167, 172–176 (1991).

self-dealing provides a reason for judges to use the Constitution to limit the ability of politicians to manipulate laws to favor their own interests. And indeed judges have done so. Those efforts, however, have opened the judges to criticism about the degree to which *they* have manipulated the political process.

1. Petition Requirements

The Supreme Court's foundational case protecting minor parties' access to the general-election ballot is *Williams v. Rhodes*.[2] *Williams* held unconstitutional Ohio's laws governing ballot access because, when those laws were considered together, they "ma[de] it virtually impossible for any party to qualify on the ballot except the Republican and Democratic Parties."[3]

Ohio had an extremely onerous signature requirement—15% of the number of voters in the last gubernatorial election—that a new party's presidential nominee had to satisfy in order to appear on the general-election ballot. The major parties, however, simply by polling 10% in the last gubernatorial election (which, of course, they were sure to do), could keep a spot on the general-election ballot without obtaining any signatures at all. Other Ohio laws added to this burden faced by minor parties by requiring all parties to choose party officials and convention delegates who have not voted in a different party's primary in the preceding four years. The effect of these rules—on top of the 15% signature requirement—was that "the new party would be required to have over twelve hundred members who had not previously voted in another party's primary, and who would be willing to serve as committeemen and delegates."[4]

The Court held that the combined effect of these laws violated the Equal Protection Clause because of the unequal burden they placed on minor parties' right of association and their supporters' right to an "effective[]" vote.[5] The Court's analysis explicitly tied those rights to ballot access, explaining that "the right to form a party . . . means little if a party can be kept off the ballot and thus denied an equal opportunity to win votes. So also, the right to vote is heavily burdened if that vote may be cast only for one of two parties at a time when other parties are clamoring for a place on the ballot."[6]

Ohio defended its laws as promoting the stability of a two-party system, but the Court responded that insulating the major parties from competition interfered with the "[c]ompetition in ideas and governmental policies [that] is at the core of our

2. 393 U.S. 23 (1968).

3. *Id.* at 25.

4. *Id.* at 25 n.1 (quoting Socialist Labor Party v. Rhodes, 290 F. Supp. 983, 995 (S.D. Ohio 1968) (three-judge court) (Kinneary, J., dissenting)).

5. 393 U.S. at 30.

6. *Id.* at 31. *See also id.* at 41 (Harlan, J., concurring in the result) ("[B]y denying the appellants any opportunity to participate in the procedure by which the President is selected, the State has eliminated the basic incentive that all political parties have for conducting such activities, thereby depriving appellants of much of the substance, if not the form, of their protected rights.").

electoral process and of the First Amendment freedoms."[7] Justice Douglas picked up on this theme in his concurrence, in which he stressed the value of vibrant third parties. Quoting an earlier opinion by Chief Justice Warren, Justice Douglas argued that "third parties are often important channels through which political dissent is aired: '... History has amply proved the virtue of political activity by minority, dissident groups, which innumerable times have been in the vanguard of democratic thought and whose programs were ultimately accepted.'"[8]

Ohio also pointed out that a three-way race might result in the selection of a candidate who gains a plurality of votes but is disfavored by a majority of voters. This result is known as the "spoiler effect" because a third-party candidate can draw votes away from the major-party candidate who is closer to the third-party candidate, thereby spoiling that candidate's chance of winning the election.

Consider an election between Candidate A and Candidate B, where 40% of voters favor Candidate A and 60% favor Candidate B. In a two-way race, Candidate B wins. Now, however, imagine that a third candidate enters the race. That third candidate, Candidate C, is close ideologically to Candidate B, so that while 40% of the voters still favor Candidate A, the other 60% wants *either* Candidate B or Candidate C. Under that scenario, a majority would prefer Candidate B to Candidate A, and a majority would prefer Candidate C to Candidate A. Nevertheless, if that majority splits its votes between Candidates B and C, the results could be that Candidates B and C would poll 30% each, but Candidate A—the candidate *least* favored by most of the voters—would win the election with 40% of the vote.

The *Williams* Court recognized that states do have an interest in avoiding the spoiler effect, but it held that they could not achieve that interest by "keep[ing] all political parties off the ballot until they have enough members to win," because doing so "would stifle the growth of all new parties working to increase their strength from year to year."[9] Similarly, although the state might have an interest in avoiding the confusion of having dozens of candidates and parties on the ballot, the Court held that a danger it termed merely "theoretically imaginable" could not "justify the immediate and crippling impact on the basic constitutional rights" to vote and associate.[10]

This conflict—between the stability of a two-party system and the vitality of a system where new parties and new ideas have ready access to the political system—is fundamental to the constitutional debates considered in this section. People who read the First Amendment or the Equal Protection Clause to protect third parties' ready access to the ballot tend to stress the value of adding third parties' voices to the political mix, or they stress the disadvantages of forcing independent voters or candidates to associate with major parties that don't reflect their beliefs. People who argue that the Constitution permits stronger limits on third parties' and independents' ballot access,

7. *Id.* at 32 (opinion of the Court).

8. *Id.* at 39 (Douglas, J., concurring) (quoting Sweezy v. New Hampshire, 354 U.S. 234, 250–51 (1957) (opinion of Warren, C.J.)).

9. *Id.* at 32 (opinion of the Court).

10. *Id.* at 33.

on the other hand, stress the stability inherent in channeling voters and candidates into two relatively moderate parties, as well as the need to combat the spoiler effect.

Williams certainly leaned toward the first of these positions, but it did not hold that Ohio must sacrifice the two-party system for the sake of third parties' rights. *Williams* did not even declare unconstitutional any particular law; rather, the Court held that "the totality of the Ohio restrictive laws taken as a whole" violated the Equal Protection Clause.[11] It is therefore difficult to extract a rule from *Williams*, and difficult for legislators and judges to know which laws will comply with constitutional requirements. The essential problem is that while it is clear that election laws can go too far in locking out third parties and protecting the two major parties, it is just as clear that "as a practical matter, there must be a substantial regulation of elections if they are to be fair and honest and if some sort of order, rather than chaos, is to accompany the democratic processes."[12]

The Court's next case, *Jenness v. Fortson*,[13] upheld Georgia's ballot-access laws against a *Williams*-based challenge but did little to clarify the doctrine.[14] The Georgia laws at issue in *Jenness* were unquestionably less restrictive than the Ohio ones struck down in *Williams*. Whereas Ohio's law featured a 15% signature requirement, Georgia's was only 5%, although Georgia required the signatures of 5% of the number of registered voters rather than, as was the case under Ohio law, the number of ballots cast in the last election. Perhaps more importantly, Georgia law featured none of the other restrictions that made it so hard to form a political party in Ohio; in fact, candidates who met the 5% requirement could have their names appear on Georgia's ballot without joining a party at all, whereas the Ohio law reserved ballot spaces for party nominees. Further, any eligible Georgia voter was eligible to sign petitions; signers did not need to pledge to support the candidate, and signers could sign multiple candidates' petitions. And if all efforts to place a candidate's name on the ballot failed, voters could still cast write-in ballots. All together, "Georgia's election laws, unlike Ohio's, d[id] not operate to freeze the political status quo,"[15] and, for that reason, the Court held that whatever burden they placed on voters' or candidates' rights was justified by "the interest, if no other, in avoiding confusion, deception, and even frustration of the democratic process at the general election."[16]

The availability of a write-in option is worth considering in isolation. It is difficult to understand how the Constitution could protect a right to vote for one's preferred candidate when that candidate is ineligible, has failed to meet the filing requirements, or simply does not want the office. And indeed the Court has held that there is no

---

11. *Id.* at 34.
12. Storer v. Brown, 415 U.S. 724, 730 (1974).
13. 403 U.S. 431 (1971).
14. The Court later admitted as much. *See Storer*, 415 U.S. at 730 ("[T]he rule fashioned by the Court to pass on constitutional challenges to specific provisions of election laws provides no litmus-paper test.... What the results of this process will be in any specific case may be very difficult to predict with great assurance.").
15. *Jenness*, 403 U.S. at 438.
16. *Id.* at 442.

constitutional right to a write-in ballot,[17] even "when other parties are clamoring for a place on the ballot," in the language of *Williams*.[18] It is doubtful, therefore, that voters could have any rights that are implicated by laws that keep their preferred candidates or parties off the ballot.

Even if voters do have some right to cast a vote for an alternative to the major-party candidates, that right would seem to be satisfied by the availability of a write-in option. Realistically, however, write-in candidates rarely have any chance of success. So if the voters not only have the right to vote for their preferred candidates but also have the right to give their candidates a decent chance of *winning*, then being able to write in those candidates' names is hardly satisfactory. But, *Williams* notwithstanding, there has never been a constitutional right to have one's favored candidate win elections. If everyone's favorite candidate had a spot on the ballot, ballots would be ridiculously long and candidates could win elections by polling a very small percentage of votes, which might interfere with the winning candidates' ability to govern after the election.

Likewise, when viewed from the perspective of candidates, there may well be a constitutional right to run for office, but not every candidate who wants an office can have the right to appear on the ballot or else ballots would be far too long. Surely there is no constitutional right to electoral success, or even to a significant chance of success. Most people who would like to hold public office have no chance of attaining it. On the other hand, the right to run for office—without the right to appear on the ballot—means little if only ballot-qualified candidates stand any chance of winning elections. Still, the hard truth is that, in an electoral system with single-member districts and plurality-winner elections, a major-party nomination is all but essential for anyone to win a general election—regardless of ballot-access rules.

This dominance of the two major parties is the effect of Duverger's Law, which holds that with single-member districts (that is, districts that elect a single representative) and with winners determined by a plurality vote (*i.e.*, with no run-off election necessary if no candidate receives a majority), two relatively centrist parties will dominate. Such domination is the result of the spoiler effect, discussed earlier, which predicts that third-party candidates will draw votes away from the major-party candidate most acceptable to people who favor the third-party candidate. In a plurality-winner system, drawing votes away from that major-party candidate will increase the chances that the other major-party candidate—the candidate least favored by the supporters of the third-party candidate—will win. Accordingly, voters will tend not to support third-party candidates in general elections, and those third parties will have a difficult time achieving electoral success; rather, voters will vote for whichever of the major-party candidates is the lesser of two evils, and major parties will continue to have success even as a large part of the electorate remains unsatisfied with the available choices.

---

17. *See* Burdick v. Takushi, 504 U.S. 428 (1992).
18. Williams v. Rhodes, 393 U.S. 23, 31 (1968).

An example may make this effect easier to understand. In 2000, the major-party presidential candidates were Republican George Bush and Democrat Al Gore. Green Party candidate Ralph Nader also ran. Most of Nader's supporters, if they had to choose, would have preferred Gore to Bush. The race between Bush and Gore was extremely close, with Bush ultimately prevailing in Florida, the state whose electoral votes would decide the election, by just over 500 votes. Nader received almost 100,000 votes. Had Nader not been in the race, it is virtually certain that Gore would have received more votes than Bush, and so Nader's participation resulted in the election of Bush—the least favored choice of Nader supporters, and the candidate who would have been *opposed* by a majority in a head-to-head race with Gore.

Duverger's Law provides that very basic elements of the electoral system itself—the use of the single-member district and the rule that the winner of the election is the candidate that receives the most votes—favor a two-party system. The example from the 2000 presidential election demonstrates not only why Duverger's Law works, but also why it might be a good thing to promote a two-party system so as to limit the spoiler effect.

Petition requirements, challenged in *Williams* and *Jenness*, advance states' legitimate interest in keeping ballots to a manageable length, but they can also add to the disadvantage faced by third parties and independents because of Duverger's Law. Petition requirements are not the only kind of election laws that obstruct third parties' and independents' success, however. We turn next to some of the other obstructions.

2. Sore-Loser Prohibitions

States often provide candidates two routes to a spot on the general election ballot. They may receive a spot on the ballot by winning a party's primary election, or they may seek to appear on the ballot as an independent candidate. Usually candidates have to choose only one of those two options, and states have implemented election laws to ensure that candidates do not run as independents in the general election after running and losing in a party's primary. Such laws permit primaries "to winnow out and finally reject all but the chosen candidates," so that the general election can be "reserved for major struggles [rather than] for continuing intraparty feuds."[19]

Storer v. Brown involved a challenge to such a law in California. The law in question prohibited candidates from appearing on the ballot as independents if they voted in the preceding primary or if they had been members of a party within a year of the primary, *i.e.*, within seventeen months of the general election. The Court upheld the law, and, in doing so, appeared to back away from the intense scrutiny that it applied in other cases. In a passage that has been repeated often in subsequent cases, the Court noted that "as a practical matter, there must be a substantial regulation of elections if they are to be fair and honest and if some sort of order, rather than chaos, is to

19. Storer v. Brown, 415 U.S. 724, 735 (1974).

accompany the democratic processes."[20] And *Storer* applied a more lenient standard than the usually fatal strict scrutiny, stressing the "hard judgments" involved in constitutional challenges to election laws and believing it to be "very unlikely that all or even a large portion of the state election laws would fail to pass muster."[21]

So, while the Court explained that the California law furthered a "compelling" interest in supporting the "stability of its political system" by discouraging "splintered parties and unrestrained factionalism," the Court did not apply strict scrutiny with its requirements of a compelling interest and narrow tailoring.[22] Rather than require the state law to be "narrowly tailored," it was enough that the law "further[ed]" the state interest.

On the other hand, an independent candidate's demand for ballot access received a much more friendly reception in *Anderson v. Celebrezze*.[23] John Anderson entered the Republican presidential primary in Ohio but then withdrew and sought to appear on the general-election ballot as an independent. Ohio had a sore-loser statute that would have prevented unsuccessful primary candidates from running as independents, but Anderson withdrew from the primary before the date that would have triggered the sore-loser statute. Anderson ran afoul of a different statute, however—one that required both independent candidates and candidates running for party nominations to declare their candidacies by a date in March.

The Court struck down the filing deadline as applied to independent candidates. Justice Stevens, writing for the Court, contended that the deadline—even though it applied to both independents and party candidates—discriminated against independents. The Court reached this counterintuitive conclusion by pointing out that although a party candidate would have to commit by March to running in the primary, the *party* would not have to commit to its candidate until the party's convention, which was set to occur in the summer. Thus, a party could take into account late-breaking developments in current events or previously unknown information about the candidates in making its selection of a nominee. "[T]hose voters whose political preferences lie outside the existing political parties," however, would be stuck with the candidates who committed in March to appearing on the ballot as independents.[24]

By handicapping independent candidacies in this way, the law "heavily burdened" independent voters' right to vote.[25] Moreover, the Court believed that such favoritism for the two major parties—far from supporting a noble interest in political stability—damaged the political system by "threaten[ing] to reduce diversity and competition in the marketplace of ideas."[26]

---

20. *Id.* at 730.
21. *Id.*
22. *Id.* at 736.
23. 460 U.S. 780 (1980).
24. *Id.* at 794.
25. *Id.* at 787 (quoting Williams v. Rhodes, 393 U.S. 23, 31 (1968)).
26. *Id.* at 794.

Significantly in terms of later doctrine (including challenges to voter-ID laws), the *Anderson* Court expanded on *Jenness*'s flexible test for assessing the constitutionality of election laws. As *Jenness* did, *Anderson* recognized that most election laws were constitutional, even though each law governing elections "inevitably affects—at least to some degree—the individual's right to vote and his right to associate with others for political ends."[27] Rather than create a two-tiered analysis, with strict scrutiny for certain laws and rational basis for others, *Anderson* adopted a sliding-scale test. The Court announced that "the State's important regulatory interests are generally sufficient to justify reasonable, nondiscriminatory restrictions."[28] But where the restrictions were not "reasonable" and "nondiscriminatory" (and the Court did not indicate what it meant by either of those terms), a more demanding (but, at the same time, vague) totality-of-the-circumstances approach would apply. In evaluating such laws, "a court must . . . first consider the character and magnitude of the asserted injury to the rights protected by the First and Fourteenth Amendments that the plaintiff seeks to vindicate. It then must identify and evaluate the precise interests put forward by the State as justifications for the burden imposed by its rule," including "the extent to which those interests make it necessary to burden the plaintiff's rights. Only after weighing all these factors is the reviewing court in a position to decide whether the challenged provision is unconstitutional."[29] Such a "test" is obviously flexible enough to allow a court to reach any outcome it desires in a particular case, so it does little either to constrain judicial discretion or to provide notice to states crafting election laws or to the people who must be bound by them.

3. Fusion Candidacies

The issue of third-party ballot access returned to the Court in 1997 with *Timmons v. Twin Cities Area New Party*.[30] At issue in *Timmons* was Minnesota's ban on fusion candidacies, *i.e.*, the nomination of the same candidate for the same office by two different parties. Both the Twin Cities Area New Party and the Democratic-Farmer-Labor Party nominated the same candidate, Andy Dawkins, for the state legislature, but Minnesota law forbade the same candidate from appearing on the ballot as the nominee of both parties. Because Dawkins had sought the major party's nomination first, the state refused to accept the New Party's request to list Dawkins on the general election ballot as the New Party's nominee.

Fusion helps minor parties because it counters the spoiler effect discussed in § B[1], *supra*. If minor parties are able to nominate the same candidates as the major party, then voters can signal their support for the ideologies of minor parties without "wasting" their votes on candidates who have no realistic chance of winning. For example, in a jurisdiction (such as New York) that allows fusion, Candidate X may be nominated

27. *Id.* at 788.
28. *Id.*
29. *Id.* at 789.
30. 520 U.S. 351 (1997).

by—and appear on the ballot as the nominee of—the Republican, Right to Life, and Libertarian Parties. That candidate may be opposed by Candidate Y, who is co-nominated by the Democratic and Green Parties. (In other races—even in other races on the same ballot—the Libertarians may nominate candidates who are also nominees of the Democratic Party. And in still other races, the third parties may nominate candidates who are not nominated by any other party.) The winner of the election is the candidate who receives the most votes when the votes on all his "lines" are added.

A voter who agrees with the philosophy of the Green Party may choose to vote for Candidate Y on the Green Party line, thus communicating not only the voter's support for Candidate Y but also the ideological reason for that support. Without fusion, the Green Party would have to choose between forgoing its ballot position and nominating a different candidate. If it chose the latter, the voter would then have to choose between supporting the Party and voting for a candidate who might have a realistic chance of winning.

But where third parties see fusion as a way of maintaining a meaningful political presence, others may see that presence as destabilizing. States may wish to ban fusion, therefore, as a way of promoting the two-party system and taking advantage of the spoiler effect to channel voters' preferences to the nominees of the major parties.

In *Timmons*, the Court upheld Minnesota's ban on fusion, concluding that the government's interests in the stability of the political system and "ballot integrity"—reserving ballots for use as "a means of choosing candidates [rather than as] a billboard for political advertising"[31]—justified the less-than-severe infringement on the minor party's rights presented by the fusion ban. The Court held that the burden was not a severe one because it did not directly prohibit the party from nominating its favored candidate: Parties could nominate whomever they wished, but their nominees could appear on the ballot only if they were not simultaneously the nominees of other parties. In the Court's view, a party was not "absolutely entitled to have its nominee appear on the ballot as that party's candidate.... That a particular individual may not appear on the ballot as a particular party's candidate does not severely burden that party's associational rights."[32]

Because the Court held that the party's rights were not severely burdened, it evaluated the constitutionality of the fusion ban by applying *Anderson*'s balancing test. The Court admitted that there were other ways the state could have protected its interests in political stability and ballot integrity, but because narrow tailoring was not required, the Court thought that the fusion ban was justified. Ballot integrity might be undermined if, without a fusion ban, third parties proliferated and major-party

31. *Id.* at 365. *See also id.* at 363 ("Ballots serve primarily to elect candidates, not as forums for political expression.").

32. *Id.* at 359. For more discussion of the difference between a party's associational right to act without interference from the state and its right to act without losing state-provided benefits, such as a place on the general-election ballot, see Michael R. Dimino, Sr., *It's My Party and I'll Do What I Want To: Political Parties, Unconstitutional Conditions, and the Freedom of Association*, 12 First Amend. L. Rev. 65, 84 (2013).

candidates tried to gain the nominations of faux parties (such as the "No New Taxes," "Conserve Our Environment," and "Stop Crime Now" parties) that served just to associate the candidate with "popular slogans and catchphrases."[33] And political stability might be threatened merely by the "factionalism" represented by the existence of multiple viable parties.

Justice Stevens, who had written the pro-third-party opinion in *Anderson*, dissented in *Timmons*. He would have held that the fusion ban put the parties to a choice that amounted to a significant burden on the party's constitutional rights. The ban forced a party to choose between nominating its first-choice candidate and forgoing its ballot line, on the one hand, and keeping its ballot line but nominating a different candidate, on the other. Because Justice Stevens viewed the law as imposing more of a burden than the majority did, he would have required the state to provide more of a justification. And when he evaluated the law, he found that the law did very little, if anything, to advance the interests in ballot integrity or political stability. Justice Stevens foresaw no risk that multiple minor parties would turn ballots into billboards, and he considered fusion to be (as the name implies) the "formulation of coalitions," rather than factionalism.[34]

As with many of the cases in this chapter, the Justices' opinions in *Timmons* reflect disagreement about the value of the two-party system and the corresponding value of the contributions of third parties to the vibrancy of a political system. It also reflects a disagreement about the purpose of ballots and elections more generally. While some Justices and policymakers see elections as opportunities for speech, most see elections in more practical terms as ways for the people to choose leaders and to decide on policies. Under this view, individuals and parties may have rights to speak and associate outside of the polling place, but they do not have a right to use a state-provided ballot to broadcast their messages.

C. Term Limits

1. Introduction

Federal and state constitutions and statutes often place limits on the number of consecutive (or nonconsecutive) times a candidate may continue to be reelected to the same office. At times, there were various informal norms that certain political offices would be subject to rotation, even without formal term limits. For example, Abraham Lincoln served only one term in the U.S. House of Representatives in the 1840s due to such an informal agreement. Until recently, most formal limits were restricted to executive offices. Most famously, the Twenty-Second Amendment to the U.S. Constitution, adopted in 1951 after Franklin Roosevelt was elected to four terms

33. 520 U.S. at 365.
34. *See id.* at 374–77 (Stevens, J., dissenting).

as President, limits Presidents to no more than two terms. Forty states place various term limits on their governors, as do 35% of major cities do for their mayors.[35]

Support for term limits grew and became more controversial in the 1990s, when twenty-four states adopted limits for state legislators and, in some cases, members of Congress from that state. Support for term limits has always been based on the notion that persons continually reelected to the same office unfairly or inappropriately aggrandize political power in ways that outweigh both the presumed advantage of greater experience and seniority and the right of voters to elect whom they want to office. This notion has gained particular currency in the past several decades, as members of Congress and state legislators have enjoyed little turnover and high reelection rates. Many argued that limiting legislative terms would lead to, among other things, fewer professional politicians, greater devotion to the public good, less spending, and less capture of public institutions by interest groups. Opponents of legislative term limits countered that such limits would degrade institutional memory and lead to the capture of less-experienced legislators by interest groups, staff, and bureaucrats, who are not affected by term limits.[36]

The empirical literature has not reached a consensus on whether the hopes of term-limits sympathizers or the fears of their opponents have been realized. One term-limits sympathizer has described the empirical studies of the effects of the limits as a "mixed bag of positives and negatives."[37]

2. The Constitutionality of Term-Limiting Members of Congress

The U.S. Constitution sets forth qualifications for the members of the House of Representatives and of the Senate. It provides that the members shall be at least 25 and 30 years old, citizens of the United States for seven and nine years, respectively, and inhabitants of the state they represent.[38] For decades, states have added qualifications, including term limits, to the Constitution's list of requirements for members of Congress. Throughout the twentieth century, federal and state courts routinely struck

35. *See* Einer Elhauge, *Are Term Limits Undemocratic?*, 64 U. Chi. L. Rev. 83 (1997); Robert Struble, Jr., *House Turnover and the Principle of Rotation*, 94 Pol. Sci. Q. 649 (1979–80).

36. For a sampling of the large popular and scholarly literature debating these points, see, *e.g.*, George F. Will, Restoration: Congress, Term Limits, and the Recovery of Deliberative Democracy (1992), and Elizabeth Garrett, *Term Limitations and the Myth of the Citizen-Legislator*, 81 Cornell L. Rev. 623 (1996).

37. Larry J. Sabato, A More Perfect Constitution 51 (2007). For a sampling of the large literature studying the effects of term limits at the state level, see, *e.g.*, John M. Carey *et al.*, *The Effects of Term Limits on State Legislators: A New Survey of the 50 States*, 31 Legis. Stud. Q. 105 (2006); H. Abbie Erler, *Legislative Term Limits and State Spending*, 133 Pub. Choice 479 (2007); Susan M. Miller *et al.*, *Reexamining the Institutional Effects of Term Limits in U.S. State Legislatures*, 36 Legis. Stud. Q. 71 (2012); Michael P. Olson & John C. Rogowski, *Legislative Term Limits and Polarization*, 82 J. Pol. 572 (2020); and Alexander Fouirnaies & Andrew B. Hall, *How Do Electoral Incentives Affect Legislator Behavior? Evidence from U.S. State Legislatures*, 166 Am. Pol. Sci. Rev. 662 (2022).

38. U.S. Const., art. I, § 2, cl. 2 (House of Representatives); art. I, § 3, cl. 3 (Senate).

down these additional requirements. The issue resurfaced in the 1990s when twenty-two states adopted term limits of various kinds for members of Congress, twenty-one by popular vote. The legality of these provisions was definitively resolved by the U.S. Supreme Court in 1995 in *U.S. Term Limits, Inc. v. Thornton.*[39]

That case began with the passage by popular vote of an amendment to the state constitution of Arkansas providing that persons elected to the U.S. House of Representatives or the Senate could not appear on the ballot after having been elected to three or two terms, respectively. Voters in that state successfully challenged the constitutionality of the new provisions in state court. The Supreme Court affirmed in a 5–4 decision.[40] The majority opinion by Justice Stevens began by observing that the case required the resolution of two questions: Does the Constitution forbid states to add to or alter qualifications found in the Constitution? And, if the answer to that question is yes, does it matter that the term limits were formulated as ballot-access restrictions, as opposed to outright disqualifications?

The majority answered the first question in the affirmative. It concluded that the power to add qualifications was not within the "original powers" of the states and, thus, not reserved to the states by the Tenth Amendment. Even if the states possessed some power in that regard, the Court concluded, the Framers intended the Constitution to be the exclusive source of qualifications. In reaching these conclusions, the Court focused on the "text and structure of the Constitution, the relevant historical materials and, most importantly, the 'basic principles of our democratic system.'"[41] The Court noted that a proposal to add term limits had been rejected at the Constitutional Convention. The Court also emphasized what it called the "egalitarian ideal" of making any citizen eligible for office. Moreover, the Court continued, the right to choose representatives belonged to the people, not to the states. With the sole exception of the limits found in the Qualifications Clauses, the Constitution "creates a uniform national body representing the interests of a single people."[42]

The majority then answered the second question in the negative. It is true that the Elections Clause permits states to regulate the "Times, Places and Manner" of elections to Congress.[43] But that provision empowers states to regulate only the procedure of elections, not any substantive qualifications. The Arkansas referendum was thus an "indirect attempt" to accomplish what the state could not do directly.[44]

In an influential concurring opinion, Justice Kennedy memorably observed that federalism "was our Nation's own discovery. The Framers split the atom of sovereignty"

---

39. 514 U.S. 779 (1995).

40. There was not a split of judicial authority on the constitutionality of such term limits, but the Court mentioned that it granted review "[b]ecause of the importance of the issues[.]" *Id.* at 786.

41. 514 U.S. at 806 (quoting Powell v. McCormack, 395 U.S. 486, 548 (1969)).

42. *Id.* at 822.

43. U.S. Const., art. I, § 4, cl. 1.

44. In a footnote, the majority stated there was no constitutional significance to the Arkansas law's being adopted by popular vote rather than by the state legislature, since the voters were acting as citizens of Arkansas, "not as citizens of the National Government." 514 U.S. at 822 n.32.

by establishing two orders of government, "each protected from incursion by the other."[45] But here, he said, neither the Constitution nor historical materials permit state interference in the electoral process between the federal government and its citizens regarding the "federal right of citizenship."

Speaking for four dissenters, Justice Thomas emphasized that the Constitution, as he saw it, was silent on the issue of whether states could add to the qualifications of their representatives in Congress.[46] Given that silence, he argued, the proper default rule under the Tenth Amendment was that the "Federal Government lacks that power and the States enjoy it."[47] Justice Thomas saw no conflict between the qualifications listed in the Constitution and those imposed by states, because the state-imposed qualifications would be in addition to the federal ones, which would still have to be satisfied.

Further, the national character of Congress would not be undermined by term limits from individual states, he argued, since the Constitution contemplates that members of Congress would be chosen from within each state. Democratic principles, he continued, permit the people in each state by popular vote to decide who can represent them in Congress. The effect of the majority's decision, Justice Thomas said, was to protect incumbents, and it would only add to the incumbent advantage already found in the franking privilege and in various aspects of federal electoral law. He did not directly address the second issue discussed in the majority opinion (state regulation of election procedures), presumably because he found it unnecessary.

3. Other State Regulation of Qualifications for Federal Office

The majority in *U.S. Term Limits* took pains to distinguish regulations that merely protect the "integrity and regularity of the election process" from ones that bar certain people from running for office. The Court recognized that it had upheld other ballot-access requirements imposed by states,[48] but it distinguished them on the ground that "they regulated election *procedures* and did not even arguably impose any substantive qualification rendering a class of potential candidates ineligible for ballot position."[49] Regulations imposing a substantive bar on certain candidates' access to the ballot

---

45. *Id.* at 838 (Kennedy, J., concurring).

46. Although Article I, §2, clause 2, and Article I, §3, clause 3, are typically referred to as the "Qualifications Clauses," they do not, as a textual matter, provide that someone is qualified for office if he meets certain criteria. Rather, both Clauses say that "[n]o person shall be a [Representative/Senator] who shall not have" satisfied the requirements of age, citizenship, and state residency. Justice Thomas would have interpreted the Clauses as they appear on their faces—as minimum qualifications. The majority interpreted the enumeration of those qualifications to imply that they were exclusive, *i.e.*, they provided both a floor and a ceiling.

47. 514 U.S. at 848 (Thomas, J., dissenting).

48. *E.g.*, Storer v. Brown, 415 U.S. 724 (1974) (upholding a state law that made independent candidates ineligible for placement on the ballot if they had been members of an existing political party in the past primary season).

49. 514 U.S. at 835.

might, therefore, be subject to challenge after *U.S. Term Limits*, at least for elections to federal offices.

Unfortunately, it may not always be easy to tell the difference between procedural regulations (permissible under *U.S. Term Limits*) and substantive prohibitions (apparently unconstitutional after *U.S. Term Limits*). For example, one court struck down provisions of Colorado law that required seekers of federal office to be registered voters in that state before the term of office began. Applying *U.S. Term Limits*, the court concluded that the requirements do not merely winnow candidates for the ballot but impermissibly exclude certain types of candidates. They were thus substantive requirements of the type forbidden by *U.S. Term Limits*.[50] In another case, a court held that state recall provisions for members of Congress were invalid after *U.S. Term Limits*.[51]

4. Constitutionality of Term Limits for State Offices

While *U.S. Term Limits* placed considerable weight on the Qualifications Clauses of the Constitution, the broader principles applied by the Court might suggest that term limits for *state* officials also violate the Constitution. Courts that have addressed this issue have concluded that the analysis of *U.S. Term Limits* was limited to congressional offices.[52] Since most courts hold that the right to run for office is not a fundamental one, term limits for state offices are usually upheld under rational-basis scrutiny.[53]

D. Ballot Design and Indirect Election Manipulation

1. Ballot Language and Term Limits

In the wake of *U.S. Term Limits*, other cases have addressed whether states may use their authority to regulate the manner of elections to impose other regulations that deal in some way with term limits. One such case was the Supreme Court decision in *Cook v. Gralike*.[54] There, Missouri had passed an amendment to the state constitution which "instructed" each member of Missouri's congressional delegation to "to use all of his or her delegated powers to pass" an amendment to the U.S. Constitution permitting congressional term limits. Candidates who refused to follow the instruction would have that fact listed by the candidate's name on all primary- and

50. Campbell v. Davidson, 233 F.3d 1229 (10th Cir. 2000).
51. Comm. to Recall Robert Menendez v. Wells, 7 A.3d 720 (N.J. 2010).
52. Bates v. Jones, 131 F.3d 843 (9th Cir. 1997) (*en banc*).
53. *See, e.g.*, Kowall v. Benson, 18 F.4th 542, 548 (6th Cir. 2021); Fouts v. Warren City Council, 97 F.4th 459, 466 (6th Cir. 2024).
54. 531 U.S. 510 (2001).

general-election ballots. A candidate for congressional office challenged the provision in federal court. Lower courts struck it down, and the Supreme Court affirmed.[55]

Missouri argued that it was merely regulating the manner in which elections were held and disclosing information about candidates. The Court, in a lead opinion by Justice Stevens, disagreed. Following *U.S. Term Limits*, the Court held that Missouri's constitutional amendment was not a mere procedural regulation. The state law was not regulating the time, place, or manner of elections, as with measures dealing with notices, registration, supervision of voting, protection of voters, counting of votes, and publication of election returns, and suchlike. This state law, on the other hand, was "plainly designed to favor candidates who are willing to favor a particular type of term limits."[56] Since the state law was attempting to influence electoral outcomes, it was not permitted by the Elections Clause.

In a concurring opinion, Justice Kennedy emphasized that states may request specific action from Congress, but here the state was improperly interposing itself between the people and the national government. A separate concurring opinion by Chief Justice Rehnquist, joined by Justice O'Connor, concluded that the state law violated the First Amendment because a candidate, "once lawfully on the ballot, [has the right] to have his name appear unaccompanied by pejorative language." The ballot's language was not viewpoint-neutral, and the state thereby improperly interjected itself into the electoral process.[57]

Cook leaves open some questions about ballot language, even outside the term-limits context. For example, it is not clear how much, if at all, *Cook* applies to election for state office, or how robustly the First Amendment analysis advanced by Chief Justice Rehnquist's concurring opinion should be interpreted.[58]

A challenge relying on *Cook* was brought against New Jersey's apparently unique practice of grouping candidates not by the office sought but rather by the candidates' slogans. New Jersey law permits candidates to have their names appear on the ballot alongside a brief slogan, but some slogans (such as ones indicating the candidate's endorsement by party leadership) may not be used without permission. The result was that endorsed candidates received prime ballot position, making it especially difficult for challengers to prevail. Furthermore, certain slogans are reserved and can be used only if a political party endorses those candidates. The Third Circuit held that the practice likely violated the Elections Clause (and therefore affirmed the grant of

55. It is not clear why the Court agreed to hear the case. As it observed, there was no split of authority in the lower courts, but it stated review was granted due to "the importance of the case." *Id.* at 518.

56. *Id.* at 524.

57. *Id.* at 530–31 (Rehnquist, C.J., concurring in the judgment). Justice Thomas also concurred, stating that while he continued to believe *U.S. Term Limits* was wrongly decided, the parties were not contesting the premises of that decision.

58. For a discussion of these issues, see Matthew M. Mannix, Comment, *Opening Ballot Access to Political Outsiders: How Third Parties Could Use* Cook v. Gralike *to Challenge the Dominance of America's Two-Party System*, 11 Roger Williams U. L. Rev. 273 (2005).

a preliminary injunction) because it did not merely regulate the orderly process of elections but rather "put[] a thumb on the scale for preferred candidates."[59]

2. Other Challenges to Ballot Designs

As might be expected, a ballot typically lists in some manner the candidates or measures that are up for a vote and provides for the voter to indicate his preference. The precise nature and design of ballots have varied throughout American history and between states. As noted at the outset of this chapter, in the nineteenth century, it was not unusual for candidates and political parties to provide their own preprinted ballots. In the twentieth century, state governments came to monopolize the design and manufacture of ballots.[60]

The design of a ballot can be subject to constitutional challenge for giving certain candidates an unfair advantage. One example is *Anderson v. Martin*,[61] which involved a 1960 Louisiana law that required the race of a candidate for elective office to be designated on the ballot. Black candidates for office sued in federal court, arguing that the law violated, among other things, the Equal Protection Clause of the Fourteenth Amendment. The Supreme Court held for the plaintiffs, reasoning that "by placing a racial label on a candidate at the most crucial stage in the electoral process—the instant before the vote is cast—the State furnishes a vehicle by which racial prejudice may be so aroused as to operate against one group because of race and for another."[62] The state defended the law on the ground that it was merely supplying information to the electorate, and it further argued that the law was nondiscriminatory since it applied to all races. On the former argument, the Court responded that the information provided—the candidate's race—did not bear on the candidate's qualifications for office. Regarding the latter argument, the Court held that the "the alleged equality [was] superficial"—that while the races of white and black candidates would appear on the ballot, that designation was an advantage for white candidates and a disadvantage for black candidates.[63] In his concurring opinion in *Cook*, Chief Justice Rehnquist relied on *Anderson* and its conclusion that the state could not use the ballot to favor some candidates and to harm others.

Voters typically choose among the candidates or other options appearing on the ballot. Many states, but not all, also provide voters with the option of writing in the name of a candidate whose name is not listed. The write-in option has important

---

59. Kim v. Hanlon, 99 F.4th 140, 159 (3rd Cir. 2024). *See also* Mazo v. New Jersey Sec'y of State, 54 F.4th 124, 140 n.14 (3rd Cir. 2022) (noting, in a different challenge to the same law brought by a congressional candidate, that the usual deference afforded to state election law was not appropriate when the state practice violated the Elections Clause).

60. *See* Erik J. Engstrom & Jason M. Roberts, The Politics of Ballot Design: How States Shape American Democracy (2020).

61. 375 U.S. 399 (1965).

62. *Id.* at 402.

63. *Id.* at 404. The Court here cited the "repressive effect" of the law on black candidates for office, "in light of 'private attitudes and pressures' towards Negroes at the time of its enactment." *Id.* at 403.

benefits. Most obviously, it allows voters to express their dissatisfaction with the candidates appearing on the ballot. Writing-in a different name allows voters to cast a none-of-the-above vote and to send a message that is less ambiguous than simply choosing not to vote in that race. A write-in option also provides a backstop in the event that one of the listed candidates dies or withdraws close to the election or that some information about the candidate becomes known that makes him an unacceptable choice. Rather than being stuck with the other candidate(s) who have qualified for the ballot, voters in a jurisdiction allowing write-in votes can vote for someone else. Write-in candidacies rarely—but occasionally—succeed. Even in races for the U.S. Senate, write-in candidates have twice defeated candidates who have appeared on the ballot (Strom Thurmond in 1954 and Lisa Murkowski in 2010).

Despite these advantages, states are not required to allow write-in voting. The Supreme Court held in *Burdick v. Takushi* that a write-in ban "imposes only a limited burden on voters' rights to make free choices and to associate politically through the vote."[64] Accordingly, the ban was a constitutional way of discouraging "sore-loser candidacies," *i.e.*, general-election campaigns by candidates who lost their primaries or who failed to take the actions necessary to secure ballot access as independents.[65] Additionally, the Court noted that while ballots allow voters to communicate their views, they are not designed to be forums for expression. Thus, states were not required to allow voters to use their ballots to cast "protest votes."[66]

3. Qualification for Elective Office

Just as states have enacted a variety of requirements for persons to vote, states have passed a parallel set of requirements for persons to run for office. These include filing a petition with a certain number of signatures, paying a filing fee, and living in the state for a certain amount of time. State law also often specifies how political parties may nominate candidates, and provides various other restrictions and options.[67]

But just as there are constitutional limits to such requirements for voters, there are constitutional limits to the requirements that may be imposed on candidates for office. For example, we already saw that *U.S. Term Limits v. Thornton* prohibited states from adding to the U.S. Constitution's list of qualifications for congressional candidates. But who gets to decide whether a candidate satisfies the qualifications that *are* in the Constitution? A high-profile case presenting this question is *Trump v. Anderson*.[68] There, the state courts of Colorado had upheld determinations by election-

---

64. 504 U.S. 428, 439 (1992).

65. *Id.* at 439–40.

66. *See id.* at 438; *see also id.* at 445 (Kennedy, J., dissenting) ("[T]he purpose of casting, counting, and recording votes is to elect public officials, not to serve as a general forum for political expression.").

67. *See* Eugene D. Mazo, *Residency and Democracy: Durational Residency Requirements from the Framers to the Present*, 43 FLA. ST. U. L. REV. 611 (2017); David B. Allen, Note, *"It's a Sham!": How Sham Political Candidates Are Threatening Democracy*, 75 FLA. L. REV. 741 (2023).

68. 601 U.S. 100 (2024) (*per curiam*).

administration officials that Donald Trump was ineligible under the Constitution to appear on the Colorado primary ballot to run for President. The basis of that decision was that his actions on January 6, 2021, allegedly fomenting the riot in Congress when Electoral College votes were counted, made him ineligible under § 3 of the Fourteenth Amendment. That section provides that no person having taken an oath to support the Constitution may serve in federal office if he "engaged in insurrection or rebellion against the [United States]."

The Supreme Court unanimously reversed. The Court observed that § 3 was designed to prevent former Confederates from serving in Congress after the Civil War. Ordinarily, states have authority to establish the qualifications of their own officials, unless prohibited by the Constitution. Relying on *U.S. Term Limits*, the Court held that such authority did not extend to candidates for federal office. Assuming § 3 applied to the Presidency (*i.e.*, assuming the President holds an "office"), the Court advanced several reasons why states could not unilaterally exclude someone from federal (as opposed to state) office in these circumstances. Congress alone had the authority to enforce § 3, through statutes or otherwise; no constitutional provision delegated such authority to states; and permitting states to enforce § 3 would create a danger of a "patchwork" of different states coming to different conclusions on the eligibilty of a single candidate for national office. The last possibility might result in "[a]n evolving electoral map [that] could dramatically change the behavior of voters, parties, and States across the country," a result that the Court deemed especially inappropriate for a federal office elected nationwide.[69]

69. *Id.* at 116. Justice Barrett filed a concurring opinion, arguing that the states lacked the authority to enforce § 3 and finding it unnecessary to "address the complicated question whether federal legislation is the exclusive vehicle through which Section 3 can be enforced." *Id.* at 118 (Barrett, J., concurring). Similarly, Justice Sotomayor, joined by Justices Kagan and Jackson, concurred in the judgment, agreeing that state enforcement could lead to a "chaotic state-by-state patchwork" and criticizing the majority for unnecessarily opining "on which federal actors can enforce Section 3, and how they must do so." *Id.* at 119.

Chapter 7
Political Speech

A. Introduction

The First Amendment "has its fullest and most urgent application . . . to the conduct of campaigns for political office."[1] Accordingly, the constitutional protections of freedom of speech and freedom of the press are particularly important when speech about candidates and public issues is at stake.

Yet the importance of speech in determining electoral outcomes means that disinformation can produce particularly meaningful negative consequences. If voters are misled about issues or candidates, the outcome of elections—and thus, the country's policies—may be altered. Further, because people are not equal in their ability to communicate effectively and to distribute political messages, free speech results in unequal political influence. Thus, ironically, elections present both a compelling context for regulating speech and the most compelling context for protecting free speech.

This chapter considers several different areas in which free-speech questions arise, but does not include campaign finance regulation, which is covered in Chapter 8, or the right to speak anonymously, which is covered in Chapter 9. Some of the regulations encountered here do not deal overtly with elections, but the resulting cases are nonetheless significant for what they say about the constitutional protection of speech on matters of public concern. They form part of the foundation for understanding the First Amendment's application to electoral politics.

Although the First Amendment by its terms applies only to Congress, other branches of the federal government are also required to respect its strictures. Further, because the Supreme Court has long considered First Amendment rights to be "fundamental," it has extended the First Amendment's protections to the states through the Fourteenth Amendment, thus prohibiting state abridgements of speech rights.[2]

Most laws regulating conduct are evaluated under the rational-basis test, which requires only that the regulation be rationally related to some legitimate government interest. If a law restricts a fundamental liberty, however, it is evaluated under a different standard. Usually, a law restricting fundamental rights is unconstitutional

1. Monitor Patriot Co. v. Roy, 401 U.S. 265, 272 (1971).
2. *See* Fiske v. Kansas, 274 U.S. 380, 386–87 (1927).

unless the government satisfies strict scrutiny, meaning that the law must be the least-restrictive means available to achieve a compelling government interest. In other words, the government must be pursuing a goal that is extremely important, and there must be no way of achieving that goal without restricting the fundamental right at least as much as the challenged law does.

Although the freedom of speech is fundamental, strict scrutiny does not apply to all laws that limit people's ability to communicate. Given the variety of behaviors that people use to communicate ideas, applying strict scrutiny to all restrictions on communication would make it practically impossible for government to regulate all manner of conduct. Rather, the standard for evaluating speech restrictions depends on the character of the regulations.

Specifically, "content-based" regulations trigger strict scrutiny, but "content-neutral" regulations are evaluated under a kind of intermediate scrutiny. That intermediate-scrutiny test permits the government to regulate the time, place, or manner of speech if the government is motivated by a purpose unrelated to suppressing speech; if that government interest is significant; and if the regulation is narrowly tailored, leaving ample alternative channels for the speech.[3] It is important to note that "narrow tailoring" in this context is not as demanding as it is under strict scrutiny. A content-neutral speech restriction may be narrowly tailored even if it is not the least-speech-restrictive way of achieving the government's interest, making this narrow-tailoring requirement, in reality, more like a requirement of substantial tailoring.[4]

A content-based restriction is one in which the harm that the government seeks to prevent is related to the message of the speaker.[5] In other words, the harm that the government wants to avoid is caused by the message—the content—that the speaker is communicating. A content-neutral restriction, by contrast, seeks to achieve a result unrelated to the message of a given speaker. It is therefore crucial to identify the government's interest—*why* the speech is being limited. After identifying that interest, one must determine whether the government's interest is implicated only by speech containing certain content, or whether the government's interest is affected identically regardless of the message that is being communicated.

The classic example of a content-neutral speech restriction is a ban on sound trucks. Such a ban limits speech, but it does so in a content-neutral way because the harm the government seeks to prevent—the disturbances caused by noise—is unrelated to the message conveyed by the sound truck. Whether the sound truck conveys a political message, a commercial advertisement, or a public-service announcement, the harm is the same. Although content-neutral speech restrictions are more apt to be constitutional than content-based restrictions are, content-neutral restrictions must still pass intermediate scrutiny. The government cannot, for example, simply

---

3. *See, e.g.*, Ward v. Rock Against Racism, 491 U.S. 781 (1989); United States v. O'Brien, 391 U.S. 367 (1968).

4. *See Ward*, 491 U.S. at 798.

5. *See id.* at 791.

ban all speech within a certain area and defend the restriction on the ground that it is content-neutral.[6]

"Viewpoint-based" restrictions are a subset of content-based ones. Viewpoint-based restrictions not only differentiate between different kinds of speech depending on the message conveyed but also go further to advantage one side in a debate. A regulation applying to speech about taxes is content-based because only speech with tax-related content would be subject to the regulation. A regulation applying to speech "supporting *lower* taxes" would not only be content-based but also viewpoint-based, because it would leave speech opposing lower taxes unregulated. Viewpoint-based regulations are almost always unconstitutional.

Accordingly, the First Amendment's protection of the freedom of speech varies, depending on the kind of restriction imposed. In that way, the First Amendment contains not so much a guarantee that people will be able to speak freely but rather protection against government discrimination against certain kinds of speech. If the government is limiting conduct without speech content, the rational-basis test applies. If the government is regulating the time, place, or manner of speech for a reason unrelated to the content of the speech, intermediate scrutiny applies. If the government is restricting speech because of the content of the speech, strict scrutiny applies. And if the government is suppressing speech on the basis of the viewpoint expressed in the speech, the speech restriction is virtually *per se* unconstitutional.

Those rules apply to restrictions on forms of expression that are entitled to protection under the First Amendment. Certain categories of communication, however, have traditionally not been considered part of the freedom of speech. Those forms of communication are treated almost like any other form of conduct, meaning that the government can impose content-based limits without triggering the strict-scrutiny test. Categories of unprotected speech include obscenity, "fighting words," threats, incitement of illegal violence, and libel.[7] Even such "low-value speech," however, is sometimes entitled to constitutional protection—especially if a government regulation may in practice chill not only the low-value speech but other expression as well.

In *New York Times v. Sullivan*, for example, the Court struck down a libel judgment as inconsistent with the First Amendment. The Court reasoned that even though libel is constitutionally unprotected, speakers might refrain from exercising their rights to speak about public officials if the threat of libel suits were too great. Accordingly, the Court held that damages for libeling a public figure may be awarded only where the speaker knew that his statement was false or where he recognized a substantial risk that the statement was false and recklessly disregarded that risk.[8] As a result, libel suits brought by public figures are extremely difficult to win. Private figures, by contrast, may recover for libel if they show that the speaker was negligent.

---

6. *See* Bd. of Airport Comm'rs v. Jews for Jesus, Inc., 482 U.S. 569 (1987).
7. *See* Chaplinsky v. New Hampshire, 315 U.S. 568, 571–72 (1942).
8. 376 U.S. 254, 280 (1964).

Another area of unprotected speech is incitement to illegal action. Obviously, crimes committed through speech, such as fraud or perjury, are constitutionally unprotected. Similarly, solicitations to commit crimes are unprotected by the First Amendment. Much valuable political speech, however, contains messages that discuss the need for illegal action, even violence. The Supreme Court has held that incitements to violence may be suppressed only when they are intended to produce, and are likely to produce, imminent lawless action.[9]

As noted above, unless speech falls within one of those unprotected categories, government may not punish the speech because of its content unless the government satisfies strict scrutiny. Despite the government's interest in ensuring fair elections, restrictions on campaign-related speech are generally unconstitutional.[10] Even judicial candidates have a First Amendment right to announce their views in campaigns,[11] although the Supreme Court has held that some restrictions on judicial candidates' speech are permissible to guard against the appearance or reality that judges would favor the interests of people who donate to their campaigns.[12]

Media outlets have occasionally been targets of "fairness" rules when regulators fear that media coverage has the capacity to slant the public's perception of candidates or issues. For the most part, such restrictions have failed to pass constitutional review. An exception exists, however, for the regulation of broadcast media. Whereas regulation of newspaper editorializing has been held flatly unconstitutional, the Supreme Court upheld the Federal Communications Commission's (since repealed) requirement that radio and television broadcasters provide criticized persons a right to respond to alleged attacks.[13] The Court reasoned that the scarcity of broadcast frequencies made it impossible for every potential speaker to have access to the airwaves, and, therefore, broadcasters could be required to hold their licenses in the public interest and permit other members of the public to use their stations.

When government acts not as sovereign but as employer, it may sometimes condition employment on the employee's agreement not to engage in political speech—provided that the employee's speech would adversely affect the workplace. But where the government agency's performance is unaffected by the speech, the government may not discipline an employee for speech that opposes the government's policy or viewpoint.[14] The Court has held, however, that the government may impose limits on employees' First Amendment rights where public confidence in government demands that workers not be seen as having their jobs depend on support for those in power.[15] The dangers of a partisan government workforce are serious enough that the Court

---

9. Brandenburg v. Ohio, 395 U.S. 444, 447 (1969) (*per curiam*).

10. Brown v. Hartlage, 456 U.S. 45 (1982).

11. Republican Party of Minnesota v. White, 536 U.S. 765 (2002).

12. *See Williams-Yulee v. Florida Bar*, 575 U.S. 433 (2015).

13. *Compare* Miami Herald Pub. Co. v. Tornillo, 418 U.S. 241 (1974), *with* Red Lion Broadcasting Co. v. Fed. Communications Comm'n, 395 U.S. 367 (1969).

14. *See* Pickering v. Bd. of Education, 391 U.S. 563 (1968).

15. *See e.g.* Broadrick v. Oklahoma, 413 U.S. 601 (1973).

has further held that party loyalty may be the basis for personnel decisions only for positions for which party affiliation is "an appropriate requirement for the effective performance of the public office involved."[16]

The rest of this chapter explores these and other issues related to the regulation of political speech.

B. Defamation and Other False Statements

This is a chapter about political speech, so perhaps it is appropriate to begin with the constitutional protection for lies.

The First Amendment states that Congress "shall make no law . . . abridging the freedom of speech," but few would argue that the Amendment was intended to prohibit such longstanding common law claims as defamation. And indeed, the Supreme Court has long held that libel is not protected speech under the First Amendment.[17] What if, however, a politician or public figure threatened to sue you for defamation any time you criticized his actions? Even if you successfully defended each case, you might decide that future criticism was not worth the time and expense, let alone the risk that a jury might (erroneously?) find you liable for monetary damages. As a result, you might refrain (*i.e.*, you might be "chilled") from speaking, thereby depriving society of the benefit that comes from freely discussing the unspoken ideas.

In *New York Times v. Sullivan*, the Supreme Court held that such a "chilling effect" is reason to provide some degree of protection even to false speech. A group of persons, many "widely known," had taken out an ad in the *New York Times* that was critical of various public officials, including (by implication) Sullivan, a City Commissioner in Montgomery, Alabama. The ad charged that the officials had violated the rights of people who were advocating for racial equality. Sullivan sued for libel. It was ultimately conceded that "some of the statements" in the ad "were not accurate." The Court held that before a public official can recover damages in a defamation action, the official must prove "actual malice" on the part of the speaker.[18]

Under the actual-malice standard of *New York Times v. Sullivan*, the defendant-speaker must make the statement knowing it to be false or with reckless disregard for whether it is false or not. The reckless-disregard rule means that, to be liable, the speaker must be aware of a substantial risk that the statement is untrue. The speaker does not need to be certain (or even virtually certain) that the statement is false, nor must he intend to lie. However, the plaintiff must show more than that the speaker acted unreasonably or that a reasonable person would have confirmed the facts before

16. Branti v. Finkel, 445 U.S. 507 (1980).
17. *See, e.g.*, Near v. Minnesota, 283 U.S. 697, 715 (1931).
18. New York Times Co. v. Sullivan, 376 U.S. 254 (1964).

making the statement. The defendant-speaker himself must harbor those doubts about the truthfulness of the statement if the reckless-disregard standard is to be met.

The Court's theory in *Sullivan* was that potential speakers will choose not to speak at all rather than risk a lawsuit if it turns out that their criticisms were factually incorrect. The consequence would be that potential listeners and readers would be deprived of much truthful speech, and the political community would ultimately suffer from reduced discussion of public affairs. Thus, false speech receives some First Amendment protection, not primarily for its own value but rather because attempts to suppress false speech would result in the suppression of truthful speech as well. The Court further noted that even false statements make valuable contributions to debate by bringing about "the clearer perception and livelier impression of truth, produced by its collision with error."[19] In other words, we often know that true statements are true only by having them challenged by false statements. And, sometimes, things that were once orthodoxy—like the belief that the sun revolved around the earth—are proven false.

The ramifications of *New York Times v. Sullivan* go beyond defamation to broader efforts to limit false speech in political campaigns. In *Brown v. Hartlage*, a candidate for county commissioner promised that if he won the election, he would reduce his commissioner's salary. He was unable to keep that promise, however, as commissioners' salaries were set by the state, not the county. Because the promise could not be kept, the state courts concluded that the candidate committed an illegal campaign practice. The Supreme Court held that the statement was constitutionally protected, even if it might have misled some voters.[20] As the Court explained, punishing a candidate "for factual misstatements in the course of political debate is incompatible with the atmosphere of free discussion contemplated by the First Amendment in the context of political campaigns."[21]

More than a dozen states have some type of law regulating false statements in political campaigns. Courts have split on the constitutionality of such laws,[22] but their survival is certainly in question in the wake of *United State v. Alvarez*, which the Supreme Court decided in 2012. In *Alvarez*, the Supreme Court invalidated a federal statute that made it a criminal offense to claim falsely to have been awarded military honors.[23]

Although the statements in *Alvarez* were made outside the context of a political campaign, there is little reason to think there would be less protection for false campaign statements. Not only do campaign statements involve core First Amendment speech, but they also present the same danger of a chilling effect that is seen with penalties imposed on other types of speech. If political speech is chilled, society suffers from the self-suppression of speech that may turn out to be truthful. Further, limits on political

---

19. *Id.* at 279 (quoting John S. Mill, *On Liberty* 15 (Blackwell ed. 1947)).
20. 456 U.S. 45 (1982).
21. *Id.* at 61.
22. *Compare* Washington ex rel. Public Disclosure Comm'n v. 119 Vote No! Comm., 957 P.2d 691 (Wash. 1998) (holding statute unconstitutional), *with* Pestrak v. Ohio Elections Comm'n, 926 F.2d 573 (6th Cir. 1991) (holding statute constitutional).
23. 567 U.S. 709 (2012).

speech present a particularly acute risk that government will use false-statement laws to suppress speech for ideological or partisan reasons. In *Susan B. Anthony List v. Driehaus*, the first post-*Alvarez* case decided by a federal court, a congressman filed a complaint against an interest group that accused him of voting for taxpayer-funded abortion. Even though the group's accusation was arguably true (Congressman Driehaus voted for the Affordable Care Act, which lacks a prohibition on abortion funding and does fund abortion at least in cases of rape and incest), the Ohio Elections Commission pursued the complaint. The group sued, and the Sixth Circuit held that even if its statement were false, the group lacked actual malice and therefore could not be held liable.[24]

Generally speaking, courts have allowed the regulation of false statements only when necessary to vindicate private rights, as in cases of defamation, fraud, or invasion of privacy.[25] The Court appears to have adopted Justice Brandeis's view that "[i]f there be time to expose through discussion the falsehood and fallacies, to avert the evil by the processes of education, the remedy to be applied is more speech, not enforced silence."[26]

C. Violent Speech

Politics is a rough-and-tumble game. Emotions run high, and political speech sometimes expresses strong disagreement with opponents or their policies. Further, sometimes speakers can inspire others to act violently, even if the speakers wish to inspire only nonviolent action. Unfortunately, recent years have seen several examples of politically motivated violence, including the January 6, 2021, attack at the Capitol, two assassination attempts on then-candidate Donald Trump in 2024, and the 2022 attempted assassination of Supreme Court Justice Brett Kavanaugh.

Suppressing speech on the basis that it might lead to violence, however, could lead to the same kind of chilling effect discussed in connection with defamation. Speakers might shy away from harsh criticism of opponents, and the public's ability to discuss policies and political leaders would be hindered. At the same time, no one doubts that incendiary speech can lead to great harm, and few think the Constitution should protect explicit threats or solicitations to commit crime, such as violent assaults on political opponents.

The Supreme Court's answer to this dilemma is the *Brandenburg* test. Clarence Brandenburg was a Ku Klux Klan leader prosecuted by Ohio for inciting violence. Brandenburg had given a speech at a Klan rally in which he announced an upcoming march and in which he said that "there might have to be some revengeance taken" if government "continue[d] to suppress the white, Caucasian race." The Court reversed

24. 814 F.3d 466 (6th Cir. 2016).

25. *Id.* at 2545; *see also* Washington *ex rel.* Public Disclosure Comm'n v. 119 Vote No! Comm., 957 P.2d at 697.

26. Whitney v. California, 274 U.S. 357, 377 (1927) (Brandeis, J., concurring).

his conviction, announcing that "the constitutional guarantees of free speech and free press do not permit a State to forbid or proscribe advocacy of the use of force or of law violation except where such advocacy is directed to inciting or producing imminent lawless action and is likely to incite or produce such action."[27] The test resembles an earlier test identified with Justice Holmes, which would allow suppression of speech where there was a "clear and present danger" that the speech would lead to unlawful activity.[28] By requiring that the speech be *intended* ("directed") to lead to violence, that the violence be *likely*, and that the violence be *imminent*, the *Brandenburg* test makes it very difficult to suppress most political speech.

Two examples make the point. In *Hess v. Indiana*, the Supreme Court reversed the conviction of a man who was part of a protest that had blocked a street. When the street was cleared by sheriffs, Hess shouted, "We'll take the f*****g street later," or "We'll take the f*****g street again." The Supreme Court held that there was no demonstration that Hess was exhorting the crowd to engage in *imminent* illegal action.[29]

NAACP v. Claiborne Hardware Co. involved a boycott of white-owned stores and threats of violence against blacks who patronized the stores. One speaker said that boycott violators would be "disciplined" and warned that the sheriff would not be able to protect them. Another speaker flatly announced that anyone entering the white-owned stores would have his neck broken. The Court recognized that, in the context of the heated controversy surrounding the boycott, the speeches "might have been understood as inviting an unlawful form of discipline or, at least, as intending to create a fear of violence whether or not improper discipline was specifically intended."[30] Nevertheless, the Court held the speech to be protected: "Strong and effective extemporaneous rhetoric cannot be nicely channeled in purely dulcet phrases. An advocate must be free to stimulate his audience with spontaneous and emotional appeals for unity and action in a common cause."[31]

D. Media Coverage

1. Private Media

Candidates, voters, and interest groups are not the only players in elections. Of crucial importance as well is the institutional press. As you will see in the pages that follow, the courts have adopted differing approaches to the First Amendment rights of print and broadcast media.

Mills v. Alabama set forth the basic doctrine quite nicely. An Alabama statute prohibited election-day "electioneering," and the state sought to apply the law to an

---

27. Brandenburg v. Ohio, 395 U.S. 444, 447 (1969) (*per curiam*).
28. Schenck v. United States, 249 U.S. 47, 52 (1919) (Holmes, J.).
29. Hess v. Indiana, 414 U.S. 105 (1973).
30. NAACP v. Claiborne Hardware Co., 458 U.S. 886, 927 (1982).
31. *Id.* at 928.

election-morning newspaper editorial. The state argued that the law would protect voters from "confusive last minute charges and countercharges," when "such matters cannot be answered or their truth determined until after the election is over."[32] The Court made short work of this argument, noting that such a rule prevented responses to charges made the day before the cutoff. Beyond that, however, the Court adopted an absolutist approach, holding that "no test of reasonableness can save a state law from invalidation as a violation of the First Amendment when that law makes it a crime for a newspaper editor to do no more than urge people to vote one way or another in a publicly held election."[33]

When it comes to broadcasting, however, the Court's record is more mixed. Here the key case is *Red Lion Broadcasting Co. v. Federal Communications Commission.*[34] For many years prior to *Red Lion*, the FCC had developed and enforced what came to be known at the "Fairness Doctrine."[35] Under the Fairness Doctrine, if an attack were made on the "honesty, character, integrity or like personal qualities" of a person or group, the station was required to notify the attacked person or group of the broadcast and offer a "reasonable opportunity" to respond.[36] In opposition to the law, the broadcaster offered up the "chilling effect" rationale that had dominated *New York Times v. Sullivan*,[37] arguing that stations would shy away from covering public affairs if doing so would require them to offer free time to speakers with whom they disagreed. Unlike *Sullivan*, however, *Red Lion* demanded actual proof of a chilling effect (how might one prove that stations were not speaking?) and suggested that if the FCC found that the Fairness Doctrine had such an effect, it could simply mandate more public programming.[38]

Particularly important to the Court's *Red Lion* decision was the issue of spectrum scarcity—the concept that the number of broadcast frequencies in a given area is necessarily limited as a matter of physics because if there are too many broadcasters using similar frequencies, the signals will interfere with each other. The Court's decision is largely based on the rationale that because not everyone can use the electromagnetic spectrum, those broadcasters that the government permits to use it may be required to act in the public interest, including by allowing opposition voices to use the station's frequency.

---

32. 384 U.S. 214, 219–220 (1966).

33. *Id.* at 220.

34. 395 U.S. 367 (1969).

35. The Fairness Doctrine should not be confused with the equal-time requirements of the Federal Communications Act. The latter requires a station that makes its facilities available to a candidate, either for free or through paid advertising, to offer equal opportunities for other candidates in the race. In other words, if you sell ad time at a particular rate to one candidate, you must sell time at the same rate to the other candidate (although different rates for different time slots, due to market pricing, are allowed). The equal-time doctrine does not apply to bona fide newscasts and interviews. *See* 47 U.S.C. § 315. Although, as discussed *infra*, the FCC has repealed the Fairness Doctrine, the equal-time requirements remain in effect.

36. 395 U.S. at 373–74.

37. 376 U.S. 254; *see* § B, *supra*.

38. 395 U.S. at 392–93.

Red Lion has been vigorously criticized by commentators on several grounds, and its ongoing vitality is questionable. Continuing advancements in broadcast and cable technology, plus the rise of satellite and internet media, have rendered the scarcity argument increasingly dubious. In any event, in 1986, a federal appeals court held that the FCC was not required by statute to maintain the Fairness Doctrine.[39] The following year, the FCC repealed it,[40] having previously found that the Doctrine restricted coverage of controversial issues, reduced the diversity of views available to the public, and created opportunities for government officials to intimidate broadcasters. The FCC also found that significant changes in technology and the marketplace had led to a vast expansion in the number of stations available.[41]

Just five years after *Red Lion*, the "chilling effect" argument of *New York Times v. Sullivan* came roaring back, and the Court rejected an attempt to extend the "scarcity" argument to print media. In *Miami Herald Publishing Co. v. Tornillo*, the Court addressed a "right of reply" statute aimed at newspapers. A Florida law provided political candidates with a right to equal space to reply to criticism and attacks made by newspapers.[42] The *Miami Herald* complained that the right of reply violated its First Amendment right to decide what to print. Tornillo raised the scarcity issue (among other arguments), noting the concentration in the newspaper industry, which resulted in a substantially smaller number of newspapers, as well as the high financial barriers to entry in the modern news market. In a 9–0 decision, the Court rejected the argument. Meanwhile, the Court again invoked concerns about a "chilling effect," with the Court arguing that "[f]aced with the penalties that would accrue to any newspaper that published news or commentary arguably within the reach of the right-of-access statute, editors might well conclude that the safe course is to avoid controversy."[43]

So does the scarcity rationale live on? Could Congress reenact the Fairness Doctrine by statute? Perhaps. But the scarcity rationale would likely face an uphill battle today, whereas the "chilling effect" doctrine remains firmly ensconced in First Amendment law, including campaign finance cases.[44]

---

39. Telecommunications Research & Action Center v. Fed. Communications Comm'n, 801 F.2d 501, 516 (D.C. Cir. 1986), *cert. denied*, 482 U.S. 919 (1987).

40. *In re* Syracuse Peace Council, 2 F.C.C. Reg. 5043 (1987), *upheld in* Syracuse Peace Council v. Fed. Communications Comm'n, 867 F.2d 654 (D.C. Cir. 1989).

41. *See* Fed. Communications Comm'n, *General Fairness Doctrine Obligations of Broadcast Licensees*, 50 Fed. Reg. 35418 (Aug. 30, 1985).

42. Miami Herald Pub. Co. v. Tornillo, 418 U.S. 241 (1974).

43. *Id.* at 257.

44. *See, e.g.*, Davis v. Fed. Election Comm'n, 554 U.S. 724, 729 (2008); Brown v. Socialist Workers '74 Campaign Comm., 459 U.S. 87 (1982); Buckley v. Valeo, 424 U.S. 1, 68 (1976) (*per curiam*).

2. Publicly Subsidized Media

Mills v. Alabama and *Miami Herald Publishing Co. v. Tornillo* set out the doctrine that applies to privately owned print media. *Red Lion Broadcasting v. FCC*, to the extent it remains good law, sets forth rules for private broadcast media.[45] The situation becomes more complex once government subsidies enter the picture. May Congress, when it is providing funding, place conditions on the use of that funding for political purposes? And if government owns the broadcast medium, does it face added obligations to be even-handed?

In *Federal Communications Commission v. League of Women Voters*, the Supreme Court held unconstitutional a federal statute prohibiting editorializing by any station that received a grant from the Corporation for Public Broadcasting. The Court distinguished *Red Lion* by arguing that the earlier case involved a "narrowly tailored" statute that furthered a "compelling government interest" in "ensuring adequate and balanced coverage of public issues." The Court recognized that stations' dependence on government funding might lead to stations' becoming mouthpieces for the government but, by a 5–4 vote, held that such interests could be addressed by less than a total ban on editorializing.[46] As the principal dissent noted, the decision seems at odds with *Regan v. Taxation with Representation of Washington*, decided just months earlier, which held that Congress could condition the tax benefits of nonprofit status on the nonprofits' refraining from participating in any political activity.[47]

In line with *League of Women Voters*, the Court has also upheld the editorial discretion of public broadcasters in the context of political news coverage and, in particular, the sponsoring of candidate debates. The Court has held that even a state-owned broadcaster (as opposed to one that merely receives some government funding, as in *League of Women Voters*) is entitled to "journalistic discretion" in deciding which candidates to invite to participate in a candidate debate. In upholding a public television station's decision to exclude third-party candidates from debates, the Court held that it was within the station's power to limit the debate to the candidates of the two major parties.[48] The decision, of course, applies with equal force to private broadcasters, at least in light of the demise of the Fairness Doctrine. The Federal Election Commission receives complaints each election year regarding broadcasters' decisions to exclude minor-party candidates from televised debates, but these claims are generally precluded by the Court's jurisprudence in the area.

---

45. *See* § D[1], *supra*.

46. Fed. Communications Comm'n v. League of Women Voters, 468 U.S. 364 (1984).

47. *See id.* at 405 (Rehnquist, J. dissenting) (citing Regan v. Taxation with Representation of Wash., 461 U.S. 540 (1983)). *League of Women Voters* is especially interesting to consider in the context of campaign finance, particularly public financing. *See* 468 U.S. at 415 (Stevens, J., dissenting) (stressing the "overriding importance" of "keeping the Federal Government out of the propaganda arena"). Public financing of campaigns is discussed in Chapter 8, § H, *infra*.

48. Arkansas Educ. Television Comm'n v. Forbes, 523 U.S. 666 (1998).

E. Speech Near Polling Places

Campaign speech occupies the core of the First Amendment. And of all the times and places to engage in campaign speech, the most valuable might well be at polling places as voters are preparing to cast their ballots. Not only is that the last time to reach voters before the election, but the messages voters receive right before they enter the polls might be the ones at the forefront of their minds when making their final decisions.

As important as it is to speak near polling places and to access speech near polling places, speech at that time and place presents dangers that are greater than those presented elsewhere. In particular, speakers near polling places may intimidate potential voters, with the effect that some voters might stay away from the polls to avoid being exposed to the speech, and others' votes might be altered because the speakers have made the voters uncomfortable. Thus, ironically, speech near polling places may interfere with democracy, and limitations on such speech may advance democracy by protecting voters' access to the polls from the possibility of intimidation or harassment. Such a rationale is in stark contrast to the usual free speech philosophy, which holds that democracy is advanced through speech because informed voters are better able to make intelligent choices at the polls.

In *Burson v. Freeman*,[49] the Supreme Court upheld Tennessee's 100-foot campaign-free zone around its polling places. Within that zone, which included streets and sidewalks, the state law banned political speech, including not just in-person solicitation of voters but also the display and distribution of campaign materials. Other kinds of speech, such as commercial speech, were not restricted.

Because the law discriminated against political speech within traditional public fora,[50] the plurality opinion by Justice Blackmun applied strict scrutiny.[51] Or, rather, it *said* that it was applying strict scrutiny. The plurality's analysis was unusually deferential for an opinion applying strict scrutiny, particularly in its analysis of the narrow-tailoring prong. Tennessee argued that its law served two compelling interests: protecting voters' free choices and ensuring that the election system maintained "integrity and reliability,"[52] *i.e.*, that it was free of voter intimidation or fraud. There was little debate about the compelling nature of those interests;[53] the question was whether the campaign-free zone was a narrowly tailored way of achieving those interests.

---

49. 504 U.S. 191 (1992).

50. Justice Scalia's opinion concurring in the judgment argued that the long history of campaign-free zones around polling places rendered those areas nonpublic fora. *Id.* at 214–16 (Scalia, J., concurring in the judgment). Justice Thomas did not participate in the decision, so the Court's split was 4–1–3.

51. The plurality used "exacting scrutiny" as well as "strict scrutiny," but it described "exacting scrutiny" in the same terms that usually apply to strict scrutiny, *viz.*, it demanded that the state show that the law was narrowly tailored to a compelling interest. *See id.* at 198, 211 (plurality opinion). The plurality therefore was using the terms interchangeably.

52. *Id.* at 199.

53. The plurality considered the compelling nature of the state's interests to be "obvious[]." *Id.*

The law's challengers first argued that if the state wanted to stop intimidation and fraud, it could simply pass and enforce laws against intimidation and fraud. Establishing a campaign-free zone was a prophylactic way of preventing intimidation and fraud, but strict scrutiny usually prevents the government from adopting prophylactic bans on speech. In this case, however, the plurality concluded that laws that were limited to stopping intimidation and fraud might not be effective. In the first place, such laws would not capture subtle means of intimidation. In the second place, for law enforcement officials to detect violations, they would have to be stationed at the places where the intimidation would occur, but having police in or near polling places might itself be intimidating. Therefore, the plurality concluded that a campaign-free zone was necessary to guard against intimidation and fraud, and it proceeded to address whether the Tennessee law's 100-foot radius was narrowly tailored.

The plurality concluded that the 100-foot zone was narrowly tailored, but it provided no reasons for why a smaller zone would have been insufficient. In fact, some states did employ smaller campaign-free zones, but that fact did not matter to the plurality. In stark contrast to the Court's usual application of strict scrutiny, the plurality announced that the geographic scope of the zone was not "a question of 'constitutional dimension.'"[54]

The plurality completely ignored another narrow-tailoring problem presented by the statute: While some aspects of campaigning could be intimidating to voters, mere display of campaign materials—say, buttons or bumper stickers—could hardly be considered necessary to guard against intimidation. Justice Stevens hit upon this point in dissent, and he further argued that the plurality conflated history with necessity—that the plurality was willing to assume that campaign-free zones were necessary just because they have been common and longstanding.[55]

The Court subsequently considered and struck down a vague ban on political speech *inside* polling places. In *Minnesota Voters Alliance v. Mansky*, the Court noted that, unlike the streets and sidewalks outside polling places, the interior of a polling place is not a public forum. Accordingly, speech restrictions there could be content-based as long as they were reasonable and viewpoint-neutral. Despite the laxity of that test, the Minnesota law flunked because its ban on the display of "political" messages on apparel was too vague and expansive, potentially encompassing any topic on which a candidate had taken a position.[56] The ban was therefore "unreasonable" and unconstitutional, even when applied to a nonpublic forum.

In *dicta*, the Court suggested that a more specific ban on speech in a polling place, for example, one limited to displays of a candidate's name or logo, might be "reasonable" and therefore constitutional because it could signal to voters that elections should be about a "shared civic obligation" rather than "partisan discord."[57] Even a

---

54. *Id.* at 210 (quoting Munro v. Socialist Workers Party, 479 U.S. 189, 197 (1986)).
55. *See id.* at 218–19, 220–21 (Stevens, J., dissenting).
56. 585 U.S. 1, 16–22 (2018).
57. *Id.* at 15–16.

narrower ban, however, is problematic. It is difficult to see how a voter's wearing of a campaign t-shirt would raise any concern about intimidating other voters, and the Court's suggestion that "partisan discord" doesn't belong in (typically partisan) elections seems curious, to say the least.

F. Judicial Candidates' Speech[58]

Thirty-nine states elect all or some of their judges, either in contested elections or retention elections.[59] Yet judges, many believe, play a role in government that is not conducive to traditional elections.[60] For example, most would think it not terribly unusual for a candidate for the legislature to proclaim, "Big Oil has ripped off the people long enough. When I'm elected and Big Oil comes to the legislature, you know whose side I'll be on." Yet a similar announcement by a judicial candidate—"When I'm elected and Big Oil comes to court, you know whose side I'll be on"—would generally be considered a gross impropriety. The reason is that judges are expected to consider each case individually, applying the law without regard to the identity of the parties before the court.

Judicial codes of conduct have long limited the campaign speech of judicial candidates. Such limits reflect the view that campaign pledges and promises are inconsistent with the judicial function. Ideally, the limits assure the public that judges act impartially, discourage voters from selecting judges based on promises of results in future classes of litigation, and remind judges of their own duty to uphold the law impartially. Opponents of such restrictions, however, see these codes not only as paternalistic and inconsistent with the very idea of elections but also as a means to keep in office judges with unpopular views on the law and to hide from the public the fact that case outcomes can depend on which judges hear the cases. As judges have more and more been called upon to decide (or, some might say, have decided to interfere in) often divisive public-policy issues such as same-sex marriage, abortion rights, and capital punishment, courts—and therefore, judicial elections—have attracted greater attention from persons and groups interested in those issues. Judicial candidates, of course, have an interest in convincing voters and interest groups to support their campaigns, and the voters and interest groups want to hear the candidates' views on the issues that matter to them. Thus, it was only a matter of time until

---

58. For judicial elections and campaign finance, see Chapter 8, § I, *infra*.

59. In a retention election, an incumbent judge runs as the only candidate. The voters are asked only whether or not he should be retained in office. Because there is no opponent, retention elections tend to involve less controversy and attacks on the judge's record, and they are designed to improve the judge's chances of reelection compared with contested elections. *See generally, e.g.*, Michael R. Dimino, Sr., *The Worst Way of Selecting Judges—Except All the Others That Have Been Tried*, 32 N. Ky. L. Rev. 267 (2005); Michael R. Dimino, Sr., *The Futile Quest for a System of Judicial "Merit" Selection*, 67 Alb. L. Rev. 803 (2004).

60. *See, e.g.*, Sandra Day O'Connor, *Project on the State Judiciary*, 21 Geo. J. Legal Ethics 1229 (2008).

First Amendment challenges to limitations on judicial-candidate speech reached the Supreme Court.

In *Republican Party of Minnesota v. White*,[61] the Court struck down Minnesota's "announce clause," a rule of judicial conduct promulgated by the Minnesota Supreme Court that prohibited an incumbent judge or a lawyer running for judicial office from "announc[ing] his or her views on disputed legal or political issues." Judges who violated the law could be suspended; lawyers running for judicial offices could be disbarred.

The significance of *White* should not be understated. Due in part to constitutional concerns, Minnesota had interpreted its rule to exempt criticism of past judicial decisions (although it minimized the value of this concession by claiming that candidates would not be exempt if the candidate also stated that he or she was against *stare decisis*). Notwithstanding the announce clause, the state had also allowed candidates to make several statements criticizing court decisions, including the following: "the Minnesota Supreme Court has issued decisions which are marked by their disregard for the Legislature and lack of common sense"; "because the Supreme Court does not trust police, it allows confessed criminals to go free"; "it's the legislature which should set our spending policies" (criticizing a decision striking down a law that restricted welfare benefits); and accusing the court of a "pro-abortion stance." Moreover, lower courts in the *White* case, in ruling for the state, had further limited the scope of the rule so that it applied only to disputed issues likely to come before the candidate if elected judge and to exempt general discussions of case law and judicial philosophy. The clause also allowed for discussion of a candidate's work habits, character, education, and other personal attributes.[62] Even as so narrowed, the Court struck down the clause, noting that almost any issue one would want to talk about in a judicial race would be likely to come before a state court of general jurisdiction—or why else talk about it?

The state argued that the speech restriction protected the appearance of judicial impartiality, but the Court noted that the state was using "impartiality" in an unusual way. Judicial impartiality usually means that a judge applies the law to one litigant in the same way as to any other litigant and that the judge has no personal interest in the cases he decides. While judicial impartiality in that sense was vital, Minnesota was pursuing a broader conception of impartiality—one in which the judge holds (or pretends to hold) no prior views on the legal issue or at least remains open-minded. That conception of impartiality, if it was even beneficial,[63] was not important enough to justify limiting candidates' speech.

Equally importantly, the Court observed that the First Amendment did not require judicial campaigns "to sound the same as those for legislative office" but held that

---

61. 536 U.S. 765 (2002).

62. *Id.* at 771–73.

63. Although it sounds good for judges to be open-minded, judges who are knowledgeable about the law will naturally come to conclusions about legal issues. *See* Michael R. Dimino, Sr., *Pay No Attention to that Man Behind the Robe: Judicial Elections, the First Amendment, and Judges as Politicians*, 21 Yale L. & Pol'y Rev. 301, 338–46 (2003).

once a state has decided to elect judges, it cannot prevent candidates "from discussing what the elections are about."[64] This point—that, having decided to elect judges, the state cannot then deprive candidates of the right to speak out on the issues—was emphasized in Justice O'Connor's concurrence. Expressing concerns about judicial campaigning, she stated, "The very practice of electing judges undermines this interest [in an impartial judiciary]."[65]

In short, a state is not required to have judicial elections, but if it does, the First Amendment gives candidates and voters the right to discuss issues they believe are relevant to the election—even if the state would prefer to treat judging as fundamentally different from policymaking.[66]

On remand in *White*, the Eighth Circuit, sitting *en banc*, struck down two other limitations on judicial campaigning. The first, a partisan-activities clause, prohibited judicial nominees from identifying themselves publicly as party members and from attending party events or soliciting party endorsements. The second, the "solicitation clause," prohibited judicial nominees from personally soliciting campaign funds.[67]

However, in *Williams-Yulee v. Florida Bar*, the Supreme Court went the other way on the question of solicitations. There, the Court upheld a Florida rule prohibiting a judicial candidate from personally soliciting contributions, even though the solicitation in question was merely signing a form letter. The Court held that the state's interest in "protecting the integrity of the judiciary" made *Williams-Yulee* "one of the rare cases in which a speech restriction withstands strict scrutiny."[68]

Lower courts have had to apply both *White* and *Williams-Yulee* to a variety of restrictions on judicial candidates. Because *White* held that judicial candidates are entitled to some First Amendment protection but *Williams-Yulee* upheld a restriction that would undoubtedly have been unconstitutional as applied to a non-judicial candidate, the essential question is which speech restrictions are justified by the concern that drove the Supreme Court to uphold the restriction in *Williams-Yulee*—the need to have judges distance themselves from the appearance that they would be influenced by money or partisanship. The Sixth Circuit's decision in *Winter v. Wolnitzek* is particularly thoughtful.[69] In that case, the court considered several provisions of Kentucky's code of judicial conduct, striking down bans on campaigning as a member or nominee of a party, giving speeches supporting or opposing a party or candidate, and making "misleading" statements, while upholding bans on

64. *Id.* at 783, 788.

65. *Id.* at 788 (O'Connor, J., concurring).

66. *See generally* Dimino, *supra* note 63.

67. Republican Party of Minnesota v. White, 416 F.3d 738 (8th Cir. 2005) (*en banc*).

68. Williams-Yulee v. Florida Bar, 575 U.S. 433 (2015). *See* Michael R. Dimino, Sr., *Image Is Everything: Politics, Umpiring, and the Judicial Myth*, 39 Harv. J.L. & Pub. Pol'y 397 (2016) (arguing that *Williams-Yulee*'s idealistic focus on promoting the appearance of an impartial judiciary is incompatible with *White*'s realistic conception of judging).

69. 834 F.3d 681 (6th Cir. 2016) (Sutton, J.).

contributing money to a party or candidate, endorsing candidates, and acting as a leader in a party.

One wonders, however, why the perception of partisan affiliation is thought to be so damaging to the judiciary. Surely the public realizes the truth—that judges (especially elected judges) tend to have been involved with partisan politics before assuming the bench. And while favoritism or partisanship *as* a judge undermines the rule of law, *becoming* a judge by winning an election requires financial support and votes, often from parties and interest groups. Restrictions like the one in *Williams-Yulee* seek to advance an image of judicial impartiality that does not reflect reality. By upholding Florida's decision to punish Williams-Yulee for signing a letter soliciting campaign funds, the Supreme Court appears to have retreated from the realistic conception of the judiciary that motivated the decision in *White*.

Finally, note that, regardless of restrictions on the speech of judicial candidates themselves, other interested parties have First Amendment rights that are at play in judicial elections. For the most part, at least, those parties may treat judicial elections as they would other elections. For example, even in states with nonpartisan ballots, political parties may endorse candidates for office.[70] And individuals are free to make unlimited independent expenditures to speak about and endorse candidates for judicial office.[71]

G. Circulation of Petitions

Although there is no provision in the U.S. Constitution permitting lawmaking by initiative or referendum,[72] every state provides for some type of citizen-initiated lawmaking at the state level.[73] Typically, the first stage in any referendum or initiative campaign is gathering enough signatures from registered voters to place the matter before the electorate, with the required number of signatures varying widely from state to state. Signatures are gathered on petitions, usually in a format prescribed by the state.

---

70. *Geary v. Renne*, 911 F.2d 280 (9th Cir. 1990) (*en banc*).

71. *But see* Caperton v. A.T. Massey Coal Co., 556 U.S. 868, 884 (2009) (holding that in rare cases where such expenditures have "significant and disproportionate influence" while a "case was pending or imminent," the judge may be required to recuse from the case). *See* Chapter 8, § I, *infra*.

72. Although the terms are often used interchangeably, or with one term intended to encompass the other, technically an initiative places a measure before the electorate, which may pass or not pass the proposed law or constitutional amendment. A referendum places a matter already passed by the legislature before the voters, who may consent to or reject the measure. Referenda can be binding on the legislature or merely advisory. The rules discussed in this section also apply to recalls, in which voters may call for an election to remove an elected official.

73. Twenty-four states provide for voter initiatives for statutes or constitutional amendments (twenty-one states allow initiatives for both); all states allow some form of referenda, although not all states allow for voter-initiated referenda. *See* National Council of State Legislatures, *Initiative and Referendum States*, https://www.ncsl.org/elections-and-campaigns/initiative-and-referendum-states (updated March 15, 2023).

Signature-gathering is "speech" protected by the First Amendment because it necessarily "involves both the expression of a desire for political change and a discussion of the merits of the proposed change."[74] Circulators discuss the merits of the petition with potential signatories, leading to "the type of interactive communication concerning political change that is appropriately described as 'core political speech.'"[75]

As discussed in Chapter 9, *infra*, the Supreme Court, in *Doe v. Reed*,[76] rejected a facial challenge to the disclosure of the names and addresses of people who signed petitions to place initiatives or referenda on the ballot. Interestingly enough, however, in *Buckley v. American Constitutional Law Foundation* (*ACLF*), the Court struck down a Colorado law requiring petition circulators to wear identification badges.[77] In *ACLF*, the Court unanimously, and on virtually no factual record, found that the badge interfered with the circulator's message and exposed the speaker to potential harassment, thus deterring persons from serving as circulators. The result might be best explained by the apparent lack of any compelling state interest supporting the badge requirement. The state suggested that the badges would deter circulator misconduct, but the Court concluded that such an interest was already accomplished because the state required circulators to identify themselves on the petitions themselves. Of course, that latter disclosure could be completed after circulating the petition, making it hard for a person approached by a circulator to identify the circulator, should misconduct occur.

The *ACLF* Court also struck down two other provisions of Colorado law. One required that petition circulators be registered voters. The state sought to justify this requirement too as an anti-fraud measure, particularly by claiming the need to subpoena circulators who might break the law. Again, however, given that the circulators must include a name and address on the completed petition, the Court found little justification for the added requirement. The majority viewed the law as a restriction on speech, akin to prohibiting people who cannot vote—for example, a newspaper corporation, a resident alien, or an out-of-state public figure—from sharing their opinions on an upcoming election. The dissenters viewed petition circulation as an act of democratic participation similar to voting itself; as Chief Justice Rehnquist wrote, "a State should be able to limit the ability to circulate initiative petitions to those people who can ultimately vote on initiatives at the polls."[78]

Finally, the Court also invalidated a provision of the Colorado law that required disclosure of the amount paid to each individual petition circulator. Given that the Court has consistently upheld compulsory disclosure of campaign expenditures (*see* Chapter 9), one might have expected the Court to uphold this provision. However, the Court held that the public interest was adequately served by knowing the identity of the payer and the amount paid in total. Knowing the names of paid circulators and the amount paid to each would not advance the public interest, according to the Court.

---

74. Meyer v. Grant, 486 U.S. 414, 421 (1988).
75. *Id.* at 421–22.
76. 561 U.S. 186 (2010).
77. 525 U.S. 182 (1999).
78. *Id.* at 228 (Rehnquist, C.J., dissenting).

As you will see in Chapter 9, § C, however, most campaign finance disclosure laws specifically require the names and addresses of vendors. Thus, this portion of *ACLF* should be viewed simply as a quirk of the law that applies to gathering signatures in ballot initiative and referendum campaigns.

This last point of *ACLF* gives rise to another question: May a state prohibit an initiative campaign from using paid petitioners at all? The answer to that is "no." In *Meyer v. Grant*, decided before *ACLF*, a unanimous Supreme Court struck down another Colorado law that prohibited the use of paid petition circulators.[79] The result of *Meyer* is less surprising than the fact that it was a 9–0 decision, with the Court's opinion written by Justice Stevens, who was usually supportive of campaign finance restrictions. In fact, the Court gave the back of its hand to Colorado's argument that allowing paid circulators would permit wealthy persons to gain undue influence in the state by paying to obtain ballot access for measures that could not gain the required signatures through a strictly volunteer effort. The Court cited *Buckley v. Valeo* and *First National Bank of Boston v. Bellotti* to argue that the government may not limit the speech of the wealthy in order to enhance the voices of others or to level the playing field.[80] *Meyer's* rejection of that argument is remarkable in that Justice Stevens, as well as Justices Brennan, White, and Marshall, have all accepted the level-the-playing-field argument in the realm of campaign finance law, as outlined in Chapter 8.

Lower federal courts have split on the constitutionality of prohibitions on paying petitioners on a per-signature basis. States have argued that petitioners paid per signature have a greater incentive to commit fraud than do volunteers or petitioners paid by the hour.[81]

H. Government Speech

The government can, and often does, speak to us. From agency websites, to "Get Vaccinated" campaigns, to town newsletters, we are confronted daily with government speech. Such speech rarely raises constitutional issues, even when the government is discriminating on the basis of viewpoint—after all, expressing a view is often the purpose of the government's speech. If the government advises us to "Just Say No" or not to drink and drive, it need not also offer an alternative view.[82]

May the government itself, however, take part in political campaigns? At one level, the answer is quite obviously "yes." To most people, there is nothing troubling about

---

79. 486 U.S. 414 (1988).

80. *Id.* at 426 n.7.

81. *See* Citizens for Tax Reform v. Deters, 518 F.3d 375 (6th Cir. 2008) (holding law unconstitutional); Prete v. Bradbury, 438 F.3d 949 (9th Cir. 2006); Initiative & Referendum Inst. v. Jaeger, 241 F.3d 614 (8th Cir. 2001) (holding laws constitutional); Pierce v. Jacobson, 44 F.4th 853 (9th Cir. 2022) (same); AZ Petition Partners LLC v. Thompson, 530 P.3d 1144 (Ariz. 2023) (same).

82. *See* Shurtleff v. City of Boston, Mass., 596 U.S. 243 (2022); Pleasant Grove City v. Summum, 555 U.S. 460 (2019); Walker v. Texas Div., Sons of Confederate Veterans, Inc., 576 U.S. 200 (2015).

the government's urging us to vote or providing incumbent officeholders with the ability to communicate with constituents through such devices as the "franking" privilege (free use of the mail) and government-maintained websites. Although federal officials are banned from using these official privileges for campaigning, obviously the ability to communicate achievements and upcoming public events and to explain one's position on public issues can influence a future campaign. Members of the government routinely defend their policies and decisions on government time and often at government expense.

When the government as an institution goes from information to electoral advocacy, however, does it cross the line? Certainly, the government, as an institution, may have expertise that could be relevant to voters. On the other hand, government participation in elections may raise even greater concerns than those implicated by corporate and union participation. The federal government is far larger than even the largest corporations or unions. A corporation or union must ultimately justify its political expenditures in terms of profits or benefits to members. Government may irritate some voters by spending on elections, but if its expenditures are effective in building public support for its policies, the government officials will prevail in elections and remain in power. As a result, there might be little limit to the government's ability to tax us to produce speech designed to convince us to support the government. Government electoral advocacy, in this view, undermines the ultimate check on government power—the views of the electorate.

Concurring in the judgment in *National Endowment for the Arts v. Finley*, Justice Scalia noted, "I suppose it would be unconstitutional for the government to give money to an organization devoted to the promotion of candidates nominated by the Republican Party [and] it would be just as unconstitutional for the government itself to promote candidates nominated by the Republican Party."[83] But Justice Scalia's hypothetical would be an easy case. In more difficult cases, lower courts have split. For example, in *Mountain States Legal Foundation v. Denver School District No. 1*, a federal district court ruled unconstitutional the school board's use of funds to urge voters to defeat a constitutional amendment that would have changed the ability of governments, including school boards, to spend public funds.[84] In *Kidwell v. City of Union*, however, the Sixth Circuit, over a dissent, upheld the use of public funds to oppose a voter-initiated referendum concerning the establishment of a fire department. *Kidwell* distinguished *Mountain States* on the ground that the referendum in *Mountain States* was not directly relevant to the school board's governance functions, whereas the *Kidwell* referendum related to the City's provision of services.[85]

---

83. 524 U.S. 569, 598 n.3 (Scalia, J. concurring in the judgment).

84. 459 F. Supp. 357 (D. Colo. 1978).

85. *Kidwell*, 462 F.3d 620 (6th Cir. 2006), *cert. denied*, 550 U.S. 935 (2007). For decisions that follow *Kidwell*, see *Page v. Lexington County School District One*, 531 F.3d 275 (4th Cir. 2008); *Montgomery County Fraternal Order of Police*, 112 A.3d 1052 (Md. Ct. Spec. App. 2015); and *Daims v. Town of Brattleboro*, 148 A.3d 185 (Vt. 2016).

Justice Scalia's comment in *Finley*, quoted above, should not be taken as suggesting that the government may not directly fund political parties and candidates. In fact, it may do so, so long as it acts on a content-neutral basis. This and other elements of public financing of campaigns are discussed in Chapter 8.

While cases seeking to limit government speech have been rare, they may become more common as government-sponsored "public service" advertising becomes more accepted, and as advocates of campaign finance reform urge publicly financed elections as a means to resolve the campaign finance issues of corruption and equality discussed in Chapter 8.

I. Public Employees

Government employees may be particularly interested in public affairs, and their knowledge may be invaluable to the public in assessing government performance. As a result, political participation by government employees may be especially valuable for society. At the same time, there has long been concern that government employees could be enlisted or pressured into serving as a political cadre in support of the government. Further, it is important that civil servants apply the law impartially, and even the appearance of partiality may undermine public confidence in government. For these reasons, both the federal and state governments have often imposed restrictions on political activities by career civil servants. Such restrictions can also be seen as protection for the workers themselves: If an employee is forbidden from taking part in a political campaign, then supervisors will have no incentive to pressure employees into political activity in support of party politics. The flip side is that some government employees want to take part in political activity outside of their work, and restrictions on their doing so raise concerns that their First Amendment rights are being abridged.

In the eighteenth century, and in some states well into the nineteenth century, government employees were expected to support the party in power. Prior to the implementation of a career government service and civil-service exams in the 1880s, all government appointments were essentially political appointments. It was even a common practice to "assess" government employees a percentage of their salary—typically around 2%—to fund the party to which they owed their jobs. Arguably, it may be beneficial to the public to have the political inclinations of government employees out in the open, and even more beneficial to give employees a strong incentive (keeping their jobs after the next election) to ensure the success of the government's policies. But by the late nineteenth century, a broad consensus had emerged to reform government service to make it more professional and less political. The passage of the Pendleton Act in 1881 created the federal civil service, and states passed similar laws during the same period, with the aim of depoliticizing government service.[86]

86. *See* BRADLEY A. SMITH, UNFREE SPEECH: THE FOLLY OF CAMPAIGN FINANCE REFORM 20 (2001).

The public-works programs of the New Deal led to a rapid increase in federal hiring, much of it outside of the traditional civil-service system. That increase created fresh concerns that these employees would become a base of political support for the Roosevelt Administration or that they were being coerced into political activity in support of the Administration. The result was the "Hatch Act" of 1939, passed by a coalition of Republicans and conservative Democrats.[87] The Hatch Act placed a variety of restrictions on political activity by federal employees. Though amended several times, it remains the principal federal law governing political activity by federal employees.[88]

The constitutionality of the Hatch Act reached the Supreme Court in 1947, in *United Public Workers of America (C.I.O.) v. Mitchell*.[89] The plaintiffs in the case wished to engage in a variety of political activities outside of working hours, including serving as an executive committee member of a local political party and as paymaster for party workers, and working the polls on election day. *Mitchell* all but abdicated any judicial responsibility for protecting the speech rights of government employees, concluding that restrictions on employee political activities are matters of congressional and presidential "judgment." The majority rejected the claim that the Hatch Act's broad prohibitions were not "narrowly drawn" to accomplish the government's ends; it held that limits on federal employee speech need not be "indispensable to a merit system" but merely "desirable."[90]

Although the Supreme Court grew generally more protective of First Amendment rights in the ensuing three decades, in its 1973 decision in *United States Civil Service Commission v. National Association of Letter Carriers*, the Court "unhesitatingly reaffirmed" the broad power of Congress and the President to restrict the political activities of federal employees.[91] Later, however, in *United States v. National Treasury Employees Union*, the Court limited *Mitchell* somewhat and held that it was unconstitutional for Congress to pass a blanket prohibition on federal employees' acceptance of any compensation for making speeches or writing articles. The Court emphasized that the ban included speeches and articles bearing no relationship to the author's duties and was not limited to speeches or articles of a political nature.[92]

It must also be pointed out that while *Mitchell* and *National Association of Letter Carriers* remain good law, the Court has been more sensitive to First Amendment claims when raised in the context of individual disciplinary actions. In those cases, the Court has attempted to assess whether the employee's activities create a serious risk of interfering with the functioning of government. The most notable case is *Pickering v.*

87. *See id.* at 27.

88. 5 U.S.C. §7321 et seq.

89. 330 U.S. 75 (1947).

90. *Id.* at 100.

91. 413 U.S. 548 (1973). In tandem with *Letter Carriers*, the Court upheld similar restrictions on state employees in *Broadrick v. Oklahoma*, 413 U.S. 601 (1973).

92. 513 U.S. 454, 465–66 (1995).

Board of Education, holding that a local school district could not terminate a teacher for writing a letter to the editor of the local newspaper attacking the school board's handling of a local bond issue and its allocation of financial resources.[93] Other cases include *Connick v. Myers* (upholding the firing of an assistant district attorney who distributed a questionnaire to other employees seeking their opinions about "transfer policy, office morale, the need for a grievance committee, the level of confidence in supervisors, and whether employees felt pressured to work in political campaigns");[94] *Rankin v. McPherson* (finding a First Amendment violation where a clerical employee in the constable's office was fired for remarking, upon hearing of an assassination attempt on President Reagan, "if they go for him again, I hope they get him");[95] and *Waters v. Churchill* (upholding the termination of a nurse for remarks critical of a supervisor).[96] In *Garcetti v. Ceballos*, the Court spelled out a two-part test for deciding such issues. First, in order to claim protection under the First Amendment, the employee's comments must be on a matter of public concern, not on private matters such as office discipline, and the employee must be speaking as a citizen rather than pursuant to his official duties. Second, if the employee is speaking as a citizen on a matter of public concern, the employee may be disciplined only if the speech has the potential to cause an adverse effect on the operations of the office—in other words, there must be a reason to treat it differently than the same speech uttered by a non-employee—and the adverse effect outweighs the employee's interest in speaking.[97]

The end result is that governments have broad authority to place general limits on political participation by their employees. However, individual disciplinary actions for public comments are handled on a case-by-case basis pursuant to the framework set forth in *Garcetti* and *Pickering*, with considerably less deference given to the state.

J. Patronage

As previously noted in this chapter, during the United States' first century, it was generally presumed that all government positions were patronage positions—that is, employees obtained and held their jobs at the whim of the political figures victorious in the last election. Early presidents frequently complained about the massive amounts of time devoted to patronage appointments. The civil-service laws that swept the nation in the late 1800s dramatically scaled back the scope of patronage, but those employees outside the scope of such statutory protections still had few or no rights against being fired or disciplined for political reasons.

93. 391 U.S. 563 (1968).
94. 461 U.S. 138 (1983).
95. 483 U.S. 378 (1987).
96. 511 U.S. 661 (1994).
97. 547 U.S. 410, 418 (2006).

This situation changed dramatically with a series of Supreme Court decisions beginning in 1976 that placed limits on the ability of government officials to engage in political patronage.

The first of those cases was *Elrod v. Burns*. After the newly elected Democratic sheriff fired all known Republicans in the office, the employees, who were bailiffs, clerks, and security guards not covered by civil-service laws against arbitrary discharge, filed suit. The Supreme Court, in a 3–2–3 decision, with Justice Stevens not participating, recognized the long history of patronage appointment but nonetheless held that the government action violated the employees' due-process rights. The state argued that patronage creates effective, accountable government; ensures representative government by preventing employees from undercutting the elected administration; and supports the party system, thus benefiting democratic government. Justice Brennan, writing for a three-member plurality, argued that efficiency could be served simply by discharging employees who were not performing their jobs; that effective policy implementation could be achieved by limiting patronage dismissals to "policymaking" positions; and that elimination of patronage would not destroy party politics. Three dissenting Justices also reviewed the history of patronage but, like the plurality opinion, ultimately rested their argument for the constitutionality of the practice on a balancing of free-speech and state interests. They concluded that patronage promoted the functioning of the two-party system—an interest those Justices characterized as "important." The decisive votes came from Justices Stewart and Blackmun. Justice Stewart's brief opinion concurring in the judgment, which was joined by Justice Blackmun, stated simply that a "nonpolicymaking, nonconfidential" government employee could not be fired simply for his political beliefs.[98]

Branti v. Finkel strengthened *Elrod* in two ways. First, it yielded a majority (not just a plurality) opinion protecting employees' right to be free from patronage dismissals. Second, it seemed to extend *Elrod*'s protection even to some policymaking officials. In *Branti*, an assistant public defender was fired due to party affiliation. In ruling for the plaintiff, the Court held that the "ultimate inquiry" is not whether the employee makes policy but "whether the hiring authority can demonstrate that the party affiliation is an appropriate requirement for the effective performance of the public office involved."[99]

Rutan v. Republican Party of Illinois[100] extended *Elrod* to cover not just dismissals but also promotions, transfers, and hiring decisions, at least for nonpolicymaking positions. And *O'Hare Truck Service v. City of Northlake*[101] extended the prohibition on political discrimination beyond employees to include government contractors as

98. Elrod v. Burns, 427 U.S. 347 (1976).

99. 445 U.S. 507, 518–520 (1980). More recent litigation in the lower courts has resulted in arguably unclear and inconsistent decisions on the scope of the policymaking exception, and the Supreme Court has not revisited the issue. *See* Michael E. Solimine, *Party Patronage*, *in* The Oxford Handbook of American Election Law 503 (Eugene D. Mazo ed., 2024).

100. 497 U.S. 62 (1990).

101. 518 U.S. 712 (1996).

well. One federal appellate court has even held that the Constitution precludes dismissal of an employee who is running against the incumbent officeholder.[102]

How far up the policymaking chain of command can the prohibition on patronage go? Is it really possible, or desirable, to staff government without political considerations? Dissenting in *Rutan*, Justice Scalia pointed out the irony that federal judges, themselves appointed by presidents on the basis, in part, of political affiliation, were holding that elected officials could not hire based on political affiliation.[103]

Perhaps inspired by Justice Scalia's analysis, in *Newman v. Voinovich*,[104] a Democratic lawyer brought suit when Ohio's Republican governor did not consider him for a judicial appointment when exercising his authority under state law to fill a vacancy. The U.S. Court of Appeals held that the governor's use of politics to choose judges did not violate the law established by the *Elrod* line of cases since "judges are policymakers because their political beliefs influence and dictate their decisions on important jurisprudential matters."[105]

The Supreme Court has not addressed the applicability of the patronage cases to judicial appointments. In *Carney v. Adams*,[106] the Court appeared to have an opportunity to resolve the issue but decided the case without reaching the merits. Adams, who was neither a Republican nor a Democrat, challenged a Delaware law requiring appointments to the state supreme court to be balanced between the two major political parties. The Court held that the plaintiff lacked standing to bring the suit in federal court because he had not shown that he was ready and able to apply for a vacancy on the court.

---

102. *See* Wilbur v. Mahan, 3 F.3d 214 (7th Cir. 1993). For cases upholding a right to discharge in such circumstances, see *Carver v. Dennis*, 104 F.3d 847 (6th Cir. 1997), and *Click v. Copeland*, 970 F.2d 106 (5th Cir. 1992).

103. 497 U.S. at 92 (Scalia, J., dissenting).

104. 986 F.2d 159 (6th Cir. 1993). One of this volume's authors served as co-counsel for the plaintiff.

105. A worthwhile nod to legal realism in its own right.

106. 592 U.S. 53 (2020).

Chapter 8
Campaign Finance

A. Introduction

Perhaps no issue in the field of election law has been so contentious for so long as that of campaign finance.

In a 1997 interview, former U.S. House Minority Leader Richard Gephardt (D-Mo.) stated, "What we have is two important values in direct conflict: freedom of speech, and our desire for healthy campaigns in a healthy democracy."[1] Although Representative Gephardt was criticized for suggesting that these values were in conflict, in fact his comment well summarized the common perception of campaign funding. There is virtually unanimous agreement that the purpose of the First Amendment is to "protect the free discussion of governmental affairs."[2] Yet many Americans are deeply concerned about the effects on governance and political equality when politicians must solicit large sums of cash to finance their campaigns. Many consider such a system to be "legalized bribery," while others are particularly concerned that the resulting influence of wealthy citizens and groups is inconsistent with basic principles of political equality.

According to the Federal Election Commission, in the elections of 2024, Americans spent approximately $12.4 billion on political campaigns—more than in any prior election. Contrary to much popular myth, the vast majority of these funds came from individual donors. Over 65% of campaign funds came from direct donations by individuals to candidates, parties, and political action committees (traditional "PACs"), and, at the federal level, these contributions are limited in size. Approximately 28% came in the form of donations, unlimited in size, by wealthy individuals to so-called "Super PACs," or from candidates paying for their own campaigns from personal wealth—including roughly $275 million in spending by Tesla and Space X magnate Elon Musk. That left approximately 6% of the total to come from nonprofit membership organizations, corporations, and union sources, with large, publicly traded corporations contributing something under 1% of the total.[3] By comparison, the total spent over the two-year

1. Quoted in Nancy Gibbs, *The Wake Up Call*, Time, Feb. 3, 1997, at 22.

2. Mills v. Alabama, 384 U.S. 214, 218 (1966).

3. *See* Fed. Election Comm'n, *Statistical Summary of 24-Month Campaign Activity of the 2023–2024 Election Cycle*, Apr. 23, 2025, https://www.fec.gov/updates/statistical-summary-of-24-month-campaign-activity-of-the-2023-2024-election-cycle/, and links therein. For perspective, see Michael E.

2023–2024 election cycle amounted to approximately 0.0004% of U.S. gross domestic product for 2024 alone. A single company, Proctor & Gamble, spent approximately $9 billion on commercial advertising in the same two-year period. Nevertheless, $12.4 billion is a lot of money to spend on electing 435 congressmen, 100 senators, and a President.

The tension between rights of speech and association, on the one hand, and anti-corruption and equality concerns, on the other, is constant in campaign finance law. Campaign finance brings to the fore deep disagreements, not only about constitutional interpretation but about theories of democratic representation, the meaning of political equality, and our fundamental attitudes toward government power.

Furthermore, the goals Americans have for campaign finance regulation are often contradictory. For example, caps on campaign spending might reduce concerns about the corrupting effects of money in politics, but they can also reduce the flow of information needed for a well-informed electorate. Disclosure of campaign contributions, which is discussed in Chapter 9, may provide information that helps the electorate monitor the behavior of public officials or learn more about candidate agendas, but disclosure can also compromise privacy, expose citizens to harassment, and even conflict with the idea of a secret ballot. Other examples of such tensions should become apparent as you go through this chapter.

But it is not just the goals of campaign finance law that are in tension. Politicians who make the law, judges who enforce it, and activists on both sides of the issue often interpret the empirical evidence in wildly different ways. The result is that the two sides often seem to be talking past one another.

Finally, behind contradictory goals, divergent theories, and differing views of empirical evidence lurks the specter of partisan politics. Few areas of law have such potential to directly affect the partisan balance of power. In the zero-sum game that is electoral politics, any change in the law that benefits one party is likely to harm the other.

B. History

1. Early Laws

Elections in colonial America and in the early United States were generally low-cost affairs before small electorates which often knew the candidates personally. Candidates were generally expected to pay any costs of campaigning from personal funds. Much campaigning was done through editorials in highly partisan newspapers, often funded

---

Toner & Karen E. Trainer, *The Fourteen-Billion-Dollar Election: Emerging Campaign Finance Trends and their Impact on the 2020 Presidential Race and Beyond*, *in* A Return to Normalcy? The 2020 Election that (Almost) Broke America 203–24 (Larry J. Sabato, Kyle Kondik, & J. Miles Coleman eds., 2021); The Committee for Econ. Dev., The Landscape of Campaign Contributions Campaign Finance After Citizens United (2017).

by officeholders or their supporters. By the 1830s, however, an expanded electorate and the rise of political parties seeking national and mass appeal required substantial campaign sums. For example, the 1830 gubernatorial race in Kentucky cost in excess of $200,000 in inflation-adjusted terms. Faced with Andrew Jackson's threats to revoke its federal charter, the United States Bank unsuccessfully spent approximately $1 million, adjusted for inflation, to defeat Jackson in the presidential election of 1832. By the election of 1876, both the Republican and Democratic candidates for President spent over $10 million in inflation-adjusted dollars.

A major source of funds in the nineteenth century was "assessments" placed on patronage employees of the government. These employees were expected to kick back a percentage of their government salaries to make certain that their political employers were reelected. Wealthy individuals and business interests were also a primary source of funds, especially after 1880, when the advent of civil-service laws began to dry up patronage assessments as a source of campaign money. Theodore Roosevelt's 1904 campaign for President was funded almost entirely by a handful of wealthy businessmen and corporations, while his Democratic opponent, Alton Parker, relied on wealthy Democratic "angels" such as financier Augustus Belmont, Jr., and a healthy influx of cash from Parker's running mate, mine owner Henry Davis.

After the election of 1896, in which Republican William McKinley steamrolled Democrat William Jennings Bryan with the help of a massive campaign fund built on corporate contributions, several states with Democratic Party legislative majorities passed prohibitions on corporate contributions in elections.

The first federal campaign finance law was the Tillman Act, passed in 1907, which prohibited federally chartered banks and corporations from making political contributions. This was followed by "Publicity Acts" in 1910 and 1911, which required the disclosure of contributors and placed limits on campaign expenditures. In 1925, in the wake of the "Teapot Dome" scandal, Congress passed the Federal Corrupt Practices Act, which retained the basic provisions of both the Tillman Act and the Publicity Acts, and attempted to update those laws to close "loopholes." The Corrupt Practices Act would remain the core federal campaign finance law for 47 years, until passage of the Federal Election Campaign Act in 1972. Important amendments, however, were enacted as part of the Taft-Hartley Act of 1947. These amendments extended the prohibition on direct corporate contributions to candidates to include all corporate spending on elections and added prohibitions on union contributions and spending as well.

None of these laws was particularly effective. The Tillman Act was circumvented by treating expenditures made separately from a campaign as not being "contributions" prohibited by the Act. The Publicity Acts applied only to contributions received in an election year and only by committees operating in two or more states, and these acts were readily avoided by running funds through state committees and by fundraising in non-election years. Although the Corrupt Practices Act sought to remedy these problems, it was equally unsuccessful. The law required reporting of all expenditures made with a candidate's "knowledge or consent," but it was interpreted to apply only to the candidate's personal funds and not to those of a campaign committee. Spending limits included in the law were circumvented by establishing numerous committees that could each spend up to the limit. Disclosure requirements continued to be evaded by the use of state committees. Although corporations could not contribute, corporate executives could and did, and they were often reimbursed by the corporation. For their part, unions formed the first "political action committees" (also known as "PACs") to make contributions. Enforcement of the laws was through U.S. attorneys, who frequently saw such prosecutions as low-priority matters and many of whom thought the law was unconstitutional in most of its applications.

State laws during this period were even more haphazard. A majority of states had no restrictions, but, even in those that did, the laws were riddled with "loopholes" and inadequate for the job they were asked to do. For example, a California law that required disclosure of campaign contributions could be met simply by filing a non-alphabetized list of donor names, with no dollar amounts and often incomplete names or inaccurate spelling.[4]

2. The Modern Reform Era and the Federal Election Campaign Act

Although these early laws had little *de facto* impact on campaign fundraising and spending, the Great Depression and the cost of two world wars reduced the funds available for political campaigns. In inflation-adjusted dollars, the presidential campaign of 1948 was the least expensive since 1880. However, the booming economy of the 1950s increased discretionary income available for political campaigning. Additionally, in 1952, the Federal Communications Commission ended a freeze on granting new broadcast licenses, and television became prevalent across America. Radio and television advertising quickly raised the costs of campaigning. The increased costs of campaigning, the perceived inadequacies of the Corrupt Practices Act, and—according to some skeptics—the desire of Democratic majorities in Congress to protect themselves from a rejuvenated Republican Party that had made major gains in the 1966 off-year elections and won the Presidency in 1968, led to the passage of the Federal Election Campaign Act (FECA) in 1972. This law closed many of the loopholes of the Corrupt Practices Act, broadened the scope of disclosure requirements, and put in place, for the first time, penalties for nondisclosure. FECA also abolished the old, unenforced spending limits on individual contributors but limited the amounts that could be spent on radio and television advertising.

FECA had been in existence only a few months when the political scandals that would be collectively known as "Watergate" began to break. These scandals created momentum for a more far-reaching law.

---

4. For background on the history of campaign financing and reform efforts, see, *e.g.*, Allison R. Hayward, *Revisiting the Fable of Reform*, 43 Harv. J. Legis. 421 (2008); John Samples, The Fallacy of Campaign Finance Reform (2006); and Robert Mutch, Campaigns, Congresses, and Courts: The Making of Federal Campaign Finance Law (1988).

The 1974 FECA amendments essentially scrapped the 1972 law and substituted in its place the most sweeping system of campaign finance regulation in American history, up to that time. The new law included comprehensive restrictions on contributions and expenditures, and new mandatory registration and reporting requirements. FECA also created an independent enforcement agency, the Federal Election Commission (FEC), to enforce civil violations of the Act. Combined with another law, the Revenue Act of 1971, FECA also created a system for government funding of presidential elections and national party nominating conventions, also administered by the FEC.

Most key provisions of FECA were immediately challenged in court, and the Supreme Court's far-reaching decision in *Buckley v. Valeo*,[5] discussed in the next section, significantly altered the law and set forth key constitutional principles that have guided the courts ever since. Despite some amendments, most notably in the Bipartisan Campaign Reform Act of 2002,[6] the FECA amendments of 1974, as shaped by *Buckley*, remain the basic framework of federal campaign finance law to this day. Unless otherwise specified, references to FECA in this chapter refer to the amendments of 1974, and subsequent amendments. Most state laws are modeled on the basic concepts included in FECA. This chapter will focus on FECA, as amended, and constitutional challenges to that statute and state statutes.

C. *Buckley v. Valeo* and Core Constitutional Concepts of Campaign Finance Law

1. Introduction

FECA was immediately challenged in federal court by a broad coalition that included the American Conservative Union, the American Civil Liberties Union (ACLU), the Libertarian Party, Senator James Buckley (Conservative-N.Y.), former Senator Eugene McCarthy (D-Minn.), and numerous other plaintiffs. The ensuing case, *Buckley v. Valeo*,[7] remains the starting point for constitutional analysis of campaign finance laws.

The Court's *per curiam* opinion, with various concurrences and dissents, makes *Buckley* one of the longest opinions in Supreme Court history, and, by some measures, the longest. Its durability in the face of substantial criticism, however, makes it well worth the effort to master. The *per curiam* opinion for the Court is complex and much

5. 424. U.S. 1 (1976)

6. Pub. L. No. 107-155 (2002). This law is sometimes referred to as the "McCain-Feingold Act," after its primary Senate sponsors.

7. 424 U.S. 1 (1976).

more deeply nuanced than many scholars give it credit for being. Any person who wishes to claim a mastery of campaign finance law will have read *Buckley* not once or twice, but many times. All of the basic concepts discussed in the following section, which continue to form the framework for constitutional analysis of campaign finance laws, originate in *Buckley.*

2. First Amendment Interests

The Court's *Buckley* opinion began by recognizing that "[t]he Act's contribution and expenditure limitations operate in an area of the most fundamental First Amendment activities. Discussion of public issues and debate on the qualifications of candidates are integral to the operation of the system of government established by our Constitution."[8]

The Court rejected the idea that the Act's limitations could be justified as a limitation on conduct—spending money—rather than speech. Because of this, it is often said that *Buckley* held that "money is speech." That may be adequate shorthand, but that is not really what the Court held. Rather, the Court recognized that the expenditure of money can be deeply entwined with speech, and that efforts to suppress communication are antithetical to the First Amendment. Consider analogies to other constitutional rights. The First Amendment right to the free exercise of religion could be eviscerated by denying believers the right to spend money to maintain facilities for worship, to purchase religious books and objects, to pay pastors, or to engage in church missionary work. The Second Amendment right to keep and bear arms would have little meaning if the government could prohibit the expenditure of money to purchase, repair, manufacture, or import guns and ammunition. The right to counsel under the Sixth Amendment would lose much force if one could not spend money to hire a lawyer. So it is with the right to speech.

While common sense tells us that money is not speech, it also tells us that limits on spending money can limit speech. The First Amendment obviously stops the government from prohibiting newspaper or online editorials, for example, but the government could achieve the same ends by prohibiting the expenditure of funds to write or publish editorials. In *Buckley*, the government attempted to argue that restrictions on campaign financing were analogous to a ban on draft-card burning, which the Court had upheld in *United States v. O'Brien*,[9] but the Court rejected the comparison. In *O'Brien*, the government did not seek to limit speech but rather to make certain that the military draft could be efficiently implemented. There was no danger that the provision would reduce the total amount of speech or that it would have more than the most marginal impact, unassociated with the content of the speech, on the plaintiff's ability to express himself. By contrast, while the government's goal in regulating campaign financing may be less to suppress speech than to prevent corruption or to

8. *Id.* at 14.
9. 391 U.S. 367 (1968).

promote equality, the means taken necessarily, directly, and substantially reduce the opportunities for, and the amount of, speech that might otherwise occur.

The Court also rejected the idea that restrictions on campaign finance were akin to "time, place, and manner" restrictions, such as limitations on picketing or using a sound truck at certain times. Limits on the use of sound trucks, for example, are tailored to serve other interests—preventing public nuisances at certain hours.[10] They do not directly limit the amount of speech and make no distinctions based on the subject matter or content of speech. Limits on campaign spending and contributions, on the other hand, "impose direct quantity restrictions on political communication and association by persons."[11]

The Court stressed two related, but nonetheless distinct, rights placed in jeopardy by campaign finance restrictions and regulations. The first is the right of free speech, and the second is the right of political association. Expenditure caps directly limit the amount of speech by placing a ceiling on efforts to communicate with people. Contribution limits, on the other hand, only indirectly limit the amount of speech. So long as one is free to continue speaking through direct expenditures (*i.e.*, spending one's own money to make and distribute speech), rather than by contributing to a particular candidate committee or party, contribution limits may not limit the total amount of communication at all. But they also infringe the ability of citizens to associate for particular purposes by limiting the degree of financial involvement that a person may have with a particular group or campaign.

Thus, although the idea that "money is speech" is often criticized, of the twenty-four Justices that have served on the Supreme Court from *Buckley* through mid-2025, only Justice Stevens and, perhaps, Justice White have concluded that contribution limits should not be analyzed under the First Amendment. (Justice Ketanji Brown Jackson, appointed in the summer of 2022, has not, as of the summer of 2025, written or joined an opinion on the issue.) But even Justices Stevens and White conceded that contributing and spending money on elections merits some constitutional protection, if not necessarily under the Free Speech Clause of the First Amendment. The question for the Court, then, is not whether "money is speech" but rather the significance of the First Amendment rights at stake and whether the government can assert interests that are sufficiently important to override these rights.

3. Government Interests in Regulation

First Amendment doctrine provides that before the government can infringe on First Amendment rights, it must normally demonstrate a "compelling interest" in doing so. In defending restrictions on contributions and expenditures, the government has typically offered two principal justifications: preventing corruption or its appearance, and promoting equality. Ancillary interests in saving officeholders' time

---

10. Kovacs v. Cooper, 336 U.S. 77 (1949).
11. *Buckley*, 424 U.S. at 18.

and providing more opportunity for people to run for office have also been invoked. The government has offered additional interests to justify mandatory-disclosure laws, which are addressed in Chapter 9.

a. Prevention of Corruption or Its Appearance

In a cursory analysis, the *Buckley* Court held that limitations on contributions could be justified by the need to prevent "corruption or its appearance." "To the extent that large contributions are given to secure a political *quid pro quo* from current and potential office holders," it wrote, "the integrity of our system of representative democracy is undermined. Although the scope of such pernicious practices can never be reliably ascertained, the deeply disturbing examples surfacing after the 1972 election demonstrate that the problem is not an illusory one."[12] The brevity of the argument notwithstanding, the Court has consistently followed *Buckley* on this point. The important constitutional question, therefore, is not whether efforts to fight corruption can justify limitations, but rather what constitutes "corruption."

Consider the many types of behavior by an officeholder that some people might call "corrupt." An obvious example of corruption would be the officeholder who demands or agrees to sell his vote for bribes. But is an officeholder "corrupt," in a manner that would justify restrictions on campaign contributions and expenditures, if he frequents prostitutes or engages in extra-marital affairs? Is an officeholder "corrupt" in a way that justifies campaign finance limits if he appoints family members to government or campaign posts? Is it corrupt for a candidate to tell a voter (or group of voters), "If you vote for me, I will fight to have contracts awarded to the factory where you work in my district" (with the implied commitment to do so even if that is not the best deal for the government), or to tell voters, "I promise that, if elected, I will forgive your student-loan debt?" Is that a "bribe"? Is it "corrupt" if an officeholder agrees to meet with supporters of his campaign before meeting with his opponents? If not, how should he decide to allocate his time? Is it "corrupt" if some individuals spend a large sum to help elect a candidate? Assume that the candidate knows of the individuals' expenditures and knows what issues are important to them, but they have made no requests of the candidate, and the candidate has made them no promises—is your answer the same?

As the example of the candidate promising to bring contracts to the district makes clear, much campaigning in a democracy consists of making promises to various constituencies and blocs of voters. At a minimum, the candidate offers policy benefits in exchange for votes, but, in many cases, the policy, such as higher Social Security benefits for seniors or ethanol subsidies for agribusinesses, will give a direct financial benefit to the voters. Of course, these policies can be justified on grounds other than the benefits that particular groups or individuals may receive—we want seniors to

12. *Id.* at 26–27 (footnote omitted).

live comfortably in retirement, we think ethanol is good for the environment, we may think student-loan-debt relief is merited and good for society as a whole—but the self-interest and exchange cannot be denied.

Almost everyone would agree that bribery is inappropriate, but broader definitions of corruption may be hotly contested. Any of the scenarios above, and many others, might loosely be deemed "corruption" by some observers, but others might simply call them democracy at work.[13]

The *Buckley* plaintiffs argued that contribution limits were unnecessary to prevent corruption because bribery was already illegal. The Court rejected this narrow reading of corruption, arguing that "the giving and taking of bribes deal with only the most blatant and specific attempts of those with money to influence governmental action."[14] But the Court was, and has remained, unwilling to accept sweeping notions that there is a compelling government interest in reducing whatever some people might term "corruption." Instead, it emphasized in *Buckley*, and in most of its decisions since, that by corruption it means a "*quid pro quo*"[15] exchange of campaign contributions for policy favors.[16]

Thus, the Court has rejected the notion that preferred access to officeholders is the type of "corruption" that can justify restrictions on campaign contributions and expenditures.[17] It has more recently rejected the notion that certain speakers—corporations—are inherently more "corrupting" than others or that unequal spending is "corrupt."[18]

Similarly, when the Court suggested that preventing the "appearance of corruption stemming from public awareness of the opportunities for abuse inherent in a regime of large individual financial contributions" is "of almost equal concern,"[19] it did not mean that any factors that might cause voters at some point to proclaim that "Congress is corrupt" were sufficient justification for regulating campaign contributions and expenditures. Rather, just as "corruption" is limited to "*quid pro quo*"

---

13. Data show that large numbers of Americans consider politicians to be "corrupt." But what they mean by "corrupt" is remarkably varied and often quite different from what the Supreme Court considers "corruption" in the context of campaign finance. *See* David M. Primo & Jeffrey D. Milyo, Campaign Finance and American Democracy: What the Public Really Thinks and Why It Matters (2021).

14. 424 U.S. at 28.

15. Literally "what for what?" but often translated as "something for something." It represents the concept of bargained-for exchange, and, thus, consideration, in contract law. *See* Russ VerSteeg, Essential Latin for Lawyers 38 (2d ed. 2024).

16. 424 U.S. at 27.

17. *See* Citizens United v. Fed. Election Comm'n, 558 U.S. 310 (2010); *cf.* McConnell v. Fed. Election Comm'n, 540 U.S. 93, 150–51 (2003).

18. *See Citizens United*, 558 U.S. 310 (2010); First Nat'l Bank of Boston v. Bellotti, 435 U.S. 765 (1978). *Austin v. Michigan State Chamber of Commerce*, 494 U.S. 652 (1990), does accept both the idea that corporate speech is particularly corrupting and that a campaign can be "corrupt[]" if large expenditures are made that do not reflect the popularity of the speaker's ideas, but *Austin*, always out of place within the *Buckley* framework, was specifically overruled by *Citizens United*. *See* § F, *infra*.

19. *Buckley*, 424 U.S. at 27.

exchanges of campaign contributions for legislative favors, the "appearance of corruption" means opportunities to make such exchanges. The "appearance of corruption" interest addresses the overbreadth argument made by the *Buckley* plaintiffs, who argued that the overwhelming majority of contributors sought no special favors from officeholders but were merely supporting candidates with whose policies they agreed. Reducing the appearance of corruption is not a separate justification for broader regulation but rather part of the basic anti-corruption rationale accepted by the Court.

In summary, while the Court's definition of "corruption" has been criticized by many as unduly limited, it allows regulation of the most egregious exchanges while attempting to prevent "corruption" from becoming a catch-all mantra that justifies any regulation of political contributions and spending. It must be understood on its own terms if one is fully to understand the many cases and distinctions that follow from it.

b. Promoting Political Equality

The second interest advanced by the government to justify FECA was, in the Court's words, "to mute the voices of affluent persons and groups in the election process and thereby to equalize the relative ability of all citizens to affect the outcome of elections."[20] In one of the strongest passages in the opinion, the Court rejected this as an inadequate justification for the infringement on speech rights, stating that "the concept that government may restrict the speech of some elements of our society in order to enhance the relative voice of others is wholly foreign to the First Amendment."[21]

The Court's rejection of the equality rationale as a compelling government interest under the First Amendment has had major consequences for campaign finance law. Many supporters of campaign finance regulation, particularly among academicians and activists who are most involved in formulating theory, support regulation primarily as a means of equalizing political voices. However, post-*Buckley*, many campaign finance measures that are largely egalitarian in nature must be justified in court as anti-corruption measures. Given the Court's narrow focus on *quid pro quo* corruption, these efforts have been largely unsuccessful, with the notable exception of the (subsequently overruled) 1990 decision in *Austin v. Michigan State Chamber of Commerce*.[22]

Note, however, that while the Court in *Buckley* struck down limits as a means to equalize speech, it blessed government subsidies to speakers as a way to try to promote equality so long as such subsidies were not mandatory or accompanied by

---

20. 424 U.S. at 25–26.

21. 424 U.S. at 48–49. *See also* Arizona Free Enter. Club's Freedom's Club PAC v. Bennett, 564 U.S. 721 (2011); Citizens United v. Fed. Election Comm'n, 558 U.S. 310 (2010).

22. 494 U.S. 652 (1990).

mandatory spending limits.[23] But the Court has struck down public subsidy provisions that appear to be an attempt to favor some candidates over others.[24]

c. Other Government Interests

While the prevention of corruption and the promotion of equality were the primary justifications offered by the government in *Buckley*, other justifications were advanced in *Buckley* and have been offered in the years since.

One justification for the law, emphasized by the government, was to lower the cost of campaigns so as to open the system to candidates lacking substantial financial resources. *Buckley* noted this rationale in passing but never discussed it. Presumably, this must fail as simply another way of stating an egalitarian rationale. Although the stated interests are somewhat different—in one case, it is to equalize voices, and in the other, it is merely to encourage or to make it possible for more persons to run for office—both require suppressing some voices so that others have a better chance to win, *i.e.*, suppressing some to enhance the relative voices of others. Thus, this rationale must fail together with the pure equalization rationale to which it is related.

Some have argued that the government has a compelling interest in limiting expenditures in order to free officeholders from the burdens of fundraising. The rationale is that officeholders feel compelled to raise large sums in order to protect their seats, taking them away from their official duties. Only by capping expenditures can the perceived necessity to keep raising funds be stopped. Although this argument was not directly addressed in *Buckley*, the Court was certainly aware of it—the desire to relieve officeholders of the "rigors of fundraising" was cited by the Court as a justification to uphold public subsidies to campaigns.[25] That the Court did not discuss it at all as a justification for limiting expenditures generally suggests it would not have found the argument convincing. The Court dealt specifically, if only briefly, with this argument in *Randall v. Sorrell*,[26] and indeed held that it was "not persuasive."

In addition to limits on contributions and expenditures, FECA imposed numerous disclosure and reporting requirements on campaigns and other political speakers. These requirements are discussed in Chapter 9.

---

23. 424 U.S. at 91–95.
24. *See* § H(3)(c), *infra*.
25. 424 U.S. at 91.
26. 548 U.S. 230 (2006).

D. Limitations on Expenditures

1. General Principles

In accordance with the general principles announced in *Buckley*, the Court has subjected limitations on expenditures to the highest level of judicial scrutiny, described in *Buckley* as "exacting," and in later decisions as "strict scrutiny."[27] The Court's decisions rest on two key observations.

First, expenditure limitations, whether on candidates, parties, committees, or individuals, directly and often substantially limit the amount of speech. As passed, FECA, in fact, limited individuals and organizations other than candidates and parties to spending just $1,000. Considering how much it would cost a group such as the Chamber of Commerce, a union, Planned Parenthood, or Right to Life to run just one television ad, the potential for limiting speech and the discussion of candidates and issues through expenditure limits should be readily apparent. Or, as the Court noted in *Buckley*, "The provision . . . would make it a federal criminal offense for a person or association to place a single one-quarter page advertisement 'relative to a clearly identified candidate' in a major metropolitan newspaper."[28]

Second, bear in mind the Court's holding that corruption, defined as *quid pro quo* exchanges, is the only constitutionally permissible justification for limits. Spending money, the Court reasoned, does not raise the possibility for *quid pro quo* exchanges nearly as much as does soliciting and receiving contributions. If a candidate can raise a large amount of money in legal contributions (ones that Congress has determined do not pose a serious threat of *quid pro quo* exchanges), there is no corruption in spending that money. Similarly, the potential for a *quid pro quo* exchange, and hence corruption, disappears when a candidate spends his own money, in whatever amounts, on his campaign.

The *Buckley* Court's emphatic rejection of the equality rationale has extended to the argument that expenditure limits will equalize the resources of candidates, thus ensuring fairer elections. The Court pointed out in *Buckley* that equalizing one facet of campaigning—cash spending—did not necessarily equalize the campaign, since various candidates will have different advantages in name recognition, incumbent status, and other areas.[29] Here, the Court is quite right—equalizing spending might further increase inequalities in the race, if, for example, one candidate has the capacity to raise more money, but his opponent has a popular political name and the endorsement of the only daily newspaper in the district. Additionally, the willingness of donors to give (thus allowing candidates to spend) allows voters to express not only the fact of their support, but also the intensity of their support. Allowing for intensity of support to be reflected in campaign donations may be particularly important to minorities (racial,

27. 424 U.S. at 16; *Citizens United*, 558 U.S. 310, 340 (2010).

28. 424 U.S. at 40.

29. *Id.* at 56–57.

ideological, and otherwise), as it may allow them to fight on relatively even terms against a majority that holds a contrary position with less intensity.

2. Defining "Expenditure": The Express Advocacy/Issue Advocacy Distinction

FECA limited expenditures, imposing limits on candidates and candidate committees, as well as on other spenders, such as political parties, political action committees, trade associations, unions, and individual citizens. The *Buckley* Court began its analysis of these provisions by addressing the plaintiffs' claim that the statutory term "expenditure ... relative to a clearly identified candidate" was unconstitutionally vague and overly broad. This discussion gave rise to two separate categories of speech that became known as "express advocacy" and "issue advocacy," and the distinction between the two drove much campaign finance litigation from the 1976 decision in *Buckley* through the 2010 decision in *Citizens United v. Federal Election Commission*.[30] Thankfully for those seeking to understand campaign finance law, be they students, politicians, campaign consultants, or citizens who simply wish to speak out on candidates, issues, and elections, a series of Supreme Court and court of appeals decisions since 2007 has dramatically simplified the law governing independent expenditures.[31] In particular, the "express advocacy"/"issue advocacy" distinction has become much less important, except concerning disclosure obligations. An understanding of the "express advocacy"/"issue advocacy" distinction is still helpful, however, not only when dealing with disclosure, but in understanding the Court's rulings on the validity of expenditure limits and the evolution of campaign finance law from *Buckley* to *Citizens United.*

The *Buckley* Court was concerned that the statutory phrase "expenditure ... relative to a clearly identified candidate" was so vague that speakers would not know what was regulated and what was not. Furthermore, read literally, it would encompass almost all speech about politics and politicians. The Court began by agreeing with the court of appeals that the problem of overbreadth might be resolved if the phrase were interpreted to apply only to communications "advocating the election or defeat of" a candidate. But the Court still considered that too vague, noting that "the distinction between discussion of issues and candidates and advocacy of election or defeat of candidates may often dissolve in practical application."[32] Thus, the Court held that "in order to preserve the provision against invalidation on vagueness grounds, [FECA] must be construed to apply only to expenditures for communications that, in express terms, advocate the election or defeat of a clearly identified candidate for federal office."[33] In a further footnote, the Court gave examples of "express words of

30. 558 U.S. 310 (2010).

31. *See id.*; Fed. Election Comm'n v. Wisconsin Right to Life, 551 U.S. 449 (2007); SpeechNow.org v. Fed. Election Comm'n, 599 F.3d 686 (D.C. Cir. 2010); Emily's List v. Fed. Election Comm'n, 581 F.3d 1 (D.C. Cir. 2010).

32. 424 U.S. at 42.

33. *Id.* at 44.

advocacy of election or defeat," such as "vote for," "elect," "support," "cast your ballot for," "Smith for Congress," "vote against," "defeat," and "reject."[34]

In the years that followed, communications that used such phrases became known as "express advocacy," while ads that avoided using such words—ads that read, for example, "Congressman Jones even supports subsidies for Big Oil. Call Congressman Jones, and tell him to fight for us, not Big Oil"—became known as "issue advocacy."

One objective of the Bipartisan Campaign Reform Act of 2002[35] was to pull these "issue ads" under the umbrella of FECA's limits. The Act amended FECA, creating a new category of speech known as "electioneering communications." "Electioneering communications" was defined as expenditures in excess of $50,000 for broadcast ads that mentioned a candidate within thirty days of a primary election or caucus, or within sixty days of a general election. Spenders were prohibited from using corporate or union funds to broadcast such ads.

This prohibition was upheld by the Supreme Court in *McConnell v. FEC.*[36] The *McConnell* Court accepted the government's contention that electioneering communications could be presumed to be intended to elect a candidate. The Court further held that "express advocacy" was not a constitutional requirement in defining expenditures but rather a narrowing statutory interpretation to avoid a constitutional issue.[37] Other ads that constituted "the functional equivalent of express advocacy" could also be regulated if the standard for identifying the regulated speech were sufficiently clear to survive a vagueness challenge. The statutory definition of "electioneering communication," the Court held, met that test.[38] Both the mention of a candidate and the thirty-/sixty-day windows were bright lines, readily discerned. The Court further rejected the plaintiffs' argument that the standard, even if not vague, was overbroad.[39]

Less than four years after *McConnell*, however, in *Federal Election Commission v. Wisconsin Right to Life*,[40] the Court substantially altered course, with a renewed emphasis on overbreadth. Wisconsin Right to Life (WRTL) had produced a series of ads critical of the Senate's failure to act on various pending judicial nominations. With the Senate still in session, the ads called on viewers to contact both of the state's senators, one of whom was on the ballot in the upcoming election, to urge action on the nominations. The Court held that to the extent that the regulation limited discussion of a pending legislative issue, with no advocacy of election or defeat, it was overbroad. The government countered the overbreadth argument by pointing to facts and circumstances indicating that WRTL's actual intent was to influence the upcoming Wisconsin election for U.S. Senate. But the Court rejected this use of a speaker's subjective intent as a factor, holding that it reintroduced the vagueness problem at

34. *Id.* at 44 n.52.
35. Pub. L. 107-155 (2002).
36. 540 U.S. 93 (2003).
37. *See id.* at 190-93.
38. *See id.* at 194.
39. *See id.* at 193-94.
40. 551 U.S. 449 (2007).

the heart of *Buckley*. The plurality held that an ad must be unambiguously campaign-related to withstand the vagueness test: "Where the First Amendment is implicated, the tie goes to the speaker, not the censor."[41]

In summary, by limiting the phrases "relative to a clearly identified candidate" and "for the purpose of influencing an election" to express advocacy, *Buckley* dramatically reduced the scope of government regulation. *McConnell* allowed the government to reach beyond "express advocacy" to regulate "electioneering communications," and potentially other speech that was the "functional equivalent of express advocacy." However, as emphasized by *Wisconsin Right to Life*, any such standard still must pass the constitutional tests for vagueness and overbreadth, keeping regulation on a short tether. And as we will see in § D[3], the narrow definition of "expenditure" became, in turn, a rationale for striking down limitations on independent expenditures.

3. Limitations on Candidate Expenditures

Following the general principles outlined above, the Supreme Court has been steadfast in striking down limitations on expenditures by candidates and their campaign committees. As discussed in § D[1], *supra*, the Court has reasoned that there is no danger of *quid pro quo* corruption in the mere spending of money raised within the source and amount limitations of FECA.

In addition to striking down limits on spending by candidate campaigns, the *Buckley* Court refused to permit any limitation on a candidate's personal expenditures on his own behalf.[42] The lack of any anti-corruption interest in limiting a candidate's personal expenditures on his campaign should be clear. (It makes no sense to say that a candidate is corruptly beholden to himself.) But the ruling illustrates that the Court's rulings were intended to be functional, not formalistic. For example, while some have suggested that a candidate's own expenditures could be limited through the expedient of calling them "contributions" to the campaign,[43] the Court's ruling focuses on the actual interest of the state and the rights of the candidate, not on a formalistic distinction between "contributions" and "expenditures." If a candidate "contributes" to his own campaign, he does not create a danger of *quid pro quo* corruption, whether that action is labeled a "contribution" or an "expenditure."

Further, in *Randall v. Sorrell*, the Court rejected a rationale, offered by the State of Vermont, that such limitations were needed to relieve candidates from the time-consuming burden of fundraising, thus allowing them to focus on legislative duties.[44] *Randall* rejected this argument in a cursory analysis, noting that the *Buckley* Court was aware of the time-saving argument and concluding briefly that "it is highly unlikely that fuller consideration of this time protection rationale would have changed

---

41. *Id.* at 474.
42. 424 U.S. at 52–54.
43. *See* Nixon v. Shrink Missouri Gov't PAC, 528 U.S. 377, 405 (2000) (Breyer, J., concurring).
44. 548 U.S. 230 (2006).

Buckley's result."[45] Although the Court made no note of the reasons officeholders spend so much time fundraising, the problem is something of a self-inflicted wound, since those officeholders have created the low contribution limits and burdensome rules that make fundraising more time-consuming than in the past. Further, given the low cost of campaigning in Vermont—the typical legislative race at the time of *Randall* cost approximately $4,000—the time-saving argument was almost specious on the facts of the particular case.

Limitations on candidate spending, whether from the candidate's own resources or from funds raised from others, are therefore unconstitutional under *Buckley* and its progeny, with one exception: The Court has upheld spending limits as a condition for receiving campaign subsidies from the state so long as the candidate is not required to participate in the public-funding system. This exception will be discussed further in § I.

4. Limitations on Independent Expenditures

Although expenditures by a candidate from his own funds, or funds raised in small amounts, raise little concern about *quid pro quo* exchanges, supporters of limits on expenditures by other individuals and groups argue that large expenditures made separately from the candidate's campaign may pose dangers of *quid pro quo* corruption similar to those found in large contributions directly to the campaign.

If a donor simply pays for a candidate's media campaign, campaign staff, or other expenses at the candidate's request, or works in conjunction with the candidate, the argument goes, then this activity is not very different than a contribution to the campaign. The *Buckley* Court did not disagree with this notion. Rather, it noted that such an expenditure would constitute a "coordinated expenditure" and be treated by FECA as a contribution to the candidate, subject to contribution limitations, as discussed in § D[5], *infra*.

But what if an expenditure is made without "coordinating" with the candidate, that is, without the candidate's request, advance knowledge, consent, or consultation? Supporters of regulating these "independent expenditures" argue that they also create opportunities for political "corruption." A person or group making large independent expenditures may have undue influence over the legislator after the election, since the legislator will naturally be thankful for the support and hope to secure it in the next election.

But this "gratitude as corruption" argument has been consistently rejected by the Court. It is neither newsworthy nor generally inappropriate if officeholders act, after the election, to reward their supporters (within legal limits) or to adopt legislative positions that drew that support. The Court's definition of corruption suggests that independent expenditures cannot corrupt in a way that is sufficient to justify the substantial First Amendment burdens of limiting the amount of speech. Where

45. *Id.* at 245.

expenditures are made independently of a candidate, the opportunity for collusion and bargaining, and hence for a *quid pro quo* exchanges, will simply be missing. Therefore, *Buckley* holds, there is no constitutional basis to limit those expenditures.

The Court has adopted two other empirically based rationales for protecting unlimited independent expenditures. The first of these was a creature of its own making. Recall that in § D[2], we noted how the Court, citing vagueness concerns, defined "expenditure" narrowly to include only "express advocacy." Having done so, the Court found that, even assuming that the independent expenditures posed dangers of *quid pro quo* arrangements, limitations on expenditures would not effectively combat that evil. Why not? Because "[s]o long as persons and groups eschew expenditures that in express terms advocate the election or defeat of a clearly identified candidate, they are free to spend as much as they want to promote the candidate and his views. . . . It would naively underestimate the ingenuity and resourcefulness of persons and groups desiring to buy influence to believe that they would have much difficulty devising expenditures that skirted the restriction on express advocacy of election or defeat, but nevertheless benefited the candidate's campaign."[46] In other words, the narrow definition of "expenditure" required to overcome vagueness and overbreadth problems rendered any limits on independent expenditures ineffective. Thus, the government had no compelling interest in their enforcement.

The Court's second rationale for protecting unlimited independent expenditures was that while independent expenditures might benefit a campaign, thereby creating some degree of gratitude, they might not. Such expenditures might be of little value or even counterproductive to the campaign. In reality, we can anticipate that most independent expenditures will have at least some value to the campaign, but the point is not totally without merit—there are periodic episodes where candidates seem positively hurt by independent expenditures intended to help them, and many interest groups would prefer to have their preferred candidate lose the race talking about their issue rather than win the race while ignoring it. In any event, this argument had something of a make-weight feel to it. The driving element was the lack of opportunity for *quid pro quo* exchanges.

The bottom line, then, is that when, in *Citizens United v. Federal Election Commission*, the Court stated that "independent expenditures, including those made by corporations, do not give rise to corruption or the appearance of corruption,"[47] the Court was not making an empirical observation about public opinion or even about the likely effects of independent expenditures on officeholders and their behavior in office. Rather, the Court should be understood as stating a legal principle flowing from *Buckley*: Independent spending cannot generally be limited consistent with the First Amendment. Such effects as it may have on officeholders are part and parcel of the Amendment's protections. Political activity is intended to shape not only who is elected to office but also how they behave once in office. Speech cannot be restricted

46. *Buckley*, 424 U.S. at 45.
47. 558 U.S. 310, 357 (2010).

simply because it affects legislative behavior or engenders gratitude. Rather, only a certain type of behavior—the exchange of favors for contributions—may be limited. But not speech.

In 1985, the Court struck down a portion of the 1974 FECA amendments and made clear that the protection for independent expenditures extended to publicly subsidized campaigns, in which the candidates had agreed to limit their own expenditures as a condition of receiving a government campaign subsidy.[48] In 1996, in *Colorado Republican Federal Campaign Committee v. Federal Election Commission*,[49] the Court struck down an FEC regulation that treated all expenditures by political parties as necessarily coordinated with their candidates' campaigns. The Court's ruling cleared the way for parties to make unlimited independent expenditures. And the Court has also struck down public-funding systems that "penalized" independent speech by awarding "matching funds" to the opposing candidate.[50]

In 2010, in *SpeechNow.org v. Federal Election Commission*, the U.S. Court of Appeals for the District of Columbia Circuit held that the Federal Election Commission could not place restrictions on the size of contributions to organizations making independent expenditures.[51] The FEC chose not to appeal this decision, and other federal courts to consider the issue have followed the D.C. Circuit.[52] As a result, individuals and other entities are free to pool their resources, in any amounts, to make independent expenditures.

However, the Supreme Court has gone back and forth on the constitutionality of prohibitions on independent expenditures by corporations and unions. Although many of the *Buckley* plaintiffs that successfully challenged FECA's general limitation on expenditures by "persons" (a defined term in FECA that includes corporations and unions) were corporations, the plaintiffs had not specifically challenged another section of FECA that prohibited corporations and unions from making expenditures—the provisions first enacted in the Taft-Hartley Act in 1947. Thus, at least some opening remained for legislatures to attempt to prohibit independent spending by corporations and unions. In 1990, the Court upheld a Michigan law that prohibited corporate spending in candidate campaigns.[53] However, in 2010, the Court reversed itself and upheld the right of corporations, and, by implication, unions, to make independent expenditures.[54] These cases are discussed more fully in § E[1] and § E[4].

The current status of the law since the 2010 decision in *Citizens United* is that corporations and labor unions, like individuals and political committees, may make unlimited independent expenditures in connection with campaigns for office.

---

48. Fed. Election Comm'n v. Nat'l Conservative Pol. Action Comm., 470 U.S. 480 (1985).

49. 518 U.S. 604 (1996).

50. Arizona Free Enter. Club's Freedom's Club PAC v. Bennett, 564 U.S. 721 (2011).

51. 599 F.3d 686 (D.C. Cir. 2010) (*en banc*).

52. *See, e.g.*, Republican Party of New Mexico v. King, 741 F.3d 1089 (10th Cir. 2013); New York Progress & Protection PAC v. Walsh, 733 F.3d 483 (2d Cir. 2013).

53. Austin v. Michigan State Chamber of Com., 494 U.S. 652 (1990).

54. Citizens United v. Fed. Election Comm'n, 558 U.S. 310 (2010).

5. Limitations on Coordinated Expenditures

a. General Principles

For purposes of FECA and most state laws, coordinated expenditures are treated as contributions to a candidate. If it were otherwise, a supporter and candidate could avoid limits on contributions by the simple expedient of having the candidate (or his agent) specify to the supporter what actions to take, ads to run, publications to print and distribute, etc., and have the supporter pay for them directly. Thus, in light of the Court's upholding of limitations on contributions (*see* § E, *infra*), the question is not whether coordinated expenditures can be limited but rather what constitutes "coordination." A finding that an expenditure is "coordinated" with a campaign or political party can have enormous ramifications because, while expenditures are otherwise unlimited, coordinated expenditures are treated like contributions and, thus, at the federal level and in most jurisdictions, they are subject to limits on source and amount.

FECA's 1974 amendments originally defined what we now call a "coordinated expenditure" as one "authorized or requested" by the candidate or his agent. The original definition was relatively unimportant since the law limited both contributions and independent expenditures to $1,000. However, once *Buckley* determined that limitations on independent expenditures were unconstitutional, the definition became extremely important. A supporter of a candidate could make unlimited independent expenditures, but if it were later determined that those expenditures fell within the definition of coordinated expenditures, they could amount to a very large, illegal "contribution" to the campaign.[55] As amended, the definition now includes expenditures made in "cooperation, consultation, or concert with, or at the request or suggestion" of a candidate or candidate's agent, as well as the "dissemination, distribution, or republication, in whole or in part" of any campaign materials prepared by the candidate or his agents.[56]

Two important questions are raised in efforts to define what constitutes a "coordinated" expenditure: what content will be considered campaign-related, and what conduct will trigger a coordination finding. In understanding the parameters of coordinated expenditures, bear in mind that the Supreme Court's approach does not allow the limitation of speech *per se* but rather seeks to focus on behavior that is akin to bribery—the *quid pro quo* exchange of campaign contributions for official action. It is this opportunity for improper bargaining, and not the effectiveness of the speech or the gratitude it may engender, that brings expenditures under the coordination umbrella.

---

55. *See Buckley*, 424 U.S. at 46 n.53.

56. 52 U.S.C. § 30116(a)(7).

b. Content Restrictions

The first issue is that of content. Recall that *Buckley* began its discussion of expenditures by giving the term "expenditure" a narrowing interpretation that included only "express advocacy" of the election or defeat of a candidate. Should a similarly narrow definition of "expenditure" apply in the context of coordinated activity? Consider that many groups and individuals that are interested in speaking out on issues also meet regularly with officeholders and may plan a campaign with supportive public officials to boost public support of (or opposition to) an issue, or to pressure other officeholders to take positions for or against the issue. Arguably, the same vagueness considerations that motivated the Court to narrow the definition of "expenditure" when discussing independent expenditures would apply in the context of coordinated expenditures. This is especially true because investigations into allegations of illegal coordination are necessarily among the most intrusive undertaken by the FEC or state enforcement agencies. Typically, they require searching emails, phone records, internal memoranda, calendars, and the like for evidence of consultation and coordination pertaining to the expenditure. This not only has high costs for respondents but may force them to reveal confidential strategies and information.[57] Applying the "express advocacy" definition to coordinated expenditures, however, would allow a candidate and a supporter to design a full ad campaign together, with the candidate's giving precise instructions, so long as the ads did not use words of express advocacy, such as "vote for," "support," or "vote against." Such a limited definition of "coordinated expenditure" would seem contrary to the goals of the coordination rule and open the door to the type of *quid pro quo* exchanges that the government has a legitimate interest in preventing.

In *Orloski v. Federal Election Commission*, the U.S. Court of Appeals for the D.C. Circuit upheld an FEC determination that assessed coordination by applying an objective express-advocacy test, rather than one dependent on the intent of a speaker to influence an election.[58] Under the objective test, a donation had to meet the definition of "expenditure" before it could qualify as a "coordinated expenditure." But two decades later, in *Shays v. Federal Election Commission*, the same Court ruled against the FEC's application of an objective test that the Court believed left open too much room for abuse.[59]

As a matter of policy, the FEC applies what it calls a "content standard" as a threshold for considering whether a given expenditure can be considered coordinated. The

---

57. *See* James Bopp, Jr. & Heidi K. Abegg, *The Developing Constitutional Standards for "Coordinated Expenditures": Has the Federal Election Commission Finally Found a Way to Regulate Issue Advocacy?*, 1 Election L.J. 209, 210 (2002); Bradley A. Smith & Stephen M. Hoersting, *A Toothless Anaconda: Innovation, Impotence, and Overenforcement at the Federal Election Commission*, 1 Election L.J. 145 (2002).

58. Orloski v. Fed. Election Comm'n, 795 F.2d 156 (D.C. Cir. 1986). Under the test, corporate sponsorship of an event featuring an incumbent member of Congress would be permissible if (1) there was no express advocacy of the congressman's reelection at the event, and (2) there were no solicitations of campaign contributions at the event. *See id.* at 160.

59. Shays v. Fed. Election Comm'n, 528 F.3d 914 (D.C. Cir. 2008).

FEC rule as of August 2024 a held that a payment for a public communication would qualify as a "coordinated expenditure," no matter the degree of actual coordination, only if it contained express advocacy; republished campaign material; referenced a candidate within 90 days of a House or Senate election or within 120 days of a presidential primary or election; or was coordinated with a candidate and aired in the candidate's district within 90 days of an election, or was coordinated with a political party and aired within a two-year time frame.[60]

Few states have followed the FEC's lead and adopted any type of content restriction, so in state and local races, as well as most federal races, the main force of the coordination analysis will fall on the spender's conduct.[61]

c. Conduct Constituting Coordination

After content, the second question is determining what behavior constitutes sufficient evidence of "coordination." The problems arise, again, because the same groups and individuals that might make campaign expenditures will often have dealings with officeholders outside of the campaign context. Determining that an expenditure is "coordinated" is easy where a candidate specifically asks a supporter to make a particular expenditure. But such requests are rare, if only because both parties know that such a request will turn any expenditure into a "contribution" subject to lower dollar limits. How specific, then, does a "suggestion" have to be to turn what would otherwise be an unlimited "independent expenditure" into a limited "coordinated expenditure"? What degree of "consultation" or "acting in concert" constitutes "coordination"? Vagueness considerations would preclude any type of "I know it when I see it" standard.

The best way to think about the standard may be to return to *Buckley*'s definition of "corruption." The goal of coordination rules is to enforce the prohibition on *quid pro quo* dealing that is at the heart of the Court's definition of corruption. It is not to limit expenditures on campaigning, which the Court ruled is generally an impermissible state goal. Rather than view coordinated communications as otherwise protected speech that can be limited, it is best to understand coordination rules as limiting certain conduct. Although the courts have not defined the problem in these exact terms, the handful of rulings interpreting coordination have generally followed this approach.

For example, for many years after *Buckley*, the FEC's regulations assumed that political parties could not make independent expenditures. The FEC's logic was that parties are inherently tied to their own candidates, share the same goal, and are part of a "team." Thus, the FEC held that any expenditure by a party was necessarily a "coordinated expenditure." In *Colorado Republican Federal Campaign Committee v.*

---

60. 11 C.F.R. § 109.21(c).

61. A notable exception is Wisconsin, where the state supreme court has interpreted the state statute to treat as coordination only those expenditures that include express advocacy. *See* Wisconsin *ex rel.* Two Unnamed Petitioners v. Peterson, 866 N.W.2d 165 (Wis. 2015). *See also* Michigan Sec'y of State Advisory Op. *In Re* Witte (Aug. 26, 2002) (limiting Michigan statute to "express advocacy").

Federal Election Committee,[62] the Court rejected this rule. The Colorado Republican Party ran a number of ads attacking the Democratic incumbent for U.S. Senate before a Republican challenger had been selected. The Republican Party did not argue that its expenditures were independent—it admitted that its behavior was "coordinated" under FEC regulations then in force—but argued that the limits on party-coordinated spending were unconstitutional. The Supreme Court, however, looked not to the regulatory definition of coordination but to the actual facts of the case. Since the Party had yet to choose a nominee, any opportunity for *quid pro quo* bargaining was literally impossible. The Court held that a finding of coordination had to rely on the actual conduct of the parties, not a definition based on mere commonality of interests. In other words, because the opportunity for *quid pro quo* exchange was not present, the Party, like other actors, could not be restricted from making independent expenditures, and the regulations were invalid.

The Colorado Republican Party, however, continued to press its case for unlimited party-coordinated expenditures, and the case again reached the Supreme Court. The Party's position was that because parties and their candidates were inherently allied, a party could not corrupt its own members/candidates. The Court specifically hinged its decision on the question "is there reason to think that coordinated spending by a party would raise the risk of corruption posed when others spend in coordination with a candidate?"[63] The Court analyzed the possibility for *quid pro quo* exchanges through party-coordinated spending and found that the parties could function as "funnels" for such spending, essentially acting as agents for donors seeking *quid pro quo* deals.[64] As with many of the Court's holdings on campaign finance, one might question the Court's view of a political party as a bagman for corrupt dealmaking, but, given that empirical view, the decision fits neatly within *Buckley*'s paradigm and narrow definition of corruption.[65]

The *Colorado Republican Federal Campaign Committee* cases are the Supreme Court's only extended ventures into the issue of coordination. Lower-court decisions are also few, but they exhibit the same reticence to allow regulation where *quid pro quo* exchanges are unlikely.

In *Clifton v. Federal Election Commission*, the Court of Appeals for the First Circuit rejected on statutory grounds an FEC regulation that prohibited any oral communication between a candidate or his campaign and an organization preparing a voter scorecard, listing, rating, or analysis of his votes.[66] The court suggested that if the reg-

62. 514 U.S. 604 (1996).

63. Fed. Election Comm'n v. Colorado Republican Fed. Campaign Comm., 533 U.S. 431, 445 (2001).

64. *Id.* at 446, 457–65.

65. In 2022, the National Republican Party again challenged the limits on coordinated party expenditures. It lost before the *en banc* Sixth Circuit, but the Supreme Court granted *certiorari* and in the 2025 Term the Court will consider whether to overrule *Colorado Republican II*. Nat'l Republican Senatorial Comm. v. Fed. Election Comm'n, 117 F.4th 389 (6th Cir. 2024) (*en banc*), *cert. granted*, 145 S. Ct. __, 2025 WL 1787717 (2025).

66. 114 F.3d 1309 (1st Cir. 1998).

ulation were a valid interpretation of the statute, it would raise serious constitutional questions under the "unconstitutional conditions" doctrine.[67] The court believed that the scorecard producer, Maine Right to Life, could not be prevented from publishing a scorecard merely because it had discussed a candidate's position orally with the campaign in order to ensure that its scorecard was correct. Again, the court simply found that there could be no corruption—no illicit bargain—in attempting to ascertain the accuracy of a candidate's position.

The FEC regulation did allow Maine Right to Life to contact candidates to ascertain their positions on issues, but only in writing. Of course, a written communication, lacking the give and take of oral exchange, might seem inadequate or at least cumbersome as a means for pinning down or understanding a candidate's position. But if we view coordination restrictions as restrictions on conduct raising the possibility of *quid pro quo* corruption, then the FEC's regulation may be a very reasonable compromise allowing the speaker to ascertain correct information but limiting the opportunity for the offending bargaining conduct,[68] and the *Clifton* majority may have been incorrect. Regardless, we see that it is not the distinctive features of the speech but rather the possibility for corrupt dealmaking that drove the court's analysis.

Similarly, only one federal-district-court decision has examined coordination in depth. In *Federal Election Commission v. Christian Coalition*, the district court rejected an insider-trading theory of "coordination" in which any use of nonpublic information by a speaker constituted "coordination."[69] Instead, the district court held that an expenditure would be deemed "coordinated" only if the campaign suggested or consented to the expenditure, if the candidate or campaign had control over the expenditure, or if there was "substantial discussion or negotiation between the campaign and the spender" over a communication's contents, timing, location, mode, intended audience (*e.g.*, choice between newspaper or radio advertisement), or "volume" (*e.g.*, number of copies of printed materials or frequency of media spots).[70] The court's opinion recognized the lack of guidance in *Buckley* but, noting that a broad prohibition on any contact would have a substantial impact on speech, concluded, "I take from *Buckley* and its progeny the directive to tread carefully[.] ... [T]he spender should not be deemed to forfeit First Amendment protections for her own speech merely by having engaged in some consultations or coordination with a federal candidate."[71] The result is a decision that requires relatively intense consultation between a candidate and a spender for the expenditure to be considered coordination.

Applying the standard, the *Christian Coalition* court held that discussion over which issues to include in a voter guide or scorecard and how those issues were phrased (the court used the example "'homosexual rights' versus 'human rights'") would be

---

67. *Id.* at 1315 (citing Regan v. Taxation with Representation, 461 U.S. 540 (1983)).

68. The dissent analyzed the case much in this manner. *See* 114 F.3d at 1317, 1320 (Bownes, C.J., dissenting).

69. 52 F. Supp. 2d 45, 90–91 (D.D.C. 1999) (Green, J.).

70. *Id.* at 92.

71. *Id.* at 91.

coordination. For conversations about a candidate's position on issues to be deemed "coordination"—the issue discussed in *Clifton* as well—"the conversation . . . must go well beyond inquiry into negotiation."[72] Similarly, "discussions of the timing, location of distribution, or volume of voter guide distribution also must transgress mere inquiry."[73] The court applied similar standards to determine if a speaker's consultations on its "get-out-the-vote" efforts rose to the level of prohibited coordination.[74] Tough on the government in theory, the court's standard proved even tougher when applied to the particular facts of the case. Recognizing substantial contact between the Christian Coalition and various campaigns, the court nonetheless found no legal coordination absent "discussion and negotiation" sufficient to establish the speaker and the candidate or campaign as "partner[s]" or "joint venture[r]s."[75]

The *Christian Coalition* ruling seemed to require consultation that went beyond creating the mere "appearance of corruption," *i.e.*, the opportunity for corrupt *quid pro quo* bargaining, to requiring conduct that would actually be corrupt, or at least would create a very heightened appearance of corruption. Whether the *Buckley* Court, had it considered the issue, would have required such a high standard is not certain. But the approach taken in *Christian Coalition* fits quite comfortably into the *Buckley* paradigm demanding *quid pro quo* exchange or the appearance that it was occurring. *Christian Coalition* implicitly rejected the idea that the Coalition's effort to instill a sense of gratitude in the various campaigns it assisted constituted corruption or that the mere efforts to make one's spending as effective as possible converted that spending from independent to coordinated.

After the *Christian Coalition* case was decided, the FEC wrote new coordination regulations based on the district court's formulation. These regulations were heavily criticized by pro-reform organizations, which sought a new legislative definition as part of the Bipartisan Campaign Reform Act of 2002.[76] But Congress could not agree on a new definition, so it settled for repealing the FEC's definition, demanding that the agency write a new one that did not require "formal collaboration" and requiring the agency to take into account the possible use of third-party common vendors and former employees to coordinate activity.

The FEC ultimately developed a rule that defined coordination to include any use of a common vendor or former campaign employee to engage in any of a number of activities for the candidate or the candidate's opponent, including development

---

72. *Id.* at 92–93. "For example, if the [speaker's] interpretation of the candidate's prior statements or votes would lead it to say he 'opposes' the issue, and the campaign tries to persuade the corporation to use 'supports' on the guide, that is coordination." *Id.* at 93.

73. *Id.* at 93 ("A [speaker's] mere announcement to the campaign that it plans to distribute thousands of voter guides in select churches on the Sunday before election day, even if that information is not yet public, is not enough to be coordination. Coordination requires some to-and-fro between corporation and campaign on these subjects.").

74. *Id.*

75. *Id.* at 92, 95.

76. Pub. L. No. 107-155. The Bipartisan Campaign Reform Act is generally known as "BCRA" or as "McCain-Feingold," after its lead Senate sponsors.

of media strategy; selecting audiences; polling; fundraising; developing content for, or producing, public communications; developing voter, mailing, or donor lists; and selecting campaign personnel. However, the FEC limited the reach of the rule to a vendor or former employee who had provided such services to the candidate or campaign within 120 days prior to assisting the otherwise-independent speaker. Beyond that point, the FEC reasoned, in the fast-moving world of political campaigns, any "inside" information was unlikely to be relevant.

In *Shays v. Federal Election Commission* (*Shays III*), the Court of Appeals struck down the 120-day limitation as arbitrary and capricious under the Administrative Procedure Act.[77] The court's analysis was cursory, holding that the FEC had not explained why a vendor or former employee's knowledge lost value after 120 days.[78] The court's ruling is questionable. The theory needed to support such a broad prophylactic rule is that common vendors and former employees serve as go-betweens or agents representing the parties in the type of *quid pro quo* bargaining that *Buckley* held could be limited. In fact, there is no evidence that vendors or former employees are particularly utilized as agents to negotiate *quid pro quo* arrangements. To the extent they might be, actions by agents are already included in determining what conduct is prohibited for coordination purposes,[79] so there is no reason to single out vendors and former employees for special treatment. Indeed, vendors are particularly poor choices for brokering a *quid pro quo* exchange, given that campaign disbursements to a vendor must be disclosed pursuant to the Act.[80] The trail to the vendor is immediately obvious. A former employee of the candidate currently in the open employ of the independent speaker would seem only a marginally less disastrous choice as the go-between for a corrupt bargain.

The focus by both the *Shays III* plaintiffs and court on the "value" of the information a former employee or vendor might convey to the speaker is directly contrary to *Buckley*'s holding on expenditures. As we have seen, what *Buckley* specifically rejected was the idea that the mere value of speech and the gratitude it would engender were sufficient bases to restrict such speech. Nothing in *Buckley* suggests that a speaker may not attempt to make his independent speech as effective and valuable as possible.

Although use of a common vendor may trigger a coordination finding, the FEC has provided a "safe harbor" by which a commercial vendor may provide services to a candidate, provided any former employees or vendors of the candidate with inside information and employed by the vendor are walled off from those persons working on the campaign.

Since the D.C. Circuit's 2010 decision in *SpeechNow.org v. Federal Election Commission*[81] allowed the creation of so-called "Super PACs,"[82] the use of former employees

---

77. 528 F.3d 914 (2008).
78. *Id.* at 928–29.
79. 11 C.F.R. § 109.20(a).
80. *See* 52 U.S.C. § 30104(a)(1).
81. SpeechNow.org v. Fed. Election Comm'n, 499 F.3d 686 (D.C. Cir. 2010).
82. *See* § E[4], *infra*.

and advisors to "coordinate" activity has drawn a good deal of commentary, with critics' arguing that Super PACs are not operating truly independently of the candidates they support because a candidate's "old consultants and . . . best buddies are setting them up," "they have former aides running this," or the candidate's "father heavily contributed."[83] But none of these facts automatically gives rise to a coordination claim. These claims constitute the sort of misguided, nonfunctional approach rejected by the Court in *Colorado Republican Federal Campaign Committee I*. Coordination cannot be presumed, and the mere fact of an affinity and unity of interest between candidate and speaker does not constitute coordination. A candidate's past advisors, "buddies," former aides, and family members are exactly the type of people who may be most interested in speaking out in favor of the candidate. Their speech does not lose its protection simply because of who they are or what they have done in the past. Nor does their "insider knowledge" turn their independent activity into coordinated activity—such an approach is the "insider trading" standard rejected in *Christian Coalition*. What is required to find coordination is actual coordination—the type of interaction that gives rise to opportunities for *quid pro quo* exchanges of official action for campaign support.

d. Summary of Coordination Law

Despite its importance and the near ubiquity of laws that treat coordinated expenditures as contributions, coordination remains one of the more inexact legal elements in campaign finance law. At the federal level, portions of the FEC's regulations have been ruled arbitrary and capricious under the Administrative Procedure Act, but the Commission has been unable to muster a majority for new rules. Most states have no definition of "coordination" or "coordinated behavior" at all. And decisions by courts interpreting such provisions are few and far between.

Generally, coordination should be found where the candidate requests or authorizes the spending at issue, or where the spender and candidate have substantial discussions over the content, timing, means, or audience for particular advertising. Coordination is not, however, a means of simply trying to limit effective independent speech. The mere fact that speakers have knowledge of a campaign's goals or resources—especially when gained through public sources—is not normally sufficient to make their speech a "coordinated" activity. Limits on coordinated spending are a means to make contribution limits effective in preventing *quid pro quo* bargaining. They are not a backdoor means to limit expenditures made separately from a candidate.

---

83. *See* Bradley A. Smith, *Super PACs and the Role of Coordination in Campaign Finance Law*, 49 Willamette L. Rev. 603, 605 (2013), and citations therein.

E. Limitations on Contributions

1. General Principles

Contribution limitations are reviewed under a lower, more permissive level of constitutional scrutiny than are limitations on expenditures. The Supreme Court has generally upheld the right of legislatures to place restrictions on the size and, in some cases, the sources of campaign contributions.

Nevertheless, contribution limits do infringe on both speech and associational rights. From the standpoint of a candidate for office, limitations on contributions burden the right to speak by making it harder for the candidate to raise the funds needed to spread his message. If set low enough, limits can effectively cut off most political dialogue by preventing candidates and parties from effectively conveying a message to the public.[84] But limits need not reduce candidate speech in a significant way. For example, a candidate planning a $1 million campaign budget may reach that total in any number of combinations, ranging from one donor contributing the entire amount to (at least theoretically) one million donors contributing $1 each. By forcing a candidate to solicit more donors, limitations on the size of contributions can increase the time and the cost of fundraising. This may reduce campaign budgets, but it does not necessarily do so, and such reduction as occurs may not be terribly substantial. The *Buckley* Court noted that at the time of the 1974 FECA amendments, only 5.1% of federal-candidate funds were raised in amounts exceeding the limits put in place by FECA.[85]

From a donor's standpoint, contribution limits directly reduce the amounts that may be given to a candidate, but they do not have to reduce the total amount of donor speech so long as donors remain free to make unlimited expenditures. Additionally, the *Buckley* Court discounted the speech right involved, suggesting that contributions amounted to mere proxy speech in that the donor relinquished control over the message once the funds were given to the candidate. (The validity of this distinction is suspect, however, since the same could be said anytime money is given to a group or organization to communicate with the public on issues or candidates, or anytime a funder gives up sole control over a message.[86]) The Court also argued that the act of contributing sent a message of support, but because it did not express the basis of support, "[t]he quantity of communication by the contributor does not increase perceptibly with the size of his contribution."[87] In other words, a donor sends more or less the same message—"I support this candidate's campaign"—by donating any amount, large or small. Again, one can question the accuracy of the Court's statement—a wealthy individual who gives $100,000 to one candidate and $100 to another sends very different messages to both the candidates and the public.

---

84. Buckley v. Valeo, 424 U.S. 1, 21 (1976) (*per curiam*).
85. *Id.* at 21 n.23.
86. *See* Fed. Election Comm'n v. Nat'l Conservative Pol. Action Comm., 470 U.S. 480, 495 (1985).
87. *Buckley*, 424 U.S. at 21.

The Court also identified burdens on the First Amendment right of association that are imposed by contribution limits. By limiting the size of contributions, FECA limited the depth of association that a donor could form with a candidate. But the donor remained free to join other groups, including other groups supporting the candidate or party, and to devote time to the candidate's campaign. Finding that the burdens on speech and association were relatively light, the Court held that the burden on association fell "where the actuality and potential for corruption have been identified."[88] Note again the emphasis on *quid pro quo* exchanges—the type of association that was limited was the provision of dollars directly to the candidate, not association with other politically oriented groups or other types of association with a candidate.

As a result, the Court has consistently given legislatures substantial leeway to regulate campaign contributions. Contributions are not reviewed under the highest "strict scrutiny" standard but rather under a more lenient standard requiring only that they be "closely drawn" to meet the state's concern.[89] In *Nixon v. Shrink Missouri Government PAC*,[90] the Court substantially lowered the evidentiary burden needed to justify limitations. In that case, the plaintiffs argued that, prior to enacting campaign contribution limits in 1994, the Missouri legislature had not demonstrated a pattern or appearance of corruption from campaign contributions that would justify such restrictions. The state's evidence of corruption consisted of little more than a handful of newspaper editorials decrying "corruption" and an affidavit from the legislation's sponsor. The court of appeals struck down the legislation as not justified by a compelling state interest. The Supreme Court reversed, however, all but doing away with any evidentiary requirement before contribution limits may be enacted. The "quantum of empirical evidence needed to satisfy heightened judicial scrutiny of legislative judgments," the Court held, "will vary up or down with the novelty and plausibility of the justification raised."[91] The Court went on to hold that *Buckley* constituted a legal determination that the threshold justifying contribution limits had been reached. In this respect, then, *Shrink Missouri Government PAC*—like *Citizens United* on the question of independent expenditures—makes clear that the Court views the issue not as one of empirical data but rather as a legal determination of the type of political activity that may be regulated consistent with the First Amendment.

The Court's distinction between contributions (generally subject to limits) and expenditures (generally not subject to limits) does not seem to depend on the substance or character of the particular speech itself. A contribution directly to a candidate's campaign may be used by the campaign to run an ad saying "Congressman Smith is the best public servant since Abraham Lincoln: Vote Smith," and an independent expenditure may say the exact same thing. Rather, the distinction lies in

---

88. *Id.* at 28.
89. *Id.* at 25.
90. 528 U.S. 377 (2000).
91. *Id.* at 391.

the opportunity for corrupt behavior—*quid pro quo* bargaining of campaign contributions for official action.

2. Limits on Contributions to Candidate Campaigns

With the Court's go-ahead in *Buckley*, reaffirmed in *Shrink Missouri Government PAC*, the federal government and thirty-eight states have placed limits on the size of contributions to legislative candidates, and forty-five states have enacted at least some type of campaign-contribution limits, although in some states the limits are nominal or apply only to certain types of donors—typically corporations, unions, and foreign nationals. Eleven states leave individual contributions to candidates unlimited.[92]

The courts have given the states broad discretion in enacting limits on contributions to candidates. Beyond the relaxed scrutiny and low evidentiary burden generally placed on states in light of *Shrink Missouri Government PAC*, courts have been reluctant to second-guess particular limits or regulatory schemes. In *Buckley*, the plaintiffs had argued that FECA's $1,000 limit was unrealistically low because such an amount could not realistically buy influence. Plaintiffs also argued that having the same limit on both presidential campaigns and House races indicated that the selection of limits was arbitrary. *Buckley* rejected both arguments, stating that "a court has no scalpel to probe, whether, say, a $2,000 ceiling might not serve as well as $1,000."[93] *Shrink Missouri Government PAC* reaffirmed the Court's unwillingness generally to police specific limits and rejected the idea that limits had to be adjusted for inflation in order to remain valid,[94] although six years later, in *Randall v. Sorrell*, the lack of any inflation adjustment was a factor in the Court's holding that Vermont's limits were unconstitutionally low.[95] Additionally, the courts have generally rejected equal-protection claims where legislators have set limits at different levels for different types of speakers, such as corporations and unions.[96]

Legislators do not, however, have free rein to set limits at any level. *Buckley* is based on the notion that speech ought not to be restricted. It allowed limits on contributions in part because the plaintiffs failed to show that such limits would actually restrict

92. Nat'l Conference of State Legislatures, *Campaign Finance Regulation: State Comparisons* (updated Oct. 24, 2022), https://www.ncsl.org/elections-and-campaigns/campaign-finance-regulation-state-comparisons.

93. 424 U.S. at 30.

94. 528 U.S. at 395–96.

95. 548 U.S. 230 (2006).

96. *See, e.g.*, Austin v. Michigan State Chamber of Com., 494 U.S. 652 (1990); Upstate Jobs Party v. Kosinski, 106 F.4th 232 (2d Cir. 2024); Thompson v. Hebdon, 7 F.4th 811 (9th Cir. 2021). *But see* Riddle v. Hickenlooper, 742 F.3d 922 (10th Cir. 2014) (holding unconstitutional a statute discriminating against write-in candidates); Protect My Check, Inc. v. Dilger, 176 F. Supp. 3d 685 (E.D. Ky. 2016) (holding unconstitutional a state law prohibiting corporate contributions but allowing contributions by unions and LLCs).

candidate speech in any meaningful way, while donors would be free to express themselves through independent expenditures. But *Buckley* did note that contribution limits would be constitutionally suspect if they "prevented candidates and political committees from amassing the resources necessary for effective advocacy."[97]

In *Randall v. Sorrell*, the Court for the first time found a state limitation on contributions to be so low as to be unconstitutional. Vermont enacted a comprehensive set of restrictions that limited contributions to $400 for statewide races, $300 for state-senate races, and $200 for state-representative races. These limits applied to all party committees combined, as well as to individuals. The law also limited individual contributions to parties to $2,000. The Court struck down the Vermont law for several reasons, which it considered in combination. Although in *Shrink Missouri Government PAC*, the Court had refused to consider the effects of inflation on Missouri's limits, in *Randall*, the Court noted that, adjusted for inflation since *Buckley*, Vermont's limits amounted to approximately $57 per election for statewide office, versus the $1,000 limit for House races approved in *Buckley*, and also that Vermont's limits were the lowest in the country. The Court noted that Vermont's limits would have reduced the funds available to various challengers by as much as 53% and would have reduced party contributions by as much as 99%.

Perhaps most importantly, the Vermont law also counted incidental costs incurred by volunteers. A campaign volunteer who made a handful of trips driving across the small state to perform volunteer activities could find himself over the contribution limit, as might a volunteer who offered the use of his house and provided coffee and doughnuts for a few dozen neighbors to meet the candidate two or three times.[98] Combined with the lack of indexing for future inflation and the lack of state evidence of particular need for such low limits, the Court's plurality of Justices Breyer and Alito and Chief Justice Roberts held that Vermont's limits were an unconstitutional restriction on speech. Justices Scalia, Thomas, and Kennedy all concurred in the judgment, but they would have gone further, to completely rethinking *Buckley*'s treatment of contributions.

In the wake of *Randall*, there was some thought that the decision might lead to a rash of decisions finding various state contribution limits unconstitutional. *Randall*'s complex, multi-factored test, however, made it of limited use to plaintiffs challenging limits.[99] Thirteen years after *Randall*, in *Thompson v. Hebdon*,[100] the Supreme Court nevertheless reaffirmed the viability of *Randall*, and, on remand, the Ninth Circuit reversed its own earlier ruling and found that Alaska's $500 limit on individual contributions was unconstitutionally low.[101]

In addition to upholding limits on contributions by individuals, the Court has also upheld limits on donations by parties and various other types of political organizations. In many states, parties may contribute considerably higher amounts than individuals

---

97. 424 U.S. at 21. *See also* Shrink Missouri Government PAC, 528 U.S. at 395–96.
98. 548 U.S. at 260.
99. *See, e.g.*, Lair v. Motl, 873 F.3d 1170 (9th Cir. 2017).
100. 589 U.S. 1 (2019) (*per curiam*).
101. Thompson v. Hebdon, 7 F.4th 811 (9th Cir. 2021).

are permitted to contribute, and some intermediate level is reserved for other political committees, often called political action committees (PACs). FECA treats parties and other political committees the same for the purpose of directly contributing to candidates and permits both to contribute more than individuals are permitted to contribute. The differing levels might seem at odds with the anti-corruption principle of *Buckley*. For example, if an individual may trade a contribution for official favors for $3,300 (the federal limit in 2024), why are PACs allowed to contribute $5,000 (the federal limit for PACs)? Surely a PAC sponsored by a corporation, union, or interest group is as capable of seeking a *quid pro quo* bargain as an individual is. Is there any reason to think that PAC money is less effective in bargaining for favors than individual contributions are? Higher levels of giving might make sense for broad-based organizations such as political parties, on the grounds that the diverse interests of their members dilute their ability to bargain for specific government favors. But that would not seem to hold true for individual corporate- or union-sponsored PACs, trade associations such as the National Association of Realtors, or single-interest groups such as Everytown USA, an anti-gun organization.

In fact, the higher limits for PACs seem themselves to have been the result of lobbying muscle, particularly by unions, at the time that FECA was passed. As for parties, many of the officeholders who passed FECA certainly felt some desire to preserve the position of political parties. The *Buckley* Court further saw value in the ability of citizens to associate through such organizations, and their higher contribution limits lessened the sting of the more-restrictive individual-contribution limits.[102] On the whole, however, it may be best merely to consider the higher limits for committees as part of the compromise of politics—they survive judicial review because of the Supreme Court's "lack of a scalpel to probe" the law, as the *Buckley* Court put it.

In addition to differential limits by type of contributor, the Court has upheld complete prohibitions on contributions to candidates by certain types of donors, including corporations and unions.[103] These prohibitions are discussed in § F, *infra*.

3. Limits on Contributions to Political Parties

FECA also limits the size and sources of contributions to political parties, and similar limits are also common in the states.[104] However, FECA and the laws of many states give political parties some special role by allowing larger contributions to parties than to nonparty committees (PACs) or candidates.

---

102. 424 U.S. at 35. The *Buckley* plaintiffs challenged the limits on contributions by committees and parties as *per se* violations of the First Amendment. They did not challenge the differential limitations on equal-protection grounds.

103. *See* Austin v. Michigan State Chamber of Com., 494 U.S. 652 (1990).

104. The limits on contributions *to* political parties and nonparty organizations, considered in this subsection and § E[4], *infra*, should not be confused with limits on contributions *by* political parties and nonparty organizations, which were considered at the end of § E[2], *supra*.

The 1974 amendments to FECA originally did not limit contributions to parties but did include an overall cap on giving.[105] The Court upheld this overall limit in order to prevent the "contribut[ion of] massive amounts of money to a particular candidate through the use of . . . huge contributions to the candidate's political party."[106] In short, the Court believed that parties and other political committees could become conduits for *quid pro quo* exchanges—a view that shapes certain of its holdings to this day. However, it would not rule specifically on the question of limits on contributions to parties for many years.

Recognizing that national and state political parties support not only federal candidates but also state and local candidates for election, in 1979 the FEC allowed party committees to accept contributions from sources and in amounts that would otherwise be illegal under FECA, provided that those contributions were used for "non-federal" activities. The original intent was to allow national and state parties to support general party-building activities and state and local candidates for office with funds raised according to state law, which might allow for larger contributions than were allowed for federal candidates under federal law, or for corporate and union contributions, which were prohibited in federal races.

Recall, however, that *Buckley* had narrowly defined the term "expenditure" under FECA to include only communications that expressly advocated the election or defeat of a candidate. By the late 1980s, national party committees had realized that they could use money raised for what the FEC termed "non-federal" activities, or what became colloquially known as "soft money," to run hard-hitting advertisements attacking the other party and its candidates or praising its own candidates. So long as such ads did not include "express advocacy," the FEC considered them "non-federal" spending. By the late 1990s, the national political parties were spending millions of dollars in "soft money" on these "issue ads" aimed at supporting their candidates for federal office. These ads were legal because they avoided "express advocacy."

Congress sought to address this practice in the Bipartisan Campaign Reform Act of 2002 (BCRA). BCRA prohibited national political parties from accepting any contributions in excess of the limits included in FECA, and it restricted the ability of state and local parties to spend money raised outside the federal limits in any election in which federal candidates were on the ballot.

These prohibitions on the receipt of "soft money" were upheld in *McConnell v. Federal Election Commission*.[107] In *McConnell*, the Court pounded on the alleged role of party committees as sources of corruption, calling the parties "willing intermediaries" in the exchange of campaign contributions for legislative favors. The Court cited evidence that federal officeholders asked donors to contribute soft money to the political parties, which kept tally sheets of races for which donors designated their soft money

105. Limits on giving to political parties were added in 1976. Pub. L. 94-283 (1976).
106. Buckley v. Valeo, 424 U.S. 1, 38 (1976) (*per curiam*).
107. 540 U.S. 93 (2003).

contributions, and then spent the money accordingly.[108] In short, the Court believed that the legislative history showed political parties to be uniquely corrupting in their influence, essentially serving as agents and bagmen of special interests.

After the Court's January 2010 ruling in *Citizens United v. FEC*, which overruled parts of *McConnell* and demonstrated a revived skepticism of campaign finance laws, a renewed challenge to the soft-money ban was raised by the Republican Party. A three-judge panel of the U.S. District Court for the District of Columbia rejected the claim in *Republican National Committee v. Federal Election Commission*, however, and the Supreme Court summarily affirmed.[109]

Although, as a matter of legislation, political parties at the federal level have benefited from substantially higher limits on contributions than the limits that apply to candidate campaigns and PACs, they have been at a disadvantage in the courts: While the Supreme Court has upheld the prohibition on party soft money, federal appellate courts have found that nonparty committees have a constitutional right to accept unlimited contributions for independent expenditures or "issue ads," as we will see in the next section. The result has been that nonparty "Super PACs" on the left and right have exploited their fundraising advantages and have sought to take over much of the traditional activities of parties in voter identification and turnout, as well as in messaging.

4. Limits on Contributions to Independent, Nonparty Organizations: PACs, "Super PACs," "527s," and Nonprofits

a. Political Action Committees (PACs)

In addition to placing limits on contributions made directly to candidates, their campaigns, and political parties, FECA and most states also place limits on the amounts that may be contributed to "political committees" or "political action committees," more commonly known as PACs.[110] FECA defines a "political committee" as an organization of two or more persons that either makes expenditures or accepts contributions in excess of $1,000 for the purpose of electing a federal candidate. Additionally, the Supreme Court has held that organizations that make no contributions, only expenditures, must be under the control of a candidate or have a "major purpose" of electing candidates before they can be subjected to the full array of constraints on "political committees."[111]

---

108. *Id.* at 146–51.

109. Republican Nat'l Comm. v. Fed. Election Comm'n, 698 F. Supp. 2d 150 (D.D.C.), *summarily aff'd*, 561 U.S. 1040 (2010).

110. Like party limits, these limits were added to FECA in 1976, post-*Buckley*. Pub. L. 94-283 (1976).

111. *Buckley*, 424 U.S. at 79.

At the federal level, PACs are limited in both the amounts they can contribute to candidates and the amounts they can accept from donors. At first glance, limits on giving to political committees may seem at odds with *Buckley*'s general theory, which focuses on bribery-like bargaining between officeholders and donors. An individual who contributes a large sum to an independent political committee does not necessarily have an opportunity to bargain directly with that candidate, and the committee's bargaining power is restricted by the limits placed on the size of its contribution to the candidate.

This line of argument was rejected, however, in *California Medical Association v. Federal Election Commission*.[112] The California Medical Association sought to make large contributions to its own PAC, arguing that since the PAC was limited to contributions of $5,000 to candidates, the threat of corruption was absent when the Association supported its own PAC. The Court, relying on *Buckley*, downplayed the Association's interest in contributing to its own PAC, arguing that such contributions constituted only "speech by proxy." The limit also prevented *quid pro quo* dealings by preventing individuals from "channeling funds through a multicandidate political committee."[113]

The plurality opinion's analysis was very short and may have reflected the internal politics of the Court. Chief Justice Burger dissented, allowing Justice Brennan, as senior Justice in the majority, to assign the opinion, which he gave to Justice Marshall. Both Justice Brennan and Justice Marshall had joined the majority in *Buckley*, but both were increasingly sympathetic to the egalitarian rationale for reform that *Buckley* had rejected. Joining in the plurality were Justices White and Stevens, the only two Justices to sit on the Court since *Buckley* who did not believe that campaign finance regulation should be analyzed under traditional First Amendment doctrines. However, it is doubtful that a fifth vote for an egalitarian justification could have been found. The deciding vote in the case, therefore, was cast by Justice Blackmun, another member of the *Buckley* majority. Justice Blackmun stressed that the reason for allowing restrictions on contributions to political committees was that such committees could otherwise become conduits for political contributions to candidates in excess of the limits, and as such could pose a threat of corruption congruent with *Buckley*'s holding. Justice Blackmun stressed that if CalPac had not made contributions to candidates but rather had made only independent expenditures, there would be no basis to limit contributions to the PAC.[114]

PACs face more restrictions than just the size of contributions they may receive. PACs that are connected to a parent organization, such as a corporation, union, or interest group, are not permitted to solicit the general public for contributions.[115] Complex FEC rules limit solicitations for these "affiliated" PACs, with rare exceptions, to what is known as the "restricted class." For corporations, this basically consists of shareholders, management, and their families; for unions, members and staff; for

112. 453 U.S. 182 (1981).
113. *Id.* at 198.
114. *Id.* at 201 (Blackmun, J., concurring in part and concurring in the judgment).
115. *See* Fed. Election Comm'n v. Nat'l Right to Work Comm., 459 U.S. 197 (1982).

trade associations and interest groups, "members," a term itself determined by complex FEC rules.[116] Thus, although in theory anybody may give to a PAC operated by such an organization, up to the legal limits, in practice the limits on solicitations drastically restrict the number of potential donors. However, the sponsors of such PACs may pay the administrative costs of the PACs from their general revenues. Since the cost of administration and legal compliance for a PAC can be considerable, this gives a substantial advantage to affiliated PACs.

b. Super PACs and Nonprofit Organizations

After *California Medical Association* upheld limits on contributions to PACs, the FEC continued to hold that contributions could be limited to any organization that fit the statutory definition of political committee, despite Justice Blackmun's controlling vote that appeared to limit the reach of FECA's committee-contribution limits only to committees that made contributions to candidates. The FEC's policy was not challenged for over a quarter-century, until *SpeechNow.org v. Federal Election Commission*,[117] decided in 2010. In that case, the U.S. Court of Appeals for the District of Columbia Circuit, sitting *en banc*, unanimously agreed with a small group, SpeechNow.org, that the government has no compelling interest in limiting the size or source of contributions to a group that makes no contributions to candidates. The FEC chose not to appeal, and the case has been generally accepted in the states and followed in all federal courts that have considered the issue.[118]

The result has been the creation of what the FEC calls "independent expenditure committees," but which are commonly known as "Super PACs." These PACs may accept contributions from previously prohibited sources, including unions and corporations, and they are not subject to limits on the size of contributions they may receive so long as they do not make contributions to candidates or parties but rather make only independent expenditures. In all other aspects, such as organizational requirements, mandatory disclosures of donors and expenditures, and reporting, these "Super PACs" operate like any other PACs.

Following *SpeechNow.org*, the plaintiffs in *Carey v. Federal Election Commission*—the National Defense PAC and various donors to the PAC—wished to make both independent expenditures and contributions.[119] They sought to have segregated bank accounts—one to operate as a traditional PAC, making contributions to

116. *See* 11 C.F.R. § 114. *See also* United States Chamber of Com. v. Fed. Election Comm'n, 69 F.3d 600 (D.C. Cir. 1995) (successfully challenging the FEC's definition of "member").

117. SpeechNow.org v. Fed. Election Comm'n, 599 F.3d 686 (D.C. Cir. 2010).

118. *See* Republican Party of New Mexico v. King, 741 F.3d 1089 (10th Cir. 2013); New York Progress & Protection PAC v. Walsh, 733 (2d Cir. 2013); Texans for Free Enter. v. Texas Ethics Comm'n, 732 F.3d 535 (5th Cir. 2013); Thalheimer v. City of San Diego, 645 F.3d 1109 (9th Cir. 2011); Wisconsin Right to Life v. Barland, 664 F.3d 139 (7th Cir. 2011); Fund for Jobs, Growth & Sec. v. New Jersey Election Law Enforcement Comm'n, Civil No. 13-2177 (D.N.J. Apr. 26, 2013); Yamada v. Weaver, 872 F. Supp. 2d 1023 (D. Haw. 2012).

119. Carey v. Fed. Election Comm'n, 791 F. Supp. 2d 121 (D.D.C. 2011).

candidates, and the other to operate as an independent-expenditure committee. Viewing the limitation as an expenditure limit, a three-judge panel of the U.S. District Court for the District of Columbia applied strict scrutiny and found that the government lacked the necessary compelling interest to force the National Defense PAC to form a second organization to make independent expenditures. The court granted a preliminary injunction against the FEC, allowing the National Defense PAC to maintain separate bank accounts: one, subject to limits, from which to make contributions, and the other, free from limits, from which to make independent expenditures. After the court granted a preliminary injunction, the FEC agreed to a consent decree barring enforcement of its regulation. As a result, an umbrella group, including a PAC, can maintain separate bank accounts, one subject to limits on contributions to the account and used to make contributions to parties and candidates, and one not subject to limits and used for independent expenditures.[120]

Like traditional PACs, Super PACs have the primary purpose of electing or defeating candidates for office (although they may also spend money on other items, such as advocating for legislation or the appointment of judges). The logic of *Buckley* and *SpeechNow.org*, however, applies equally to nonprofit organizations that engage in candidate advocacy.

Many nonprofits—primarily advocacy-oriented organizations such as the National Rifle Association and Planned Parenthood Action Fund, or trade associations such as the American Banking Association or the National Association of Realtors—make occasional independent expenditures in political races. After *SpeechNow.org*, these organizations may also accept unlimited contributions from for-profit corporations, unions, and individuals, and still make these occasional political expenditures. If such organizations wish to contribute directly to candidates or campaigns, however, they must organize a political action committee. Additionally, these nonprofits' tax-exempt status subjects them to limits on their political activity. But they have fewer obligations to disclose the identity of their donors. Those obligations are discussed in Chapter 9.

In summary, limits may be placed on contributions to accounts or organizations that, in turn, make contributions to candidate campaigns or political parties. However, limits may not be placed on contributions to funds or organizations that make only independent expenditures, and a single organization may maintain separate bank accounts: one to function as a traditional PAC, contributing to candidates but subject to limits on contributions to the PAC, and the other to make only independent expenditures.[121]

---

120. *But see* Vermont Right to Life Comm. v. Sorrell 875 F. Supp. 2d 376 (D. Vt. 2012) (holding that separate accounts are not sufficient to permit independent expenditures when the groups operated as a single entity).

121. Note that a traditional PAC may also make unlimited independent expenditures, *see* Fed. Election Comm'n v. Nat'l Conservative Pol. Action Comm., 470 U.S. 480 (1985), but must do so from funds raised under the FECA limits for giving to political committees.

5. Aggregate Contribution Limits

Aggregate caps on giving limit the total amount that a donor may contribute to all candidates, parties, or committees in a year. An aggregate cap on total contributions was a feature of the 1974 FECA amendments and was upheld by the Supreme Court in *Buckley* as a means of preventing circumvention of limits on contributions through contributions to numerous party committees and PACs that were expected to support particular candidates.[122]

In *McCutcheon v. Federal Election Commission*,[123] however, the Supreme Court held that aggregate contribution limits were unconstitutional. The Court reasoned that the government's interest in preventing corruption was met by the limits on giving to a particular candidate or committee, combined with restrictions on "earmarking" contributions to PACs and party committees for the support of particular candidates.

To illustrate, if the aggregate cap on giving in a campaign cycle were set at $100,000 and the maximum per-candidate contribution were $3,300 (which it was in 2024), a donor could contribute that legal maximum to just thirty candidates. But suppose a well-heeled donor wished to support all of his party's candidates for Congress with a maximum contribution, or perhaps just the fifty or so in the most competitive races, or, in a large state such as California, all of the party's candidates for Congress in that state. The aggregate cap would prohibit the donor from doing so.

The Court reasoned that giving the same amount to the thirty-first or thirty-second candidate would be no more likely to corrupt that candidate than would the same amount contributed to any of the first thirty candidates. Thus, aggregate caps serve primarily to restrict the number of candidates or committees an individual might support, rather than to prevent any of those candidates or committees from being corrupted through a large contribution. For that reason, the Court held aggregate caps unconstitutional.

6. Exemptions from Contribution Limits

This chapter thus far has focused on cash contributions to campaigns and committees. However, FECA and most state laws define "contribution" to include more than monetary gifts. For example, FECA defines a "contribution" as including not only cash donations and loans but "anything of value . . . [given] for the purpose of influencing an election for Federal office."[124]

In fact, there are numerous statutory and regulatory exceptions to this sweeping language. This part deals with three of the most common: volunteer services, the "press" exemption, and sponsorship of debates.

---

122. 424 U.S. 1, 38 (1976) (*per curiam*).
123. 572 U.S. 185 (2014).
124. 52 U.S.C. § 30101(8)(A)(i).

a. Volunteer Services

FECA excludes from the definition of "contribution" volunteer services provided without compensation, nominal expenditures of funds by volunteers to do things such as print invitations or provide food and beverages for gatherings in the home, nominal discounts on food and beverage by commercial vendors, and travel expenses incurred by volunteers.[125] Most states similarly exempt volunteer services and incidental expenses by volunteers.

While the exemption is intended to allow for low-level volunteer services, it might be noted that some services can be of considerable value, as, for example, when a prominent singer performs at a rally, or an actor, athlete, or other celebrity agrees to appear at an event. Such volunteer services could violate both the equality rationale for limits that was rejected by *Buckley* and the anti-corruption rationale behind limits that was accepted by *Buckley*. Nevertheless, such exemptions are ubiquitous in the law, and, in *Randall v. Sorrell*,[126] the strict limitations imposed on volunteers' incidental expenses were one reason the Court struck down Vermont's contribution limits as unconstitutionally low.

b. The "Press" Exemption

Also exempt from contribution limits, by federal statute and by statutes in most states, are news reports and editorial commentary, unless the publisher is owned or controlled by a candidate.[127] Although the federal statute exempts "broadcasting station[s], newspaper[s], magazine[s], [and] other periodical publication[s]," the FEC and the courts have interpreted the exemption broadly. Among protected speakers are publishers of newsletters, airline magazines, and publications such as shopping-store magazines.[128]

The question of who constitutes the "press," however, has grown more complex in recent years. The federal statutory exemption, read literally, does not cover books or movies, but the FEC has not attempted to enforce the statute against them, at least ones produced by established publishers and movie houses. One notable exception was *Citizens United*, which grew out of the FEC's attempt to enforce the prohibition on

---

125. 52 U.S.C. § 30101(8)(B).

126. 548 U.S. 230 (2006).

127. 52 U.S.C. § 30101(9)(B)(i).

128. *See* Reader's Digest Ass'n v. Fed. Election Comm'n, 509 F. Supp. 1210 (S.D.N.Y. 1981) (exemption includes advertising for publication as well as publication itself); Fed. Election Comm'n v. Phillips Publ'g, Inc., 517 F. Supp. 1308 (D.D.C. 1981) (press exemption covers investment newsletter); Fed. Election Comm'n, MUR 5315 (Wal-Mart Stores), Aug. 25, 2003 (Statement of Reasons of Vice Chairman Bradley A. Smith and Commissioners Michael E. Toner and David M. Mason) (finding press exemption applied to retail store magazine that was published on regular basis, included articles of general interest, employed an editor and paid writers, and was distributed for free in stores and through the mail); Fed. Election Comm'n, MUR 3607 (Northwest Airlines, Inc.), Nov. 12, 1993 (press exemption covers airline in-flight magazine).

corporate expenditures against Citizens United, a lobbying group that had produced several documentary movies prior to producing *Hillary: The Movie*, a partisan documentary about presidential candidate Hillary Clinton.[129]

The development of the internet has also raised questions about the scope of the press exemption. The FEC has largely deregulated the internet, including blogs, news sites, reader forums, and user-made videos, but these efforts, as well as statutory efforts, have been met with sharp opposition.[130]

FECA, including its exemption for broadcasters and periodicals, was passed at a time when most homes in America were served by three (or perhaps just two) television networks, a handful (if that) of radio stations, one daily newspaper, and national magazines such as *Time*, *Newsweek*, *Look*, and *Life*. Entry into publishing or operating a broadcast station was prohibitively expensive for most persons. Today, opinion sites on the internet are ubiquitous—many grow from hobbies to become significant businesses. Movies can be made cheaply in the home and distributed on DVD or uploaded to YouTube and other internet sites, and short videos dominate TikTok and some other platforms. Self-publishing is available for authors unable to find a traditional publisher for political books. In this environment, it is not clear that there is any longer a definable "press" covered by the exemption.[131]

This democratization of the media raises a series of questions: Can campaign finance laws exist without a definable press exemption? Who qualifies for it? Is an exemption constitutionally required, and, if so, for whom? In *Corsi v. Ohio Elections Commission*, an Ohio appellate court held that blogging is not covered by the state's press exemption and required the blogger to register with the state as a "political committee."[132] The lower court in *San Juan County v. No New Gas Tax* similarly held that on-air commentary by radio-talk-show hosts constituted a campaign contribution under state law, not covered under a press exemption. The Washington Supreme Court reversed, but it did so on statutory grounds, declining to consider if the state or federal constitution required an exemption for press commentary.[133]

---

129. *See* Citizens United v. Fed. Election Comm'n, 558 U.S. 310, 310; *see also* Fed. Election Comm'n, Adv. Op. 2004-30 (Citizens United), Sep. 10, 2004 (finding documentary movie *Celsius 41.11* was not covered by the press exemption); Fed. Election Comm'n, Adv. Op. 2004-15 (David T. Hardy), June 25, 2004 (finding *The Rights of the People*, a Second Amendment documentary movie featuring footage of President George W. Bush, not to be covered by the press exemption).

130. *See* 11 C.F.R. § 114 (FEC regulations). *See also* Shays v. Fed. Election Comm'n, 337 F. Supp. 2d 28, 65–71 (D.D.C. 2004), *aff'd*, 414 F.3d 76 (D.C. Cir. 2005) (lawsuit successfully contesting FEC internet exemption as contrary to statute); Trevor Potter, *Say No to Online Soft-Money Loophole*, Roll Call, Oct. 28, 2005, *at* https://rollcall.com/2005/10/28/say-no-to-online-soft-money-loophole/.

131. *See* Bradley A. Smith, *The John Roberts Salvage Company: After* McConnell, *a New Court Looks to Repair the Constitution*, 68 Ohio St. L.J. 891, 895–99 (2007).

132. Corsi v. Ohio Elections Comm'n, 981 N.E.2d 919 (Ohio Ct. App. 2012), *cert. denied*, 984 N.E.2d 29 (Ohio 2013).

133. 157 P.3d 831 (Wash. 2007).

Citizens United makes the question of the press exemption less important because any corporation can now make independent expenditures. However, in theory at least, much press coverage still might be limited as "coordinated" with a campaign or in close cooperation with a campaign. Additionally, whether or not an entity is covered under a press exemption will determine the extent of its disclosure obligations and whether it might need to register and report as a political committee. As more and more individuals and political organizations begin to assume traditional "press" functions—reporting online, tweeting news events and opinion, posting videos, blogging, producing low-budget movies for distribution online or by DVD—the exemption is likely to be seen as a "loophole" for undue influence and an Achilles heel for legal regulation of campaign speech.

c. Sponsorship of Debates

Debates have become common in U.S. elections, but, perhaps curiously, they are rarely organized or paid for directly by the candidates; rather, they are typically sponsored by news or civic organizations. U.S. presidential debates were for many years sponsored by a private corporation, the Commission on Presidential Debates, established for that purpose.

When debates do not include all candidates, as when minor-party candidates are excluded from general-election debates or "fringe" candidates are excluded from primary debates, privately sponsored debates arguably constitute a "contribution" ("anything of value") to the candidates included in the debate because they are given exposure unavailable to other candidates. Debates, however, have largely been exempted from regulation as contributions, either under the press exemption, when sponsored by press entities, or under FEC regulations, so long as the selection of candidates is based on objective criteria and is not structured to benefit particular candidates.[134] Such "objective" criteria can include minimal showings in polling data, media coverage, and a variety of other factors. Since the decision to sponsor a debate is usually made after the basic contours of the race, such as whether there will be a significant third-party or independent candidate, are known, it is not particularly difficult for sponsoring entities to develop "objective" criteria for inclusion that predictably exclude certain candidates. The courts and the FEC have been reluctant to attempt to police debate criteria, instead giving sponsors considerable leeway in the selection of criteria for inclusion and, therefore, the selection of candidates.[135]

---

134. 11 C.F.R. § 110.13.

135. *See* Level the Playing Field v. Fed. Election Comm'n, 961 F.3d 462 (D.C. Cir. 2020); *cf.* Arkansas Educ. Television Comm'n v. Forbes, 523 U.S. 666 (1998).

F. Expenditure and Contribution Limits: Treatment of Special Entities

1. Corporations and Unions

The first campaign finance laws, both federally and in the states, were prohibitions on corporate contributions to political campaigns. Such prohibitions began to be enacted around the turn of the twentieth century. The federal ban on corporate contributions was enacted in 1907. It was extended to unions in 1943 as a temporary measure and made permanent in the Taft-Hartley Act of 1947. Taft-Hartley also extended the prohibition on corporate and union contributions to cover expenditures as well as contributions. This prohibition remained until *Citizens United v. Federal Election Commission*[136] held that corporations had a First Amendment right to spend on elections from their general treasuries.

Despite the relatively lengthy history of prohibitions on corporate and union participation, the extent to which such bans were deeply rooted in American political life before *Citizens United* is frequently overstated. The original Tillman Act of 1907, for example, applied only to federally chartered corporations and banks, and was readily circumvented by making "expenditures" rather than contributions. In the 1930s, the Democratic Party began the practice of selling advertising space to corporations in souvenir books sold at the party's national convention, a practice soon adopted by Republicans and maintained into the 1960s. The lack of clear guidelines allowed corporate executives to make personal contributions that were reimbursed as expenses by their corporate employers.[137]

Nor did passage of FECA freeze corporations and unions out of the process. After passage of the Taft-Hartley Act, unions quickly established the first "political action committees," which were funded by automatic dues deductions from union members. Only a few corporations followed suit, but the 1974 FECA Amendments clarified the legal status of corporate PACs, and the number of corporate PACs quickly swelled.[138] Commonly called "connected PACs," these PACs may solicit voluntary contributions from members (in the case of unions) or corporate officers, executives, and shareholders (in the case of corporations) to contribute directly to candidate campaigns. Additionally, corporations and unions continued to fund "issue ads" that fell outside the narrowing construction of "express advocacy" given by *Buckley* to FECA's definition of "expenditure." Until passage of the Bipartisan Campaign Reform Act of 2002, corporate and union expenditures also included "soft money" to political parties. And, more directly, on the eve of *Citizens United*, a majority of states still allowed explicit corporate advocacy in state elections, with twenty-four

136. 558 U.S. 310 (2010).

137. For a brief history of such practices, see Bradley A. Smith, Unfree Speech: The Folly of Campaign Finance Reform 25–27 (2001).

138. *Id.* at 28–29.

states allowing unlimited corporate spending. Several states allowed direct corporate contributions to candidate campaigns and parties. In fact, as of 2025, twenty-eight states still allowed direct corporate contributions to candidates,[139] even though courts have continued to uphold limits on such contributions.[140] Thus, while *Citizens United* is a very important benchmark in campaign finance law, its practical impact is often overstated.

Citizens United involved an incorporated, nonprofit, ideological group—Citizens United—that produced a documentary film about then-presidential candidate Hillary Clinton, titled *Hillary: The Movie*. Citizens United not only was a corporation itself; it also accepted corporate contributions into its general treasury. When the organization sought to air and advertise the film, it was threatened with prosecution by the FEC for making an illegal corporate expenditure in the form of the movie, which the FEC argued was merely a piece of political advocacy.

Contrary to much popular understanding, *Citizens United* was not decided by creating the legal fiction of "corporate personhood." Indeed, the issue was not even discussed in the opinion. All nine Justices agreed that Citizens United was a legal "person" entitled to some level of constitutional protection, and the decision broke no new ground on the doctrine of "corporate personhood."[141] Rather, the opinion in *Citizens United* followed a straightforward application of the *Buckley* framework. Since Citizens United was operating independently of any candidate, the Court applied "strict scrutiny" to the law, as it had been doing since *Buckley* when considering expenditure limits. The question, then, was whether the government could cite sufficiently compelling evidence that the unique features of corporations, and such legal advantages as they might receive from the state in the form of limited liability and perpetual life, were sufficient to justify a complete ban on corporate spending from general-treasury funds. Returning to its traditional emphasis on *quid pro quo* corruption, the Court ruled in favor of Citizens United. Essential to the Court's holding was the understanding that there is no particular reason to find an independent expenditure by a corporation to be more corrupting than an independent expenditure by a wealthy individual or any other entity. The Court also rejected the idea that

139. National Conference of State Legislatures, *State Limits on Contributions to Candidates*, May 2023, *available at* https://documents.ncsl.org/wwwncsl/Elections/Contribution-Limits-to-Candidates-2023-2024.pdf.

140. United States v. Danielczyk, 683 F.3d 611 (4th Cir. 2012), *cert. denied*, 568 U.S. 1193 (2013).

141. The legal doctrine of "corporate personhood" is in fact a very old doctrine with roots in pre-Revolutionary common law. *See* Carl J. Mayer, *Personalizing the Impersonal: Corporations and the Bill of Rights*, 41 Hastings L.J. 577 (1990). "Corporate personhood" was clearly recognized by the Supreme Court by 1819 at the latest, when the Court decided *Trustees of Dartmouth College v. Woodward*, 17 U.S. 518 (1819). Soon after enactment of the Fourteenth Amendment, the Court made clear that the protections of that Amendment also applied to corporations. Southern Pacific Railroad v. Santa Clara County, 118 U.S. 394 (1886). No Supreme Court Justice in a campaign finance case has ever argued against the doctrine of corporate personhood or denied that corporations have rights under the First Amendment. The question for the Court has always been the extent to which legislatures could restrict those rights.

any unique advantages conferred by corporate status were sufficient to truncate First Amendment rights.

In reaching its decision, the majority overruled a 1990 case, *Austin v. Michigan State Chamber of Commerce*.[142] In *Austin*, the Court applied a much broader definition of "corruption," which it described as "the corrosive and distorting effects of immense aggregations of wealth that are accumulated with the help of the corporate form and that have little or no correlation to the public's support for the corporation's political ideas."[143] While *Austin* lays forth what many believe to be a compelling case for regulation, *Austin*'s use of "corruption" is very different from the *quid pro quo* meaning in *Buckley*, *First National Bank of Boston v. Bellotti*,[144] and other leading cases that preceded and, indeed, followed it.[145] In short, while many disagree that corporations should be treated the same as other speakers, the case itself is not particularly difficult to understand if one returns to the core principles of *Buckley*. Even critics of *Buckley* and *Citizens United* had long recognized that *Austin* fit very uneasily into the Court's line of cases.[146]

Citizens United directly addressed only corporate spending, but it has generally been presumed that the Court's analysis would hold for any challenge to the ban on union spending as well.[147] In fact, since the 1940s, federal law and most state laws have treated corporations and unions in parallel fashion, either allowing or prohibiting contributions to both types of entities, and by setting similar contribution limits for both unions and corporations. The treatment is not always identical due to the different features of the two types of organizations, but political accommodation has made similar treatment a seeming necessity in most cases. However, the law does not require such parallel treatment, so, outside of limiting expenditures, a state can treat unions and corporations differently if it has compelling reasons to do so. Similarly, a state may in some circumstances discriminate between types of corporations. In *Austin*, for example, the Supreme Court rejected the Chamber of Commerce's claim

142. 494 U.S. 652 (1990).

143. *Id.* at 660.

144. 435 U.S. 765 (1978).

145. *See* Citizens Against Rent Control/Coalition for Fair Housing v. City of Berkeley, 454 U.S. 290 (1981); *see also* Fed. Election Comm'n v. National Conservative Pol. Action Comm., 470 U.S. 480 (1985).

146. *See* Richard L. Hasen, Buckley *Is Dead, Long Live* Buckley: *The New Campaign Finance Incoherence of* McConnell v. Federal Election Commission, 153 U. Pa. L. Rev. 312 (2004); *see also* Daniel Hays Lowenstein, *A Patternless Mosaic: Campaign Finance and the First Amendment After* Austin, 21 Cap. U. L. Rev. 381 (1992); Prescott M. Lassman, *Breaching the Fortress Walls: Corporate Political Speech and* Austin v. Michigan Chamber of Commerce, 78 Va. L. Rev. 759 (1992) ("The United States Supreme Court's decision in *Austin v. Michigan Chamber of Commerce* ... is, as Justice Scalia points out, contrary to prior case law and a clear rejection of an integral feature of the Court's First Amendment jurisprudence.... ").

147. Both the corporate and union bans are included in federal law now at 52 U.S.C. § 30118.

that equal protection was violated because media corporations were free to editorialize and endorse candidates, but other corporations were not.[148]

Similarly, in *California Medical Association v. Federal Election Commission*,[149] the Court rejected an equal-protection challenge to differential treatment of corporations and unincorporated entities, with the law in this case favoring corporations by allowing them, but not unincorporated entities, to pay the legal and administrative costs of their PACs.

Citizens United allowed corporations (and presumably unions) to make expenditures from their general treasuries; it did not address the right of corporations to make contributions. Does *Citizens United* undercut the rationale for restricting direct corporate contributions to candidates? The case that it does is at least superficially appealing. If, as *Citizens United* says, "[g]overnment cannot restrict political speech based on the speaker's corporate identity,"[150] then one might question the justification for the outright prohibition on corporate contributions to candidates. Does a $3,300 contribution from a corporation really offer more opportunity for *quid pro quo* exchanges than a $3,300 contribution from that corporation's CEO does? Similarly, the Court's opinion noted that due to the costs and burden of maintaining a political action committee, "fewer than 2,000 of the millions of corporations in this country have PACs."[151] If PACs are an inadequate substitute for corporate expenditures, should the Court extend this reasoning to hold that PACs are an inadequate substitute for most corporations to make contributions?

Apparently not. William Danielczyk was criminally prosecuted for, *inter alia*, using straw donors to contribute corporate funds to a campaign. Danielczyk argued that, after *Citizens United*, a complete ban on corporate contributions was unconstitutional. The Fourth Circuit, however, upheld the ban, and the Supreme Court denied *certiorari*.[152] Recall that *Buckley* held that a limit on independent expenditures was a greater First Amendment burden than a limit on contributions was and that contributions posed a greater danger of corruption than independent expenditures did. This distinction arguably, if not entirely convincingly, explains the difference.

Danielczyk aside, it is important to understand that corporate and union PACs, which are technically called "separate segregated funds" in the FECA, operate under extensive restrictions governing most every aspect of the PAC, including who may be solicited for contributions and how (and how often) such solicitations may be made.[153] As a result, as the *Citizens United* majority noted, most small and mid-sized corporations cannot afford the administrative costs of operating PACs, the odd effect

148. *But see* Protect My Check, Inc. v. Dilger, 176 F. Supp. 3d 685 (E.D. Ky. 2016) (holding unconstitutional a Kentucky statute that prohibited corporate contributions but allowed union contributions).

149. 453 U.S. 182 (1981).

150. 558 U.S. at 346.

151. *Id.* at 338.

152. United States v. Danielczyk, 683 F.3d 611 (4th Cir. 2012), *cert denied*, 568 U.S. 1193 (2013).

153. *See* 11 C.F.R. § 114.

being that the PAC requirement provides large corporations with a means to contribute to campaigns that, as a practical matter, is not available to smaller corporations.

2. Government Contractors

A federal prohibition on contributions and expenditures by federal contractors dates back to 1940, when the Hatch Act was amended to prohibit contributions by federal contractors.[154] However, because most federal contractors are corporations, and corporate contributions had been prohibited by the Tillman Act and its successors since 1907, the provision has rarely been invoked. Following the 2010 *Citizens United* decision freeing corporations to make independent expenditures, however, the contractor ban has taken on renewed importance.

In *Wagner v. Federal Election Commission*,[155] the D.C. Circuit upheld the ban. The court held that the blanket prohibition was closely drawn to address the government's interest in preventing *quid pro quo* exchanges, noting that the ban was passed after a series of scandals involving federal contractors, and further noting evidence of more recent scandals in state governments. The plaintiffs, individuals holding personal-services contracts with the government, also argued that the ban violated the equal-protection guarantee of the Fifth Amendment because corporate contractors can form PACs with which to make contributions, while individuals have no such option. The court held that individual contractors are not similarly situated under the law to corporate contractors' PACs, which are legally distinct from the corporation. The court also rejected the contractors' similar argument that it was unconstitutional to prohibit their speech when federal employees were not subject to the same restriction. The court held that the distinction was justifiable, as employees typically had less to gain from making contributions.

Meanwhile, even before *Citizens United*, so-called "pay-to-play" laws were proliferating at the state and local levels. These laws range from narrow laws prohibiting state contractors from making contributions, to broader laws requiring the disclosure of contributions to other groups that make political contributions, to sweeping laws that loop in persons only tangentially related to the contractor, such as low-level employees and family members.[156] States and municipalities have generally met with suc-

---

154. 5 U.S.C. §§7321–7326. The ban is currently codified at 52 U.S.C. §30119.

155. 793 F.3d 1 (D.C. Cir. 2015), *cert. denied sub nom.* Miller v. Fed. Election Comm'n, 577 U.S. 1102 (2016).

156. *See, e.g.*, CAL. GOV'T CODE §8880.57(b)(7) (requiring California State Lottery contractors to disclose all reportable campaign contributions to any local, state, or federal political candidate or political committee in California for the past five years); CONN. GEN. STAT. §9-612(g)(2)(A)–(B) (prohibiting state government contractors from making political contributions to candidates running for statewide and state legislative offices and also political party committees); ILL. COMP. STAT. §500/50-37(a)–(b) (prohibiting business entities with aggregate annual state contracts totaling over $50,000 and certain of their affiliates from making contributions to political committees established to promote the candidacy of any incumbent or declared candidate for various state offices).

cess in early court challenges to these laws.[157] However, an Ohio law that prohibited contributions from any Medicaid provider or person with an ownership interest in a Medicaid provider was struck down as overly broad in *Lavin v. Husted*.[158] The court noted that the ban would affect over 93,000 Medicaid providers, mainly physicians, and that in a typical year, 0.003% of such providers were even investigated for fraud.

Because the potential for *quid pro quo* dealing seems relatively clear in most situations involving government contractors, successful future challenges to such laws, as in *Lavin*, will likely be focused on the alleged overbreadth of particular laws.

3. Regulated Industries and Lobbyists

Several states have enacted specific limitations or disclosure requirements for contributions by registered lobbyists.[159] The constitutionality of these laws should, as always, focus on whether the limitations serve a government interest in preventing corruption or its appearance, as defined in *Buckley*. In *Preston v. Leake*,[160] the Fourth Circuit ruled that a complete ban on lobbyists' contributions met the "closely drawn" requirement of *Buckley* and its progeny. The court cited North Carolina's recent history of scandals that prompted the legislation, and it noted that lobbyists were uniquely involved in legislative dealmaking. The scandals cited by the state in *Preston* were only marginally related to campaign finance—for example, in the most prominent scandal, the state agricultural commissioner and several aides were found guilty of extorting bribes and illegal campaign contributions in exchange for government contracts, perjury, and obstruction of justice. The payments were made by local businesses and their owners/executives, not necessarily lobbyists. The only connection to legal campaign finance contributions was that the officials doctored campaign finance reports to cover up their activities.[161] Another scandal involved the speaker of the state house, who accepted illegal campaign contributions—not from lobbyists but from chiropractors; the speaker also paid another legislator a $50,000 bribe in exchange for switching parties. The speaker also accepted illegal campaign contributions from business owners and lobbyists.[162]

---

157. *See* Ognibene v. Parkes, 671 F.3d 174 (2d Cir. 2011), *cert. denied*, 567 U.S. 935 (2012); Yamada v. Weaver, 872 F. Supp. 2d 1023 (D. Haw. 2012).

158. 689 F.3d 543 (6th Cir. 2012).

159. *See, e.g.*, CAL. GOV'T CODE § 85702, Reg. 18572 (lobbyist may not contribute to a state officeholder's or candidate's committee if the lobbyist is registered to lobby the agency of the elected officer or the agency to which the candidate is seeking election); N.C. GEN. STAT. § 1630278.13C (limiting lobbyist campaign contributions to legislators); MINN. STAT. § 10A.27-11 (limiting contributions by lobbyists).

160. 660 F.3d 726 (4th Cir. 2011).

161. *See* Cullen Browder, *Phipps to Spend Four Years in Prison for State Ag Department Scandal*, WRAL NEWS (Mar. 2, 2004), http://www.wral.com/news/local/story/109254/.

162. *See* Susan Ebbs et al., *Under the Dome: Jim Black*, RALEIGH NEWS-OBSERVER, Mar. 28, 2007.

In contrast to *Preston*, in *Green Party of Connecticut v. Garfield*,[163] the Second Circuit struck down a ban on lobbyist contributions on the grounds that the state had produced insufficient evidence to support the law. The court noted that the law banned contributions as opposed to limiting them, prohibited contributions by lobbyists' family members in addition to the lobbyists themselves, and prevented even attendance at fundraising events.

Preston and *Garfield* both relied on the courts' assessments of the strength of the state's evidence. Differing assessments leave open the question of whether a law may be constitutional in one state and unconstitutional in another. In *Nixon v. Shrink Missouri Government PAC*, the Supreme Court held that the plausibility of Missouri's asserted interest in preventing corruption was sufficient to overcome a paucity of actual evidence of corruption.[164] Similarly, in *American Tradition Partnership v. Bullock*,[165] the Court reversed a decision by the Montana Supreme Court holding that an evidentiary record concerning Montana's unique history justified a ban on corporate political expenditures in spite of the Court's decision in *Citizens United*. If and when the lobbyist issue reaches the Supreme Court, the fate of outright bans on lobbyists' contributions, as opposed to limits on the size of contributions, may depend on whether the Court sees the issue in categorical terms, as in *Nixon* and *American Tradition Partnership*, or believes that states can produce individual legislative histories that may justify restrictions in some states and not in others.

Other rules have been imposed on regulated industries through the regulatory process. For many years, the Municipal Securities Rulemaking Board (MSRB) has had a rule that municipal-finance professionals may not make contributions to candidates who have authority over bond underwriting. Violations can disqualify the professional's firm from bond underwriting in the candidate's jurisdiction for two years.[166] In 2010, the Securities and Exchange Commission enacted a similar rule covering investment advisors.[167] The rule prohibits an investment advisor from providing advisory services for compensation to a government client for two years after a contribution to certain elected officials or candidates made by the advisor or by particular executives or employees. The broad scope of the rule, reaching low-level advisors with no connection to the advisory services rendered and applying retroactively for two years, may make the rule constitutionally suspect, along the reasoning in *Garfield*, but the law has not been challenged in court as yet.

Other state laws that attempt to impose limits on particular industries must similarly demonstrate that they are closely drawn to address the state's legitimate anticorruption interests.

---

163. 616 F.3d 189 (2d Cir. 2010).

164. 528 U.S. 377 (2000).

165. 567 U.S. 516 (2012), *rev'g* Western Tradition P'ship v. Bullock, 271 P.3d 1 (Mont. 2011).

166. Mun. Sec. Rulemaking Bd. R. G-37.

167. 11 C.F.R. § 275.

4. Foreign Nationals

Federal law imposes blanket bans on campaign contributions and spending by aliens,[168] although permanent-resident aliens are exempt from the ban.[169] In the wake of *Citizens United*, this prohibition was challenged in *Bluman v. Federal Election Commission*, with plaintiffs, Israeli and Canadian nationals in the United States on long-term non-immigrant visas, arguing that, per *Citizens United*, their identities should not matter to the anti-corruption analysis.[170] A three-judge panel of the D.C. District upheld the prohibition in an opinion written by future-Justice Brett Kavanaugh. The court did not rely on the anti-corruption rationale of *Buckley* but rather on the ground that foreign citizens may be denied political rights available to U.S. citizens, including the rights to vote and to hold public office. The decision was summarily affirmed by the Supreme Court. It should be noted that the federal ban on contributions by foreign nationals applies to state and local elections as well as to federal ones.[171]

Similarly, companies that are incorporated or headquartered outside the United States are not permitted to make contributions or expenditures in U.S. elections. But American-headquartered and incorporated subsidiaries of foreign-owned corporations are permitted to operate political action committees (a rule that long predates *Citizens United*) so long as decisions on contributions and expenditures by the PACs are made exclusively by U.S. citizens.[172]

The federal law provides that a corporation that is both headquartered and incorporated in the United States is a U.S. corporation, even if a majority, or all, of its stock is owned by foreign nationals. Thus, under FEC regulations, subsidiaries of foreign corporations can also take advantage of *Citizens United*, provided that decisions on political spending are made by U.S. citizens. Claiming to follow *Bluman* (and ignoring *Bluman*'s statement that "American corporations . . . [are] members of the American political community"[173]), some states have considered or enacted laws defining companies with as little as 1% foreign ownership as foreign-owned and have barred them from spending in state and local elections. However, in *Minnesota Chamber of Commerce v. Choi*, the first reported decision on a challenge to such a law, the federal district court granted a permanent injunction against the law's enforcement. The court found that mere ownership did not constitute participation in American elections and that, while a ban on participation by corporations "funded predominately by foreign shareholders" might be justified, banning speech by corporations with merely

168. 52 U.S.C. § 30121.

169. *See* 52 U.S.C. § 30121(b)(2).

170. 800 F. Supp. 2d 281 (D.D.C. 2011), *summarily aff'd*, 565 U.S. 1104 (2012).

171. 52 U.S.C. § 30121(a)(1).

172. *See* 52 U.S.C. § 30121; 11 C.F.R. § 110.20; Fed. Election Comm'n Advisory Ops. 1992-16 (Nansay Hawaii), June 26, 1992; 1990-8 (CIT Group Holdings), June 18, 1990; 1989-29 (GEM), Dec. 19, 1989; 1989-20 (Kuilima Development), Oct. 27, 1989; 1985-3 (Rod Diridon), Mar. 4, 1985; and 1982-10 (Syntex, Inc.), Mar. 29, 1982.

173. *Bluman*, 800 F. Supp. 2d at 290.

1% or 5% foreign ownership was not "narrowly tailored" to address the problem and primarily served to burden the rights of American citizens.[174]

5. Minors

In the late 1990s, reform advocates became concerned that minors were being used as conduits for contributions. In response, as part of the Bipartisan Campaign Reform Act of 2002, Congress banned all contributions by persons seventeen years old or younger.

In one of the few victories for the plaintiffs in *McConnell v. FEC*, the Supreme Court struck down this blanket prohibition.[175] The plaintiffs in this portion of the suit were well-chosen—they were teenagers who had their own money from part-time work and sought to contribute to the campaigns of candidates personally known to them. The Court held that the categorical ban was unnecessary, since contributions in the name of another are already prohibited, and noted that the government had produced little evidence to show that contributions by minors were a source of corruption, either directly or as a means to circumvent contribution limits. Presumably, there is some age level at which donations by minors could be banned as tools for circumvention (six-month-olds?); however, where a minor child has his own income or some cognitive understanding of politics, or both, a categorical ban will fail.

G. Summary of Rules Governing Campaign-Spending Entities

Consistently more than 90% of campaign funds in the United States are donated by individuals. Corporations and unions account for most of the remainder. However, the vast majority of political spending is done through intermediaries; donors contribute to organizations that then spend money to support candidates and campaigns. This section summarizes the main types of organizations through which campaign expenditures are made and the basic rules governing different types of campaign donors at the federal level. States may have somewhat different rules of governance, but in most cases they are substantially modeled after federal law.

1. *Individuals*: Individuals may make unlimited expenditures on behalf of their own candidacies, or independently in support of other candidates and parties, including through contributions to independent-expenditure committees, or "Super PACs," and nonprofit membership organizations. Direct independent expenditures over $250 must be reported to the FEC. Individuals may

174. Minnesota Chamber of Com. v. Choi, 765 F. Supp. 3d 821 (D. Minn. 2025).

175. 540 U.S. 93, 231–232 (2003).

contribute directly to candidates, parties, and PACs, but these contributions may be limited in size. As of 2024, individuals were limited to contributing $3,300 to any one candidate per election, and $5,000 per year to a PAC, with significantly higher limits for giving to various political-party committees.

2. *Corporations and Unions*: Corporations and unions may make unlimited independent expenditures, including through Super PACs and nonprofit membership organizations. They must disclose direct independent expenditures in excess of $250. They are prohibited from contributing to candidates or political-party committees from their general treasuries. Corporations and unions may establish affiliated PACs and pay the administrative and fundraising costs of those PACs. These "affiliated" PACs may solicit funds only from management and shareholders and their families, in the case of corporate-affiliated PACs; or members, in the case of union-affiliated PACs.
3. *Candidate and Party Committees*: Candidate and party committees are the core vehicle for organizing political campaigns. These committees are subject to limitations on the size and source of contributions they may receive—including, under FECA, a prohibition on corporate and union contributions—and party committees are limited in how much they may contribute to candidate campaigns. They have substantial disclosure obligations, being required to disclose all donors and all expenditures above relatively low threshold amounts (for example, $200 for contributions to federal-candidate campaigns).
4. *Traditional PACs*: Traditional PACs register with the FEC[176] and report all donors over $200. They may make contributions to candidates and party committees (currently limited to $5,000 per candidate per election), or make independent expenditures. Like candidate and party committees, they are subject to limits on the size of contributions they may receive and the source of those contributions (no corporate or union money). Examples include Emily's List Political Action Committee and Microsoft Political Action Committee.
5. *Independent Expenditure Committees (Super PACs)*: Super PACs are subject to the same registration and reporting requirements as traditional PACs, but they may make only independent expenditures.[177] They may accept contributions without limit from U.S. citizen and permanent resident individuals, corporations, and unions. Examples include WinSenate PAC, which promotes liberal candidates for U.S. Senate, and Make America Great Again, which supports the candidacy and agenda of Donald Trump.

---

176. The Federal Election Commission requires PACs to fill out a Statement of Organization. *See* FEC Form 1, FED. ELECTION COMM'N, https://www.fec.gov/resources/cms-content/documents/policy-guidance/fecfrm1.pdf (viewed Mar. 25, 2025).

177. *See Registering as a Super PAC*, FED. ELECTION COMM'N https://www.fec.gov/help-candidates-and-committees/filing-pac-reports/registering-super-pac/ (viewed Mar. 25, 2025); *Making Independent Expenditures*, FED. ELECTION COMM'N, https://www.fec.gov/help-candidates-and-committees/making-independent-expenditures/ (viewed Mar. 25, 2025).

6. *527s*: A 527 is an organization that is deemed by the IRS to have political activity as its primary purpose but that does not qualify as a "political committee" under FEC or relevant state regulations, usually because it makes no expenditures "expressly advocating" the election or defeat of a candidate. Such organizations may make "electioneering communications" or other political messages, including discussion of candidates and issues, that do not include "express advocacy." The organizations are not subject to contribution restrictions but must publicly disclose donors through the Internal Revenue Service. They may not contribute directly to parties or candidates. Such organizations, including Swift Boat Veterans for Truth and MoveOn.org in the 2004 presidential campaign, were popular in the past but have dramatically declined in use since the advent of Super PACs following the *Citizens United* and *SpeechNow.org* decisions in 2010.
7. *Trade Associations and Nonprofit Advocacy Organizations*: These organizations, sometimes referred to as "501(c)" organizations after the section of the Internal Revenue Code under which they operate, cannot make direct contributions to candidates but may make independent expenditures so long as those expenditures do not become their "major purpose." They do not have to disclose their donors to the public unless those donors have earmarked contributions for political use. The NAACP Voter Education Fund and the National Rifle Association are examples of nonprofits operating under § 501(c)(4) of the tax code; the U.S. Chamber of Commerce and National Association of Realtors are examples of trade associations operating under § 501(c)(6).

It is possible for one umbrella organization to operate any combination of the above forms of organizations. For example, a 501(c)(4) nonprofit group may establish a traditional PAC to contribute to directly to candidates, a Super PAC to make independent expenditures, and also make limited expenditures from its general treasury (allowing some donors to remain confidential), provided it keeps the various funds separate.[178]

In choosing the best campaign vehicle, practitioners in the field will need to discover and sometimes balance the various interests of spenders and donors, including the desire for anonymity, tax status, the desire to make contributions directly to candidates and parties, whether or not political campaign activity is an organization's primary purpose, and the perceived effectiveness of various types of activities in accomplishing the organization's goals.

178. *See* Carey v. Fed. Election Comm'n, 791 F. Supp. 2d 121 (D.D.C. 2011).

H. Government Financing of Campaigns

1. Introduction

Direct government funding of campaigns was recommended by President Theodore Roosevelt in 1907 and has been a major goal of many progressive reformers ever since.

This section discusses government plans that provide money directly to candidates for the purpose of campaigning. These government programs include those that provide lump-sum grants to candidates, and others that provide a bewildering array of formulas for "matching funds" (where funds raised by a candidate are "matched" in some ratio by the government).[179]

This section does not discuss indirect methods that governments may use to subsidize campaigns, such as through tax credits or tax deductions for contributions, or state statutes allowing taxpayers to contribute to political parties by checking a box on their tax returns.[180] This section is limited to programs that pay funds directly from the state treasury to candidates for the purpose of campaigning.

2. General Principles

In addition to placing restraints on contributions and expenditures, FECA provided for public, or government, funding of presidential primary and general-election campaigns. The plaintiffs in *Buckley v. Valeo*[181] challenged these systems on several constitutional grounds.

The *Buckley* Court held first that Congress's power to spend for the "general Welfare"[182] included the power to fund campaigns directly. The Court also found significant government interests in preventing corruption and relieving candidates from "the rigors of soliciting private contributions."[183] The Court did not mention the goal of equality in this portion of the opinion, either as a significant government interest supporting such programs or as an illegitimate government interest.[184]

Having determined that subsidies were within Congress's spending power, the Court rejected the plaintiffs' claim that the programs—by providing more money

---

179. *See, e.g.*, 26 U.S.C. §§ 9001 *et seq.* (presidential general-election fund); New York City, N.Y., Local Law No. 8 of 1988, § 1.

180. *See, e.g.*, Ohio Rev. Code §§ 3517.16, 5747.081 (2005); Or. Rev. Stat. § 316.102.

181. 424 U.S. 1 (1976).

182. U.S. Const. art. I, § 8, cl. 1.

183. 424 U.S. at 96.

184. For arguments that the "general Welfare" clause does not support such government subsidies, see Bradley A. Smith, *Separation of Campaign and State*, 81 Geo. Wash. L. Rev. 2038 (2013); Robert G. Natelson, *The Original Scope of the Government Power to Regulate Elections*, 13 U. Pa. J. Const. L. 1 (2010); and *Buckley v. Valeo*, 424 U.S. at 247–49 (Burger, C.J., dissenting).

to the general-election candidates of the Republican and Democratic parties, using prior vote levels as the sole criterion for pre-election funding, limiting new-party candidates to post-election funds, and denying general-election funds to candidates of parties receiving less than 5% of the vote in an election—constituted invidious discrimination under the Fifth Amendment. The Court argued that there were valid reasons for discriminating in amounts based on past vote totals, and it noted that there was no evidence that small parties would have less money by not qualifying for the subsidy than they would if the subsidies did not exist at all. The Court's decision in *Buckley* is a practical one, recognizing that the major barriers to small parties are not public-financing systems but rather ballot-access laws, which the Court had upheld in other cases, and, of even greater importance, the "two-party" system fostered by election through single-member districts.[185]

In upholding the funding systems, the Court recognized that they required participating candidates to limit their spending in the general election to the amount of the federal grant plus a small amount for personal spending by the candidate, and to a fixed amount, including private and public funds, in the primaries. The question immediately arose as to whether this conclusion contradicts *Buckley*'s holding that expenditure limits are constitutionally suspect. The answer for the Court was "no," provided that participation in the government-financing system was voluntary. Candidates, therefore, were free to spend more simply by forgoing the subsidy.

Buckley, then, permits states and the federal government to subsidize candidate campaigns directly so long as participation on the part of the candidate is voluntary and nonparticipating candidates are permitted to raise and spend unlimited sums.[186] However, those nonparticipating candidates may still be subject to the contribution limits and reporting rules. Additionally, the government cannot prevent or limit independent spending merely because a candidate participates in a government-funded program.[187]

A fundamental problem for government campaign financing systems is how to convince candidates to participate without causing unacceptable increases in the costs of the programs. If the funds provided to candidates are set too high, the cost to the state may rise, increasing political opposition to the system. Additionally, government campaign financing systems may draw more candidates into the system, including frivolous candidates looking to propagate a message at taxpayers' expense, corrupt

---

185. This is known among political scientists as "Duverger's Law," for the French political scientist Maurice Duverger, who published a series of articles in the 1950s, 1960s, and 1970s demonstrating that plurality elections in single-member districts tended to result in two dominant parties. *See* Maurice Duverger, Party Politics and Pressure Groups 23–32 (1972); *see also* Chapter 6, § B, *supra*.

186. In theory, a public-funding system does not have to include limits on the amounts that may be spent but could simply provide subsidies to candidates, in the hope that the subsidies would be sufficiently large to displace the desire for private fundraising. *See* Joel L. Fleishman & Pope McCorkle, *Level-Up Rather Than Level Down: Towards a New Theory of Campaign Finance,* 1 J. L. & Pols. 211 (1984). In fact, that approach has not been enacted in the United States.

187. Arizona Free Enter. Club's Freedom Club PAC v. Bennett, 564 U.S. 721 (2011); Fed. Election Comm'n v. Nat'l Conservative Pol. Action Comm., 470 U.S. 480 (1985).

candidates using funds for personal use, and publicity seekers. However, if the funds made available to candidates are too low in amount, many candidates will decide that the benefits of exceeding the expenditure limit outweigh the costs of additional time spent fundraising and any backlash in public opinion. If candidates decline to participate in the system, the system will have no value in preventing corruption or promoting political equality.

As a result, governments have attempted a variety of incentives for participation and handicaps for nonparticipation to try to ensure that candidates take part in the government-funding programs. Most of the legal questions about government-funding programs have arisen around the issue of how far the government may go in attempting to ensure participation by candidates before the incentives for participation become coercive and thus violate *Buckley*.

3. Designs of Government-Funding Programs

a. Presidential General-Election and Fixed-Sum Grant Programs

The simplest government-funding programs provide cash grants for candidates. The presidential general-election system, which went into effect in 1976, is an example of this type of system. Under the presidential funding system, each major-party nominee receives a cash grant from the government after presenting evidence of nomination. The candidates agree not to spend above the grant level except for a small allowance for the candidate's personal spending.

Additionally, in the presidential system, candidates have been allowed to raise supplemental private funds, subject to contribution limits, to pay for legal and accounting fees for the campaign.[188] These funds can be substantial, exceeding 10% of the amount of the public-funding grant, as campaigns stretch the definition of "legal and accounting" to pay more bills with this supplemental private funding.

In the federal system, nominees of the two largest vote-getting parties each receive a fixed cash grant. Nominees of other parties that received at least 5% of the vote in the prior election are eligible for a grant proportional to their share of the vote versus the average of the top two parties. Party nominees not qualifying for funds in advance of the election may be eligible for funding after the election by receiving at least 5% of the vote. However, in practice, candidates have found it nearly impossible to borrow funds for the campaign in the hope that the lender will be repaid with federal funds after the election.

Although the size of the presidential general-election grant is regularly adjusted for inflation, the grants have increasingly been seen as inadequate because the costs

188. These funds are called General Election Legal and Accounting Compliance Funds, or "GELAC." *See* 11 C.F.R. §§ 9003 *et seq.*

of campaigning have risen considerably faster than general inflation. In 2008, Barack Obama became the first major-party nominee to decline to participate in the government-funding program, and he went on to raise record amounts in the general election, far outspending his government-funded opponent, Senator John McCain. Since then, no major-party presidential candidate has participated in the government-funding program, opting instead to raise money privately. Federal budget deficits and lack of popular support make it unlikely that the grants will be sufficiently increased to attract candidates back to the system in the near future.

b. Presidential-Primary and Matching-Grant Systems

FECA actually created two separate financing systems: one for the presidential general election and one for the presidential primaries. The primary system is a matching-grant system. A candidate qualifies to receive primary matching funds by raising $5,000 or more in amounts of $250 or less in each of at least twenty states. Once the candidate qualifies, the federal government matches the first $250 of each contribution until the candidate hits a spending limit determined by a statutory formula. A candidate loses matching benefits by failing to get 10% or more of the vote in two consecutive primaries but may re-establish eligibility by receiving 20% or more of the vote in a later primary.

Like the presidential general-election fund, the spending limits and grants in the primary matching-fund program are adjusted, by law, for inflation, but, as with the general-election system, candidates have increasingly found the amounts inadequate and have chosen to opt out of the system. By 2004, neither of the eventual major-party nominees participated in the primary program, and no significant candidate in either major party has participated in the primary program since 2012. Matching-fund programs in the states have similarly fallen into desuetude, existing on the books but rarely being used by serious candidates in competitive races.[189]

In an effort to keep matching-fund systems viable, some commentators have proposed matches of $3, $4, and even $8 in public funds for each dollar raised privately. The most prominent example is New York City's Campaign Finance Program, which matches contributions of up to $175 from city residents with an eight-to-one government match. Thus, a $175 contribution triggers an additional $1,400 in government subsidies for the candidate. New York City's system has been called a glowing success and a colossal flop.[190] As a one-party city with relatively few competitive council

---

189. *See, e.g.*, MINN. STAT. §§ 290.06, 10A.322, 10A.25. The low subsidies and consequent withdrawal from the programs by many of the most competitive candidates have led to the suggestion that participation in government funding systems is "for losers." Michael Malbin, *Are Matching Funds Only for Losers?*, *in* WELFARE FOR POLITICIANS 251 (John Samples ed., 2005) (citing Tod Linberg, *Dancing Dollars*, WASH. TIMES, Jan. 27, 2004).

190. *See* Angela Migally & Susan Liss, *Small Donor Matching Funds: The NYC Election Experience*, BRENNAN CENTER FOR JUSTICE (Sep. 17, 2010), https://www.brennancenter.org/our-work/research-reports/small-donor-matching-funds-nyc-election-experience; *see also* Jason M. Farrell, *Clean Elections and Scandal: Case Studies from Maine, Arizona, and New York City*, INST. FOR FREE SPEECH

races, and three consecutive mayoral races from 2001 through 2009 dominated by the wealthy self-funder Michael Bloomberg, New York is probably a unique case from which it is impossible to draw many lessons either way.

c. Variable Grants, Spending Limits, and "Rescue Funds"

By the mid-1990s, it was becoming clear that traditional fixed-sum and matching-grant programs were squeezed between two forces. If the grants were too low, the candidates with the greatest ability to raise money—and usually the candidates with the best chances of winning—would decline to participate. If the grants were set too high, the cost of the program would rise and voters would see tax dollars going to significant numbers of fringe candidates, candidates in noncompetitive races, or simply to candidates with whom they disagreed, costing the program political support.

The solution that was developed was a system based on a fixed-sum grant that could be augmented by what were called "rescue funds" or, somewhat confusingly, "matching funds." The programs were often promoted under the name "clean elections."

These programs essentially worked off a variable grant that could increase as money was spent against a candidate. In other words, the "match" referred not to funds provided by the government to match those raised *by* the candidate, but to funds provided by the government to match funds raised *against* the candidate by independent spenders or by opponents who had not agreed to participate in the public-financing system.

Under this variable-grant approach, a qualifying candidate would receive an initial grant from the state. If an opponent not participating in the program raised more money than the initial grant, however, the state would match those funds for the participating candidate, to prevent that candidate from being outspent. In some plans, this match feature could be triggered not only by spending by a nonparticipating candidate but also by independent expenditures by another individual or entity, over which the nonparticipating candidate had no control. In a three-way race with two participating candidates, "excess" expenditures by a nonparticipating candidate, or independent expenditures on his behalf, would trigger matching funds to each participating opponent, meaning each dollar in spending by the nonparticipating candidate triggered two dollars in spending by his opponents. However, if independent spending favored a participating candidate, the participating candidate's grant was not reduced. A Kentucky program offered a variation in which contributions to participating candidates were matched by the state up to a set amount; however, if an opposing, nonparticipating candidate raised more than the spending ceiling for a participating candidate, the participating candidate was allowed to continue raising funds and to continue drawing the two-for-one state match indefinitely.

Opponents of these systems argue that the financing systems amount to the government putting its thumb on the scale to attempt to ensure that favored candidates—those

(formerly Cent. for Competitive Politics) (Sep. 23, 2011), https://www.ifs.org/research/clean-elections-scandal-case-studies-from-maine-arizona-new-york-city/.

participating in the system—win. Opponents further argue that the systems discourage spending by nonparticipating candidates as well as independent expenditures by supporters because such expenditures merely trigger opposition speech—in some cases, greater amounts of speech—with state funds.

Lower courts initially tended to uphold such programs, including the Kentucky plan discussed above.[191] However, the Supreme Court's 2008 decision in *Davis v. Federal Election Commission*[192] threw into doubt the ability of legislatures to apply different rules to different candidates based simply on their spending or that of their opponents. In 2011, the Supreme Court specifically considered "rescue fund" features in government-financing systems for the first time and struck them down in *Arizona Free Enterprise Club's Freedom Club PAC v. Bennett.*[193]

The *Bennett* opinion is not a model of clarity, but, in the end, the Court seemed to sense that the government was penalizing some speech in a manner that was unfair. Quoting *Davis*, the Court noted that, under a program providing "rescue funds," "the vigorous exercise of the right to . . . finance campaign speech" leads to "advantages for opponents in the competitive context of electoral politics."[194] Indeed, as noted above, in multi-candidate races, spending above the state-imposed trigger could actually result in multiples of the amount spent being given to the combined opposition. What the Court recognized is that, ultimately, political races are zero-sum games in which one candidate's advantage is always another's disadvantage. The Court brushed aside the state's argument that, in order to encourage candidates' participation, it needed to assure participating candidates that they would not likely be outspent. The Court reasoned that the purpose of encouraging participation was to get candidates to abide by spending ceilings and, thus, to discourage speech. The Court was also skeptical of the state's claim that participation would battle "corruption," pointing to evidence in the state's own promotional material, legislative history, and the statute itself, that the primary purpose was to promote equal spending.[195]

Without such "rescue fund" provisions, government-financing systems have foundered politically, since voters seem unwilling to finance them at high levels, and candidates seem unwilling to participate if funding is set at low levels.

---

191. Gable v. Patton, 142 F.3d 940 (6th Cir. 1998), *cert. denied*, 525 U.S. 1177 (1999); *see also* North Carolina Right to Life Comm. Fund for Indep. Pol. Expenditures v. Leake, 524 F.3d 427 (4th Cir. 2008) (raising spending ceiling and providing dollar-for-dollar match with nonparticipating candidate up to twice the original spending limit); Daggett v. Comm'n on Governmental Ethics & Election Pracs., 205 F.3d 445 (1st Cir. 2000) (providing matching funds up to twice the original limit, and labeling participating candidates as "clean"); *cf.* Vote Choice, Inc. v. DiStefano, 4 F.3d 26 (1st Cir. 1993) (allowing participating candidates to raise more funds, under higher contribution limits, when a nonparticipating candidate exceeded the spending limit).

192. 554 U.S. 724 (2008) (raising contribution limits for candidates who were outspent by candidates using personal funds).

193. 564 U.S. 721 (2011).

194. *Id.* at 736.

195. *Id.* at 748–49.

d. Qualifying Provisions

An ongoing issue for government-funding programs is determining who qualifies for government subsidies. The government seeks to limit the candidates eligible for funding lest the subsidy draw more fringe candidates into the race, thus raising the costs of the program. Such limits are particularly important because public support for financing such "welfare for politicians" has long been tepid.[196] At the same time, restricting the program to too few candidates could raise equal-protection problems under the Constitution.

The Court has long held that the government's interest in orderly elections allows it to demand that candidates demonstrate some modicum of public support in order to secure a spot on the ballot.[197] The Court relied on this line of cases in *Buckley* to uphold the presidential public-financing system against equal-protection claims.[198] At the same time, those ballot-access cases make clear that the state's rules must be tailored to the state's legitimate interest in election administration and may not become a substitute for entrenching particular political interests—normally the two major political parties.[199]

Similarly, then, a government-financing system must allow some means for participation by minor-party and independent candidates, although the state is not required to treat them on equal terms with the major-party candidates. The Court has never attempted to draw this line, but it is probably fair to say that so long as there is a reasonable probability that a popular independent or minor-party candidate could qualify for funding, the system will pass constitutional scrutiny.[200] In fact, the most popular minor-party and independent candidates have usually been able to qualify for funding, if only barely.[201]

e. Funding Government Subsidies

Public opinion on government financing of campaigns has proven to be highly sensitive to polling language.[202] Support for funding such systems, however, does not appear to be strong.

---

196. CATO INSTITUTE, WELFARE FOR POLITICIANS? TAXPAYER FINANCING OF CAMPAIGNS (John Samples ed., 2005).

197. *See* Jenness v. Fortson, 403 U.S. 431 (1971); *see also* Chapter 6, § B, *supra*.

198. Buckley v. Valeo, 424 U.S. 1, 96 (1976) (*per curiam*).

199. Williams v. Rhodes, 393 U.S. 23 (1968).

200. *Buckley*, 424 U.S. at 96–102.

201. These candidates include John Anderson in 1980, who obtained 6.6% of the popular vote, Ross Perot in 1996 at 8%, and Patrick Buchanan at 0.42% in 2000 as the nominee of Perot's Reform Party. *See* Federal Election Commission, *Federal Elections 2000: President*, *at* https://www.fec.gov/introduction-campaign-finance/election-results-and-voting-information/federal-elections-2000/president2000/ (visited Jun. 16, 2025).

202. *See* David M. Primo, *What Does Research Say About Public Funding for Political Campaigns?*, INST. FOR JUSTICE (Aug. 2010), https://ij.org/report/what-does-research-say-about-public-funding

The common method for funding programs in the 1970s was through tax check-offs, by which taxpayers could earmark a small portion of their tax returns to a public fund that would finance candidate campaigns; this is the system used for presidential campaigns.[203] This voluntary-contribution system was initially favored because of both policy and constitutional concerns over forcing taxpayers to pay for opposing political beliefs. Participation in the voluntary check-off plan peaked at under 30% in 1980 and has declined regularly since, to less than 4% in 2023.[204] The result has been that, in some years, the fund has not had enough money to pay candidates the full amounts to which they were entitled, resulting in delays in payments while the FEC waited for more tax returns. This lack of funds has led to more candidates deciding to abandon the system.

Funding the systems through traditional appropriations by state legislatures has also proven unreliable. Kentucky's system was repealed in 2005.[205] North Carolina's government funding of judicial races ended in 2013.[206] Wisconsin defunded its program in 2011.[207] In Massachusetts, the legislature refused to fund a program passed by voter initiative; the measure was eventually repealed following the overwhelming approval of a different voter initiative, one that called for repeal and was less favorably worded toward government financing.

To overcome these funding obstacles, supporters of government financing in some states, notably Arizona, have sought to establish dedicated funding sources. The Arizona plan provided for funding through a 10% surcharge on civil and criminal violations of the law, including motor-vehicle violations, and a tax on a politically unpopular group, lobbyists. The surcharge was upheld as a valid exercise of taxing power in *May v. McNally*.[208] However, the fee on lobbyists was struck down as unconstitutional by an Arizona court in 2001, and the decision was not appealed.[209] Similarly, a Vermont law imposing a tax on lobbyists to provide funds for campaign subsidies was struck down as unconstitutional in *Vermont Society of Association Executives v. Milne*.[210]

-for-political-campaigns/.

203. 26 U.S.C. § 6096. The amount was originally set at $1, and increased to $3 in 1993.

204. *See* Federal Election Commission, *Presidential Fund Income Tax Check-Off Chart*, *at* https://www.fec.gov/resources/cms-content/documents/Pres_Public_Funding.pdf (June 10, 2025).

205. http://statutes.laws.com/kentucky/121A00.

206. Matthew Burns et al., *Voting Changes Head to Governor*, WRAL.com (updated July 26, 2013), https://www.wral.com/voting-changes-head-to-governor/12703982/.

207. Bill Lueders, *Public Financing of Elections a State Budget Casualty*, Wisconsin St. J. (updated May 23, 2012), https://host.madison.com/news/local/govt-and-politics/elections/public-financing-of-elections-a-state-budget-casualty/article_3dfcc38a-a63f-11e0-ad5d-001cc4c03286.html.

208. 55 P.3d 768 (Ariz. 2002), *cert. denied*, 538 U.S. 923 (2003).

209. Lavis v. Bayless, No. CV 2001-006078 (Ariz. Super. Ct. 2001).

210. 779 A.2d 20 (Vt. 2001).

I. Judicial Elections

Most state and local judges in the United States are elected. These elections may be nonpartisan, partisan, or some type of hybrid; other judges face retention elections in which they have no opponent, but the voters decide whether to retain them in office. It has been argued that the unique role of judges necessitates different constitutional rules for campaign finance in judicial races than in races for legislative and executive offices. However, the courts have generally not been receptive to such arguments, and, for the most part, judicial elections are subject to the same constitutional limits on campaign finance rules that apply to other races.

As a basic matter, nothing in *Buckley*, *Citizens United*, or the Court's other decisions suggests that judicial elections are so different in kind as to provide for different constitutional rules. However, state codes of judicial ethics and the Supreme Court decision in *Caperton v. A.T. Massey Coal Company*[211] do place some constraints on fundraising that do not apply in legislative and executive races.

In *Caperton*, the elected chief justice of a state supreme court opted not to recuse himself as the court considered an appeal of a $50 million verdict against the Massey Coal Company. The CEO of Massey Coal had committed nearly $3 million of his personal funds to independent expenditures supporting the chief justice in the prior election. Although the case had not been appealed to the state supreme court at the time of the election, it was widely recognized that the case would be appealed if the company's motion for a new trial were denied. The company itself spent nothing, and the CEO was not personally a party to the lawsuit. The state supreme court ruled 3–2, with the chief justice in the majority, for the company. The Supreme Court, in a 5–4 opinion by Justice Kennedy, held that the decision by the chief justice not to recuse himself violated Caperton's due-process rights. The Court's opinion went to great lengths to note the "extreme" facts of *Caperton*, and it stressed that these unique facts should differentiate the case from more common instances in which litigants or counsel have supported the election of judges who ultimately hear their cases.

The Court's test for when recusal must take place, however, was vague. The Court emphasized that there must be a "serious risk of actual bias—based on objective and reasonable perceptions"[212]—and that "a person with a personal stake in a particular case" must have a "significant and disproportionate influence in . . . raising funds or directing the campaign when the case was pending or imminent."[213] Such an inquiry, according to the Court, required consideration of such factors as "the contribution's size in comparison to the total amount of money contributed to the campaign, the total amount spent in the election, and the apparent effect of such contribution on the outcome."[214]

211. Caperton v. A.T. Massey Coal Co., Inc., 556 U.S. 868 (2009).
212. *Id.* at 884.
213. *Id.* at 883.
214. *Id.* at 884.

To the dismay of many, the relief of others, and the surprise of almost all, *Caperton* does not appear to have led to a major increase in recusal motions. Ultimately, *Caperton* is not a campaign finance case but rather a due-process case. The Court's opinion does not disqualify a CEO or corporation from making expenditures but merely requires the judge to recuse in "extreme" situations. In a coda to the case, on remand, with the chief justice recused, Massey won again, this time by a 4–1 vote of the state supreme court.[215]

While states may not limit spending in judicial races, several states have enacted ethics codes that limit a judge's ability to accept or solicit campaign funds personally.[216] Such restrictions were upheld in *Williams-Yulee v. Florida Bar*.[217] However, attempts to use judicial-ethics rules to impose the type of spending restrictions struck down in *Buckley* have been rejected by lower courts.[218]

J. Ballot Issues

Buckley allowed for some limitations on campaign contributions in order to prevent corruption, but it rejected the idea that the government could limit speech in order to promote a form of political equality, and it also rejected the notion that spending limitations served a compelling government interest in preventing corruption.

Thus, it is not surprising that just two years after *Buckley*, in *First National Bank of Boston v. Bellotti*,[219] the Court struck down a Massachusetts law that prohibited corporate spending concerning a ballot proposition to impose a state income tax. Because a ballot initiative or referendum must be approved by the voters, there is not a great danger of *quid pro quo* exchanges of contributions for official action. The electorate may be persuaded to vote in one manner or another, but that is the essence of, and rationale for, political speech and campaigning. Voters are not going to "corrupt" themselves as the term "corruption" is used in campaign finance law.

Recent years have seen a growth of ballot initiatives and referenda that have been closely identified with officeholders who seek to use these propositions to achieve policy objectives and to boost their political fortunes. Arguably, this practice could allow a reconsideration of the Court's position, but, in fact, such reconsideration seems unlikely, and spending and contributions in ballot initiative and referenda campaigns are likely to remain unlimited.

---

215. Caperton v. A.T. Massey Coal Co., Inc., 690 S.E.2d 322 (W. Va. 2009).
216. *See, e.g.*, OHIO JUD. CONDUCT R. 7(B); PA. CODE JUD. CONDUCT R. 7(B)(2).
217. 575 U.S. 433 (2015).
218. *See* Suster v. Marshall, 951 F. Supp. 693 (N.D. Ohio 1996), *aff'd*, 149 F.3d 523 (6th Cir. 1998).
219. 435 U.S. 765 (1978).

Chapter 9
Anonymous Speech and Mandatory Disclosures

A. Introduction

Almost everyone would agree that robust free speech is a fundamental component of a functioning democracy.[1] The right to speak, however, may mean little in practice if one will suffer negative consequences after the fact for speaking. For that reason, modern First Amendment doctrine prohibits not only "prior restraints" on speech but also *ex post* punishments on speech, whether those punishments are criminal or civil.[2] Even the *possibility* of subsequent punishment might produce a "chilling effect" by causing would-be speakers to censor themselves rather than risk negative consequences for speaking. The chilling of speech both interferes with the free-speech rights of the speaker and deprives the rest of society of the benefits that come from the free exchange of ideas. The Court has attempted to counter this chilling effect by employing doctrines such as "overbreadth" to protect speech that might otherwise be suppressed through the prospect of future sanctions.[3]

But one may be dissuaded from speaking even if there is no risk of criminal or civil punishment by the government. While many speakers are eager to be publicly identified or to endorse candidates or causes publicly, others are not. People may be reticent to speak if their words might upset a spouse, a boss, a friend, or a neighbor. Business executives may wish to speak in a personal capacity and not have their thoughts tied to the business, as that might lead some consumers to boycott the enterprise, thus harming employees and stockholders of the company. Proponents of civic and charitable organizations may not want their personal political views to create problems for

1. *See, e.g.*, Mills v. Alabama, 384 U.S. 214, 218 (1966) ("[T]here is practically universal agreement that a major purpose of th[e First] Amendment was to protect the free discussion of governmental affairs.").

2. *See, e.g.*, Brandenburg v. Ohio, 395 U.S. 444 (1969) (striking down a criminal conviction for the advocacy of violence as violating the First Amendment); *New York Times Co. v. Sullivan*, 376 U.S. 254 (1964) (holding that a libel judgment against a newspaper violated the publisher's First Amendment rights).

3. *See, e.g.*, Washington State Grange v. Washington State Republican Party, 552 U.S. 442 (2008).

their charitable endeavors. Others may wish to protect family, friends, or business associates from controversy. Speech can be chilled because it might cause someone to lose a job, a contract, or a friend.

Perhaps the most obvious ways to prevent this chilling is to allow speakers to speak anonymously and to protect the privacy of persons who join or financially support clubs and organizations engaged in civic affairs. If speakers are able to keep their identities secret, then they will be less likely to face consequences for their speech and, therefore, less likely to censor themselves. Further, speakers may wish to encourage the audience to focus on the merits of the speech itself, uncolored by whatever feelings the audience might have about the speaker. This last was a primary reason that the Federalist Papers were published anonymously. Anonymity permits speech to reach the public even when the speaker, for any number of reasons, is not willing to be publicly associated with the speech.

On the other hand, permitting speakers to be anonymous might lead to harmful results. If an anonymous speaker falsifies a story and defames someone, the victim of the defamation might have a hard time recovering. Likewise, if speech is obscene or reveals national-security secrets, perhaps the speaker should not be immune from the consequences of making the speech. Additionally, anonymity itself might deprive the public of useful information. Readers might find an argument more or less persuasive knowing the biases of its author. Lastly, society may wish to know the identities of particular speakers. For example, if a politician were supported by people aligned with a certain industry or interest group, the identities of those supporters may be information that voters could use to predict how the candidate would likely act in office, which could be of assistance in deciding whether to vote for that politician.

This chapter considers the conflict between promoting speech and encouraging people to participate in politics, on the one hand, and giving the public useful information about the identities of people who are attempting to influence politics, on the other. Because people can try to influence politics in different ways, speakers, and the funders of speech, may wish to remain anonymous when they are engaged in a variety of different tasks, from writing and publishing to contributing to campaigns and signing petitions. The chapter covers compulsory disclosure of political contributions as well as other efforts to compel disclosure of the identity of individuals engaged in the discussion of elections and public affairs.

B. First Amendment Principles

During the post-World War II campaign for civil rights, segregationist southern officials often sought to use compulsory disclosure to undercut the efforts of the NAACP and other civil-rights organizations and activists. The first, and most prominent, of these cases to reach the U.S. Supreme Court was *National Association for the Advancement of Colored People v. Alabama ex rel. Patterson* (*NAACP v.*

Alabama).[4] The attorney general of Alabama filed suit against the NAACP to enjoin it from further activities in the state, on the ground that the organization had failed to file proper paperwork required of all businesses operating within the state. The state then demanded, among other records of the organization, the names and addresses of members of the association. When the NAACP refused to turn over membership lists, it was held in contempt of court, and it was an appeal of this contempt order that reached the U.S. Supreme Court.

The Supreme Court noted at the outset that "it is hardly a novel perception that compelled disclosure of affiliation with groups engaged in advocacy may constitute a restraint on freedom of association" and that privacy of groups' associates may be "indispensable," especially for groups espousing "dissident beliefs."[5] Considering evidence of past economic reprisal, loss of employment, and physical coercion against the NAACP's members and donors, the Court held that only a "compelling" government interest could justify the intrusion on association. The state failed to meet that burden, as the state's only interest was in determining whether the NAACP was complying with the state's requirement that out-of-state corporations register before carrying out certain business in the state, and the membership list had nothing to do with that issue.[6]

Importantly, the Court also rejected the government's claim that there was no First Amendment violation because any negative consequences to members, or deterrent effects on their future speech, would not come from punishment by the government but rather from private actors. "The crucial factor," the Court held, "is the interplay of governmental and private action, for it is only after the initial exertion of state power . . . that private action takes hold."[7]

NAACP v. Alabama is perhaps the most dramatic, forceful, and paradigmatic of many cases decided in the 1950s and 1960s involving anonymous expression. In addition to its speech-protective rulings in several other cases involving the NAACP,[8] the Warren Court was broadly protective of other organizations' and individuals' right to privacy in association and anonymous speech. In *Shelton v. Tucker*,[9] for example, the Court struck down an Arkansas statute requiring public-school teachers to disclose the names and addresses of all organizations to which they had belonged or donated in the preceding five years. Similarly, in *Sweezy v. New Hampshire*, the Court reversed the contempt conviction of a college professor who refused to answer questions from a state legislative body regarding various political organizations to which he belonged or had contact.[10] In *Shelton*, the Court's stated concern was less the validity of the

4. 357 U.S. 449 (1958).
5. *Id.* at 462.
6. *See id.* at 464.
7. *Id.* at 463.
8. Gibson v. Florida Legis. Comm., 372 U.S. 539 (1963); Talley v. California, 362 U.S. 60 (1960); Bates v. Little Rock, 361 U.S. 516 (1960).
9. 364 U.S. 479 (1960).
10. 354 U.S. 234 (1957).

state's stated interest (weeding Communist teachers out of the public schools) than the method used, writing, "[e]ven though the governmental purpose be legitimate and substantial, that purpose cannot be pursued by means that broadly stifle fundamental personal liberties when the end can be more narrowly achieved."[11]

Not until 1976, in the landmark campaign finance case of *Buckley v. Valeo*, did the Court begin to flesh out an "exacting scrutiny" test for laws mandating disclosure. The Court held that the state must demonstrate a "sufficiently important" interest that is substantial enough to "outweigh the possibility of infringement" of First Amendment rights.[12] It further demanded that there be a "substantial relation" between the government interest and the information required to be disclosed.[13] Finally, the Court declined to provide blanket protection from any adverse consequences of disclosure, concluding that "*NAACP v. Alabama* is inapposite where, as here, any serious infringement on First Amendment rights brought about by the compelled disclosure of contributors is highly speculative."[14]

NAACP v. Alabama—highly skeptical of compelled disclosure—and *Buckley*—skeptical, but ultimately upholding broad campaign finance disclosure—set forth competing considerations that have vexed both the Supreme Court and lower courts since. As the next two sections explore, most of the conflict over mandatory-disclosure laws has focused on three issues: (1) What passes as a sufficient government interest? (2) Does the required "substantial relation" between the law and the government interest mean that the government solution must be "narrowly tailored" to address that issue? and (3) What level of harassment, threat, or inconvenience is sufficient to defeat the government interest?

C. Reporting and Disclosure of Campaign Contributions and Expenditures

1. General Principles

In 1890, New York imposed the nation's first law requiring disclosure of campaign contributions and expenditures, and the first federal "publicity" act—the term then used—was adopted in 1910.[15] Mandatory disclosure of campaign contributions and

11. 364 U.S. at 489.

12. 424 U.S. 1, 66 (1976) (*per curiam*). Elsewhere in the opinion, discussing FECA's government-financing provisions, the Court described "exacting scrutiny" as requiring a "vital" government interest. *Id.* at 94.

13. *Id.* at 64.

14. *Id.* at 70.

15. *See* Earl R. Sikes, State and Federal Corrupt Practices Legislation 122, 284–91 (1928).

expenditures has been a mainstay of campaign finance law in the United States ever since. Today, every state and the federal government require some disclosure of campaign contributions and expenditures by campaign committees. Just four states do not specifically require disclosure of independent expenditures.

Although disclosure laws are perhaps the most universally accepted and most deeply entrenched element of campaign finance regulation, they are not without controversy. Disclosure requirements can substantially burden political speech, both by requiring the disclosure of an organization's donors and members, and by the direct burden of complying with the administrative requirements themselves.[16] Yet prior to *Buckley v. Valeo*, in 1976, there was little litigation over compelled disclosure of campaign contributions and expenditures.

The Federal Election Campaign Act (discussed extensively in Chapter 8) imposes substantial organizational, administrative, and registration and reporting requirements on political committees.[17] Many of these requirements were challenged in *Buckley v. Valeo.* And so, as usual, we turn to that case for the general principles that have governed the Court's treatment of compulsory-disclosure laws in the campaign finance arena.

Buckley's analysis of FECA's compulsory-disclosure requirements began by citing the civil rights cases from the 1950s and 1960s, emphasizing *NAACP v. Alabama.*[18] Having placed this marker, however, the Court went on to identify three government interests of sufficient magnitude to pass the "exacting scrutiny" test: First, disclosure provides information to voters to help them evaluate candidates and identify interests to which the candidate is likely to be responsive. Second, disclosure deters corruption by exposing contributions to public scrutiny, thus interfering with *quid pro quo* deals at the heart of *Buckley*'s definition of corruption. Third, disclosure provides the government with information needed to enforce the contribution limits in FECA.[19]

The Court found that the burdens and threats of disclosure faced by the *Buckley* plaintiffs were not so great as those in the civil-rights cases and that the government's interest in disclosure was more legitimate. Further, on the facts presented in *Buckley*, the Court held that FECA's disclosure requirements were appropriately tailored to that interest.

The Court saw greater problems with the Act's broad disclosure requirements for independent expenditures. Beyond the possibilities of official or unofficial harassment, the Court noted that disclosure places "very real, practical burdens" on speakers and is a "direct intrusion on privacy of belief." As a result, disclosure may cause

16. *See* Fed. Election Comm'n v. Massachusetts Citizens for Life, 479 U.S. 238, 266 (1986) (O'Connor, J., concurring). One study has found that corporate PACs spend almost half of what they raise on administration and legal compliance. Stephen D. Ansolabehere et al., *Why Is There So Little Money in American Politics?*, 17 J. ECON. PERSPECTIVES 105 (2003).

17. *See* 52 U.S.C. §§ 30102–30104; 11 C.F.R. §§ 102–106.

18. 424 U.S. at 64 (citing Gibson v. Florida Legis. Comm., 372 U.S. 539 (1963); NAACP v. Button, 371 U.S. 415 (1963); Shelton v. Tucker, 364 U.S. 479 (1960); Bates v. Little Rock, 361 U.S. 516 (1960); NAACP v. Alabama, 357 U.S. 449 (1958)).

19. *Buckley*, 424 U.S. at 66–67.

persons to restrict their speech, particularly in light of possible criminal penalties for failure to disclose properly.[20] Thus, the same concerns of vagueness and overbreadth that underlay the Court's discussion of independent "expenditures"[21] and its narrowing construction of "express advocacy" came into play regarding disclosures.

As it had in discussing contributions and expenditures, the Court avoided vagueness and overbreadth concerns by narrowing the category of political committees subject to disclosure requirements. The definition of a political committee, the Court held, could survive a vagueness challenge only if it were limited to "encompass organizations that are under the control of a candidate or the major purpose of which is the nomination or election of a candidate."[22] For organizations that did not fit that definition, the Court held that FECA, "as construed, imposes independent reporting requirements on individuals and groups that are not candidates or political committees only in the following circumstances: (1) when they make contributions earmarked for political purposes or authorized or requested by a candidate or his agent, to some person other than a candidate or political committee, and (2) when they make expenditures for communications that expressly advocate the election or defeat of a clearly identified candidate."[23]

The Court's narrowing construction here is often overlooked but extremely important. While the Court went on to uphold the recordkeeping, reporting, and disclosure provisions of FECA, the narrowed definition actually excluded, as a matter of constitutional law, a great deal of the disclosure that otherwise would have been covered by the Act.

Moreover, an organization's disclosure obligations depend substantially on whether the organization qualifies as a "political committee." Political committees—groups that either make contributions to candidate campaigns or that have the "major purpose" of electing or defeating candidates for office through independent expenditures—are subject to far-reaching disclosure of all but *de minimis* contributions and expenditures. However, groups that make only independent expenditures, and lack a major purpose of contributing to campaigns, need only disclose the actual independent expenditures they make, and only the names of funders who have earmarked their donations to fund those expenditures. Thus, the extent of a group's disclosure obligations often turns on whether it has a "major purpose" of electing candidates to office.

Unfortunately, the Supreme Court has not taken a case that might further define what constitutes "major purpose." The closest it has come is in *Federal Election Commission v. Massachusetts Citizens for Life* (*MCFL*), which concerned a grassroots organization that rarely endorsed candidates. In *MCFL*, the Court simply noted that

---

20. *Id.* at 75 (citing Talley v. California, 362 U.S. 60 (1960), and Thomas v. Collins, 323 U.S. 516 (1945)).

21. *See* Chapter 8, § D[2], *supra*.

22. *Buckley*, 424 U.S. at 79, 80. The Court also explicitly referenced the definition of "express advocacy" from footnote 52 of the decision to make clear its meaning. *See id.* at 80 n.108. *See also* Chapter 8, § D[2], *supra*.

23. *Id.* at 80.

it was "undisputed" that the group's "central organizational purpose [wa]s issue advocacy, although it occasionally engages in activities on behalf of political candidates."[24] Most lower courts seem to have implicitly assumed that an organization lacks the requisite "major purpose" unless a majority, or at least a plurality, of its spending goes for activity other than express advocacy of the election or defeat of a candidate.[25] Others, however, have asserted that as long as campaign advocacy is among the major purposes of the organization, it may qualify.[26]

Although the Supreme Court has left "major purpose" undefined, since *Buckley*, the Court has upheld most laws mandating disclosure of political campaign contributions and spending. In *McConnell v. Federal Election Commission*,[27] the Court permitted Congress to extend disclosure by requiring groups that did not qualify as "political committees" to disclose contributions and expenditures for "electioneering communications"—broadcast ads airing in a candidate's district within thirty days of a primary or caucus or sixty days of a general election.[28] The Court ruled that the "electioneering communications" standard was not vague and that such ads were "the functional equivalent of express advocacy." Indeed, the *McConnell* Court upheld requirements that executory contracts be disclosed even if the actual expenditures for such ads had not been made, on the ground that the short time frames in elections made such early disclosure necessary.

Four years later, in *Federal Election Commission v. Wisconsin Right to Life* (*WRTL*), the Court narrowed the definition of "electioneering communications" for purposes of the funding limits for such ads, but it did not address whether this narrowing construction applied as well to disclosure requirements.[29] But three years after that, in *Citizens United v. Federal Election Commission*, the Court refused to extend *WRTL*'s narrowing construction to mandatory disclosure of "electioneering communications."[30] The Court held that "prompt disclosure of expenditures can provide shareholders and citizens with the information needed to hold corporations and elected officials accountable for their positions and supporters," and, therefore, "we reject Citizens United's contention that the disclosure requirements must be limited to speech that is the functional equivalent of express advocacy."[31] While this holding should not be taken as a green light to regulate non-campaign speech, it has provided considerably more leeway for state experimentation than existed before.

---

24. Fed. Election Comm'n v. Massachusetts Citizens for Life, 479 U.S. 238, 252 n.6 (1986).

25. *See, e.g.*, New Mexico Youth Organized v. Herrera, 611 F.3d 669 (10th Cir. 2010); North Carolina Right to Life v. Leake, 525 F.3d 274, 289 & n.6 (4th Cir. 2008); Fed. Election Comm'n v. Machinists Non-Partisan Pol. League, 655 F.2d 380 (D.C. Cir. 1981).

26. *See* Human Life of Washington v. Brumsickle, 624 F.3d 990, 1009–11 (9th Cir. 2010).

27. 540 U.S. 93 (2003).

28. *Id.* at 101.

29. 551 U.S. 449 (2007).

30. 558 U.S. 310 (2010).

31. *Id.* at 369–70.

2. Disclosure Rules for Political Committees

The most extensive disclosure requirements are reserved for "political committees." "Political committee" is defined variously by FECA at the federal level and by state statutes for state and local races, but generally the term includes candidate campaign committees, political party committees, and political action committees (both traditional PACs and Super PACs).[32]

Under FECA, political committees must report to the FEC detailed information on contributors and expenditures, usually above some *de minimis* threshold. As described by the Supreme Court in *Federal Election Commission v. Massachusetts Citizens for Life*,

> [A political committee] must . . . see that its treasurer keeps an account of every contribution regardless of amount, the name and address of any person who makes a contribution in excess of $50, all contributions received from political committees, and the name and address of any person to whom a disbursement is made regardless of amount; and preserve receipts for all disbursements over $200 and all records for three years. [It] must file a statement of organization containing its name, address, the name of its custodian of records, and its banks, safety deposit boxes, or other depositories; [and it] must report any change in the above information within 10 days. . . .
>
> [It] must file either monthly reports with the FEC or reports on the following schedule: quarterly reports during election years, a pre-election report no later than the 12th day before an election, a postelection report within 30 days after an election, and reports every 6 months during nonelection years. These reports must contain information regarding the amount of cash on hand; the total amount of receipts, detailed by 10 different categories; the identification of each political committee and candidate's authorized or affiliated committee making contributions, and any persons making loans, providing rebates, refunds, dividends, or interest or any other offset to operating expenditures in an aggregate amount over $200; the total amount of all disbursements, detailed by 12 different categories; the names of all authorized or affiliated committees to whom expenditures aggregating over $200 have been made; persons to whom loan repayments or refunds have been made; the total sum of all contributions, operating expenses, outstanding debts and obligations, and the settlement terms of the retirement of any debt or obligation.[33]

Federal political committees must also separately report any independent expenditures they make exceeding $250. Inadvertent violations of these requirements, in

---

32. *See* § C[1], *supra*.

33. 479 U.S. at 253–54 (citations omitted).

particular missed filing deadlines, make up a considerable portion of the FEC's workload. State laws vary, of course, but largely adopt the same approach to disclosure of campaign contributions and expenditures.

3. Disclosure Rules for Campaign Spending by Individuals and by Organizations That Do Not Meet the Definition of Political Committee

Individuals and organizations that do not qualify as political committees, including corporations, unions, partnerships, trade associations, and nonprofit advocacy organizations operating under § 501(c)(4) of the Internal Revenue Code (such as the Sierra Club, or, to name a rather famous player in campaigns, Citizens United), have considerably more-limited reporting and disclosure requirements than political committees do.

As we saw in § C[1], *supra*, *Buckley v. Valeo* substantially limited reporting requirements for "individuals and groups that are not candidates or political committees" by requiring reporting only of independent expenditures expressly advocating for the election or defeat of a candidate, and only to donors who have earmarked their contributions for that purpose.

Under FECA, any independent expenditure in excess of $250, along with the identity of any person contributing more than $200 for the purpose of furthering an independent expenditure, must be reported to the FEC. The FEC has interpreted the rule narrowly to apply only when the donor to a group or organization was solicited to fund particular independent expenditures, or when the donor designated the donation for independent expenditures. The rule has the salutary effect of shielding members of established groups from being designated as contributors to ads they might have had no idea would be run or might not have wanted to pay for, but, at the same time, it means that few donors are reported since relatively few give to nonpolitical committees specifically to make independent expenditures.

Additionally, individuals and other entities that spend $10,000 for "electioneering communications"—broadcast ads that mention a candidate's name and are run in the candidate's electoral district within sixty days of a general election or thirty days of a primary or caucus—must also file reports with the FEC, with regular follow-up reports for succeeding communications.[34]

Registered lobbyists have additional reporting obligations under the Honest Leadership and Open Government Act. They must report not only their own contributions but also any "bundled" contributions, that is, contributions that they have asked others

34. See 52 U.S.C. § 30104 for disclosure requirements.

to make to a campaign and that are either forwarded to the campaign by the lobbyist/bundler or otherwise recorded by the campaign as having been raised by the bundler.[35]

A final set of disclosure requirements applies to organizations that are colloquially known as "527s." The name comes from § 527 of the Internal Revenue Code, which is the section of the Code under which political organizations—including political committees—operate. Some organizations are classified as political organizations under § 527, but because they do not expressly advocate for the election or defeat of candidates, they are not regulated as political committees by the FEC or state authorities. Between 1990 and 2010, these organizations were quite important in political campaigns. Because they did not expressly advocate the election or defeat of candidates, they were not regulated by the FEC, and so they could accept unlimited individual, corporate, and union contributions, with no disclosure obligations. However, the "issue ads" they produced were often nearly indistinguishable from campaign ads. For example, an ad might harshly criticize a public official's voting record, but instead of concluding with a pitch to vote against that official's reelection or in favor of his opponent, the ad would urge some other action, such as signing a petition, contributing to the group funding the ad, or calling the incumbent's office.

The Bipartisan Campaign Reform Act's creation of "electioneering communications" as a regulated category of speech[36] was largely aimed at curtailing 527 activity. Before that, however, in 2000, Congress required any organization operating under § 527 and not reporting to the FEC as a political committee to report expenditures of $500 or more, and donors of at least $200, to the IRS.[37] Despite both BCRA and the 2000 law, 527s remained important campaign players until the 2010 decision in *Citizens United*. That decision, by allowing corporations, unions, and individuals to fund independent expenditures, largely killed any advantage to operating a 527, as opposed to simply filing as a political committee or working through trade associations or advocacy groups, which had the advantage of being able to advocate expressly for and against candidates. But 527s still play an important, albeit considerably lesser, role in campaigns, spending over $150 million in the 2020 federal election cycle.[38]

---

35. Pub. L. No. 110-81, § 204 (2007); 52 U.S.C. § 30104(i).

36. *See* § C[1], *supra*.

37. Pub. L. No. 106-230 (2000).

38. *527s: Advocacy Group Spending*, OpenSecrets, https://www.opensecrets.org/527s/index.php (visited August 15, 2024).

D. Mandatory Disclosure Outside of Campaign Contributions and Expenditures

Buckley upheld substantially narrowed, but still extensive, disclosure provisions as part of FECA. Although *Buckley* cited *NAACP v. Alabama* and other early disclosure cases several times, those decisions mainly involved the funding of, and membership in, groups that were engaged in discussion of political affairs by means other than making campaign contributions and expenditures. What are the limits of compulsory disclosure as applied to speech that constitutes broad advocacy in civic life but that does not expressly promote the election or defeat of a candidate?

In *Doe v. Reed*,[39] the Supreme Court rejected an effort to block public disclosure of the names of persons who had signed a referendum petition. The petition sought to place a referendum on the Oregon ballot that would have repealed a law expanding the rights of same-sex partners in the state. The Court emphasized that the disclosed information was closely related to the election, and it found the important state interest demanded by *NAACP* and *Buckley* present in the need to "preserv[e] the integrity of the electoral process by combating fraud, detecting invalid signatures, and fostering government transparency and accountability."[40] The Court also highlighted the "scant evidence" plaintiffs provided that disclosure would subject signers to threats, harassment, or reprisals.[41] A concurrence by Justice Sotomayor and a dissent by Justice Thomas debated whether the "substantial fit" required by *Buckley* and the *NAACP* line of cases required "narrow tailoring" by the government,[42] but Chief Justice Roberts, writing for the Court, apparently found it unnecessary to address the issue.

In 2021, in *Americans for Prosperity Foundation v. Bonta* (*AFPF*), the Court finally decided that narrow tailoring was required under the "exacting scrutiny" formula.[43] The case involved an order by then-California Attorney General Kamala Harris requiring each charitable organization wishing to solicit donations in the state to submit a form to her office identifying the organization's large donors. The Court agreed that California had an interest in policing charitable organizations but noted the "dramatic mismatch" between the interest and the means chosen. Over 60,000 charitable entities renewed registrations with California each year, but the district court had found that there was not "a single, concrete instance in which pre-investigation collection of [donor information] did anything to advance the Attorney General's investigative, regulatory or enforcement

39. Doe v. Reed, 561 U.S. 186 (2010).
40. *Id.* at 197.
41. *Id.* at 201.
42. *See id.* at 213 (Sotomayor, J., concurring); *id.* at 232 (Thomas, J., dissenting).
43. 594 U.S. 595 (2021).

efforts."[44] Narrow tailoring, the Court held, did not require a "least restrictive means" analysis, but "we still require a fit that is not necessarily perfect, but reasonable; that represents not necessarily the single best disposition but one whose scope is in proportion to the interest served, that employs not necessarily the least restrictive means but a means narrowly tailored to achieve the desired objective."[45] Moreover, such tailoring was required in all cases reviewed under "exacting scrutiny," not merely for laws imposing "severe burdens."[46] The Court specifically rejected "administrative convenience" as a justification for the burden on First Amendment rights.[47] And because the law was not narrowly tailored, the plaintiffs were not required to bear the evidentiary burden of demonstrating widespread harassment and threats.[48]

The breadth of the ruling in *AFPF*, and the Court's grounding its decision in the 1950s civil-rights cases, may be indicative of a new sensitivity to privacy issues in a world of "cancel culture."

E. Disclaimer Requirements

Political advertisers and speakers are subject to various "disclaimer" requirements in addition to the public-disclosure requirements discussed above. The word "disclaimer" is something of a misnomer, since the requirements generally exist to force the speaker to claim—not to disclaim—responsibility for the ad or otherwise to provide information about the speaker, but the "disclaimer" label has stuck. While donor-reporting requirements and disclaimer mandates are usually lumped together as "disclosure" laws, recognizing the difference can help to make sense of certain court decisions and to gain a better perspective and understanding of the protection granted to anonymous speech.

The laws discussed in §§ C and D require speakers to disclose information about a group's political activities—including its financial supporters, the entities to which it has made payments, and the purpose of those payments—to the government. The government then typically discloses the information to the public. The disclosed information is typically reported to the government after the contributions have been received and after the expenditures have been made, or, in some cases, after they have been contracted.

Additionally, however, federal law and most states require speakers to include notices—"disclaimers"—on the face of political advertising. At a minimum, these notices must contain a statement of who paid for the ad. More elaborate "disclaimers"

---

44. *Id.* at 613 (citing Americans for Prosperity Found. v. Harris, 182 F. Supp. 3d 1049, 1055 (C.D. Cal. 2016)).

45. 594 U.S. at 609.

46. *Id.* at 611.

47. *Id.* at 615.

48. *Id.* at 617.

may include contact information for the speaker, a statement that the ad was or was not authorized by a candidate, and, in some states, the names of the largest contributors to the speaker. The ubiquitous and often-mocked "stand by your ad" statement that appears in all federal ads ("I'm Candidate X, and I approved this message") is another such requirement.[49]

Because virtually all political advertising is required to have a notice stating who paid for the ad, and because campaign ads are subject to reporting requirements federally and in every state, it is wrong to say that organizations that do not disclose the names of all their members and/or donors in their ads are speaking "anonymously." Reporting and disclaimer requirements should be viewed as complementary. Notices on the face of the advertising provide the viewer or listener with minimal but immediate information that may be used to evaluate the ad or to look for more information about the speaker. Disclosure reports filed with the government, with their detail about funding and expenditures, provide that added information.

Unlike disclosure rules, disclaimer requirements have produced relatively little litigation. The most important cases are *Talley v. California*[50] and *McIntyre v. Ohio Elections Commission*.[51] In *Talley*, the Court invalidated a Los Angeles city ordinance prohibiting all anonymous picketing. More relevant to elections is *McIntyre*, in which the Court invalidated an Ohio disclaimer law that required political advertising to include an identification of the person or organization funding the communication. A third Supreme Court ruling, *Buckley v. American Constitutional Law Foundation*, relied on *McIntyre* in finding unconstitutional a Colorado law requiring petition signature-gatherers to wear name badges—in effect, in-person "disclaimers."[52]

While *Talley* and *McIntyre* appeared to strike down the challenged laws facially, a strong case can be made that they depended on their unique facts. *Talley* was a civil-rights case involving picketers of a business with allegedly discriminatory hiring practices. *McIntyre* concerned a parent and taxpayer in the Westerville, Ohio, school district, who designed various leaflets on her home computer opposing a local school tax and paid a small amount (less than $100) to print copies at a local print shop. Working with her son and a friend, she distributed the leaflets at public meetings. Contrary to Ohio law, however, the leaflets did not disclose her name and address as the person paying for them. And despite the lack of a disclaimer on her pamphlets, school officials knew that Ms. McIntyre was responsible for distributing the handbills. Five months after the election, an apparently vindictive school official filed a complaint with the Ohio Elections Commission, which fined McIntyre $100. The Court found the law unconstitutional.

---

49. See 52 U.S.C. § 30120 and 11 C.F.R. § 110.11 for disclaimers required by FECA, including the requirement of contact information, an authorization statement, and the so-called "stand by your ad" requirement. For an example of a state statute that requires the disclosure of a spokesperson, see Cal. Code Regs. tit. 2, § 18450.11 (2010).

50. 362 U.S. 60 (1960).

51. 514 U.S. 334 (1995).

52. 525 U.S. 182 (1999).

Although the cases, on their face, suggest a broad right to anonymous speech, the result in *McIntyre* seems in tension with the Court's endorsement of sweeping campaign reporting requirements. But, more importantly, *Talley* and *McIntyre* are in tension even with other Court rulings on disclaimer requirements. Most notably, in *McConnell v. Federal Election Commission*, the Court upheld, in two cursory paragraphs, a requirement that political ads contain on their face an "unobscured, full-screen view" of the ad's sponsor expressing his approval of the ad.[53] Following *McConnell*, lower federal courts have upheld disclaimer requirements far more intrusive than those at issue in *McIntyre* or *McConnell*. For example, in *No on E v. Chiu*, the U.S. Court of Appeals for the Ninth Circuit upheld a San Francisco ordinance that required the names of up to nine donors to be printed, in large type, on the face of an ad (including secondary donors, *i.e.*, donors to groups that donated to the group funding the ad), with detailed requirements on formatting and language.[54]

Without further guidance from the high Court, and notwithstanding *Talley* and *McIntyre*, disclaimers requiring minimal information—the name of the person or entity paying for ad, and some contact information—have a reasonable claim to constitutionality, at least so long as they relate to electoral campaigns, with the possible exception of ads placed by individuals such as Margaret McIntyre, or perhaps small, grassroots organizations, such as the protest organizers in *Talley*.

F. As-Applied Exemptions from Disclosure Requirements

In *NAACP v. Alabama* and other early cases, the Supreme Court did not hold that the state was categorically prohibited from gathering the information it sought concerning the organization's membership and donors. Rather, the Court held that the information sought was too far removed from any legitimate investigatory reason offered by the state.[55] In *Roberts v. Pollard*, for example, the Court summarily affirmed a three-judge district-court panel that had quashed a subpoena seeking names of Republican Party donors as part of investigation into election fraud.[56] In *Roberts*, the district-court had concluded that there was "no showing here that the identities of Party contributors and the amounts of their contributions are reasonably relevant to defendant's investigation of alleged vote buying."

53. 540 U.S. 93, 230–31 (2003).

54. 85 F.4th 493 (9th Cir. 2023), *cert. denied*, 145 S. Ct. 136 (2024).

55. *See, e.g.*, NAACP v. Alabama, 357 U.S. 449, 464 (1958); Bates v. Little Rock, 361 U.S. 516 (1960) (striking down a statute requiring charitable organizations to provide lists of their members as a condition of maintaining favorable tax status); Gibson v. Florida Legis. Comm., 372 U.S. 539, 572 (1963) (reversing a contempt citation against the president of the local NAACP chapter for refusing to identify members from a list of known Communists during a legislative investigation of Communist infiltration of community organizations).

56. 393 U.S. 14 (1968), *sum. aff'g* Pollard v. Roberts, 283 F. Supp. 248, 257 (E.D. Ark. 1968).

In *Buckley*, the Court distinguished these cases, in particular *Roberts*, because the disclosure requirements of FECA were statutes of general applicability, not aimed at any one organization, and presumably, in the Court's view, bore a reasonable-enough "substantial relation" to the important government interests involved.[57] However, while upholding the statute against a facial challenge, the Court added that "[t]here could well be a case, similar to those before the Court in *NAACP v. Alabama* and *Bates*, where the threat to the exercise of First Amendment rights is so serious, and the state interest furthered by disclosure so insubstantial, that the Act's requirements cannot be constitutionally applied," thereby opening the door to as-applied challenges in the future.[58]

The leading post-*Buckley* decision on as-applied exemptions from a general disclosure statute is *Brown v. Socialist Workers '74 Campaign Committee*.[59] In *Socialist Workers*, the Court provided an as-applied exemption from Ohio's campaign reporting requirements for the Socialist Workers Party (SWP), based on a history of harassment from government officials and private individuals.

The level of such harassment necessary to escape compulsory disclosure, however, is unclear. In *Buckley*, the Court held that "[t]he evidence offered need show only a reasonable probability that the compelled disclosure of a party's contributors' names will subject them to threats, harassment, or reprisals from either Government officials or private parties" and that "unduly strict requirements of proof could impose a heavy burden" on minor parties.[60] The evidence that the Court found sufficient to grant a disclosure to the SWP included "threatening phone calls and hate mail, the burning of SWP literature, the destruction of SWP members' property, police harassment of a party candidate, ... the firing of shots at an SWP office ... [and] in the 12-month period before trial, 22 SWP members, including four in Ohio, were fired because of their party membership." It also included evidence of government harassment and hostility, including long-time surveillance that was continuing at the time the case was brought.[61]

More recently, however, in *Doe v. Reed*,[62] the Court managed to produce no fewer than seven opinions discussing the burden necessary to gain an exemption from disclosure requirements. The case did not involve campaign finance disclosure but rather public disclosure of the names of persons who had signed a petition to put an initiative before the voters. Chief Justice Roberts's brief opinion for the Court merely noted that the case was brought as a facial challenge and there was little evidence that harassment would befall signers of most petitions. Concurring opinions, however, ranged from Justice Scalia's, which not only argued that virtually any mandatory disclosure of petition signers' names would be constitutional but seemed to go out of its way to

57. Buckley v. Valeo, 424 U.S. 1, 69 (1976) (*per curiam*).

58. *Id.* at 71–72.

59. 459 U.S. 87 (1982).

60. 424 U.S. at 74.

61. *Brown*, 459 U.S. at 98–101.

62. 561 U.S. 186 (2010).

argue against even any right to a secret ballot, to Justice Stevens's, which argued that "[f]or an as-applied challenged to ... succeed, there would have to be a significant threat of harassment ... that cannot be mitigated by law enforcement measures,"[63] to Justice Sotomayor's, which suggested that "[c]ase-specific relief may be available ... in the rare circumstance in which disclosure poses a reasonable probability of serious and widespread harassment that the state is unwilling or unable to control,"[64] to Justice Breyer's, which discussed the need to balance interests, to Justice Alito's, which argued that "the as-applied exemption plays a critical role in safeguarding First Amendment rights. ... [S]peakers must be able to obtain an as-applied exemption without clearing a high evidentiary hurdle."[65] Meanwhile, Justice Thomas, in dissent, reiterated his opinion that compulsory disclosure is generally unconstitutional, citing fears of both official and unofficial retaliation.[66] An additional complicating factor in *Doe v. Reed*, however, was the nature of the speech involved—signing a petition to place a measure on the ballot—which has direct legal ramifications if enough people sign. All of the concurring Justices, save Justice Alito, noted the relatively low speech interest at stake in signing petitions as compared to more direct campaign speech.

The high Court's latest pronouncement on disclosure came in *Americans for Prosperity Foundation v. Bonta*.[67] The Court found the donor-disclosure requirement facially unconstitutional, citing its lack of tailoring to the government's alleged interest in preventing fraud or other misconduct.[68] However, the Court also held that the district court had properly found the state practice unconstitutional on an as-applied basis.[69] In *Bonta*, the plaintiffs' evidence included testimony that a technology contractor working at one plaintiff's headquarters had posted online that he was "inside the belly of the beast" and "could easily walk into [the CEO's] office and slit his throat," as well as evidence that another plaintiff had received "threats, harassing calls, intimidating and obscene emails, and even pornographic letters."[70]

At a minimum, *Bonta* suggests that the Court will take a hard line against compulsory-disclosure statutes that are not closely tied to either political campaigning or election operations. But the Court has yet to show much inclination to reconsider the facial constitutionality of campaign finance disclosure laws, and as-applied challenges to those laws face substantial, though hardly insurmountable, evidentiary burdens.

63. *Id.* at 218 (Stevens, J., concurring in part and concurring in the judgment).

64. *Id.* at 215 (Sotomayor, J., concurring).

65. *Id.* at 203–04 (Alito, J., concurring).

66. *Id.* at 244–45 (Thomas, J., dissenting); *see also Citizens United*, 558 U.S. 310, 480, 481–85 (2010) (Thomas, J., dissenting).

67. 594 U.S. 595 (2021).

68. *Id.* at 612.

69. *Id.* at 619; *see also id.* at 621 (Thomas, J., concurring in part and concurring in the judgment). The dissent disagreed but admitted it would be "sympathetic" to such a holding. *Id.* at 646 (Sotomayor, J., dissenting).

70. 594 U.S. at 604.

G. Summary of Disclosure

At first blush, the concept of disclosure of campaign contributions and spending, and other politically related speech, seems simple: Political donations and expenditures are disclosed, but no one's speech is limited. But, in fact, disclosure has turned out to pose some of the hardest First Amendment questions, and the result is a jumble of decisions often in conflict with one another. As one federal appellate court put it: "The arc of campaign finance law has been ambivalent, bending toward speech and disclosure. Indeed, what has made this area of election law so challenging is that these two values exist in unmistakable tension. Disclosure chills speech. Speech without disclosure risks corruption. And the Supreme Court's track record of expanding who may speak while simultaneously blessing robust disclosure rules has set these two values on an ineluctable collision course."[71]

In *NAACP v. Alabama* and the other early civil rights cases, *Buckley v. Valeo*, *McIntyre*, *Americans for Prosperity Foundation v. Bonta*, and numerous other cases, the Supreme Court has recognized the ways in which association—including (and perhaps especially) anonymous association—fosters free speech and the ways in which compulsory-disclosure laws burden First Amendment rights. Yet the Court has also—often in the same case, as in *Buckley*—upheld laws mandating public disclosure of individuals' memberships and donations, as a necessary means to fight corruption in office and to inform voters. The disclosure reports filed with the Federal Election Commission and various state agencies now constitute an easily accessible database of the political views and participation by millions of American citizens, stretching back literally decades.

Together, the decisions of the Supreme Court make up something of a "patternless mosaic." Each decision of the Court acts as a stone turned over to reveal one of two colors, flipped over in a somewhat random pattern, and stones are rarely, if ever, removed from the work.[72] The legal test, as summarized in *AFPF v. Bonta*, is "exacting scrutiny," which requires that disclosure laws address a "sufficiently important" government interest, that there be a "substantial relationship" between the law and that interest, and that the regulation be "narrowly tailored" to achieve the government interest.[73] But, in application, the test tends to break down.

Broad, generally applicable laws, such as those at issue in *Buckley v. Valeo* and *McConnell v. Federal Election Commission*, tend to fare better under exacting scrutiny than do individual investigatory decisions, such as those in *NAACP v. Alabama*, unless they are so broad such that they fail to meet the narrow-tailoring standard, as in *AFPF v. Bonta*. Laws requiring disclosure of campaign contributions and expenditures or laws that are closely related to election administration, as in *Doe v. Reed*, will tend to fare better than

71. Van Hollen v. Fed. Election Comm'n, 811 F.3d 486, 488 (D.C. Cir. 2016) (Brown, J.).

72. *See* Daniel Hays Lowenstein, *A Patternless Mosaic: Campaign Finance and the First Amendment After* Austin, 21 Cap. U. L. Rev. 381, 382–83 (1992).

73. 594 U.S. at 607–08.

laws more broadly regulating public discourse, as in *AFPF v. Bonta*. Disclaimer requirements are generally unconstitutional (*Talley*, *McIntyre*) except when they seem integral to a major campaign finance law (*McConnell*). Where there is a possibility of threats, boycotts or other economic reprisals, or another form of harassment, individuals and organizations may obtain as-applied relief from mandatory-disclosure requirements, but there is neither agreement among the Justices nor a consistent majority on the Court for determining what constitutes sufficient evidence of harassment—compare the minimal burden of *Shelton v. Tucker* and *Talley* with the record in *NAACP v. Alabama* or *Brown v. Socialist Workers '74 Campaign Committee*, or consider the multiple opinions in *Doe v. Reed* and *AFPF v. Bonta*.

The problem, as the court of appeals wrote in *Van Hollen v. Federal Election Commission*, the case quoted above, is that "the Supreme Court's campaign finance jurisprudence subsists, for now, on a fragile arrangement that treats speech, a constitutional right, and transparency, an extra-constitutional value, as equivalents."[74]

In *Majors v. Abell*,[75] the plaintiff challenged an Indiana law mandating lengthy disclaimers, including an identification of the funder of the ad, on political advertising. The Court of Appeals for the Seventh Circuit was left to try to make sense of *McIntyre* and *McConnell*, the Supreme Court's recent, and conflicting, precedents regarding disclaimers. Judge Posner, writing for the court, summed up the Supreme Court's jurisprudence in the area as "a balancing of imponderables."[76] The panel majority rather hesitantly upheld the Indiana statute, concluding as follows: "Reluctant, without clearer guidance from the [Supreme] Court, to interfere with state experimentation in the baffling and conflicted field of campaign finance law . . . , we hold that the Indiana statute is constitutional."[77] The third judge on the panel, Judge Easterbrook, took the opportunity to write a rarely seen "*dubitante*" (meaning "doubtful") opinion—a label used by a judge who expresses doubt about the correctness of the opinion yet is insufficiently convinced to dissent. Judge Easterbrook concluded, "I cannot be confident that my colleagues are wrong in thinking that five Justices [on the Supreme Court] will go along. But I also do not understand how that position can be reconciled with established principles of constitutional law."[78]

---

74. 811 F.3d at 501.
75. 361 F.3d 349 (7th Cir. 2004).
76. *Id.* at 352.
77. *Id.* at 355.
78. *Id.* at 358 (Easterbrook, J., *dubitante*).

Chapter 10
Election Day and Counting the Votes

A. Introduction

Most of the cases that we identify with the right to vote concern limits on voter registration. We considered those cases in Chapter 1. But the right to vote can be limited by regulations that affect voters throughout the electoral process, including at the polls themselves. Additionally, other constitutional rights, such as the right to free speech, are implicated at the polls—the crucial juncture where the public's attitudes are translated into political action.

B. Fraud Prevention and Burdens on Casting Ballots

Laws that limit the franchise to certain people (*e.g.*, residents, citizens, men, property owners, or non-felons) impose rather obvious burdens on the right to vote—obvious, that is, once it is determined that the excluded voters have the right to vote in the elections from which they are excluded. The controversial issues presented by laws that exclude certain classes of people tend to center on whether the right to vote encompasses those classes of people. Chapter 1 considered such regulations.

Regulations governing polling places and the casting of ballots also implicate the right to vote by burdening the exercise of that right. Such regulations may deter some individuals from voting, but they are not based on a judgment that any class of eligible voters should be prevented from voting. Usually, the regulations are efforts to protect some form of the "integrity" of the elections—for example, by ensuring that the elections are not undermined by fraud or intimidation, or by ensuring that only eligible voters participate.

Many election regulations thus present a conflict between protecting the right to vote—making sure that eligible voters are not unduly hindered in their ability to exercise the right—and protecting government's ability to run orderly, fair elections.[1] The conflict is analogous to the one we saw in Chapter 6 between the right of independents and third parties to access the ballot, on the one hand, and the ability of states to limit ballot access so as to promote order and stability, and to protect against the chaos and factionalism that might result from lengthy ballots, on the other. It may, therefore, not be surprising that the cases evaluating the constitutionality of burdens presented by election-day voting and vote-counting rules apply the same tests we first saw being applied in analyzing the cases on third-party ballot access.[2]

1. Voter-ID Laws

An extremely controversial area of election law in recent years has been laws requiring voters to show identification when voting. The laws do not formally exclude anyone from casting a ballot—those persons who do not already possess an acceptable form of identification may obtain one for free—but critics claim that the inconvenience associated with obtaining an ID may have the effect of "disenfranchising" eligible voters. Moreover, those voters lacking IDs are believed to be disproportionately poor and elderly and, perhaps, also disproportionately minority and disabled. Because those constituencies tend to favor more liberal candidates, support for voter-ID laws tends to be divided along party lines. Democrats sometimes charge Republicans with supporting voter-ID laws in order to disenfranchise likely Democratic voters; Republicans argue that the laws are designed to ensure that elections are not undermined by fraud.

The Supreme Court faced a facial challenge to Indiana's voter-ID law in *Crawford v. Marion County Election Board*.[3] Six of the nine Justices rejected the challenge and upheld the law, but those Justices were split 3–3 as to the rationale. Justice Stevens wrote the lead opinion, which was joined by Chief Justice Roberts and Justice Kennedy. Justice Stevens began by invoking *Harper v. Virginia Board of Elections*, the case declaring unconstitutional Virginia's poll tax in state elections.[4] *Harper*, in the view of Justice Stevens, stood for the proposition that "even rational restrictions on the right to vote are invidious if they are unrelated to voter qualifications."[5] Indiana provided ID cards to voters for free, so the voter-ID law did not impose the same kind of direct financial burden as did the poll tax. Nevertheless, there were costs associated with obtaining the ID. Voters who did not already have ID had to travel to the Bureau of Motor Vehicles (BMV) and present proof of voter eligibility, such as a birth certificate. Because it might be expensive, time-consuming, or impossible for some voters to obtain those documents, the voter-ID law imposed indirect costs on voters who

---

1. *See* Bradley A. Smith, *Crisis and Disconnect: Electoral Legitimacy and Proposals for Election Reform*, 24 U. Pa. J. Const. L. 1053 (2022).
2. *See* Chapter 6, § B.
3. 553 U.S. 181 (2008).
4. 383 U.S. 663 (1966).
5. 553 U.S. at 189 (opinion of Stevens, J.).

lacked ID. Further, voters who went to the polls but failed to present ID were limited to casting a provisional ballot, which would be counted only if the voter went to the county seat within ten days of the election and presented an ID there. That trip also added to the time and expense of voting.

The Court, however, found these allegations of burdens insufficient to justify striking down the law. The test Justice Stevens applied was the same open-ended balancing test he had announced in *Anderson v. Celebrezze*.[6] Under the *Anderson* test, as applied in *Crawford*, non-"severe" restrictions on the right to vote would be constitutional if the state's "precise interests" in favor of the law outweighed the burden imposed on the right to vote. Even "slight" burdens "must be justified by relevant and legitimate state interests 'sufficiently weighty to justify the limitation.'"[7]

For most voters, Justice Stevens noted, the burden of obtaining and presenting an ID was not substantial. The vast majority of voters already had a qualifying ID (a driver's license, for example), and most of those who did not already have one could make a trip to the BMV to obtain one without much difficulty. Surely some voters would face greater burdens in obtaining the ID, but the challengers had not demonstrated how many voters would face significant burdens. Without knowing how much the right to vote was burdened, the Court was unwilling to strike down the entire law, or even to place much weight on the side of the scale measuring the extent of the law's limitation on the right to vote.[8]

Because Justice Stevens believed the burden on voters to be small, the state was not required to demonstrate much of a justification. The state's interest was in preventing in-person voter-impersonation fraud, *i.e.*, ineligible voters or people who have already voted pretending to be eligible voters, and Justice Stevens accepted that interest as sufficient. Everyone agrees that preventing such fraud is a valid interest, but the interest is controversial because that kind of fraud has not been shown to be a significant problem. In fact, *Crawford* noted that there was no record of such fraud having taken place—ever—in Indiana, and it cited only sporadic instances of such fraud elsewhere.

On the one hand, the fact that there have been very few proven instances of fraud does not mean that the fraud has not occurred. If the fraud was successful, there would be no record of it, and states surely have an interest in deterring and preventing fraud (and other crimes) without having to demonstrate a rash of similar crimes. On the other hand, however, we would hardly expect voter-impersonation fraud to be epidemic. Someone inclined to commit the fraud would have to go to a polling place pretending to be someone else, risking discovery (and severe punishment) if a poll worker knew that he was not the voter he was pretending to be, or if the real

---

6. 460 U.S. 780 (1983).

7. 553 U.S. at 190–91 (opinion of Stevens, J.) (quoting Norman v. Reed, 502 U.S. 279, 288–89 (1992)).

8. *See Crawford*, 553 U.S. at 200 (opinion of Stevens, J.) ("[O]n the basis of the evidence in the record it is not possible to quantify either the magnitude of the burden on this narrow class of voters or the portion of the burden imposed on them that is fully justified.").

voter later came to the polling place and found that someone else had already signed his name in the registry. And even if the fraudulent voter were entirely successful and managed to avoid detection, he would only be able to cast a single extra vote for his favored candidate. Potential defrauders would be facing extremely high risk for the possibility of very little reward.

Further, Democrats charged that the anti-fraud interest was a sham; the real objective, according to critics, was a partisan power play by Republicans to suppress the votes of Democratic supporters. Justice Stevens was unwilling to invalidate a law supported by "valid neutral justifications" even though partisan considerations may have played a role as well.[9]

The most important part of Justice Stevens's opinion was not the result he reached but his method of calculating the burdens the law placed on voters. Justice Stevens analyzed the burden on individual voters rather than on the electorate as a whole. That is, even though *most* voters would face virtually no burden at all (because they already had an acceptable ID), and even though most voters who did not already have an ID could obtain one without "a substantial burden on the right to vote, or even . . . a significant increase over the usual burdens of voting," the ID requirement *would* place "a somewhat heavier burden . . . on a limited number of persons."[10]

That "somewhat heavier burden," however, did not justify striking down the statute in all its applications. In the first place, it was unclear how many voters would have trouble obtaining an ID, and it was unclear how much trouble they would encounter. In the second place, a voter lacking the resources to obtain an ID could cast a provisional ballot that would be counted as long as he later executed an affidavit attesting to indigency. "[E]ven assuming that the burden may not be justified as to a few voters," Justice Stevens mused, "that conclusion is by no means sufficient to establish" that the law should be struck down as applied to all voters.[11]

Justice Stevens's individual analysis of the burdens imposed by Indiana's voter-ID law left open the possibility that a narrower, as-applied challenge to a voter-ID law might succeed. And in the years since *Crawford*, Pennsylvania's courts have applied a similar analysis to invalidate voter-ID laws when challenged under the state constitution.[12] Other courts, however, have upheld voter-ID laws against challenges based on both the Federal Constitution and state ones.[13]

In sum, Justice Stevens saw the law in *Crawford*—as the facts were developed in that case—as presenting a quite limited incursion on the right to vote caused by a law

---

9. *Id.* at 204.

10. *Id.* at 198.

11. *Id.* at 199–200.

12. Applewhite v. Commonwealth, 2014 Pa. Commw. Unpub. LEXIS 379 (Pa. Commw. Ct. 2014). *See also* North Carolina Conference of the NAACP v. McCreary, 831 F.3d 204 (4th Cir. 2016) (invalidating voter-ID law under the U.S. Constitution and § 2 of the Voting Rights Act).

13. *See* Democratic Party of Georgia v. Perdue, 707 S.E.2d 67 (Ga. 2011) (upholding Georgia's law); Frank v. Walker, 768 F.3d 744 (7th Cir. 2014) (upholding Wisconsin's law and overturning a district-court judgment striking it down).

that was designed to combat an important (if overblown) problem. Because the rationale of Justice Stevens's opinion was limited by what the parties had demonstrated in the *Crawford* case itself (particularly the burdens facing individual voters who lacked the proper ID), it was a narrow opinion, leaving room for later cases to reach different results on different facts. Justice Scalia's separate opinion, joined by Justices Thomas and Alito, was not so limited.

Justice Scalia began by taking issue with Justice Stevens's use of the sliding-scale test of *Anderson*. Rather than simply comparing the burden on the right to vote with the state's interest, Justice Scalia preferred to classify burdens on the right to vote as either severe or not. Severe burdens would be evaluated under strict scrutiny, while non-severe burdens serving "important regulatory interests" would be upheld as long as they were "reasonable [and] nondiscriminatory."[14]

The burden in this case, according to Justice Scalia, was not severe. Justice Scalia admitted that the impact of the voter-ID law fell more heavily on certain voters than others, but he rejected the idea that individual impacts were enough to render a burden severe. He pointed out that if states had to satisfy strict scrutiny every time an election law imposed a severe burden on *somebody*, then strict scrutiny would apply to *every* law, and states would effectively be disabled from regulating elections. Laws requiring voters to register or to cast their ballots at designated polling places may present a severe burden for those voters who would have a difficult time complying with those laws. But they are not considered to be "severe" burdens because they do not have a severe impact on the overall electorate.[15]

Justice Scalia is surely correct that election laws are not unconstitutional because *someone* may face a significant burden under them.[16] Laws establishing a single day for elections, or laws establishing certain polling places instead of permitting internet voting or voting by mail, are not unconstitutional—and do not even trigger strict scrutiny—simply because some people have difficulty going to their polling places on that day.

On the other hand, Justice Scalia's methodology seems inconsistent with *Harper*. Virginia's $1.50 poll tax did not present a severe burden on the average voter, and yet the Court struck it down because *some* voters would have a difficult time paying the tax. Justice Scalia addressed *Harper* but did not provide a principled rationale for distinguishing the case. He acknowledged that *Harper* (as well as *Bullock v. Carter*[17]

---

14. Crawford v. Marion Cnty. Election Bd., 553 U.S. 181, 204–05 (Scalia, J., concurring in the judgment) (citing *Burdick v. Takushi*, 504 U.S. 428, 433–34 (1992)).

15. *See* 553 U.S. at 208 (Scalia, J., concurring in the judgment).

16. The Pennsylvania Supreme Court's *Applewhite* decision, in the litigation noted above, failed to deal with this problem and fails to establish a limiting principle. The court announced that the state's voter-ID law should be enjoined unless the lower court was "convinced" that there would be "*no* voter disenfranchisement" as a result of the law. Applewhite v. Commonwealth, 54 A.3d 1, 5 (Pa. 2012) (*per curiam*) (emphasis added). The no-voter-disenfranchisement standard, if applied literally, is impossible to meet.

17. 405 U.S. 134 (1972).

and *Lubin v. Panish*,[18] two cases involving ballot-access fees) "strictly scrutinized nondiscriminatory voting laws requiring the payment of fees" but suggested that such an approach should be used in evaluating only laws that imposed direct monetary conditions for participating in elections.[19] One might ask, however, whether there is a reason to apply strict scrutiny if a state law requires voters to pay a $1.50 tax but a more lenient standard of review if the state gives voters a "free" ID but requires them to spend money and time obtaining documents and making trips to the BMV or the county seat. It appears, therefore, that under Justice Scalia's analysis, *Harper* was wrongly decided; his apparent willingness not to overrule the case may be based on nothing more than *stare decisis*.

However much Justice Scalia's approach appears inconsistent with *Harper*, there does not appear to be a viable alternative. As pointed out above, strict scrutiny cannot be applied (and certainly has not been applied) to all laws that have the effect of requiring voters to spend money or time before they are permitted to vote. Millions of voters spend a considerable amount of time as well as money (*e.g.*, for gasoline or bus fare) to register, to get to their polling places, and to cast their ballots.

The three dissenters, in opinions by Justice Souter and Justice Breyer, endorsed Justice Stevens's interpretation of the *Anderson* balancing test (making six votes for that method of assessing constitutional challenges to laws burdening the right to vote), but the dissenters believed that *Anderson*'s balance should have tilted in favor of the law's challengers. The dissenters did not dispute that the state had an interest in preventing fraud, but given that in-person voter-impersonation fraud had not been much of a problem, they believed that the burdens placed on voters without IDs were disproportionate to the state's interests.

At this point, it is difficult to assess the impact of *Crawford*. Even within the voter-ID controversy itself, *Crawford* has not clarified the law. Justice Stevens's opinion—and the *Anderson* balancing test it applied—were so focused on the facts as proven in one individual case that it is hard to tell whether burdens faced in other cases would be sufficient to result in the invalidation of other voter-ID laws. Factors that might be significant include how many voters in a state lack IDs, the number and location of facilities where voters can obtain IDs, the procedures for casting provisional ballots and ensuring that they are counted, the kinds of IDs that are accepted (*e.g.*, Must the ID have a photo? Must it be issued by the government? Are expired IDs sufficient? How recently must the ID have been issued?), and whether the state has a history of election fraud.[20]

---

18. 415 U.S. 709 (1974).

19. *Crawford*, 553 U.S. at 207 n.* (Scalia, J., concurring in the judgment).

20. One study of the effect of voter-ID laws on state legislative, gubernatorial, congressional, and presidential elections from 2003 to 2020 concluded that such laws motivate and mobilize supporters of both parties, resulting in negligible effects overall on election results. *See* Jeffrey J. Harden & Alejandra Campos, *Who Benefits from Voter Identification Laws?*, 120 Proceedings Nat'l Acad. Scis. no. 7, e2217323120 (Feb. 6, 2023), https://doi.org/10.1073/pnas.2217323120.

Outside of voter-ID cases, *Crawford*'s impact is even less certain. *Anderson* and *Burdick* create a framework for assessing the constitutionality of all types of election laws that burden the right to vote. *Crawford* (if we are willing to combine the votes in the Stevens, Souter, and Breyer opinions) does seem to clarify *Anderson* and *Burdick* by comparing a law's burdens and benefits on a sliding scale rather than adopting a two-tiered approach that separates "severe" from "non-severe" burdens. But *Crawford* does nothing to clarify (indeed, it seems to muddy) how to measure the burden that a law places on the right to vote.

2. Vote Buying and Vote Trading

Federal and state statutes prohibit buying and selling votes. Professor Richard Hasen has explained that prohibitions on vote buying can be justified by three rationales: equality, efficiency, and inalienability.[21] The equality concern centers on the belief that poor voters are the ones most willing to sell their votes because they have the most need for the extra money they could receive by selling their votes. On the flip side, rich voters with plenty of disposable income are the ones most willing to dispose of some of that income by buying the votes of others. Thus, permitting vote buying would allow the rich to control more votes than the poor and therefore to have more influence over policy.

The efficiency rationale flows from that same concern. If vote buyers can have more votes and therefore more political influence than vote sellers, then public policy will tilt toward the interests of vote buyers rather than toward the interests of the general public. The inalienability rationale more simply holds that voting is a personal right that should not be transferable.

Bans on vote buying are largely accepted without much controversy, although certainly not everyone would accept all of the rationales identified by Professor Hasen. Bans on vote *trading*, however, have not received the same broad acceptance. Before considering the legality of vote trading, it is necessary to address why anyone would want to trade votes. In the era of one person, one vote, aren't all votes worth the same? No, they are not.

The most obvious inequality of votes is that different jurisdictions hold different elections. Thus, a person (call him Voter X) who lives in District A but wishes to elect a certain candidate for Congress in District B might be willing to trade his vote in District A to a voter in District B (call him Voter Y) who would agree to vote for Voter X's favorite candidate. Thus, Voter X would vote for the candidate favored by Voter Y, and Voter Y would vote for the candidate favored by Voter X.

In presidential elections featuring at least three candidates, the Electoral College provides a different reason to trade votes.[22] We do not hold one unified election for

21. Richard L. Hasen, *Vote Buying*, 88 Calif. L. Rev. 1323 (2000).

22. Technically, the Electoral College provides the same rationale for vote trading, because each state's voters vote for that state's delegates to the Electoral College—not for the presidential nominee

president; rather, each state holds its own election to decide how to allocate its votes in the Electoral College. Some of those statewide votes are never in doubt; others (in the so-called "battleground" or "swing" states) are close. As a result, votes in some states have a greater chance of affecting the outcome than do votes in other states. So a voter in a blow-out state might want to trade his vote for a vote in a battleground state.

But why would someone be willing to trade away his vote in a close election for a vote in an election when the outcome is a foregone conclusion? The answer is that third parties benefit from getting more votes even if they do not win the election. In the 2000 election, for example, nobody thought that Green Party candidate Ralph Nader had any realistic chance of winning the presidency. But if he were able to poll 5% in the election, the party would qualify for federal funding in the future. It was therefore important for Nader and his supporters that he receive at least 5% of the votes, even if he did not win. Because of the "spoiler effect" discussed in Chapter 6,[23] however, some Nader supporters were reluctant to vote for Nader when doing so could result in the election of George Bush (their third-choice candidate) over Al Gore (their second-choice candidate).

Nader supporters in close states were therefore willing to trade their votes and vote for Gore, while Gore supporters in blow-out states were willing to trade their votes and vote for Nader. After such a trade, Nader would get votes in blow-out states—votes that would contribute to his goal of receiving 5% of votes nationwide. Because those votes would come from blow-out states, however, they would not jeopardize a Gore victory. Gore, meanwhile, would get votes in close states, which were far more valuable to him and his supporters.

Vote trading thus benefits third-party candidates because it mitigates the spoiler effect. It undermines the Electoral College, however, by allowing a state's election to be affected by the preferences of voters in other states. Moreover, one might question whether there is any principled difference between vote trading and vote buying. In the typical instance of vote buying, one voter sells his vote for money or some other consideration. In vote trading, one voter is in effect selling his vote in exchange for the buyer's promise to vote for the candidate favored by the seller. Vote trading doesn't involve an exchange of cash, but both vote buying and vote trading involve an exchange of votes for a kind of consideration.

The Supreme Court has never ruled on the legality of vote trading, although it has indicated in dictum that it is constitutional for the government to ban the exchange of votes for "money or other things of value."[24] Despite this language, the Ninth Circuit struck down a ban on vote trading in *Porter v. Bowen*,[25] concluding that a web-

---

himself. Thus, even though people throughout the country think that they are voting for presidential candidates, the voters of each state are actually voting in different elections for different candidates for the Electoral College. Therefore, if two voters in different states trade votes with each other, each voter would be able effectively to vote in an election outside his own jurisdiction.

23. *See* Chapter 6, § B.

24. Brown v. Hartlage, 456 U.S. 45, 54 (1982).

25. 496 F.3d 1009 (9th Cir. 2007).

site facilitating vote trading featured constitutionally protected speech. The court distinguished vote buying from vote trading by pointing out that vote buying involves the exchange of votes for *private* profit, whereas "the only benefit a vote swapper can receive is a marginally higher probability that his preferred electoral outcome will come to pass."[26]

C. Constitutional Constraints on Vote Counting: *Bush v. Gore*

1. Introduction

The administration of elections in general, and the counting of votes in particular, have become, or at least have come to be perceived as, partisan. In thirty-three states, the chief election officer, usually the Secretary of State, is elected as a partisan candidate. Critics have often accused such officers of making decisions for partisan reasons. This perception has led to calls for selecting election officials in nonpartisan ways.[27] Recently, there have been increasing efforts to centralize and nationalize the counting of votes. Those efforts resulted in the Help America Vote Act (HAVA) of 2002,[28] passed by Congress in the wake of controversies surrounding the 2000 presidential election, among other measures. HAVA and other such statutes are discussed below.[29]

Federal and state courts have been involved in reviewing the counting of votes in elections for many decades,[30] but the most high-profile example of such litigation in American history is surely the U.S. Supreme Court's decision in *Bush v. Gore*,[31] which in effect determined who won the presidency in 2000.

---

26. *Id.* at 1020.

27. For overviews of this controversy and calls for reform, see Jocelyn Friedrichs Benson, *Democracy and the Secretary: The Critical Role of Election Administrators in Promoting Accuracy and Access to Democracy*, 27 St. Louis U. Pub. L. Rev. 343 (2008); Richard L. Hasen, *Beyond the Margin of Litigation: Reforming U.S. Election Administration to Avoid Electoral Meltdown*, 62 Wash. & Lee L. Rev. 937 (2005); Michael J. Ritter, Joseph A. Coll, & Caroline J. Tolbert, *Can Election Administration Overcome the Effects of Restrictive State Voting Laws?*, 23 Election L.J. 19 (2024); Daniel P. Tokaji, *The Future of Election Reform*, 28 Yale L. & Pol'y Rev. 125 (2009). *Compare* Michael J. Pitts, *Defining "Partisan" Law Enforcement*, 18 Stan. L. & Pol'y Rev. 324 (2007) (arguing that charges of partisan actions in this context are made too easily and positing objective criteria to define true partisan actions).

28. 52 U.S.C. § 20901 *et seq.*

29. *See* § D[3], *infra.*

30. Further examples are found in Chapter 11, which addresses judicial remedies to resolve election disputes. *See also* Edward B. Foley, Ballot Battles: The History of Disputed Elections in the United States (2d ed. 2024).

31. 531 U.S. 98 (2000) (*Bush II*).

2. The Presidential Election of 2000

While most choices about the methods of casting and tabulating votes are made at the state and local levels, federal law—including the Constitution—imposes limits on those choices. The most famous instance of federal-court oversight of state decisions concerning vote counting was the Supreme Court's decision striking down Florida's recount procedures in the 2000 presidential election between Republican George W. Bush and Democrat Al Gore. The practical result was that Bush obtained a sufficient number of electoral votes to become President.

On election day, Gore had a substantial lead in the nationwide popular vote, but the Electoral College was much closer. As election night came to an end, it became clear that the winner of Florida's electoral votes would win the presidency. Initial counts there showed that Bush had prevailed by 1,784 votes out of approximately 6,000,000 cast.

The closeness of the election triggered a recount under state law. A machine recount was held, with Bush determined still to be the winner. Gore then asked for a manual recount in four counties, prompting controversy over the procedures governing such a recount. Although voters were supposed to vote by locating the "chad" (the detachable rectangle) next to the preferred candidate's name and using a stylus to dislodge the chad from the ballot completely, several voters left chads attached by at least one of the four corners. The question then became whether to count such votes, or, in the terms of the relevant Florida statute, whether those ballots indicated an "intent of the voter" to vote for a particular candidate. Perhaps unavoidably, given the vagueness of the "intent of the voter" statutory rule, different vote counters in different counties used different standards to assess whether the marks sufficiently indicated an intent to cast a vote. Some, for example, might count a ballot as a legal vote if two corners of the "hanging chad" were attached, while others would require at least three corners to be pushed through. For other officials, one corner, or even a "dimpled" or "pregnant" chad (one with an indentation but all four corners intact) might be enough. For still others, it might matter how a voter voted in other races—if the voter completely dislodged the chad for all races except the presidency, an ambiguous vote in the presidential race might be viewed differently than if the voter poked through only one corner for several different races. Whether the differences in vote counting were consistent with the constitutional guarantee of the Equal Protection Clause was the principal (though not the only) question ultimately faced by the U.S. Supreme Court.

The Supreme Court's first entry into the 2000 election controversy was *Bush v. Palm Beach County Canvassing Board*,[32] where the Court was presented with a challenge to the recount deadline established by the Florida Supreme Court. The Florida court, after noting the Florida Constitution's protection of the right to vote and the importance of counting every vote, had imposed a deadline of November 26, despite the relevant statutes' apparent selection of November 14. The Secretary of State objected that the court's reliance on the state constitution undermined the

32. 531 U.S. 70 (2000) (*Bush I*).

legislature's choice in violation of Article II, § 1, clause 2, of the United States Constitution, which vests authority for determining the method of selecting presidential electors in state legislatures.[33]

The Supreme Court did not decide the Article II issue. Instead, it vacated the Florida judgment and remanded to permit the Florida court to clarify the source of its holding. On remand, the Florida Supreme Court maintained that its decision was strictly an interpretation of the Florida statutes, and it therefore professed to be following, rather than contravening, the intent of the Florida legislature.[34]

Simultaneously with the recount-deadline litigation, Gore pressed separate election contests seeking manual recounts in two counties, and eventually the Florida Supreme Court permitted the recounts to go forward.[35] Republicans again appealed to the Supreme Court, which by a 5–4 vote stayed the lower-court decision while the appeal was briefed and argued.[36]

3. The *Per Curiam* Opinion

The Court handed down a decision four days after oral argument. Five Justices joined in the lead, *per curiam*, opinion. As the opinion noted, two questions were presented: (1) whether the Florida Supreme Court decision "established new standards for resolving Presidential elections" when interpreting Florida statutes, thereby violating Article II of the U.S. Constitution and 3 U.S.C. § 5, and (2) "whether the use of standardless manual recounts violates the Equal Protection Clause."[37] The *per curiam* opinion focused entirely on the second question.

The Court began by observing that there was no federal constitutional right to vote for the members of the Electoral College. Under the Constitution, the state legislature has plenary authority either to choose the electors itself or to institute a voting process to pick the electors.[38] But all states now hold popular votes to choose electors, and, citing iconic voting-rights cases, the opinion noted that equal-protection principles hold that a state "may not, by later arbitrary and disparate treatment, value one person's vote over that of another."[39]

Applying these principles to the facts, the *per curiam* opinion concluded that the Florida recount procedures were unconstitutional. The problem was not the abstract "intent of the voter" standard in the Florida statutes; rather, the problem was that the

---

33. U.S. Const. art. II, § 1, cl. 2 ("Each state shall appoint, in such Manner as the Legislature thereof may direct, a Number of Electors, equal to the whole Number of Senators and Representatives to which the State may be entitled in the Congress. . . . ").

34. Palm Beach Cnty. Canvassing Bd. v. Harris, 772 So. 2d 1273 (Fla. 2000).

35. Gore v. Harris, 772 So. 2d 1243 (Fla. 2000).

36. Bush v. Gore, 531 U.S. 1046 (2000).

37. *Bush II*, 531 U.S. at 103.

38. *Id.* at 104 (citing McPherson v. Blacker, 146 U.S. 1 (1892), discussed *infra*, § D[1]).

39. *Id.* at 104–05 (citing Harper v. Virginia Bd. of Elec., 383 U.S. 663 (1966), and Reynolds v. Sims, 377 U.S. 533 (1964)).

standards for accepting or rejecting contested ballots (namely, the conditions of ballots and how much of the chads could be left attached) varied from county to county and even within the same county. The Court also emphasized that the votes were being counted by *ad hoc* teams of judges, some with no previous training in interpreting ballots. The Court concluded that the recount process "is inconsistent with the minimum procedures necessary to protect the fundamental right of each voter in the special instance of a statewide recount under the authority of a single state judicial officer. Our consideration is limited to the present circumstances, for the problem of equal protection in election processes generally presents many complexities."[40]

Florida statutes required that this type of election contest be completed by six days before the presidential electors were set to meet. That deadline turned out to be the very day of the Supreme Court's decision. Given that deadline, the Court held that the only appropriate remedy was to reverse the decision of the Florida Supreme Court, as opposed to remanding for a proper recount.[41]

4. The Concurring Opinion

Chief Justice Rehnquist, joined by Justices Scalia and Thomas, wrote an opinion concurring in the reasoning of the *per curiam* opinion but also addressing the first question presented by the case—one that went unaddressed by the *per curiam* opinion. The concurring opinion concluded that the holding of the Florida Supreme Court violated the language of Article II, § 1, clause 2, which provides that each state's electors shall be appointed "in such Manner as the Legislature thereof may direct."

Normally, the opinion noted, federal courts defer to state courts concerning the interpretation of state law. But that deference was not due here, in the view of the Chief Justice, because the Constitution conferred lawmaking authority on a specific branch of state governments.[42]

In addition, 3 U.S.C. § 5 created a safe harbor that a state's selection of electors "shall be conclusive" if the electors are chosen under laws enacted prior to election day and the selection process is completed six days prior to the meeting of the Electoral College. Here, the decisions of the Florida court were frustrating the "legislative desire" to attain the safe harbor because they had interpreted Florida statutes to extend certain deadlines for the certification of votes, even after certification by the Secretary of State. As Chief Justice Rehnquist read the Florida statutes, however, they vested authority in the Florida Secretary of State and state circuit courts to resolve election disputes. Moreover, the concurring opinion stated, the Florida court unreasonably

---

40. *Id.* at 109.

41. *Id.* at 110. The Court observed that "[s]even Justices of the Court [namely, the five Justices joining the *per curiam* opinion, and Justices Souter and Breyer] agree that there are constitutional problems with the recount," and the "only disagreement is as to the remedy." *Id.* at 111.

42. The Court revisited the issue in *Moore v. Harper*, 600 U.S. 1 (2023), in the context of a challenge to redistricting. *See* Chapter 2, § E.

read Florida law to require the counting of improperly marked ballots, since that law instructed voters to punch out ballots cleanly (*i.e.*, to leave no hanging chads). All of these actions "significantly departed from the statutory framework" and improperly prevented completion of the selection of electors by the safe-harbor date, by which the statute required the recount to be completed.

5. The Dissents

The four dissenting Justices each wrote a dissent. Justice Stevens's dissent, which was joined by Justices Ginsburg and Breyer, was primarily responsive to the concurring opinion. Justice Stevens argued that the concurring opinion took too narrow a view of the constitutional language referring to the state legislature's determining the selection of members of the Electoral College. That language, he argued, assumed that legislatures under state constitutions work in conjunction with other branches, including state courts. Thus, it was proper for the Florida courts to interpret and apply the election provisions passed by the legislature. From that perspective, the inability of the Florida courts precisely to define "intent of the voter" was not problematic, no more so than the "beyond a reasonable doubt" standard used in criminal cases.[43] The Florida courts were not making any substantive change in Florida electoral law; rather, they were only interpreting those provisions.

Justice Souter's dissent was joined by Justice Breyer. Justice Souter argued that the different standards used to determine voters' intent with respect to ballots with identical markings seemed wholly arbitrary and thus raised significant constitutional problems. Nonetheless, he asserted that a mere reversal of the state court was inappropriate. The better course was to remand, in order to permit the state courts to establish uniform standards to evaluate ballots—standards that would be applied in all counties conducting recounts. In his view, it would have been difficult, but not impossible, for a recount to be accomplished before the Electoral College was to meet on December 18.[44]

Justice Ginsburg's dissent was joined in full by Justice Stevens. The initial part of her dissent was also joined by Justices Souter and Breyer. In that part, she agreed with Justice Stevens that the Florida Supreme Court was merely engaging in a reasonable construction of state law. In the second part of her dissent, she argued that equal protection principles did not require perfection in the recount. That recount, "flawed as it may be," would not be "any less fair or precise than the certification that preceded it."[45] Finally, she contended that the majority was giving too much weight to the December 12

---

43. Justice Stevens observed that a majority of states applied either an "intent of the voter standard" or an "impossible to determine the elector's choice" standard in ballot recounts. *Bush II*, 531 U.S. at 124 n.2 (Stevens, J., dissenting).

44. *See* 3 U.S.C. § 7 (providing for the Electoral College to meet "on the first Tuesday after the second Wednesday in December next following their appointment").

45. *Bush II*, 531 U.S. at 143 (Ginsburg, J., dissenting).

safe-harbor deadline. Florida, she noted, could still deliver electoral votes even after that date, although Congress would have the prerogative to reject those votes.

Finally, Justice Breyer's dissent focused on whether the Court should have taken this case at all. He argued it should not have. He acknowledged that the use of different standards to count ballots did "implicate principles of fundamental fairness," but the appropriate remedy was a remand, not a reversal. Whether there was time for a recount prior to the meeting of the Electoral College was for the state courts to determine. More fundamentally, he argued, federal statutes governing the counting of electoral votes (*e.g.*, 3 U.S.C. § 5) contemplated a role for state courts and for Congress, but no role for the U.S. Supreme Court.[46] He recounted the controversy attending the commission established to resolve the 1876 presidential election between Rutherford Hayes and Samuel Tilden, and concluded that the participation of five Justices in that commission "did not lend that process legitimacy."[47] He regretfully concluded that the Court's deciding *Bush v. Gore* would similarly lead to suspicions that the Justices were voting based on political considerations.

6. The Reaction

It is difficult to overstate the attention and controversy that accompanied the *Bush v. Gore* litigation and its aftermath. The complex litigation played out over but a few weeks and was predicated on one of the closest presidential elections in American history. It is also difficult to overstate the controversy in the legal academy's response to *Bush v. Gore*. One branch of scholarly response took seriously the doctrinal and statutory analysis of the various opinions and subjected them to traditional academic scrutiny. The focal point of much of this literature was whether the equal-protection analysis of the *per curiam* opinion properly followed from *Reynolds v. Sims* and other one-person, one-vote decisions. A second branch of scholarship took the analysis of the opinions (particularly those of the Justices constituting the majority) less seriously and, to varying degrees, charged that the decision was a result-oriented attempt by Republican-appointed Justices to install a Republican President.[48] Most scholars were very critical of the decision, although the decision has not gone unsupported by academics.[49]

---

46. While Justice Breyer did not explicitly make the argument, his observations on the roles of Congress and the Court on this matter came close to suggesting that the entire case was a nonjusticiable political question. The political question doctrine is addressed in Chapter 2.

47. *Bush II*, 531 U.S. at 157 (Breyer, J., dissenting).

48. For a small sampling of the enormous scholarly literature, see the essays collected in Bush v. Gore: The Question of Legitimacy (Bruce Ackerman ed., 2002); The Vote: Bush, Gore, and the Supreme Court (Cass R. Sunstein & Richard A. Epstein eds., 2001); and *Symposium: The Law of Presidential Elections: Issues in the Wake of Florida 2000*, 29 Fla. St. U. L. Rev. 325 (2001). For an overview of the considerable literature, see Richard L. Hasen, *A Critical Guide to* Bush v. Gore *Scholarship*, 7 Ann. Rev. Pol. Sci. 297 (2004).

49. *Compare, e.g.*, Jack M. Balkin, Bush v. Gore *and the Boundary Between Law and Politics*, 110 Yale L.J. 1407 (2001), which itself is criticized as being partisan in Robert J. Pushaw, Jr., *Politics,*

The Article II rationale applied by the concurring opinion of Chief Justice Rehnquist in *Bush v. Gore* also attracted its share of scholarly attention.[50] Although the Electors Clause obviously applies only in the context of presidential elections, its meaning has implications for related constitutional questions. For example, Article I, § 4, similarly vests the power to set rules for congressional elections in state legislatures (subject to Congress's power to make or alter those rules). Both provisions, therefore, raise the question whether they provide state legislatures the freedom to act independently of other branches of state government.[51]

7. *Bush v. Gore*, Equal Protection, and the Elections Clause

Despite (or perhaps because of) the political and seeming jurisprudential significance of the case, for several years after the decision, *Bush v. Gore* had relatively little effect in the lower courts.[52] Perhaps courts were affected by the Court's enigmatic statement (in the *per curiam* opinion) that the decision was "limited to the present circumstances" and, thus, not expected to have significant precedential effect. While there were exceptions,[53] most lower courts upheld state election procedures challenged under *Bush v. Gore*.[54]

Ideology, and the Academic Assault on Bush v. Gore, 2 ELECTION L.J. 97 (2003), *with, e.g.*, Einer Elhauge, *The Lessons of Florida 2000*, 110 POL'Y REV. 15 (Dec. 2001 & Jan. 2002), *and* Nelson Lund, Bush v. Gore *at the Dawning of the Age of Obama*, 61 FLA. L. REV. 1101 (2009).

50. *See, e.g.*, Harold J. Krent, *Judging Judging: The Problem of Second-Guessing State Judges' Interpretation of State Law in* Bush v. Gore, 29 FLA. ST. U. L. REV. 493 (2001) (arguing that the Florida Supreme Court's interpretation of state law was plausible); Richard A. Posner, *Florida 2000: A Legal and Statistical Analysis of the Election Deadlock and Ensuing Litigation*, 2000 SUP. CT. REV. 1, 26 (arguing that the Florida court engaged in a "patent misreading of the election statute").

51. *See* Moore v. Harper, 600 U.S. 1 (2023) (rejecting the independent-state-legislature theory in a challenge to congressional districts); Arizona State Legis. v. Arizona Indep. Redistricting Comm'n, 576 U.S. 787 (2015) (upholding the use of an independent commission, created by ballot initiative, to bypass state legislatures in drawing congressional districts).

52. *See* Richard L. Hasen, *The Untimely Death of* Bush v. Gore, 60 STAN. L. REV. 1 (2007); Richard L. Hasen, *The Supreme Court's Shrinking Election Law Docket: 2001–2010: A Legacy of* Bush v. Gore *or Fear of the Roberts Court?*, 10 ELECTION L.J. 325 (2011).

53. One prominent exception was *Stewart v. Blackwell*, 444 F.3d 843 (6th Cir. 2006) (2–1), which struck down Ohio's then-in-use punch-card system for counting votes. *Bush v. Gore* and other cases, the court held, called for strict scrutiny to be applied to state practices that impaired the right to vote. The Sixth Circuit granted rehearing *en banc* but eventually dismissed the case as moot, 473 F.3d 692 (6th Cir. 2007), because Ohio had replaced the punch card system. For an analysis of the case and other lower-court litigation addressing these topics, see Richard B. Saphire & Paul Moke, *Litigating* Bush v. Gore *in the States: Dual Voting Systems and the Fourteenth Amendment*, 51 VILL. L. REV. 229 (2006).

54. *E.g.*, Wexler v. Anderson, 452 F.3d 1226 (11th Cir. 2006) (holding that Florida's recount procedures for counties employing paperless touch-screen voting machines did not violate equal protection or due process, since strict scrutiny was not appropriate and the state had rational regulatory reasons to employ different recount procedures in different counties); Sw. Voter Registration Project v. Shelly, 344 F.3d 914 (9th Cir. 2003) (*en banc*) (upholding the continued use of punch-card technology).

The dormancy of the decision in the lower courts came to an end about a decade later. Later election cycles generated several significant decisions that addressed the application of *Bush v. Gore* in conjunction with earlier voting cases. Some cases involved the counting of ballots, not unlike the facts in *Bush v. Gore*. For example, in one case, a U.S. Senator was defeated in the party primary but retained her office by running as an independent write-in candidate in the general election. The losing candidate then filed litigation, in state and federal court, on the basis of spelling errors on some write-in ballots. The state court rejected the challenges, holding that abbreviations, misspellings, or other minor errors in write-in ballots would not invalidate the ballot if the voter's intent could be ascertained.[55] Shortly afterward, the federal court also rejected the challenge, holding that the state was using uniform standards to count write-in ballots and that the state court had not violated Article II by amending state statutes to allow misspelled write-in ballots to be accepted, since the state court had rendered an acceptable interpretation of a "poorly drafted state statute."[56]

In another case, the incumbent loser of an election for the U.S. Senate challenged the counting of absentee ballots, in part on the basis that different election officials used different standards in the acceptance or rejection of the return envelopes that contained the ballots. A state supreme court rejected the challenge, holding that, while there was some variation among counties, the different resources available justified the variations, and, unlike in *Bush v. Gore*, "there were clear statutory standards for acceptance or rejection of absentee ballots, about which all election officials received common training." And only the ballot-return envelopes, not the ballots themselves, were at issue.[57]

Some cases have involved the counting of provisional ballots, which all states now provide under the mandate of the Help America Vote Act.[58] In one case, an unsuccessful candidate in a juvenile-court election challenged the result on the basis that, as the result of improper directions given by poll workers, certain ballots were cast in the wrong precinct and not counted. Federal courts held that all of the provisional ballots must be counted, in part because there was evidence that some miscast ballots, contrary to the holding of *Bush v. Gore*, had been treated more favorably than others.[59] In another case, the court held that disparate treatment of deficient provisional ballots violated equal-protection principles, drawing on *Bush v. Gore* and other cases[60] that required judicial inquiry into the burdens placed on voters and the reasons for the state's action. That case, however, also held that a provisional ballot incorrectly completed by the voter could be discarded without violating equal protection, because

---

55. Miller v. Treadwell, 245 P.3d 867 (Alaska 2010).

56. Miller v. Treadwell, 736 F. Supp. 2d 1240 (D. Alaska 2010).

57. Coleman v. Franken, 767 N.W.2d 453 (Minn. 2009). This case is also addressed in Chapter 11, §C[1].

58. *See* §D[3], *infra*.

59. Hunter v. Hamilton Cnty. Bd. of Elections, 635 F.3d 219 (6th Cir. 2011), *on remand*, 850 F. Supp. 2d 795 (S.D. Ohio 2012). The challenger won the election upon the recount.

60. *E.g.*, Burdick v. Takushi, 504 U.S. 428 (1992).

state law placed the burden on the voter, not the poll worker, to execute the ballot correctly.[61]

Finally, some cases have used *Bush v. Gore* principles in evaluating other aspects of election administration besides ballot-counting. In one case, Ohio adopted no-fault absentee voting and, at the same time, created early in-person voting. Later, due to additional amendments to various election statutes, military and overseas voters had the entire weekend before election day for in-person voting, while non-military voters had only until the Friday evening preceding election day. Organizations representing non-military voters brought suit, and federal courts held that the distinction violated equal protection. The courts, drawing on *Bush v. Gore* and related cases, found that the limits on non-military voters disproportionately harmed women, older, and lower-income voters and were not justified by the administrative burdens placed on local election boards by weekend voting or by the assertedly unique challenges faced by military voters and their families.[62]

Most recently, the Supreme Court has returned to Chief Justice Rehnquist's argument that Article II gives state *legislatures*—and not other parts of state government—the ability to choose the manner of selecting presidential electors. In *Moore v. Harper*,[63] the Court considered the Elections Clause of Article I, § 4, which, similarly to the Electors Clause addressed in Chief Justice Rehnquist's concurrence, gives power to state legislatures to choose the manner of holding elections for members of Congress. *Moore* held that, in carrying out that function, state legislatures could be restrained by provisions of state constitutions, such as provisions that forbid state legislatures from engaging in partisan gerrymandering.[64] The *Moore* Court went on, however, to insist that "the Elections Clause expressly vests power to carry out its provisions in 'the Legislature' of each State, a deliberate choice that this Court must respect.... [S]tate courts may not transgress the ordinary bounds of judicial review such that they arrogate to themselves the power vested in state legislatures to regulate federal elections."[65] Although the Court did not adopt any test for "the ordinary bounds of judicial review," it expressly referred to Chief Justice Rehnquist's *Bush v.*

---

61. Northeast Ohio Coalition for the Homeless v. Husted, 696 F.3d 580 (6th Cir. 2012) (*per curiam*) (*NOCH*). *But see* Serv. Emps. Int'l Union v. Husted, 698 F.3d 341 (6th Cir. 2012) (*per curiam*) (holding that a state need not count provisional ballots cast in the wrong polling place, even due in part to poll-worker error (the "wrong-place/wrong-precinct" problem), because voters are not entirely dependent on poll workers to arrive at the correct polling place, and distinguishing *Hunter* and *NOCH* as "right-place/wrong-precinct" cases); Donald J. Trump for President, Inc. v. Boockvar, 493 F. Supp. 3d 331 (W.D. Pa. 2020) (holding that alleged uneven use of drop-boxes for mail-in ballots did not violate *Bush v. Gore* because the plaintiffs had not shown that votes were diluted in different counties).

62. Obama for Am. v. Husted, 697 F.3d 423 (6th Cir. 2012). Some federal statutes address voting by military and overseas voters. *See* § D[4], *infra*. For an analysis of the application of the equal-protection principles of *Bush v. Gore* in the lower courts, see Michael T. Morley, Bush v. Gore*'s Uniformity Principle and the Equal Protection Right to Vote*, 28 Geo. Mason L. Rev. 229 (2020).

63. 600 U.S. 1 (2023).

64. *See id.* at 22–34.

65. *Id.* at 34, 36.

Gore concurrence, which asked whether the state courts gave state law a "fair reading," as providing a possible standard.[66]

8. *Bush v. Gore* and Due Process

Plaintiffs in *Bush v. Gore* had also advanced due-process arguments, but the lead *per curiam* opinion in that case directly addressed only the equal-protection claim. Several later cases in the lower courts have nonetheless addressed how due-process concerns can interact with the equal-protection principles of the Supreme Court decision. Cases predating *Bush v. Gore* have held that, apart from other constitutional or statutory protections, the Due Process Clause protects against extraordinary voting restrictions that are "fundamentally unfair." Routine voting irregularities do not rise to that level, but due process can be implicated by substantial changes made to election procedures after the casting of ballots or by the implementation of non-uniform standards that result in significant disenfranchisement and vote dilution.[67]

Some of these principles have been applied in a way that interacts with the equal-protection analysis of *Bush v. Gore*. For example, one court held that a state could insist on strict compliance with voting requirements when counting absentee ballots, despite arguments that the state previously had required only substantial compliance.[68] Another case held that due process was violated when poll-worker error led to voters' casting provisional ballots in the wrong precinct. To penalize the voter by not counting a ballot in those circumstances was, according to the court, fundamentally unfair.[69]

D. Federal Regulation of State-Run Elections

Through most of American history, elections for federal, state, and local elective offices have been administered almost entirely at the state and local levels. This presumption, however, has eroded since the second half of the twentieth century as a result of, for example, federal-court decisions under the Equal Protection Clause dealing with malapportionment,[70] and the passage and implementation of the Voting

66. *Id.* at 36 (quoting Bush v. Gore, 531 U.S. 98, 115 (2000) (Rehnquist, C.J., concurring)).

67. *See, e.g.*, Griffin v. Burns, 570 F.2d 1065 (1st Cir. 1978); Roe v. Alabama, 43 F.3d 574 (11th Cir. 1995) (*per curiam*); Bennett v. Yoshina, 140 F.3d 1218 (9th Cir. 1998). For further discussion of these cases, see Chapter 11, § C.

68. Coleman v. Franken, 767 N.W.2d 453 (Minn. 2009).

69. Northeast Ohio Coalition for the Homeless v. Husted, 696 F.3d 580, 597–98 (6th Cir. 2012) (*per curiam*). *But see* Fitrakis v. Husted, 2012 U.S. Dist. LEXIS 159017, 2012 WL 5411381 (S.D. Ohio 2012) (declining to hold that due process was violated when the plaintiff did not submit sufficient evidence on the claim that computer software used by election officials could be hacked).

70. *See* Chapter 2.

Rights Act of 1965.[71] As outlined below, in more recent decades, Congress has passed statutes addressing more directly the mechanics of voting and the types and counting of ballots. These statutory developments have not been without controversy. While many applaud them for expanding the franchise by easing the registration and ballot-counting processes, others worry that they amount to unfunded mandates on states, that some of their provisions are attempts to advantage certain parties or interests, or that they might make it easier for persons to vote unlawfully.[72] Still others wonder if these reforms can or should be achieved without federal intervention as such, by encouraging competition among states to achieve best practices on voting.[73]

1. The Electoral College

As discussed in § C, *supra*, sometimes the Constitution itself provides rules for conducting federal elections. One such set of rules relates to the Electoral College, the institution created by Article II, § 1, clauses 2 and 3 (as modified by the Twelfth Amendment), for the selection of the President. Clause 2 calls for "[e]ach State [to] appoint, in such Manner as the Legislature thereof may direct, a Number of Electors, equal to the whole Number of Senators and Representatives to which the State may be entitled in the Congress."

In *McPherson v. Blacker*, the U.S. Supreme Court emphasized the interest in deferring to state decisions on selecting electors to the Electoral College.[74] In that case, Michigan had changed from a statewide, winner-take-all system to one that allocated electors on the basis of the presidential vote in each congressional district. (Maine and Nebraska use versions of the latter system today.) The district-based system was challenged on the ground that, among other things, it violated Article II, § 1, because the state was not acting as a whole and was instead delegating electoral selection to political subdivisions. The Court rejected the argument, holding that the state legislature had plenary authority to determine the manner of appointing electors. The constitutional language, the Court held, was broad enough to endorse several possible methods of selection, and indeed various states had followed various methods since the adoption of the Constitution.

McPherson played a role in the Supreme Court's resolution of the Article II issue in *Bush v. Gore*.[75] It is also relevant in considering recent proposals to change the distribution of presidential electors from a winner-take-all system to a proportional

---

71. *See* Chapters 3 and 4.

72. For discussion, see, *e.g.*, J. Kenneth Blackwell & Kenneth A. Klukowski, *The Other Voting Right: Protecting Every Citizen's Vote by Safeguarding the Integrity of the Ballot Box*, 28 Yale L. & Pol'y Rev. 107 (2009); Daniel J. Tokaji, *The Future of Election Reform: From Rules to Institutions*, 28 Yale L. & Pol'y Rev. 125 (2009).

73. *See* Heather K. Gerken, The Democracy Index: Why Our Election System is Failing and How to Fix It (2009).

74. 146 U.S. 1 (1892).

75. 531 U.S. 98, 104 (2000) (*per curiam*); *see also id.* at 113 (Rehnquist, C.J., concurring).

system, whether based on the statewide popular vote or the results in each congressional district. *McPherson* could bear on the method by which such a system could be adopted, whether by action of the state legislature or some other way, such as a referendum or initiative. A broad reading of *McPherson* might suggest that only the state legislature itself could adopt the change.[76]

More recently, the Supreme Court addressed the issue of so-called "faithless electors"—those members of the Electoral College who do not vote for the presidential and vice-presidential candidates to whom they are pledged. States appoint a slate of electors chosen by the political party whose candidates for those offices won the most votes, and most states compel electors to pledge in advance to support the nominee of that party.[77] Some of those states impose sanctions on electors who violate their pledges. Such sanctions include a monetary fine or the removal of the elector from his position and the substitution of an alternate.

The Court upheld such sanctions in *Chiafalo v. Washington*.[78] There, the State of Washington imposed a $1,000 fine on electors who voted for someone other than the candidate nominated by the party who won the most votes in that state. The electors argued that the purpose of the College (restraining the popular will by insisting that the President be chosen not by the people directly but by a select group of electors), and the language of the Electors Clause in Article II, § 1, of the Constitution, implied independent choice by the electors. The argument appeared reasonably strong; after all, if states could require electors to vote a certain way, there would be little reason to require the appointment of electors rather than allowing the state to cast its electoral votes directly.

Nevertheless, the Court unanimously rejected the argument, concluding that the constitutional text and decisions such as *McPherson* give states "far-reaching authority over presidential electors," including the regulation of faithless electors. The Court conceded that some of the Framers seemed to contemplate that electors would exercise discretion, but reasoned that "[w]hether by choice or accident," that understanding was not reflected in the "sparce instructions" found in the Constitution. The Court also emphasized that the vast majority of electors who have voted since the first presidential election in 1788 have done so faithfully, which undermined a claim of a supposed "historical tradition" to the contrary.[79]

And most recently, Congress has passed legislation clarifying how the votes of the Electoral College should be counted by Congress. On January 6, 2021, supporters

---

76. For discussion, see Nicholas P. Stabile, Comment, *An End Run Around a Representative Democracy? The Unconstitutionality of a Ballot Initiative to Alter the Method of Distributing Electors*, 103 Nw. U. L. Rev. 1495 (2009).

77. Such requirements were upheld in *Ray v. Blair*, 343 U.S. 214 (1952).

78. 591 U.S. 578 (2020).

79. Justice Thomas, joined in part by Justice Gorsuch, concurred in the judgment on the basis that the Constitution "is silent on States' authority to bind electors in voting." Given that silence, he argued that the people of each state were free to regulate faithless electors, citing his dissent in *U.S. Term Limits, Inc. v. Thornton*, 514 U.S. 779 (1995).

of the incumbent President, Donald Trump, stormed the U.S. Capitol. The rioters believed President Trump's false claims that he was the rightful victor of the 2020 presidential election, and they went to the Capitol to "stop the steal." The riot resulted in the death of one of the rioters, several injuries, damage to the Capitol, and the temporary disruption of Congress's counting of electoral votes. President Trump had urged Vice President Mike Pence, who, pursuant to the Twelfth Amendment, presided over the electoral count, to reject the votes in states where Trump was contesting the validity of the results.[80] Pence refused, believing that he had no such authority.

The following year, in an attempt to avoid repeating the calamity of January 6, 2021, Congress passed the Electoral Count Reform Act (ECRA).[81] The ECRA explicitly provided that the Vice President's role in counting the votes is purely ceremonial, and it increased the number of members of Congress necessary to challenge any state's electoral votes. The previous law provided that a challenge to a state's votes would be considered by the Houses of Congress if only one member of each House supported the challenge. Under the new law, no such challenge will be considered unless it has the support of one-fifth of each chamber.

Other provisions of the ECRA specify the governor as the official responsible for certifying each state's electors, provide for expedited judicial review of electoral challenges by presidential and vice-presidential candidates with a direct appeal to the Supreme Court, and require Congress to defer to slates of electors chosen pursuant to court orders. Together, these reforms were aimed at allowing Congress to identify conclusively a single slate of electors from each state and to have challenges resolved expeditiously. Finally, the ECRA amended prior law that had allowed each state to declare a "failed election" after the fact; the law now provides that the presidential election day may be moved from the Tuesday after the first Monday in November only in the event of an "extraordinary and catastrophic" event.

2. The National Voter Registration Act

In 1993, Congress passed the National Voter Registration Act (NVRA),[82] among other reasons, to "increase the number of eligible citizens who register to vote in elections for Federal office."[83] To that end, provisions of NVRA establish national procedures for voter registration for elections for federal office by requiring that states permit such registration (1) when citizens also apply for or seek renewal of drivers'

---

80. *See* U.S. Const. amend. XII ("The President of the Senate shall, in the presence of the Senate and House of Representatives, open all the certificates [of the electors' votes] and the votes shall then be counted.").

81. Division P, Title I of the Consolidated Appropriations Act, Pub. L. 117-328, 136 Stat. 4459 (2022).

82. 52 U.S.C. § 20501 *et seq.*

83. 52 U.S.C. § 20501(b).

licenses,[84] (2) by mail,[85] or (3) at various public offices to be designated by the state.[86] NVRA also provides for procedures for confirming voter registration and removing persons from voting rolls[87] and for enforcement of its requirements by the Attorney General and by private parties.[88]

The Supreme Court in *Arizona v. Inter Tribal Council of Arizona Inc.*[89] considered the preemptive effect of NVRA's mandate that states "accept and use" the federal voter registration form for elections to federal office.[90] The form required the applicant to aver that he was a citizen but did not require any evidence of citizenship. Arizona required that applicants using the form also present documentary evidence of citizenship. A majority of the Court, in an opinion by Justice Scalia, held Arizona's evidentiary requirement to be preempted by NVRA. The Court noted that the Elections Clause[91] imposes upon states the duty to prescribe the time, place, and manner of elections to the House and Senate while conferring power upon Congress to alter or supplant those regulations, including those dealing with voter registration. The Clause thus "empowers Congress to regulate *how* federal elections are held, but not *who* may vote in them."[92] The Court held that while the "accept and use" language of NVRA might be subject to different interpretations, the "fairest reading of the statute is that a state-imposed requirement of evidence of citizenship not required by the Federal Form" was inconsistent with the mandate. The traditional presumption against interpreting statutes to preempt state laws did not apply when Congress legislated under the Elections Clause, the Court held, because the Clause "necessarily displaces some element of a pre-existing legal regime erected by" a state. The Court allowed that Arizona could request the Federal Election Assistance Commission to alter the federal form to include additional information.[93]

NVRA's private right of action states that a "person who is aggrieved by a violation" of the law may bring suit in federal court to enforce it. Courts have held that interest groups seeking to expand voter registration, among others, are included within the

84. 52 U.S.C. § 20504.
85. 52 U.S.C. § 20505.
86. 52 U.S.C. § 20506.
87. 52 U.S.C. § 20507.
88. 52 U.S.C. § 20510.
89. 570 U.S. 1 (2013).
90. 52 U.S.C. § 20505.
91. U.S. Const. art. I, § 4, cl. 1.
92. 570 U.S. at 16 (emphasis in original).
93. Justices Thomas and Alito dissented, the former on the basis that the Elections Clause, properly understood, permitted states to determine whether voter qualifications have been satisfied, and the latter on the basis that a presumption against preemption had not been satisfied by the NVRA language. The state of Arizona took the advice of the Court and made the indicated request to the EAC. The EAC denied its request, and that decision was affirmed upon court review. Kobach v. U.S. Election Assistance Comm'n, 772 F.3d 1183 (10th Cir. 2014).

class of "person[s]" who may enforce the law in court.[94] It is not clear that the NVRA in and of itself has led to an increase in voter registration.[95]

3. Help America Vote Act

The 2000 election debacle produced widespread agreement that America's voting processes needed to be improved. One of the responses from Congress was the passage of the Help America Vote Act of 2002 (HAVA),[96] which was designed to aid and encourage states to improve and upgrade their election administration. The law reflected Democratic desires to improve access to the ballot as well as Republican concerns over the integrity of the voting process. HAVA authorized federal funds to states for replacing punch-card or lever-based voting systems with more modern technology;[97] set up a new agency, the Election Assistance Commission (EAC);[98] imposed certain requirements on states with regard to voting-equipment standards, registration databases, identification requirements for first-time voters, and the establishment of provisional voting;[99] and authorized the Attorney General to bring enforcement actions.[100]

HAVA has been relatively controversial since its inception. For example, the EAC consists of two members from each major party, with a majority required for action. That and the limited powers granted by Congress have rendered the EAC largely toothless. It is authorized to distribute HAVA funds for election improvements and to engage in research, but it cannot issue regulations and otherwise is given relatively little power. Moreover, it has been plagued by disputes over commissioner appointments, limited funding, and failure to exercise what limited powers it does have.[101]

---

94. *E.g.*, ACORN v. Fowler, 178 F.3d 350 (5th Cir. 1999). *See also* Scott v. Schedler, 771 F.3d 831 (5th Cir. 2014) (potential voter lacked standing to sue for alleged violations of NVRA due to failure to give notice to the state's chief election officer).

95. *See* Robert D. Brown & Justin Wedeking, *People Who Have Their Tickets But Do Not Use Them: "Motor Voter," Registration, and Turnout Revisited*, 34 AM. POL. RES. 479 (2006). Much of the empirical literature appears to support a similar, broader point that changes to increase registration and turnout often have relatively little of the intended effect. *See, e.g.*, James W. Endersby & Steven Jokinsky, *State Electoral Innovation and Voter Turnout in Midterm and Presidential Elections*, 23 ELECTION L.J. 132 (2024); Justin Grimmer & Eitan Hersh, *How Election Rules Affect Who Wins*, 16 J. LEGAL ANALYSIS 1 (2024); Brian T. Hamel, Jan Leighley & Robert M. Stein, *Why Making Voting Easier Isn't Enough: Early Voting, Campaigns, and Voter Turnout*, 52 AM. POL. RES. 343 (2024).

96. 52 U.S.C. § 20901 *et seq.*

97. 52 U.S.C. § 20902.

98. 52 U.S.C. § 20921.

99. 52 U.S.C. § 21081.

100. 52 U.S.C. § 21111.

101. *See* Ray Martinez III, *Is the Election Assistance Commission Worth Keeping?*, 12 ELECTION L.J. 190 (2013); Daniel P. Tokaji, *The Future of Election Reform: From Rules to Institutions*, 28 YALE L. & POL'Y REV. 125, 134–36 (2009).

HAVA's requirements, including those relating to provisional ballots,[102] have generated litigation. In one leading case, *Sandusky County Democratic Party v. Blackwell*,[103] the Sixth Circuit made two important holdings. The first was that private parties could sue to enforce § 302 of HAVA, the core provision requiring states to provide voters with the opportunity to cast provisional ballots.[104] In particular, the court determined that § 302 conveyed an enforceable individual right by providing that a voter "shall be permitted to cast a provisional ballot" upon affirming that he is registered and eligible to vote; thus, § 302 could be enforced in a suit brought under 42 U.S.C. § 1983.[105]

The second holding, on the merits, was that neither HAVA's text nor its legislative history required the state to count a provisional ballot cast in the wrong precinct, where it would be invalid under state law. To hold otherwise, the court held, would empower political parties to "marshal their supporters at the last minute from shopping centers, office buildings, or factories, and urge them to vote at whatever polling place happened to be handy."[106] The HAVA provision that permitted provisional votes to be cast in the "jurisdiction in which the individual desire[d] to vote" did not require states, the court held, to ignore otherwise applicable state law that required voters to register and to cast votes in particular precincts.

Other courts have interpreted other portions of HAVA as not empowering private parties to bring suit. For example, later cases have distinguished *Sandusky* and held that §§ 301 (requiring voting systems to meet certain standards)[107] and 303 (requiring states to maintain a computerized voter-registration list)[108] of HAVA confer no private right of action on plaintiffs. If there is no private right of action to enforce HAVA, then (absent voluntary compliance) the responsibility falls on the federal government to ensure that the law is followed.[109]

HAVA has been credited with encouraging states to abandon the traditional paper punch-card ballots and to adopt newer technologies, such as optically scanned ballots or electronic voting machines. Refinements to the voting process have continued at the state level, even without the mandate of HAVA or other federal laws. For example,

---

102. Daniel P. Tokaji, *HAVA in Court: A Summary and Analysis of Litigation*, 12 Election L.J. 203 (2013).

103. 387 F.3d 565 (6th Cir. 2004) (*per curiam*).

104. 52 U.S.C. § 21082.

105. Under 42 U.S.C. § 1983, a person whose federal rights have been violated by someone acting under color of state law (*i.e.*, a state- or local-government official) has an express private right of action against the violator. That cause of action requires the plaintiff to prove a violation of a federal *right*, not simply a violation of federal law, so it is essential that the plaintiff establish that the federal law that the defendant violated conferred a right on the plaintiff. *See* Medina v. Planned Parenthood South Atlantic, 606 U.S. __, __, 145 S. Ct. 2219, 2234 (2025); Gonzaga Univ. v. Doe, 536 U.S. 273, 283 (2002). That is why *Sandusky* focused on § 302's language giving *voters* the ability to cast a provisional ballot, rather than merely imposing an obligation *on the state* to make provisional ballots available.

106. 387 F.3d at 568.

107. Crowley v. Nevada, 678 F.3d 730 (9th Cir. 2012).

108. Brunner v. Ohio Republican Party, 555 U.S. 5 (2008) (*per curiam*).

109. For a discussion of these issues, see Daniel P. Tokaji, *Public Rights and Private Rights of Action: The Enforcement of Federal Election Laws*, 44 Ind. L. Rev. 113 (2010).

HAVA did not require that states implement a voter-verifiable paper record, but at least twenty-nine states have adopted some version of that requirement.[110]

4. Other Federal Laws

Aside from NVRA and HAVA, other federal laws regulate the manner in which states manage their voting systems when conducting elections for federal office. For example, the Voting Accessibility for the Elderly and Handicapped Act (VAEHA), passed in 1984, requires states to facilitate voting in federal elections by voters who are handicapped or age sixty-five or older.[111] The Uniformed and Overseas Citizens Absentee Voting Act (UOCAVA), passed in 1986, requires states to facilitate absentee voting in federal elections by voters, including those in the military, who are overseas.[112] And the Military and Overseas Voter Empowerment Act (MOVE Act), passed in 2009, amended UOCAVA and requires states to facilitate mail and electronic absentee voting in federal elections by members of the armed forces stationed outside the United States.[113]

The Civil Rights Act of 1964 forbids states from denying any person the right to vote "because of an error or omission on any record or paper relating to any application, registration, or other act requisite to voting, if such error or omission is not material in determining whether such individual is qualified under State law to vote in such election."[114] A controversy has arisen recently concerning whether that "materiality provision" is violated when a mail-in vote is rejected for reasons that do not establish the voter's ineligibility. Pennsylvania law requires that mail-in ballots be placed in an envelope and that the voter sign and date the envelope. The date on the envelope serves no meaningful purpose; the ballot's timeliness is determined by the date it is *received*, so the date the voter claims to have *marked* the ballot is irrelevant. Nevertheless, state law requires ballots sent in undated envelopes to be rejected.[115] Voters whose ballots were rejected sued, claiming that, by rejecting their ballots, the

---

110. For discussion of HAVA, its implementation, and the litigation it has generated, see Martha Kropf & David C. Kimball, Helping America Vote: The Limits of Election Reform (2011); Symposium, *HAVA@10*, 12 Election L.J. 130 (2013); Kathleen Hale & Ramona McNeal, *Election Administration Reform and State Choice: Voter Identification Requirements and HAVA*, 38 Pol'y Stud. J. 281 (2010); and Daniel Palazzolo *et al.*, *Election Reform after HAVA: Voter Verification in Congress and the States*, 38 Publius: J. Federalism 515 (2008). For further discussion of HAVA, related statutes, and voter registration in general, see Presidential Comm'n on Election Admin., The American Voting Experience: Report and Recommendation of the Presidential Commission on Election Administration (2014).

111. 52 U.S.C. § 20101.

112. 52 U.S.C. § 20301.

113. Pub. L. 111-84, 123 Stat. 2318 (2009). For overviews of NVRA, HAVA, and UOCAVA, see Justin Weinstein-Tull, *Voting Under Federal Election Laws*, *in* The Oxford Handbook of American Election Law 221 (Eugene D. Mazo ed., 2024); Justin Weinstein-Tull, *Election Law Federalism*, 114 Mich L. Rev. 747 (2016).

114. 52 U.S.C. § 10101(a)(2)(B).

115. *See* 25 Pa. C.S. § 3150.16(a); *Ball v. Chapman*, 289 A.3d 1, 20–23 (Pa. 2023).

state abridged their right to vote based on a nonmaterial error, in violation of the Civil Rights Act's materiality provision. The Third Circuit rejected the argument, pointing out that the federal statute was applicable to errors in paperwork used to "determin[e] whether [the voter] is *qualified* under State law to vote." In other words, the statute makes it illegal for states to rely on a nonmaterial error in deciding *who* may vote, but it has no relevance to state laws that govern *how* a person is supposed to vote.[116]

E. Determining a Winner

In Chapter 6, § B, we discussed the "spoiler effect" caused by a third-party candidate's participation in a plurality-winner ("first past the post") election. Under plurality-winner systems, the third candidate tends to work as a spoiler, taking votes from the major-party candidate who is ideologically closer to the third-party candidate, thereby increasing the electoral chances of the candidate likely to be least palatable to supporters of the third-party candidate.[117]

Alternative methods of vote counting give minor parties a much better chance of gaining representation in elected bodies. They also produce results that are more representative of the range of voters' true preferences. Proportional representation, for example, seeks to divide seats in a legislature proportionately according to the votes received by various parties. Thus, a minor party that receives 20% of the vote might receive no seats in a plurality system but might receive 20% of the seats in a proportional system.

Single-transferable-vote (STV), or instant-runoff, systems provide a different means to enable voters to express a preference for minor parties. Under those systems, voters do not simply select their first-choice candidates. Rather, voters rank the candidates. First-choice votes are tabulated, and if one candidate receives a majority, that candidate is the winner. If no candidate receives a majority, however, the candidate with the least first-place votes is eliminated from contention. Voters who chose the eliminated candidate have their second-choice votes counted in the next round, with the process repeating until one candidate receives a majority. For elections to fill multiple seats, STV systems not only attempt to solve the problem of "wasted" votes for losing candidates but also attempt to solve the problem of extra votes cast for winning candidates (*i.e.*, more votes than the candidate needs to secure election). Once a candidate reaches a majority, an STV system applies all future votes cast for that candidate to the voters' second choices. That way, each voter has an increased opportunity to affect the outcome.

---

116. *See* Pennsylvania State Conf. of NAACP Branches v. Sec'y, Commonwealth of Pennsylvania, 97 F.4th 120, 125, 130 (3d Cir. 2024). As this book went to press, however, the Third Circuit held that Pennsylvania's law violated the Federal Constitution's right to vote. *See Eakin v. Adams Cty. Bd. of Elections*, 149 F. 4th 291 (3d Cir. 2025).

117. William H. Riker, *The Two-Party System and Duverger's Law: An Essay on the History of Political Science*, 76 Am. Pol. Sci. Rev. 753 (1982).

Other voting systems involve giving voters multiple votes to allocate to the candidates. One such system allocates zero votes to the voter's least-preferred candidate, one to the candidate the voter prefers next, two to the next-preferred candidate, and so on. A second such system gives each voter a certain number of votes and permits the voter to allocate votes as he sees fit. For example, a voter might have five votes to allocate between ten candidates running for five seats in a legislature, and the voter might decide to give three votes to Candidate A and two to Candidate B. Because voters can pool their votes, such a system permits voters who strongly support minor-party candidates to overcome some of the disadvantages they face because of their smaller numbers. Such a system also may inure to the benefit of racial minorities or other minority groups that can unite behind a small number of candidates, making it more likely that the group will receive some representation.

Ranked-choice voting (RCV), which includes STV and instant-runoff systems, is enjoying a resurgence of popularity in states and political subdivisions. Some critics argue that RCV should not be adopted because it is confusing to voters (*e.g.*, if some voters do not rank all of the choices, the advantages of an RCV system will not be realized, and the voters who do rank their preferences will have outsized influence on the outcome), unduly undermines the major political parties, and conflicts with state constitutional and statutory provisions which, using various language, seem to require that the candidate receiving a plurality of votes be declared the winner. Supporters of RCV contend that, properly understood, RCV ultimately ascertains the preference of a majority of voters and thus is consistent with requirements that the winner be the candidate who receives the most votes.[118] It seems likely that policy and legal arguments over STV and RCV will continue.

---

118. *See, e.g.*, Op. of the Justices, 162 A.3d 188 (Me. 2017) (advisory opinion by the Maine Supreme Judicial Court); Richard H. Pildes & G. Michael Parsons, *The Legality of Ranked-Choice Voting*, 109 Calif. L. Rev. 1773 (2021). *See also* Edward B. Foley, *The Constitution and Condorcet: Democracy Protection Through Electoral Reform*, 70 Drake L. Rev. 543 (2023).

Chapter 11

Remedying Errors in Elections

A. Introduction

Much election-law litigation is undertaken to remedy perceived errors in the electoral process, particularly in elections that have already taken place. Chapter 10 considered one high-profile, if now-dated, example: the Supreme Court's decision in *Bush v. Gore*,[1] which had its genesis in state-court litigation to recount certain ballots that were improperly cast. This chapter considers more systematically the ways legislatures and courts deal with perceived and actual electoral errors.

There is no common-law basis to contest elections.[2] Rather, most states have fairly detailed statutory schemes that set out procedures for state and local officials to follow when confronting problems in an election. These statutes typically provide for an administrative process, followed, if necessary, by review in the state courts. Among the issues that state officials encounter are fraudulent votes, mistaken votes, and recounts when elections are extremely close. If and when a dispute reaches the judicial branch, a court must consider, often with little substantive guidance from the relevant statutes, whether an error has taken place and, if so, what the remedy should be.[3]

Any resolution of election disputes—whether by a legislature or by a court—involves inevitable trade-offs. Among the potentially conflicting values at stake are the perceived fairness, accuracy, and legitimacy of the remedial process itself; the desire of voters to be anonymous; the desire to resolve an election dispute with promptness and finality; and the efficiency (or lack thereof) and costs associated with any remedy.

1. 531 U.S. 98 (2000) (*per curiam*).

2. *E.g.*, Taylor v. Roche, 248 S.E.2d 580, 582 (S.C. 1978); Taylor v. Cent. City Comm. Sch. Dist., 733 N.W.2d 655, 657 (Iowa 2007).

3. For helpful discussion of these issues, see Edward B. Foley, Ballot Battles: The History of Disputed Elections in the United States (2d ed. 2024); Richard L. Hasen, Election Meltdown: Dirty Tricks, Distrust, and the Threat to American Democracy (2020); Joshua A. Douglas, *Procedural Fairness in Election Contests*, 88 Ind. L.J. 1 (2013); Richard L. Hasen, *The Democracy Canon*, 62 Stan. L. Rev. 69 (2009); and Steven F. Huefner, *Remedying Election Wrongs*, 44 Harv. J. Legis. 265 (2007). The American Law Institute in 2023 approved the launch of a Restatement of the Law on Election Litigation to provide guidance to federal and state judges adjudicating election disputes.

B. Correcting Faulty Elections

1. New Elections

The simplest but most drastic remedy a court can order in the face of evidence of improper voting is ordering a new election. The request can be based on alleged violations of federal constitutional or statutory law, or of state law.

The leading case ordering a new election for violations of federal law is *Bell v. Southwell*.[4] That case emerged from the civil-rights era and involved an election in Georgia for a justice of the peace. Amid "racial discrimination which was gross, state-imposed, and forcibly state-compelled,"[5] the black plaintiff had lost the election to her white opponent, who was one of the defendants in the case. There was evidence that, among other things, voting lists and voting booths were segregated on the basis of race; qualified black voters were not permitted to vote in "white" booths; and various state officials intimidated the plaintiff and her black supporters from voting or monitoring the voting process. Less than one-third of the registered and qualified black voters participated in the election. Despite the constitutional violations, the U.S. district judge refused to order relief, on the basis that even if all registered black voters had voted for the plaintiff, she still would have lost, and federal courts "simply [did] not have the power to void a state election."

The Fifth Circuit reversed. It held that in many circumstances, prospective-only relief would be appropriate, but in egregious, "outrageous" instances, retrospective voiding of an election can be ordered. Here, the court emphasized, the "body politic as a whole, both Negro and white," had suffered. Nor was it appropriate to assume that black voters would have voted only for a black candidate, and white voters only for a white candidate, in a "free, untainted election." The discriminatory practices had so infected the election process that ordering a new election was the only effective relief.

As the *Bell* court acknowledged, it is extraordinary for a court (particularly a federal court) to take the "drastic" step of ordering a new election for a state office. According to the court, the remedy was necessary given the seriousness and pervasiveness of the voting-rights violations. Federal[6] and state courts[7] have rarely found such circum-

---

4. 376 F.2d 659 (5th Cir. 1966).

5. *Id.* at 659. *See also* Keyes v. Gunn, 890 F.3d 232 (5th Cir. 2018) (holding that, under 28 U.S.C. § 1344, federal courts lack jurisdiction to adjudicate election contests to state legislative bodies, but concluding that *Bell* did not violate that prohibition since it did not concern an election contest as such).

6. *E.g.*, Bodine v. Elkhart Cnty. Election Bd., 788 F.2d 1270 (7th Cir. 1986); Curry v. Baker, 802 F.2d 1302 (11th Cir. 1986); Gold v. Feinberg, 101 F.3d 796 (2d Cir. 1996); Hamer v. Ely, 410 F.2d 152 (5th Cir. 1969); Hutchinson v. Miller, 797 F.2d 1279 (4th Cir. 1986); Pope v. Cnty. of Albany, 687 F.3d 565 (2d Cir. 2012); Scheer v. City of Miami, 15 F. Supp. 2d 1338 (S.D. Fla. 1998). *But see* Hunter v. Hamilton Cnty. Bd. of Elections, 635 F.3d 219 (6th Cir. 2011) (finding federal intervention appropriate in a dispute regarding the counting of provisional ballots in a state election, given non-frivolous allegations of violations of federal rights).

7. *E.g.*, Putter v. Montpelier Pub. School Sys., 697 A.2d 354 (Vt. 1997) (in a § 1983 action brought in state court, even assuming election was tainted by public officials spending public funds in favor of a ballot proposal, a new election was held not to be appropriate, given high standard for relief found in federal cases).

stances, and so the remedy in *Bell*, or indeed any judicial intervention at all, is rarely ordered. Courts frequently state that mere "garden variety election disputes" are not enough to justify judicial relief.[8]

Although modern courts may not often follow *Bell* in ordering new elections, *Bell* continues to frame debate concerning judicial intervention in election disputes. For example, one scholar argued that the federal judges in *Bell* "courageously" voided the election, but he also argued that "court intervention should be used sparingly" and he criticized *Bush v. Gore* for failing to follow such an approach.[9] Another noted appraisal of *Bell* addressed the pros and cons of retroactively remedying an illegal election by ordering a new one, as opposed to prospectively forbidding the challenged practice. The former provides a more complete remedy and seemingly returns voters to the *status quo*. The latter is less intrusive and avoids difficult, perhaps futile, efforts to restore the *status quo*, since not all of the same voters may vote, time has passed, and it is almost impossible to rerun the same election. Given the subjectivity of the "outrageous" test of *Bell*, the author argued that a new election should be ordered only when improprieties might have affected the outcome of the election.[10]

Although federal judges rarely order new elections, the remedy is more common in local elections being reviewed by state judges, often primarily or exclusively on state-law grounds.[11] One well known example is the decision of Hawaii's Supreme Court in *Akizaki v. Fong*.[12] That case involved an election to the Hawaii House of Representatives, in which the winner prevailed by two votes. The dispute turned on certain absentee ballots postmarked too late but nonetheless mistakenly counted by election officials. Those ballots were then commingled with validly cast absentee ballots. The lower court discarded all of the absentee ballots and ruled that the winner should be the candidate who won the most election-day votes, but the Hawaii Supreme Court ordered an entirely new election. The court held that, given the commingling, there was no way to determine the winner. Drawing on federal cases, the court proceeded on the principle that implicit in the right to vote "is the right to have one's vote count and the right to have as nearly as perfect an election proceeding as can be provided." Eliminating all absentee ballots, in the view of the court, "inflicts too harsh a result on those absentee voters whose votes are validly cast." The court added that ordering

---

8. *E.g.*, Northeast Ohio Coalition for Homeless v. Husted, 696 F.3d 580 (6th Cir. 2012); Scheer v. City of Miami, 15 F. Supp. 2d 1338 (S.D. Fla. 1998).

9. Richard L. Hasen, Bush v. Gore *and the Future of Equal Protection Law*, 29 Fla. St. U. L. Rev. 377 (2001).

10. Kenneth W. Starr, *Federal Judicial Intervention as a Remedy for Irregularities in State Elections*, 49 N.Y.U. L. Rev. 1092 (1974). For an in-depth discussion of the materiality of election errors, see Justin Levitt, *Resolving Election Error: The Dynamic Assessment of Materiality*, 54 Wm. & Mary L. Rev. 83 (2012). *See also* Edward B. Foley, *Assessing the Validity of an Election's Result: History, Theory, and Present Threats*, 95 N.Y.U. L. Rev. Online 171 (2020) (distinguishing between the negation and manipulation of voter choice and arguing that only the former undermines the validity of elections).

11. *See, e.g.*, Nickelson v. Whitehorn, 375 So. 3d 1132 (La. Ct. App. 2023) (ordering a new election in a race decided by one vote when, due to alleged irregularities in in-person and absentee ballot voting, six votes were invalidated and it was "legally impossible to determine the result of the election").

12. 461 P.2d 221 (Haw. 1969).

a new election did not violate separation-of-powers concerns and thus a case asking for such a remedy did not present a nonjusticiable political question.

A more-recent example going in the other direction is *Fladell v. Palm Beach County Canvassing Board*,[13] issued by the Florida Supreme Court during the *Bush v. Gore* controversy and growing out of the same dispute. That case focused on one county's "butterfly ballot," which listed candidates' names on both the right and left sides, with arrows pointing to spaces in a center column which voters would mark to indicate their choices. Plaintiffs argued that the ballot violated statutory requirements and was so confusing that votes may have been cast for unintended candidates. One of the remedies sought was a new election. To order a new election, the court held, there must be "substantial noncompliance" with statutory requirements for the ballot. Courts should be wary of ordering a new election, the court further observed, since it was tantamount to disenfranchising voters. Those high bars were not met in the case, and no new election was ordered.[14]

2. Adjusting Vote Totals

Another remedy for election errors is to adjust the vote totals. That remedy is closely related to the issues raised in the prior section because a request for a new election can be based on vote totals being changed by a recount, and adjusting vote totals is often requested as an alternative remedy. Courts have taken several approaches in deciding how to determine if a ballot was validly cast, whether to adjust vote totals, and when election errors should lead to a new election. Some states will order a new election, more or less automatically, simply if the number of invalid votes exceeds the margin of victory. Other states, in contrast, will order a new election only if there is a significant chance that the invalid votes would have affected the outcome. Some states require direct evidence that an illegal vote was cast for a particular candidate before a court will deduct a vote from that candidate. Finally, some states undertake proportionate reduction, where the court estimates the likely vote cast invalidly, by examining the location of the votes or other factors, and then appropriately reduces the vote total of one candidate or another.[15]

One leading example is *Ippolito v. Power*,[16] from the New York Court of Appeals. That case involved a primary election for a local district leader of the Democratic Party. The winning margin was seventeen votes, but over one hundred of the total

13. 772 So. 2d 1240 (Fla. 2000) (*per curiam*).

14. For a critical analysis of the case, see Stephen J. Mulroy, *Right Without Remedy? The "Butterfly Ballot" Case and Court Ordered Federal Election "Revotes,"* 10 Geo. Mason. L. Rev. 215 (2001).

15. For further discussion of these different approaches, see *Developments in the Law: Voting and Democracy*, 119 Harv. L. Rev. 1127, 1157–61 (2006); Kevin J. Hickey, Note, *Accuracy Counts: Illegal Votes in Contested Elections and the Case for Complete Proportionate Deduction*, 83 N.Y.U. L. Rev. 167 (2008); and Sarah E. LeCloux, Comment, *Too Close to Call? Remedying Reasonably Uncertain Ballot Results with New Elections*, 2001 Wis. L. Rev. 1541.

16. 241 N.E.2d 232 (N.Y. 1968).

cast were suspect or invalid for various reasons, albeit without evidence of fraud or intentional misconduct. The relevant statute stated that courts could order a new election if "frauds or irregularities" made it impossible to determine who was rightfully elected. Distinguishing prior cases where the margin of victory was much closer to or exceeded the number of invalid votes, the court held that the "irregularities [in the election under review were] sufficiently large in number to establish the probability that the result would be changed by a" shift in the questioned votes.[17]

Other cases, in various factual settings, have been presented with sometimes difficult questions about how, if at all, to adjust vote totals. One example is when the names of candidates on ballots are not randomly listed on printed ballots, as is required in many jurisdictions. Such requirements are in place to prevent some candidates from being systematically advantaged by the "primacy effect" of voters simply voting for those at the top of a ballot. In one such case, the court refused to shift votes based on expert testimony that purported to quantify the primacy effect.[18]

A particularly controversial recount and adjustment of votes took place after the 2004 gubernatorial election for the State of Washington. Initially, Republican Dino Rossi led Democrat Christine Gregoire by 261 votes out of more than 2.8 million cast. It was apparently the closest race for governor in American history. Two sets of recounts led to a lead by Gregoire of 129 votes. Rossi filed suit in state court, requesting a new election. Discovery in the case revealed that over 1,600 voters had voted illegally, many of them disenfranchised felons. The challengers did not undertake the heavy burden of providing direct evidence of how the invalid voters voted. The trial judge found that proportionate reduction, the alternative remedy posited by the challengers, was not appropriate, in part because it could not assume that the mostly male felons had voted proportionately like non-felons. The challengers did not appeal the trial court's decision. Proportionate adjustment of vote totals seems to be done relatively rarely.[19]

---

17. One much-discussed effort to address the role of statistical evidence has some criticism of *Ippolito*. In Michael O. Finkelstein and Herbert E. Robbins, *Mathematical Probability in Election Challenges*, 73 COLUM. L. REV. 241 (1973), the authors set out a formula to help determine whether invalid votes altered the outcome of an election. The formula considers the winner's plurality, the total number of votes cast, and the number of invalid votes cast, and it assumes that the invalid votes were randomly distributed, *i.e.*, not biased toward any candidate. The authors contend that under their formula, there was only a 5% chance that the outcome of the election in *Ippolito* would have been different without the invalid votes. *Id.* at 243. Apparently no court has ever applied this formula. Most, if not all, courts appear unwilling to engage in a precise measurement of the "probabilities" of a different outcome.

18. *See* Bradley v. Perrodin, 106 Cal. App. 4th 1153, 131 Cal. Rptr. 2d 402 (2003). For a discussion of the ballot-order effect, see R. Michael Alvarez *et al.*, *How Much Is Enough? The "Ballot Order Effect" and the Use of Social Science Evidence in Election Disputes*, 5 ELECTION L.J. 40 (2006), and Mary Beth Beazely, *Ballot Design as Fail-Safe: An Ounce of Rotation Is Worth a Pound of Litigation*, 12 ELECTION L.J. 18 (2013).

19. For further discussion of the Washington election and of proportionate reduction in general, see RICHARD L. HASEN, THE VOTING WARS: FROM FLORIDA 2000 TO THE NEXT ELECTION MELTDOWN 149–52 (2012), and Kevin J. Hickey, Note, *Accuracy Counts: Illegal Votes in Contested Elections and the Case for Complete Proportionate Reduction*, 83 N.Y.U. L. REV. 167 (2008).

An historically high-profile example of a legal challenge to vote totals took place in 2020, when President Donald J. Trump claimed that his loss in his bid for reelection was due to fraud in several states, and several lawsuits were brought alleging that fraud had tainted the results. Almost all the suits were dismissed on the merits for lack of plausible allegations or proof, though some were dismissed for lack of standing by plaintiffs or on other grounds.[20] The episode generated extensive commentary on whether and how U.S. elections can be secure from fraud and subversion.[21]

C. State Remedies for Federal Elections

Previous portions of this chapter discussed cases where federal courts contemplated whether and to what extent they should intervene to regulate elections for state offices. This section considers the opposite issue, of state courts contemplating remedies for errors in elections for federal office. The U.S. Constitution and federal statutes speak to this issue in several ways. For presidential elections, Article II establishes the Electoral College but largely leaves to states, specifically state legislatures, the methods of choosing their electors. The Electoral Count Act of 1887[22] establishes deadlines for states to select their electors and for Congress to count any disputed electoral votes.

A separate set of provisions deals with congressional elections. For example, Article I, § 4, of the Constitution gives state legislatures the power to regulate the time, place, and manner of such elections but also states that Congress may "make or alter such regulations."[23] Congress is vested with power to be the exclusive judge of the elections, returns, and qualifications of its own members,[24] and, since 1842, Congress

---

20. *See, e.g.*, Donald J. Trump for President, Inc. v. Boockvar, 502 F. Supp. 3d 899 (M.D. Pa. 2020). For a list, see www.democracydocket.com. This is not to say that the election was free from legitimate concerns or controversy. For example, the Pennsylvania Supreme Court held that mail-in ballots should be counted even if they were received after the statutory deadline. Pennsylvania Democratic Party v. Boockvar, 238 A.3d 345 (Pa. 2020). In Wisconsin, officials authorized the use of ballot drop boxes that the state supreme court later held to be illegal. Teigen v. Wisconsin Elections Comm'n, 976 N.W.2d 519 (Wisc. 2022), *overruled by* Priorities USA v. Wisconsin Elections Comm'n, 8 N.W.3d 429 (Wisc. 2024).

21. *See, e.g.*, Richard L. Hasen, *Identifying and Minimizing the Risk of Election Subversion and Stolen Elections in the Contemporary United States*, 135 Harv. L. Rev. F. 265 (2022) (suggesting increased transparency in vote counting; limiting the discretion of those who certify votes; limiting politicization of election administration; and countering election-related disinformation); Derek T. Muller, *Election Subversion and the Writ of Mandamus*, 65 Wm. & Mary L. Rev. 327 (2023) (arguing that writs of mandamus can and should be used by courts to prevent election subversion).

22. 3 U.S.C. §§ 1–21.

23. U.S. Const. art. I, § 4, cl. 1 ("The Times, Places and Manner of holding Elections for Senators and Representatives, shall be prescribed in each State by the Legislature thereof; but the Congress may at any time by Law make or alter such Regulations, except as to the Places of chusing Senators.").

24. U.S. Const. art. I, § 5, cl. 1 ("Each House shall be the Judge of the Elections, Returns, and Qualifications of its own Members. . . . ").

has required members of the House of Representatives to be elected in single-member districts, as opposed to being elected statewide.[25]

Nonetheless, these provisions are not comprehensive, and much of the details of federal elections are left to the individual states.

1. Selecting Members of Congress

As noted above, absent congressional action, the Constitution leaves most of the details of electing members of Congress to the states. A recent case that highlights how states resolve disputes involving congressional elections is *Coleman v. Franken*.[26] There, incumbent Minnesota Senator Norm Coleman initially appeared to have defeated challenger Al Franken by 206 votes out of 2.9 million cast. Given the close margin, a manual recount was required under state law. The statewide recount included certain absentee ballots that had been rejected on or before election day. Franken was eventually declared the winner by 312 votes. Coleman then brought suit, arguing, among other things, that the recount violated due process and equal protection.

The due-process challenge focused on whether the election process itself was fundamentally unfair. That inquiry in turn focused on voter reliance on established procedures and any significant disenfranchisement that resulted from a change in those procedures.[27] Minnesota statutes established a multi-step procedure for voters to apply for and cast absentee ballots, which procedure included the proper marking of return envelopes. Coleman argued that Minnesota precedent permitted "something less than strict compliance with" statutory procedures when determining whether an absentee ballot was properly cast. The court disagreed, holding that absentee voting was a privilege, not a right, and that the recount's strict compliance with Minnesota statutory requirements "was not a deviation from our well-established precedent."[28]

The court drew on *Bush v. Gore* to analyze the equal-protection argument. Coleman argued that different election officials throughout the state used different standards to access the propriety of absentee ballots. The court again disagreed, holding that "equal protection is not violated every time public officials apply facially neutral state laws differently." There was evidence that various election boards used different procedures, depending on available resources, but there was no intentional discrimination. *Bush v. Gore*, itself a manual-recount case, was distinguished on the basis

25. 2 U.S.C. § 2c.

26. 767 N.W.2d 453 (Minn. 2009) (*per curiam*). For an in-depth study of *Coleman*, see Edward B. Foley, *The Lake Wobegone Recount: Minnesota's Disputed 2008 U.S. Senate Election*, 10 Election L.J. 129 (2011).

27. The Minnesota court cited federal cases, *e.g.*, *Bennett v. Yoshina*, 140 F.3d 1218 (9th Cir. 1998), for this proposition.

28. 767 N.W.2d at 466. The court contrasted such strict compliance regarding errors by absentee voters with errors by election officials, where only "substantial compliance" is required. The court noted that, in the latter situation, voters have no control over what an election official does with the ballot.

that, in *Coleman*, there were "clear statutory standards for acceptance or rejection of absentee ballots, about which all election officials received common training." Moreover, unlike in the earlier case, the markings on the outside return envelope were the subject of the dispute in *Coleman*, so the actual votes inside were not known to the election officials.

Coleman is also notable for making a "right/privilege" distinction in explaining the need for strict compliance with statutory requirements regarding absentee ballots. In contrast, other state courts have not made this distinction, instead permitting absentee votes to be counted as long as there was substantial compliance with statutory requirements.[29]

Another, earlier, example of the importance of state law and state courts in regulating federal elections is *Roudebush v. Hartke*.[30] There, incumbent Senator C. Vance Hartke, Democrat from Indiana, defeated Republican challenger Richard Roudebush in an extremely close race. Roudebush filed a petition in state court to order a recount, and Hartke responded by filing suit in federal district court, requesting the district court to enjoin the state-court litigation. The federal court eventually did issue the requested injunction, on the basis that the state recount procedures would interfere with the Senate's power to judge the qualifications of its own members. On appeal, the Supreme Court reversed. The 5–2 majority held that the states possessed broad authority to regulate federal elections and further held that a manual recount is "within the ambit" of those powers. Such a recount would not prevent the Senate from later independently evaluating the election or from conducting its own recount. There was no evidence to support the district court's holding that a recount "would increase the probability of election fraud and accidental destruction of ballots." The dissent argued that the Senate had a long tradition of independently resolving disputed Senate elections by convening a special committee. There was a federal interest, the dissent contended, "in preserving the integrity of the evidence" of the disputed ballots, and for that reason it agreed with the district court.

The *Roudebush* decision gave a good deal of power to states, and to state courts in particular, to resolve disputed congressional elections. But it apparently left intact the ability of the houses of Congress to take action concurrently to resolve such disputes. Since *Roudebush*, some disappointed candidates have simultaneously pursued remedies in state courts and in Congress.[31]

---

29. For an overview, see Richard L. Hasen, *The Democracy Canon*, 62 Stan. L. Rev. 69, 86–87 (2009). The strict/substantial compliance distinction can also arise in contexts other than absentee ballots. *See, e.g.*, Miller v. Treadwell, 245 P.3d 867 (Alaska 2010) (holding that it was proper to count misspelled write-in votes because state election statutes should be construed in favor of voter enfranchisement); State *ex rel.* Painter v. Brunner, 941 N.E.2d 782 (Ohio 2011) (*per curiam*) (holding that provisional ballots cast in wrong precinct due to poll-worker error should not be counted, given the mandatory language of state statutes and the need for strict compliance).

30. 405 U.S. 15 (1972).

31. *See* Lisa Marshall Manheim, *Judging Congressional Elections*, 51 Ga. L. Rev. 359 (2017); Kristen R. Lisk, Note, *The Resolution of Contested Elections in the U.S. House of Representatives: Why State Courts Should Not Help with the House Work*, 83 N.Y.U. L. Rev. 1213 (2008).

2. Federal and State Judges in Election Disputes

There is a long-running debate among federal-courts scholars over whether federal judges are in various ways better able than state-court judges to protect federal constitutional and statutory rights. Many point out that, unlike the vast majority of state judges, federal judges enjoy lifetime tenure and thus are presumably insulated from electoral pressure when making decisions, and that federal judges often possess higher qualifications and are better paid, or have more institutional resources, than do most state-court judges. Others argue that these differences and the electoral pressures on state judges can be overstated, and that empirical evidence does not support the proposition that state judges on the whole are systematically undermining the adjudication and enforcement of federal law.[32]

In a similar fashion, some argue that the state political process, including state courts, is not an appropriate venue to settle election disputes for federal offices. The fear is that state officials, judges included, would act in parochial and partisan ways to resolve the disputes. While it is hard to argue that the members of the House and Senate would be any less partisan than state officials in resolving election disputes, some might nonetheless contend that federal judges with lifetime tenure would be less partisan than their state counterparts. Anecdotal evidence on this debate cuts in different ways. Consider, for example, *Coleman*, where a state supreme court made up primarily, though not exclusively, of Democrats ruled unanimously in favor of the Democratic candidate. On the federal court side, consider the three-judge district-court decision in *Roudebush*. There, the Republican appointee (then-Circuit Judge John Paul Stevens) ruled in favor of the Republican candidate, while the other two judges, both Democratic appointees, ruled in favor of the Democratic candidate.[33] The extant empirical evidence on partisan decisionmaking by judges in election-related cases is mixed, making it hazardous to draw definitive conclusions.[34]

---

32. For an overview of the debate, compare Burt Neuborne, *The Myth of Parity*, 90 Harv. L. Rev. 1105 (1977), with Michael E. Solimine & James L. Walker: Respecting State Courts: The Inevitability of Judicial Federalism (1999). *See also* Kyle C. Kopko, *Litigant Partisan Identity and Challenges to Campaign Finance Policies: An Examination of U.S. District Court Decisions, 1971–2007*, 36 Justice Sys. J. 212 (2015) (concluding that federal judges did not systematically favor challenges by litigants who shared the judges' partisan affiliations, but that judges were less likely to favor challenges filed by plaintiffs of the opposing major political party).

33. Hartke v. Roudenbush, 321 F. Supp. 1370 (S.D. Ind. 1970) (*per curiam*) (three-judge court), *rev'd*, 405 U.S. 15 (1972).

34. On the state-court side, compare Scott Graves, *Competing Interests in State Supreme Courts: Justices' Votes and Voting Rights*, 24 Am. Rev. Pol. 267 (2003) (state supreme courts acted in partisan ways in some circumstances in ballot-access cases), and Rebecca L. Brown, Lee Epstein, & Michael J. Nelson, *In Electoral Disputes, State Justices Are Less Reliable GOP Allies than the U.S. Supreme Court—That's the "Problem" the Independent State Legislature Claim Hopes to Solve*, 708 Annals Am. Acad. Pol. & Soc. Sci. 208 (2023) (same), with Kyle C. Kopko, *Partisanship Suppressed: Judicial Decision-Making in Ralph Nader's 2004 Ballot Access Litigation*, 7 Election L.J. 301 (2008) (state-judge partisan affiliation relatively insignificant in voting on cases where Nader sought placement on presidential ballot). On the federal-court side, compare Michael E. Solimine, *Institutional Process, Agenda Setting, and the Development of Election Law on the Supreme Court*, 68 Ohio St. L.J. 767, 790–92 (2007) (arguing that

D. Federal Remedies for State Elections

1. Federal Civil and Criminal Enforcement

Federal statutes create a wide range of potential remedies that public entities or private parties can use to address election-related irregularities. Many of those statutes and their remedial provisions have already been discussed in this book. For example, the Voting Rights Act is addressed in Chapters 3 and 4, the Federal Election Campaign Act and its predecessor statutes are addressed in Chapter 8, and the Help America Vote Act (HAVA) and the National Voter Registration Act are discussed in Chapter 10.

These statutes can be enforced, in various ways, by the federal government. Thus, the Federal Election Commission (FEC) can undertake to enforce the campaign finance laws. The FEC can seek a variety of penalties against violators of those laws but must request that courts enforce its orders.[35] The Civil Rights Division of the U.S. Department of Justice is charged with enforcing provisions of the Voting Rights Act, HAVA, and other laws. Both civil and criminal remedies are available.[36]

Not surprisingly, court decisions have played a major role in shaping the scope of the power of the branches of the federal government in enforcing these laws. For example, various statutes[37] make it a crime for persons acting under color of state law to deprive persons of their constitutional right to vote. In the leading case of *United States v. Classic*,[38] the Supreme Court upheld criminal prosecutions under these statutes of state election officials who had committed various frauds in a Democratic Party primary election for a seat in the U.S. House of Representatives. The officials argued that a mere primary election, as opposed to a general election, was an internal matter for the party, and hence they were not acting under color of state law. The Court rejected the argument, holding that primaries (especially in a state politically

---

evidence does not show that lower-court federal judges systematically vote in a partisan fashion in election-law cases), with Adam C. Cox & Thomas J. Miles, *Judicial Ideology and the Transformation of Voting Rights Act Jurisprudence*, 75 U. CHI. L. REV. 1493 (2008) (federal judges often voted in partisan fashion in Voting Rights Act cases), and Mark Jonathan McKenzie, *The Influence of Partisanship, Ideology, and the Law on Redistricting Decisions in the Federal Courts*, 65 POL. RES. Q. 799 (2012) (arguing that "constrained partisanship" along with other factors, best explains federal-court decisions in this context). *See generally* Richard L. Hasen, *Judges as Political Regulators: Evidence and Options for Institutional Change, in* RACE, REFORM, AND REGULATION OF THE ELECTORAL PROCESS 101 (Guy-Uriel E. Charles, Heather K. Gerken & Michael S. Kang, eds. 2011); Michael S. Kang & Joanna M. Shepherd, *The Long Shadow of* Bush v. Gore: *Judicial Partisanship in Election Cases*, 68 STAN. L. REV. 1411 (2016).

35. 52 U.S.C. §§ 30106–30110.

36. For helpful overviews of the scope and enforcement of federal election law by federal authorities, see David C. Rothschild & Benjamin J. Wolinsky, *Election Law Violations*, 46 AM. CRIM. L. REV. 391 (2009); U.S. DEP'T OF JUSTICE, FEDERAL PROSECUTION OF ELECTION OFFENSES (8th ed. 2017).

37. *E.g.*, 18 U.S.C. §§ 241–242.

38. 313 U.S. 299 (1941).

dominated by one party) were "an integral part of the procedure for the popular choice of Congressman."[39] *Classic* gave greater power to federal authorities to regulate elections for federal offices in the states, and it emboldened private parties to use federal law to challenge practices such as the white primary, as discussed in Chapter 5.

Private plaintiffs who are injured in some way by state law or by the actions of state officials in election matters can bring suit themselves under various federal statutes[40] that are often used in conjunction with general civil-rights statutes.[41]

Where federal statutes do not explicitly provide for a private right of action, there can be a question as to whether the statutes may be enforced in lawsuits brought by private parties or, instead, whether only government officials may bring enforcement proceedings. Courts have inferred a private right of action to enforce many election-related federal statutes, including portions of the Voting Rights Act.[42] Thus, the remedial enforcement of federal election law is, as a practical matter, often a mix of administrative and legal actions by public and private entities. In recent years, however, the Supreme Court has greatly limited the ability of private parties to enforce federal law absent an express cause of action.[43] Following that trend, the Eighth Circuit has held that § 2 of the Voting Rights Act—often used to challenge district maps for allegedly not providing an equal opportunity for racial minorities to elect their candidates of choice—may not be enforced via private lawsuits.[44] That issue has never explicitly been addressed in a majority opinion of the Supreme Court,[45] but several Justices have at least assumed the availability of a private right of action to enforce VRA § 2.[46]

There are advantages and disadvantages to relying on federal prosecutors or other federal officials, as opposed to private parties, to enforce these laws. The U.S. Department of Justice and other federal offices typically have limited resources and can therefore pursue only a limited number of investigations and court actions. Private enforcement would seem to be a necessary supplement to public prosecutions if a high degree of compliance is expected, but private plaintiffs (often, interest groups) will have their own agendas and may not pursue or serve the public interest. Courts

---

39. *Id.* at 314.

40. *E.g.*, 52 U.S.C. §§ 10101, 10301.

41. Especially 42 U.S.C. § 1983.

42. *See, e.g.*, Allen v. State Bd. of Elections, 393 U.S. 544, 556–57 (1969) (finding an implied private right of action under § 5 of the Voting Rights Act as a necessary supplement to public enforcement); Morse v. Republican Party of Virginia, 517 U.S. 186, 230–34 (1996) (same with respect to § 10 of the Voting Rights Act); Sandusky Cnty. Democratic Party v. Blackwell, 387 F.3d 565 (6th Cir. 2004) (inferring a private right of action under § 302 of HAVA). For an overview of these cases and an argument for greater reliance on private enforcement, see Daniel P. Tokaji, *Public Rights and Private Rights of Action: The Enforcement of Federal Election Laws*, 44 Ind. L. Rev. 113 (2010).

43. *See, e.g.*, Alexander v. Sandoval, 532 U.S. 275 (2001).

44. Arkansas State Conference of the NAACP v. Arkansas Bd. of Apportionment, 86 F.4th 1204 (2023), *reh'g denied*, 91 F.4th 967 (8th Cir. 2024).

45. *See also* Brnovich v. Democratic Nat'l Comm., 594 U.S. 647, 690 (2021) (Gorsuch, J., concurring) (noting that the question is an open one).

46. *See* Morse v. Republican Party of Virginia, 517 U.S. 186, 232 (1996) (Stevens, J., joined by Ginsburg, J.); *id.* at 240 (Breyer, J., joined by O'Connor and Souter, JJ., concurring in the judgment).

have faced these issues when considering whether to infer a private right of action in a federal statute, when textually it provides for only administrative enforcement.

2. Remedies for the Wrongful Denial of the Right to Vote

a. Damage Remedies

Most often, suits to vindicate the rights of voters seek injunctions. Nevertheless, an award of damages is possible as well,[47] and the propriety of awarding damages for a wrongful denial of the right to vote was recognized in England as early as 1703.[48] Courts have awarded more than trivial amounts of damages for unlawful restrictions of the right to vote.[49]

Nonetheless, affixing a dollar value to the right to vote is difficult for several reasons. First, there is no market against which to measure a damages award. All states and the federal government have laws prohibiting the buying or selling of votes,[50] and, as a result, we cannot be certain how much a vote is "worth" in that sense. Second, if we were to approximate the value of a vote based on the behavior of voters, the behavior of the Americans who decide not to vote might indicate that the right has very little value.[51] Third, if we view the right in narrow instrumental terms—the chances that one vote will make the difference in an election—the value is infinitesimally small. Fourth, taking a broader view, the value of voting—of subjecting government to popular accountability—is infinitely high. Indeed, the behavior of generations of Americans who have fought and died to protect democracy might indicate that the right has a very large value.

---

47. Murphy v. Ramsey, 114 U.S. 15, 37 (1885); Wiley v. Sinkler, 179 U.S. 58 (1900) (holding that a damages suit in federal court for state restriction of the right to vote satisfied the $2,000 amount-in-controversy requirement then in effect for federal-question cases).

48. Ashby v. White, 92 Eng. Rep. 126, *rev'd*, 1 Eng. Rep. 417-HL (1703). The Queen's Bench, 3–1, held for the defendant and against the would-be voter, over Chief Justice Holt's dissent. The judgment was reversed, however, in the House of Lords.

49. *E.g.*, Taylor v. Howe, 280 F.3d 1210 (8th Cir. 2002) (affirming a compensatory-damages award to seven plaintiffs of between $500 and $2,000 each for unlawful restrictions on the efforts of black citizens to vote or to serve as poll-watchers). For an overview of the British and American cases addressing the awarding of damages in these circumstances, see Delaney Herndon, Note, *Voting Rights and Remedial Gaps*, 137 Harv. L. Rev. 1182, 1183–91 (2024).

50. *See, e.g.*, 18 U.S.C. §§ 597, 598; Richard L. Hasen, *Vote Buying*, 88 Calif. L. Rev. 1323 (2000).

51. *Cf.* Crawford v. Marion Cnty. Election Bd., 472 F.3d 949, 951 (7th Cir. 2007) (Posner, J.), *aff'd*, 553 U.S. 181 (2008) ("A great many people who are eligible to vote don't bother to do so. Many do not register, and many who do register still don't vote, or vote infrequently. The benefits of voting to the individual voter are elusive (a vote in a political election rarely has any *instrumental* value, since elections for political office at the state or federal level are never decided by just one vote), and even very slight costs in time or bother or out-of-pocket expense deter many people from voting, or at least from voting in elections they're not much interested in."); Anthony Downs, An Economic Theory of Democracy 260–76 (1957).

The Supreme Court has indicated that the narrower vision of the right is appropriate for assessing the proper amount of damages. "The 'value of the right' [to vote] is the money value of the particular loss that the plaintiff suffered—a loss of which 'each member of the jury has personal knowledge.' It is *not* the value of the right to vote as a general, abstract matter, based on its role in our history or system of government."[52]

b. Remedies for Unsuccessful Candidates

Federal courts have also held that unsuccessful candidates for state elective office cannot pursue damage relief for election-law violations. The leading case on point is the Fourth Circuit decision of *Hutchinson v. Miller*.[53] Unsuccessful candidates for elective office, including for the U.S. House of Representatives, alleged that local officials combined with private citizens to predetermine the election results by fixing vote tabulations. They sued for damages but not injunctive relief. The court acknowledged the "significant duty of federal courts to preserve constitutional rights in the electoral process," but that role, the court held, is subject to significant limitations when damages are sought. Both federal and state authorities are able to investigate and rectify election irregularities. To permit post-election suits for damages, the court held, would be to "intrude on the role of states and the Congress, to raise the possibility of inconsistent judgments concerning elections, to erode the finality of results, to give candidates incentives to bypass the procedures already established, and to constitute the jury as well as the electorate as an arbiter of political outcomes."[54] This was true, the court concluded, even if the same conduct might be the basis for injunctive relief.[55]

c. Injunctive Relief and Due Process Violations

Plaintiffs in election suits can seek both damages and injunctive relief, but in many, or perhaps most, suits, the latter type of relief is sought. This may be due to the difficulties in measuring damages in this context, coupled with the desire of plaintiffs to have their voting rights vindicated in short order, often in light of upcoming (or ongoing) elections.[56] But the desire and preference for injunctive relief does not make

52. Memphis Cmty. School Dist. v. Stachura, 477 U.S. 299, 312 n.14 (1986).

53. 797 F.2d 1279 (4th Cir. 1986).

54. *Id.* at 1285.

55. For decisions following *Hutchinson*, see *Soules v. Kauaians for Nukolii Campaign Comm.*, 849 F.3d 1176 (9th Cir. 1988); *Lecky v. Virginia State Board of Elections*, 285 F. Supp. 3d 908 (E.D. Va. 2018); *White-Battle v. Democratic Party of Virginia*, 323 F. Supp. 2d 696 (E.D. Va. 2004); and *Hill v. Stowers*, 680 S.E.2d 66 (W. Va. 2009). *See also* Roberts v. Wasmer, 883 F.2d 617 (8th Cir. 1989) (holding that an unsuccessful candidate was not an "aggrieved person" entitled to bring suit for violations of § 2 of the Voting Rights Act).

56. While it appears that for "most of the nation's history, the standard remedy for a voting wrong was damages," Herndon, *supra* note 49, at 1182 (footnotes omitted), by "the 1950s and 1960s, injunctive relief became far more common." *Id.* The change is attributed to, among other things, advocacy by civil-rights organizations, injunctions' being more efficient to achieve structural change, and federal-court remedial doctrines' being more receptive to granting injunctions against government action. *Id.* at 1194–96.

it easier to obtain. Under typical formulations of the standard for obtaining injunctive relief in any context, plaintiffs must demonstrate a strong likelihood of succeeding on the merits of their claim and of suffering irreparable injury if injunctive relief is not immediately obtained.[57]

In theory, a great variety of actions under state law or by state officials can impair the right to vote, in violation of various provisions of the U.S. Constitution and federal statutory law. Many examples are found elsewhere in this book. Particularly noteworthy examples are cases challenging state election practices under the Due Process Clause of the Fourteenth Amendment. In those situations, federal courts frequently state that mere "garden variety election irregularities" cannot be the basis for federal court intervention.[58] Rather, for federal courts to intervene, the election process must be "patently and fundamentally unfair." Mere fraud, mistake, human error, and technical difficulties are not enough.[59] Instead, courts typically ask whether voters likely relied on established election procedures or pronouncements about a coming election and whether significant disenfranchisement or vote dilution resulted from a change in those procedures.[60] It is rare but not unheard of for plaintiffs to satisfy this demanding standard.[61]

A particularly noteworthy illustration of federal courts' grappling with this due-process standard is *Roe v. Alabama*.[62] That case grew out of an extremely close election for two statewide offices in Alabama in 1994. The dispute was over the counting of absentee ballots under Alabama law, which statutorily required that absentee voters have their signatures notarized and witnessed by two people. A post-election decision by a state court required officials to count even those absentee ballots that did not satisfy those requirements. Federal-court action followed, and the federal courts held that election officials would violate due process if they followed the state court's order. Invoking the tests outlined above, the federal courts held that counting the contested absentee ballots would constitute a post-election departure from previous practice in Alabama and would dilute the votes of those voters, absentee and

57. *E.g.*, Northeast Ohio Coalition for Homeless v. Husted, 696 F.3d 580, 591 (6th Cir. 2012) (*per curiam*); *Lecky*, 285 F. Supp. 3d at 913. On the standards to obtain injunctive relief, see generally *Winter v. Natural Resources Defense Council*, 555 U.S. 7 (2008).

58. *E.g.*, Griffin v. Burns, 570 F.2d 1065, 1070 (1st Cir. 1978); *Northeast Ohio Coalition for Homeless*, 696 F.3d at 597.

59. Gold v. Feinberg, 101 F.3d 796 (2d Cir. 1996); Bodine v. Elkhart Cnty. Election Bd., 788 F.3d 1270 (7th Cir. 1986); Hendon v. North Carolina State Bd. of Elections, 710 F.2d 177 (4th Cir. 1983); Gamza v. Aguirre, 619 F.2d 449 (5th Cir. 1980); Scheer v. City of Miami, 15 F. Supp. 2d 1338 (S.D. Fla. 1998).

60. *See, e.g.*, Bennett v. Yoshina, 140 F.3d 1218, 1226–27 (9th Cir. 1998); Warf v. Bd. of Elections of Green Cnty., 619 F.3d 553, 559 (6th Cir. 2010).

61. *See, e.g.*, Northeast Ohio Coalition for the Homeless v. Husted, 696 F.3d 580, 597–98 (6th Cir. 2012) (*per curiam*) (disqualification of wrong-precinct ballot due to poll-worker error); Griffin v. Burns, 570 F.2d 1065 (1st Cir. 1978) (absentee voting was disallowed post-election after it had been allowed in previous elections); Briscoe v. Kusper, 453 F.2d 1046 (7th Cir. 1970) (signature requirements enforced for the first time).

62. 43 F.3d 574 (11th Cir. 1995) (*per curiam*).

otherwise, who followed the proper procedure. Counting the disputed votes would also, in effect, have disenfranchised those who would have voted but for the notarization and witness requirements.[63]

d. The Timing of Injunctive Relief

The Supreme Court has signaled that courts should be wary of becoming involved in last-minute challenges to election procedures. The principal decision is *Purcell v. Gonzalez*.[64] There, the Court reversed a lower court's preliminary injunction that had blocked enforcement of a voter-ID law one month before an election. Without ruling on the merits of the challenge, the Court relied on the need for "clear guidance" to election officials and the risk of "voter confusion."

Purcell was unanimous, but, since then, the Court has not been clear on the factors to be applied or how those factors interact with the other criteria courts consider when deciding a request for injunctive relief. But *Purcell* does appear to have strengthened the presumption against late judicial remedies. Thus, in *Republican National Committee v. Democratic National Committee*,[65] the Court, in a 5–4 decision, held that the "lower federal courts should ordinarily not alter the election rules on the eve of an election." There, the lower court had, five days before the election, ordered that absentee votes sent after election day should be counted as long as they were received within six days of election day. Concluding that the order would "fundamentally alter the nature of the election by allowing voting for six additional days after the election,"[66] the Supreme Court rebuked the lower court.

In *Merrill v. Milligan*, another case involving a change of election rules relatively close to an election, Justice Brett Kavanaugh wrote a concurring opinion in which he expounded on the criteria that courts should consider in applying *Purcell*.[67] Justice Kavanaugh argued that the *Purcell* principle was a "bedrock tenet of election law" because "[l]ate judicial tinkering with election laws can lead to disruption and to unanticipated and unfair consequences for candidates, political parties, and voters." However, he did not read *Purcell* as an absolute rule. Acknowledging that the Court had yet to "fully spell out all of its contours," he argued that the principle can be overcome if a plaintiff establishes that the underling merits are clear-cut in his favor;

---

63. The *Roe* litigation was particularly controversial, given its circuitous journey through federal and state courts. The Eleventh Circuit certified an issue of state law to the Alabama Supreme Court regarding whether state law permitted the counting of the disputed absentee ballots. The latter court held that they were valid under state law, but the federal courts then held that the uniform practice in the state prior to the election had been to exclude absentee ballots like those in question. Hence, they ordered state authorities to certify the election results without including the contested absentee ballots. For an overview of the complicated litigation, see *Roe v. Alabama*, 68 F.3d 404 (11th Cir. 1995) (*per curiam*). For a discussion of allegations in the case of politicized judging and excessive federal-court intervention, see Richard L. Hasen, *The Democracy Canon*, 62 Stan. L. Rev. 62, 119–22 (2009).

64. 549 U.S. 1 (2006) (*per curiam*).

65. 589 U.S. 423 (2020) (*per curiam*).

66. *Id.* at 426.

67. 142 S. Ct. 879 (2022).

that he would suffer irreparable harm absent the injunction; that he has not unduly delayed in filing suit; and that the relief in question may be granted before the election without significant cost, confusion or hardship. Even with such additional guidance, lower courts have taken different positions on whether and to what extent the *Purcell* principle interacts with the traditional criteria for granting injunctive relief or for a stay of a lower-court decision while it is on appeal.[68]

The COVID-19 pandemic disrupted primary and general elections in 2020, requiring courts, along with the rest of government, to make alterations to election procedures, sometimes at the last minute.[69] In one notable case, as a result of the large increase in requests for mail-in ballots, Wisconsin election officials were unable to issue mail-in ballots to voters in advance of the April 7 primary election. A federal district court responded by requiring election officials to accept mail-in ballots as long as they were received by April 13.[70] The Supreme Court applied *Purcell* and reversed in part, holding that it was permissible for the district court to order election officials to count ballots that arrived late, but it was impermissible to order election officials to count ballots that were sent (and possibly filled out) after election day.[71]

Predictably, some COVID-related changes were criticized as attempts to manipulate election procedures to give a partisan advantage. Often critics also claimed that the alterations weakened protections against election fraud. Michigan's Secretary of State, for example, drew criticism for issuing mail-in ballot applications to registered voters, including voters who did not request them, but the Michigan Court of Appeals, by a 2–1 vote, upheld the action.[72]

Late changes can lead to other controversies as well. Pennsylvania's Supreme Court "interpreted" a statute that required mail-in ballots to be returned by 8:00 p.m. on election day to permit ballots to be received as late as three days after election day.[73] That decision was attacked as not only an implausible reading of an unambiguous state statute but also as potentially usurping the state legislature's prerogative to make

68. For a canvassing of lower-court decisions on these issues, see *Tennessee Conf. of the NAACP v. Lee*, 105 F.4th 888 (6th Cir. 2024) (*per curiam*). For varying commentary on these issues, see, *e.g.*, Brooks M. Chupp, *Equitable Balancing in the* Purcell *Framework*, 16 Drexel L. Rev. 507 (2024); Richard L. Hasen, *Reining in the* Purcell *Principle*, 43 Fla. St. U. L. Rev. 427 (2016); and Harry B. Dodsworth, *The Positive and Negative* Purcell *Principle*, 2022 Utah L. Rev. 1081. For the application of *Purcell* in state-court litigation, see Robert Yablon & Derek Clinger, Purcell *Principles for State Courts*, 2024 Wis. L. Rev. 1637.

69. For discussion of election-related lessons to be learned from COVID, see Richard L. Hasen, *Three Pathologies of American Voting Rights Illuminated by the COVID-19 Pandemic, and How to Treat and Cure Them*, 19 Election L.J. 263 (2020).

70. *See* Democratic Nat'l Comm. v. Bostelman, 451 F. Supp. 3d 952 (W.D. Wisc. 2020).

71. *See* Republican Nat'l Comm. v. Democratic Nat'l Comm., 589 U.S. 423 (2020) (*per curiam*).

72. Davis v. Secretary of State, 963 N.W.2d 653 (Mich. Ct. App.), *appeal denied*, 951 N.W.2d 911 (Mich. 2020).

73. *See* Pennsylvania Democratic Party v. Boockvar, 238 A.3d 345 (Pa. 2020).

rules for conducting federal elections.[74] The Supreme Court, by a 4–4 vote, denied a request for a stay,[75] and, by a 6–3 vote, ultimately denied *certiorari*.[76]

COVID-19 is surely not the last emergency that will affect elections. Indeed, in 2024, Hurricane Helene caused extensive damage, especially to parts of North Carolina, causing some observers to worry about a potential impact on that year's elections, in addition to the death and destruction that the storm caused. Election officials must deal with whatever emergencies arise, ideally by having procedures in place well ahead of any potential emergency, in a way that protects both voting rights and the public's confidence in election results.[77]

---

74. *See* Moore v. Harper, 600 U.S. 1, 34–36 (2023).

75. 141 S. Ct. 643 (2020). Justices Thomas, Alito, Gorsuch, and Kavanaugh would have granted the stay. Justice Ginsburg had died earlier that year, and Justice Barrett had not yet been confirmed, so the Court had only eight Justices.

76. 141 S. Ct. 732 (2021).

77. *See* Michael T. Morley, *Election Emergencies*, *in* The Oxford Handbook of American Election Law 1055 (Eugene D. Mazo ed., 2024); Michael T. Morley, *Election Emergencies: Voting in the Wake of Natural Disasters and Terrorist Attacks*, 67 Emory L.J. 545 (2018).

Table of Cases

Table of Authorities

David B. Allen, Note, *"It's a Sham!": How Sham Political Candidates Are Threatening Democracy*, 75 FLA. L. REV. 741 (2023), 152

R. Michael Alvarez, et al., *How Much Is Enough? The "Ballot Order Effect" and the Use of Social Science Evidence in Election Disputes*, 5 ELECTION L.J. 40 (2006), 293

Stephen D. Ansolabehere et al., *Why Is There So Little Money in American Politics?*, 17 J. ECON. PERSPECTIVES 105 (2003), 247

STEPHEN ANSOLABEHERE & JAMES M. SNYDER, JR., THE END OF INEQUALITY: ONE PERSON, ONE VOTE AND THE TRANSFORMATION OF AMERICAN POLITICS 3 (2008), 30, 31

Matt Apuzzo, *Holder Urges States to Lift Bans on Felons' Voting*, N.Y. TIMES, Feb. 12, 2014, 23

Jack M. Balkin, Bush v. Gore *and the Boundary Between Law and Politics*, 110 YALE L.J. 1407 (2001), 274

Rachel E. Barkow, *More Supreme Than Court? The Fall of the Political Question Doctrine*, 102 COLUM. L. REV. 237 (2002), 26

William Baude et al., HART AND WECHSLER'S THE FEDERAL COURTS AND THE FEDERAL SYSTEM 881–907 (8th ed. 2025), 60

Mary Beth Beazely, *Ballot Design as Fail-Safe: An Ounce of Rotation Is Worth a Pound of Litigation*, 12 ELECTION L.J. 18 (2013), 293

Jocelyn Friedrichs Benson, *Democracy and the Secretary: The Critical Role of Election Administrators in Promoting Accuracy and Access to Democracy*, 27 ST. LOUIS U. PUB. L. REV. 343 (2008), 269

ALEXANDER BICKEL, THE LEAST DANGEROUS BRANCH (1962), 26

J. Kenneth Blackwell & Kenneth A. Klukowski, *The Other Voting Right: Protecting Every Citizen's Vote by Safeguarding the Integrity of the Ballot Box*, 28 YALE L. & POL'Y REV. 107 (2009), 279

James Bopp, Jr. & Heidi K. Abegg, *The Developing Constitutional Standards for "Coordinated Expenditures": Has the Federal Election Commission Finally Found a Way to Regulate Issue Advocacy?*, 1 ELECTION L.J. 209, 210 (2002), 200

Curtis A. Bradley & Eric A. Posner, *The Real Political Question Doctrine*, 75 STAN. L. REV. 1031 (2023), 28

Rebecca L. Brown, Lee Epstein, & Michael J. Nelson, *In Electoral Disputes, State Justices Are Less Reliable GOP Allies than the U.S. Supreme Court — That's the "Problem" the Independent State Legislature Claim Hopes to Solve*, 708 ANNALS AM. ACAD. POL. & SOC. SCI. 208 (2023), 297

Einer Elhauge, *The Lessons of Florida 2000*, 110 POL'Y REV. 15 (Dec. 2001 & Jan. 2002), 275

Michael Ellement, *Preclearance Without Statutory Change: Bail-In Suits Post-*Shelby County, 32 YALE L. & POL'Y REV. INTER ALIA 1 (2013), 71

James W. Endersby & Steven Jokinsky, *State Electoral Innovation and Voter Turnout in Midterm and Presidential Elections*, 23 ELECTION L.J. 132 (2024), 283

ERIK J. ENGSTROM & JASON M. ROBERTS, THE POLITICS OF BALLOT DESIGN: HOW STATES SHAPE AMERICAN DEMOCRACY (2020), 151

H. Abbie Erler, *Legislative Term Limits and State Spending*, 133 PUB. CHOICE 479 (2007), 146

Jason M. Farrell, *Clean Elections and Scandal: Case Studies from Maine, Arizona, and New York City*, CENTER FOR COMPETITIVE POLITICS (September 2011), 235

Michael O. Finkelstein & Herbert E. Robbins, *Mathematical Probability in Election Challenges*, 73 COLUM. L. REV. 241, 243 (1973), 293

Joel L. Fleishman & Pope McCorkle, *Level-Up Rather Than Level Down: Towards a New Theory of Campaign Finance*, 1 J. L. & POLS. 211 (1984), 233

Edward B. Foley, *Assessing the Validity of an Election's Result: History, Theory, and Present Threats*, 95 N.Y.U. L. REV. ONLINE 171 (2020), 291

EDWARD B. FOLEY, BALLOT BATTLES: THE HISTORY OF DISPUTED ELECTIONS IN THE UNITED STATES (2016), 269, 289

Edward B. Foley, *The Constitution and Condorcet: Democracy Protection Through Electoral Reform*, 70 DRAKE L. REV. 543 (2023), 287

Edward B. Foley, *The Lake Wobegone Recount: Minnesota's Disputed 2008 U.S. Senate Election*, 10 ELECTION L.J. 129 (2011), 295

Forum: Responses to Shelby County, 12 ELECTION L.J. 317 (2008), 70

Alexander Fouirnaies & Andrew B. Hall, *How Do Electoral Incentives Affect Legislator Behavior? Evidence from U.S. State Legislatures*, 166 Am. Pol. Sci. Rev. 662 (2022), 146

BARRY FRIEDMAN, THE WILL OF THE PEOPLE 268–70 (2009), 34

James A. Gardner, *A Post-*Vieth *Strategy for Litigating Partisan Gerrymandering Claims*, 3 ELECTION L.J. 643 (2004), 34

Elizabeth Garrett, *Term Limitations and the Myth of the Citizen-Legislator*, 81 CORNELL L. REV. 623 (1996), 146

Heather K. Gerken, THE DEMOCRACY INDEX: WHY OUR ELECTION SYSTEM IS FAILING AND HOW TO FIX IT (2009), 279

Heather K. Gerken, *Understanding the Right to an Undiluted Vote*, 114 HARV. L. REV. 1663, 1681–89 (2001), 39, 85

Scott Graves, *Competing Interests in State Supreme Courts: Justices' Votes and Voting Rights*, 24 AM. REV. POL. 267 (2003), 297

Justin Grimmer & Eitan Hersh, *How Election Rules Affect Who Wins*, 16 J. LEGAL ANALYSIS 1 (2024), 283

Kathleen Hale & Ramona McNeal, *Election Administration Reform and State Choice: Voter Identification Requirements and HAVA*, 38 POL'Y STUD. J. 281 (2010), 285

Brian T. Hamel, Jan Leighley & Robert M. Stein, *Why Making Voting Easier Isn't Enough: Early Voting, Campaigns,*

cial Function, 114 HARV. L. REV. 1833 (2001), 33

Kevin J. Hickey, Note, *Accuracy Counts: Illegal Votes in Contested Elections and the Case for Complete Proportionate Deduction*, 83 N.Y.U. L. REV. 167 (2008), 292, 293

RICHARD HOFSTADTER, THE IDEA OF A PARTY SYSTEM: THE RISE OF LEGITIMATE OPPOSITION IN THE UNITED STATES, 1780–1840 (1969), 113

Steven F. Huefner, *Remedying Election Wrongs*, 44 HARV. J. ON LEGIS. 265 (2007), 289

Samuel Issacharoff, *Beyond the Discrimination Model on Voting*, 127 HARV. L. REV. 95 (2013), 70

Samuel Issacharoff, *Groups and the Right to Vote*, 44 EMORY L.J. 869 (1995), 39

Michael S. Kang & Joanna M. Shepherd, *The Long Shadow of* Bush v. Gore: *Judicial Partisanship in Election Cases*, 68 STAN. L. REV. 1411 (2016), 298

Pamela S. Karlan, *Two Section Twos and Two Section Fives: Voting Rights and Remedies After* Flores, 39 WM. & MARY L. REV. 725 (1998), 88

Kyle C. Kopko, *Litigant Partisan Identity and Challenges to Campaign Finance Policies: An Examination of U.S. District Court Decisions, 1971–2007*, 36 JUS. SYS. J. 212 (2015), 297

Kyle C. Kopko, *Partisanship Suppressed: Judicial Decision-Making in Ralph Nader's 2004 Ballot Access Litigation*, 7 ELECTION L.J. 301 (2008), 297

Harold J. Krent, *Judging Judging: The Problem of Second-Guessing State Judges' Interpretation of State Law in* Bush v. Gore, 29 FLA. ST. U. L. REV. 493 (2001), 275

MARTHA KROPF & DAVID C. KIMBALL, HELPING AMERICA VOTE: THE LIMITS OF ELECTION REFORM (2011), 285

Prescott M. Lassman, *Breaching the Fortress Walls: Corporate Political Speech and* Austin v. Michigan Chamber of Commerce, 78 VA. L. REV. 759 (1992), 223

Sarah E. LeCloux, Comment, *Too Close to Call? Remedying Reasonably Uncertain Ballot Results with New Elections*, 2001 WIS. L. REV. 1541, 292

Justin Levitt, *Resolving Election Error: The Dynamic Assessment of Materiality*, 54 WM. & MARY L. REV. 83 (2012), 291

Kristen R. Lisk, Note, *The Resolution of Contested Elections in the U.S. House of Representatives: Why State Courts Should Not Help with the House Work*, 83 N.Y.U. L. REV. 1213 (2008), 296

Leah M. Litman, *Inventing Equal Sovereignty*, 114 MICH. L. REV. 1207 (2016), 70

Daniel Hays Lowenstein, *A Patternless Mosaic: Campaign Finance and the First Amendment After* Austin, 21 CAP. U. L. REV. 381 (1992), 223, 259

Bill Lueders, *Public Financing of Elections a State Budget Casualty*, WISCONSIN ST. J. (updated May 23, 2012), 239

Nelson Lund, Bush v. Gore *at the Dawning of the Age of Obama*, 61 FLA. L. REV. 1101 (2009), 275

Michael Malbin, *Are Matching Funds Only for Losers?*, *in* WELFARE FOR POLITICIANS 251 (John Samples ed., 2005), 235

Lisa Marshall Manheim, *Judging Congressional Elections*, 51 GA. L. REV. 359 (2017), 296

Matthew M. Mannix, Comment, *Opening Ballot Access to Political Outsiders:*

Daniel J. Tokaji, *The Future of Election Reform: From Rules to Institutions*, 28 YALE L. & POL'Y REV. 125 (2009), 269, 279, 283

Daniel P. Tokaji, *HAVA in Court: A Summary and Analysis of Litigation*, 12 ELECTION L.J. 203 (2013), 284

Daniel P. Tokaji, *If It's Broke, Fix It: Improving Voting Rights Act Preclearance*, 49 HOW. L.J. 785 (2006), 61

Daniel P. Tokaji, *Public Rights and Private Rights of Action: The Enforcement of Federal Election Laws*, 44 IND. L. REV. 113 (2010), 284, 299

Caroline J. Tolbert, Daniel A. Smith & John C. Green, *Strategic Voting and Legislative Redistricting Reform*, 62 POL. RES. Q. 92 (2009), 55

Michael E. Toner & Karen E. Trainer, *The Fourteen-Billion-Dollar Election: Emerging Campaign Finance Trends and their Impact on the 2020 Presidential Race and Beyond*, *in* A RETURN TO NORMALCY? THE 2020 ELECTION THAT (ALMOST) BROKE AMERICA 203–24 (Larry J. Sabato, Kyle Kondik, & J. Miles Coleman eds., 2021), 181–82

RUSS VERSTEEG, ESSENTIAL LATIN FOR LAWYERS 38 (2d ed. 2024), 189

Hans von Spakovsky, *Destroying Election Integrity: The Unnecessary and Unconstitutional John R. Lewis Voting Rights Advancement Act* (S.4/H.R.4), HERITAGE FOUND. (Oct. 29, 2021), 71

THE VOTE: BUSH, GORE, AND THE SUPREME COURT (Cass R. Sunstein & Richard A. Epstein eds., 2001), 274

EARL WARREN, THE MEMOIRS OF EARL WARREN 306 (1977), 3

Justin Weinstein-Tull, *Election Law Federalism*, 114 MICH. L. REV. 747 (2016), 285

Justin Weinstein-Tull, *Voting Under Federal Election Laws*, *in* THE OXFORD HANDBOOK OF AMERICAN ELECTION LAW 221 (Eugene D. Mazo ed., 2024), 285

ROBERT F. WILLIAMS & LAWRENCE FRIEDMAN, THE LAW OF AMERICAN STATE CONSTITUTIONS 336 (2d ed. 2023), 33

GEORGE F. WILL, RESTORATION: CONGRESS, TERM LIMITS, AND THE RECOVERY OF DELIBERATIVE DEMOCRACY (1992), 146

Robert Yablon & Derek Clinger, Purcell *Principles for State Courts*, 2024 WIS. L. REV. 1637, 304

TINSLEY E. YARBROUGH, RACE AND REDISTRICTING: THE *SHAW-CROMARTIE* CASES (2002), 99

Table of Statutes

Index

[References are to sections.]